UN-COMMON SOCIALITY

SÖDERTÖRN
PHILOSOPHICAL STUDIES
2016

Un-common Sociality
Thinking sociality with Levinas

Ramona Rat

SÖDERTÖRN
PHILOSOPHICAL STUDIES

Södertörns högskola
(Södertörn University)
The Library
SE-141 89 Huddinge

www.sh.se/publications

© The author

Cover image: *le film oscille entre archives de spectacle et prononciation, anagramme et synonyme* (56 x 81 cm),
Irina & Silviu Szekely, 2012.

Graphic Form: Per Lindblom & Jonathan Robson

Stockholm 2016

Södertörn Philosophical Studies 19
ISSN 1651–6834

Södertörn Doctoral Dissertations 124
ISSN 1652–7399

ISBN 978-91-87843-60-0 (print)
ISBN 978-91-87843-61-7 (digital)

Acknowledgements

First and foremost I would like to sincerely thank my supervisors Fredrika Spindler and Marcia Sá Cavalcante Schuback for their guidance and endless support throughout my doctoral years. Their vast knowledge and insightful advice, along with their countless careful readings of my text in its different stages, helped me develop this thesis and bring clarity to my thoughts. Thank you for your tireless help and infinite patience!

I would also like to express my gratitude to the School of Culture and Education from Södertörn University and especially the Philosophy Department, for the highly professional and friendly environment that I had the privilege to enjoy during my studies. The opportunity to present my work on various occasions at the Higher Seminars in Philosophy made possible for me to benefit from a number of useful comments from both senior staff and fellow doctoral candidates. I would like to thank in particular Hans Ruin, Irina Sandomirskaja, Nicholas Smith, Fredrik Svenaeus, Sven-Olov Wallenstein, Charlotta Weigelt, Anders Bartonek, Jonna Bornemark, Erik Bryngelsson, Carl Cederberg, Lovisa Håkansson, Krystof Kasprzak, David Payne, Johan Sehlberg, Anna-Karin Selberg, Gustav Strandberg, Gabriel Itkes Sznap and Björn Sjöstrand. I also remain greatly indebted to my opponents on these seminars, Paulina Remes, Bettina Bergo, Carl Cederberg and Susanna Lindberg, for their attentive reading and constructive critique.

An important role in rendering possible the writing of this thesis has The Centre for Baltic and East European Research (CBEES) and The Baltic and East European Graduate School (BEEGS). CBEES and BEEGS have offered a fruitful academic milieu where I always felt welcomed. For this, I am deeply thankful to director Rebecka Lettevall, all the faculty and staff. I also thank Ewa Rogström, Nina Cajhamre, Lena Arvidson and Karin Lindebrant for their cheerful spirit and kind assistance, especially regarding the administrative tasks. During my studies I have received the generous financial support of The Foundation for Baltic and East European Studies, for which

I am truly thankful. I am also grateful to Helge Ax:son Johnsons Stiftelse and to Gunvor och Josef Anérs Stiftelse for offering financial support for the final stage of my writing.

In the course of my studies I had the opportunity to meet and have inspiring discussions with wonderful people, among them Tanya Jukkala, Anne Kaun, Paul Karlsson, Jaska Turunen, Florence Fröhlig, Eva Schwarz, Steffen Werther, Mirey Gorgis, Maryam Adjam, Karin Edberg, Péter Balogh, Carina Guyard and Ola Svenonius. I am profoundly grateful for their supporting friendship. I thank my dear friends Andreea and Silviu Székely for allowing their beautiful artwork to be on the cover of this book, as well as for the many hours of our long-distance philosophical conversations.

Last but not least, I would like to express my gratitude to those who are closest to me. Thank you Beni, Cristina, Klári and Tati for always helping me out and staying by my side, no matter what. *Vă mulțumesc!*

Contents

Abbreviations 11
    Works by Levinas 11
    Other works 12

Introduction 13
    Reading Levinas 13
    General aims and structure of the argument 18
    Reading about Levinas 24

PART I
Subjectivity and Multiplicity 31

CHAPTER 1
Substitution 33
    1.1. De-posed subject 35
    1.2. Inside-out 40

CHAPTER 2
Bad Consciousness and Bad Time 55
    2.1. The an-archy of the hither side 56
    2.2. Non-intentional consciousness 59
    2.3. Diachrony of Time 71

CHAPTER 3
Self and Multiplicity 79
    3.1. The radicalization of multiplicity 80
        3.1.1. Subjectivity in *"Totality and Infinity"* 81
        3.1.2. Radical multiplicity 88
    3.2. Radical multiplicity in *"Otherwise than Being"* 94
        3.2.1. The continuity in thinking subjectivity 96
        3.2.2. For the other(s) 97

CHAPTER 4
The Question of Justice 101

4.1. An outside dimension.. 102
4.2. "Inside-out" and "outside" intertwined 106
    4.2.1. Ethics and justice 106
    4.2.2. The saying and the said.. 119
4.3. Singular and plural... 127

PART II
Sociality 133

CHAPTER 5
Sociality: the Word and the Notion.. 135

5.1. Sociality – the notion 136
5.2. The word 'sociality' 144

CHAPTER 6
The Presence and Absence of Sociality in Levinas's Early- and Middle-period Works 149

6.1. "Existence and Existents" and "Time and the Other"...... 151
6.2. "Totality and Infinity" 159

CHAPTER 7
The Presence and Absence of Sociality in Levinas's Later Works 171

7.1. The 'correction' of the I-Thou... 172
7.2. Sociality and proximity.. 181
7.3. Sociality and love.. 187
7.4. Sociality and society... 196

CHAPTER 8
Thinking Sociality with Levinas against Levinas 201

8.1. The critique of the dyad 202
8.2. Sociality as Facing 206

PART III
Un-common Sociality 215

CHAPTER 9
Levinas's Community... 217

9.1. Side-by-side with a shared common 219
9.2. Fraternal Community.. 226
    9.2.1. Thinking community through fraternity 227

9.2.2. Some problems with fraternity 231
9.2.3. Fraternal community and sociality 237

CHAPTER 10
Without a Common 243
10.1. Inoperative community 244
10.2. Unavowable community 255

CHAPTER 11
Sociality and the Un-common 269
11.1. Thinking the un-common with Levinas 269
11.1.1. Beyond the ontology/ethics alternative 269
11.1.2. On the same and the other 276
11.2. Un-common and irreciprocal facing 281

Instead of a Conclusion
Un-common Turned Inside-out 293

References 295
Works by Levinas 295
Other references 300

Abbreviations

Works by Levinas

AE - *Autrement qu'etre ou au-dela de l'essence* [1974]. Paris: Le Livre de Poche, 1978.

AT - *Alterity and Transcendence*. [1995]. Translated by Michael B. Smith. New York: Columbia University Press, 1999.

BPW - *Basic Philosophical Writings*. Edited by Adriaan Peperzak, Simon Critchley and Robert Bernasconi. Bloomington, IN: Indiana University Press, 1996.

BV - *Beyond the Verse. Talmudic Readings and Lectures* [1982]. Translated by Gary D. Mole. Bloomington IN: Indiana University Press, 1994.

CPP - *Collected Philosophical Papers*. Translated by Alphoso Lingis. Pittsburgh, PA: Duquesne University Press, 1987/1998.

DEE - *De l'existence a l'existant* [1947]. Paris: Vrin, 1990/2004. (Seconde édition augmentée)

DF - *Difficult Freedom* [1976]. Translated by Seán Hand. Baltimore: The John Hopkins University Press, 1990.

DQVI - *De Dieu qui vient a l'idée* [1986]. Paris: Vrin, 2004. (Seconde édition augmentée. Quatrième tirage).

EE - *Existence and Existents* [1947]. Translated by Alphonso Lingis. Dordrecht: Kluwer Academic Publishing, 1978 (Third Printing 1995).

EI - *Ethics and Infinity. Conversations with Philippe Nemo* [1982]. Translated by Richard A. Cohen. Pittsburgh, PA: Duquesne University Press, 1985.

EN - *Entre Nous. Thinking of the Other* [1991]. Translated by Michael B. Smith and Barbara Harshav. New York: Columbia University Press, 1998.

ENEPA - Entre Nous. Essais sur le penser-à-l'autre. Paris: Grasset, 1991.

GDT - *God, Death and Time* [1975-6]. Translated by Bettina Bergo. Stanford, CA: Stanford University Press, 2000.

OGCM - *Of God who Comes to Mind* [1986]. Translated by Bettina Bergo. Stanford, CA: Stanford University Press, 1998.

HS - *Hors Sujet*. Montpellier: Fata Morgana, 1987.

IIRB - *Is it righteous to be?* Edited by Jill Robbins. Stanford, CA: Stanford University Press, 2001.

TO - *Time and the Other* [1947]. Translated by Richard A. Cohen. Pittsburgh, PA: Duquesne University Press, 1987.

LR - *The Levinas Reader*. Edited by Seán Hand. Oxford, UK: Basil Blackwell, 1989.

NTR - *Nine Talmudic Readings*. Translated by Annette Aronowicz. Bloomington, IN: Indiana University Press, 1990/1994.

OB - *Otherwise than Being or Beyond Essence* [1974]. Translated by Alphonso Lingis. Pittsburgh, PA: Duquesne University Press, 1999.

OS - *Outside the Subject* [1987]. Translated by Michael B. Smith. Stanford, CA: Stanford University Press, 1993.

PN - *Proper Names* [1975]. Translated by Michael B Smith. Stanford, CA: Stanford University Press, 1996.

TeI - *Totalité et infini* [1961]. Paris: Le Livre de Poche, 1990.

TI - *Totality and Infinity. An essay on exteriority* [1961]. Translated by Alphonso Lingis. Pittsburgh, PA: Duquesne University Press, 1969.

Other works

BSP - Nancy, Jean-Luc. *Being Singular Plural* [1996]. Translated by Robert D. Richardson and Anne E. O'Byrne. Stanford, CA: Stanford University Press, 2000.

CD - Nancy, Jean-Luc. *La communauté désœuvrée*. Edited by Christian Bourgois. Paris: Galilée, 1986/1990.

CI - Blanchot, Maurice. *La communauté inavouable*. Paris: Les Éditions de Minuit, 1983.

IC - Nancy, Jean-Luc, *The Inoperative Community*. Edited by Peter Connor. Foreword by Christopher Fynsk. Minneapolis, MN: Minneapolis University Press, 1991.

UC - Blanchot, Maurice. *The Unavowable Community* [1983]. Translated by Pierre Joris. Barrytown, NY: Station Hill Press, 1988.

Introduction

The following pages invite the reader on a quest to think the meaning of sociality in a manner inspired by the philosophy of Emmanuel Levinas, and to explore its significance by engaging in the larger debate on the question of community without foundation in a shared common. Important landmarks in this quest will be thinking subjectivity as de-position and a consideration of the relation to the other(s) from the "inside-out," ideas which will help us carry forward Levinas's understanding of sociality towards a refusal of determination, of becoming a common ground. This resistance to forming a common, which nevertheless gives sense to any communion, reveals an *un-common sociality*, a sociality thought beyond the ethical dyad, and also beyond the reciprocity required by the implication of the third. Thus, our aim is not merely to read exegetically, but to shed light on the meaningfulness of pursuing directions opened up by Levinas's work and of thinking, from out of that work, an *un-common sociality*.

Reading Levinas

Most readers of Levinas would agree that deciphering his texts is not the easiest task. His words are often cryptic and metaphorical, and his writing lacks a straightforward conceptual framework. Transparency and structure seem not to be among his priorities.[1] Although, on his own account, his writings owe much to the phenomenological method,[2] Levinas does not

---

[1] Levinas's criticizes the philosophical approach that gives priority to 'light,' that is, to bringing forth, clarifying and showing. We will return to this critique when we discuss the question of consciousness in Chapter 2.

[2] See for example in TI 28.

seem to follow strictly any specific philosophical method, and in general does not appear to place much weight on methodology.[3]

In trying to unravel Levinas's writing, it seems particularly fitting to recall the words of Derrida, who compared his work to the "infinite insistence of waves on a beach," washing over and over again the same shore, returning each time renewed and enriched.[4] Levinas himself, in a discussion with Dutch philosophers at the University of Leyden in March 1975, designates his "method" as being one of *emphasis*: "I am treating emphasis (*emphase*), as you see, as a method (*procédé*)."[5] For Levinas, emphasis carries the double meaning of bringing forth and of excess.[6] There is an overflow of meaning, a surplus that pours outside the containments of showing. In a way, Levinas's method of emphasis reflects the philosophical question imprinted in many of his discussions (e.g. the discussion on alterity, the Saying, the self—discussions which are clearly connected), that is, the question of the unthematized that goes beyond determination.

The excess of meaning implied by Levinas's method of emphasis is also evident in the way in which he builds his terminology. The notions are not simply determined or given a straightforward meaning, but are rather 'over-determined' through the excess, the overflow of meanings that cannot be directly shown. Indeed, in *Otherwise than Being* Levinas presents his ethical language as emerging from this over-determination:

> Here the over-determination of the ontological categories is visible, which transforms them into ethical terms.[7]

The surplus of meaning cannot be captured by a language of determination, which Levinas identifies with the ontological language that he has mostly learned from Heidegger. Nonetheless, it is this surplus of meaning, and the

---

[3] "I do not believe that there is transparency possible in method. Nor that philosophy might be possible as transparency. Those who have worked on methodology all their lives have written many books that replace more interesting books that they could have written.," "Questions and answers" (1977), in OGCM 89.
[4] Jacques Derrida, "Violence and Metaphysics" (1964) in *Writing and Difference*, trans. Alan Bass (London and New York: Routledge, 2001), 397–8, n. 7.
[5] "Questions and answers," in OGCM 89.
[6] Ibid.
[7] OB 115.

over-determination it involves, that enables the engagement of an ethical language.[8]

Levinas's mixing of ethical vocabulary with many phenomenological and ontological concepts form a distinctive writing style; when we add to this the lack of rigorous method, the reading indeed becomes difficult; but at the same time, it is this that opens his texts toward a variety of interpretations and possible inflections. The reading that we propose is one in which certain lines of interpretation are prioritized, but will always be seen to be permitted by Levinas's text; it corresponds to a general approach towards Levinas's philosophy, one which will help us take up in a fruitful way the question of sociality. This approach is guided by an effort to break the modes of thinking that prioritize determination and operate through alternatives, even if this means leaving behind Levinas's remarks on sociality as face-to-face or as dyadic ethical relation, and his occasionally strong separation between the Same and the Other or between ontology and ethics. We can say that we are applying the same method in dealing with Levinas's writings that Levinas himself promotes, of going beyond determination, embracing the paradoxes instead of attempting to resolve them. In this sense, we will turn Levinas against himself, whilst, paradoxically, remaining faithful to the spirit of his writings.

According to this particular mode of reading Levinas, we find that the ethical language that comes fully into its own in his later work, although seemingly presented as an alternative to ontological categories, is not in fact simply placed over against the ontological. On the contrary, it has the role of emphasizing the ontological through its very surplus of determination, in a way that renders the ethical language more ontological than the ontological language itself. We find in the following words of Levinas an important indication, one that resonates profoundly with the approach we will adopt here, as it prevents the ethical from being turned into a separate sphere, or into an alternative to the ontological:

---

[8] "Through emphasis one passes from the order of presence and representation into another, ethical order. Emphasis is no argumentation.," "What one asks of oneself, one asks of a saint" (1980–81), interview conducted and translated by Johan F. Goud, in *Levinas Studies. An Annual Review, Vol. 3*, ed. Jeffrey Bloechl (Pittsburgh: Duquesne University Press, 2008), 15.

> [E]thical language seems to me closer to the adequate language [...] for me, ethics is not at all a layer that covers over ontology, but rather that which is in some fashion more ontological than ontology; an emphasis of ontology.[9]

Levinas's refusal to think ethics as something separated from ontology,[10] offers important support for our interpretation, which endorses the importance of the ontological expressed through the ethical in Levinas's philosophy. However, the intention is not that of turning Levinas's philosophy into the kind of ontology that he criticized, but rather of overcoming a dichotomy of ethics and ontology.[11]

The way one reads the notion of responsibility has an important role in breaking down the ethics/ontology dichotomy. Levinas's texts suggest that responsibility is not a matter of individual choice and that, as such, it cannot be categorized in terms of good or bad, or in terms of altruistic and non-altruistic attitudes or behaviours.[12] When following Levinas via this line of thought, we find responsibility irreducible to a responsive *act*, but already deeply imprinted in the self as self. Responsibility is connected to the 'birth' of the self: it means the response to the other who calls the self into uniqueness, the response through which subjectivity itself emerges.[13] In this sense, it needs to be detached from the designation of a kind of moral conduct, and considered instead in terms of responsiveness, as a responding to the other.

Our reading of the notion of ethics is consistent with the reading of responsibility described above, and is thus disconnected from prescriptive or normative ethics and moral theory. This reading finds its support in many of Levinas's texts, among them this often-cited passage from *Totality and Infinity*, in which Levinas explains the meaning of ethics:

---

[9] "Questions and answers," in OGCM 89–90.
[10] Here it is important to note that the refusal of separation between ethics and ontology is not at all the same as the intertwinement of the ethical and justice, which we will discuss in Chapter 4. The most important difference is perhaps that the ontological includes the question of self as unique singularity, while justice always engages comparison and measuring.
[11] This issue will be addressed more directly in Chapter 11.
[12] "Egoism and altruism are posterior to responsibility, which makes them possible." OB 197, n. 27.
[13] Nevertheless, this "birth" does not denote a beginning or origin. We will see in Chapter 2 that the emergence of the self is an-archical, that is to say, an-originary.

> A calling into question of the same—is brought about by the other. We name this calling into question of my spontaneity by the presence of the Other ethics.[14]

For Levinas, ethics is the very calling into question of the self by the other. This calling into question marks the emergence of the self itself and is not a mere characteristic attached to the self, or a matter of choice. Thus, Levinas's task is not that of building an ethical or moral theory.[15] In *Ethics and Infinity* Levinas is very clear on this point: "My task does not consist in constructing ethics; I only try to find its meaning."[16] Readers of Levinas have become quite accustomed to calling his project an "ethics of ethics" or a "meta-ethics" instead of just calling it simply "ethics."[17] This re-naming is undertaken precisely in order to underscore that Levinas is not proposing a prescriptive ethical theory, but rather that he is concerned to raise the more fundamental question of how there can be an ethical attitude in the first place—a question that underlies any kind of an ethical theory.

By offering a reading of responsibility as responsiveness, and by connecting ethics to the emergence of the self, we will attempt consistently to displace Levinas's writings from their categorization as ethical theory and underline instead the role they hold in examining the relation of the self in responsiveness to the other(s). Viewed in this way, Levinas's project can be seen to place a far greater focus on sociality as the relation to the other(s) in responsiveness, rather than on the general question of ethics as such.[18]

---

[14] TI 43.
[15] As for example, Joshua James Show' reading suggests: "At the foundation, my goal is to share a reading of Levinas that does justice to his claims about the priority of ethics. The Levinas I admire is the one who tells us that nothing matters more in this world than helping others," says Show in the preface of his book, *Emmanuel Levinas on the Priority of Ethics: Putting Ethics First* (Amherst: Cambria Press, 2008), XX.
[16] *Ethics and Infinity. Conversations with Philippe Nemo* (1982), trans. Richard A. Cohen (Pittsburgh: Duquesne University Press, 1985), 90.
[17] Perhaps most famously Derrida named Levinas's ethics an "ethics of ethics" (see "Violence and Metaphysics," in *Writing and Difference*, 138) or "ethics beyond ethics" (see "Adieu" [1995], in Jacques Derrida, *Adieu to Emmanuel Levinas*, trans. Pascale-Anne Brault and Michael Naas [Stanford: Stanford University Press, 1999], 4). It subsequently became quite common among commentators to refer to 'ethics of ethics,' 'meta-ethics' or 'proto-ethics.'
[18] In his commemorative words delivered at Levinas's funeral (later published under the title "Adieu"), Derrida recalls a conversation with Levinas about the role of ethics for his work: "One day on the rue Michel-Ange, during one of those conversations whose memory I hold so dear [...] he said to me: 'You know, one often speaks of ethics to

Labeling Levinas as an ethical thinker carries the risk of placing most of the weight of his work on 'the Other' as an ethical notion, which in its turn shadows the philosopher's efforts of de-posing the subject from its own foundation, a de-posing that is characteristic of his later work. Perhaps it is not a coincidence that, especially in his later writings, Levinas explicitly announces that his philosophical project is to be considered a "phenomenology of sociality."[19] If we want to take Levinas's thoughts seriously, we need to situate his philosophical achievements beyond making 'the Other' into an ethical concept, and highlight instead the strong connection between de-position and sociality. This approach enables us to think sociality otherwise than as a dyad, but also differently from the third (these representing the traditional interpretations of the relation to the other in Levinas's work), and show its meaningfulness in the effort to think a de-position of community, community that does not find its foundation in a shared common.

General aims and structure of the argument

By means of the approach described above, our goal is to open up the meaning of sociality from out of Levinas's work and contribute to the development of this notion beyond mere exegesis. In order to understand the potential value of exploring sociality in this way, we must first address

---

describe what I do, but what really interests me in the end is not ethics, not ethics alone, but the holy, the holiness of the holy.'" Jacques Derrida, "Adieu," in *Adieu to Emmanuel Levinas*, 4. Here, it needs to be mentioned briefly Levinas's distinction between holy (or saintly) and sacred: holiness (*sainteté*) signifies "separation and purity, the essence without admixture that can be called Spirit," while the sacred (*la sacré*) "is in fact the half light in which the sorcery the Jewish tradition abhors flourishes," "Desacralization and Disenchantment" (1977), in NTR 141. Other times, while focusing on the development of the notion of hospitality, Derrida views the Levinasian ethics, as an ethics of hospitality. For more on this topic see François Raffoul. "The Subject of the Welcome," *Symposium* 2, no.2 (1998): 211-222.

[19] "I have attempted a 'phenomenology' of sociality starting from the face of the other person—from proximity—by understanding in its rectitude a voice that commands before all mimicry and verbal expression, in the mortality of the face, from the bottom of this weakness.," "Diachrony and representation" (1985), in TO 109. Or again, in his interview from 1986: "The thought of Buber pushed me to engage in a phenomenology of sociality, which is more than the human. Sociality is for me the better – than - human," "The Proximity of the Other" (1986), trans. Bettina Bergo, in IIRB 215.

the rather basic yet necessary question: why is it of importance to *develop the notion of sociality* from Levinas's work? This question is more than a search for a general motivation. All three elements of the question: "development," "notion," and "sociality," can raise serious problems in the context of Levinas's work. We shall explore their problematic nature and show how we intend to overcome the problems they might pose.

Levinas is well known for his exploration of different forms of relation to the other. In this sense, if we considered sociality loosely as the relation to the other, one could easily argue that Levinas's whole oeuvre is about sociality. Although from time to time, Levinas explicitly announces sociality to be at the centre of his work, due to the manifold aspects of the relation to the other addressed throughout his work one can only wonder whether there is in fact a specific meaning that he would attribute to "sociality" as such; ultimately we need to ask: what is it that is supposed to be central for Levinas? Scholars of his work tend to follow Levinas's own model and treat the task of clarifying the meaning of sociality as being of secondary importance. Consequently, the reading of this notion differs considerably from interpretation to interpretation, ranging from an understanding of sociality as my relation with one other person, to allowing the term to designate the relations established between all members of a society.[20] So, if we want to address the question of sociality in relation to Levinas's thought, we should clarify first exactly what it is that sociality means for Levinas. Since Levinas's philosophy does not offer a straightforward response, and the meaning of sociality is rather emphasized by means of other notions than addressed directly, a process of disclosure is required, and the notion of sociality

---

[20] To mention just a few examples: some read sociality as the face-to-face encounter seen as *dual relation* between me and you (as for example Richard Cohen does in *Levinasian Meditations. Ethics, Philosophy and Religion* [Pittsburgh: Duquesne University Press, 2010]). Another reading of sociality understands it as *the implication of the third* in the face-to-face relation (an example in this sense is Adriaan Peperzak's reading, that considers sociality as the "social philosophy" of Levinas, which, at least as it is reflected in *Totality and Infinity*, is concerned with the relation between the face-to-face and society, with all the others. See *To the Other: An Introduction to the Philosophy of Emmanuel Levinas* [West Lafayette, IN: Purdue University Press, 1993], especially Ch. V); and there are readers who stretch the meaning of sociality "beyond the human," not by suggesting a moral demand that an animal would have, but rather an ethical responsibility that man carries towards the shared world. (See Alphonso Lingis, "Objectivity and of justice: A Critique of Emmanuel Levinas's explanations," *Continental Philosophy Review* 32, no.4 [1999]: 395–407, or *The Community of Those Who Have Nothing in Common*, [Bloomington and Indianapolis: Indiana University Press, 1994]).

developed gradually from Levinas's work. However, this is just the first aspect of the need for development, one which regards the meaning of sociality within Levinas's work itself. The second aspect comes from moving beyond this preliminary investigation and open up the meaning of sociality in Levinas's work towards a more complex discussion involving the resistance to the formation of common ground, resistance given by the meaning of sociality itself. We call this two-fold movement a *development* of the notion of sociality because it is not taken directly from Levinas's work, but rather extrapolated from that work, in thinking along with Levinas. At times, as has already been mentioned, this process will also involve confronting Levinas with himself in order to explore the true potential of a Levinasian sociality.

One counter-argument to any attempt to "develop" the notion of sociality from Levinas's work could be that the very reason behind Levinas's lack of clarity regarding the meaning of sociality is his insistence on avoiding the construction of a purely theoretical notion, since according to him, the way such a notion functions necessarily implies abstraction and universalization. In this sense, to speak about a *notion* of sociality might appear to run counter to Levinas's philosophical stand of refusing generalization and determination when it comes to the relation to the other. Nevertheless, the notion of sociality proposed by this thesis takes into consideration Levinas's insistence on leaving the relation to the other outside determination, as well as his critique of universalization and abstraction. Our reading of sociality implies precisely the breakdown of any unifying principle that a universalized abstract concept would presuppose through the strong role that we attribute to the hither side (the inside-out dimension of the relation to the other, characteristic of sociality). This approach gives sociality the role of interrupting determination, while not forming a separate realm or a determined essence that causes the interruption. In this sense, sociality interrupts, and coincides with this interruption without the notion of sociality congealing into universal determinations.

Still, even if it does not establish a separate realm or a determined essence through universalization, sociality nevertheless represents a rather wide-ranging notion, one that can be found both in philosophy and in social theories. Indeed, it is reasonable to think that Levinas's intention in avoiding terminologically the use of the notion of sociality was to distinguish firmly his philosophy from the sociological spirit of the time. In an interview from 1986 he makes it rather clear that during his studies at Strasbourg it was customary to engage in sociological debates (about

Durkheim in particular), something which always remained far from Levinas's objectives.[21] Thus, again, the question arises: why develop the notion of *sociality*? Why not just follow Levinas in focusing on the different aspects of the relation to the other? This would be a legitimate question if one's sole goal were an exposition of Levinas's philosophy. However, as we have already pointed out, our aim here is different. Our goal is to explore the possibilities that Levinas's philosophy offers for thinking the question of sociality by pointing out its un-grounding character, in strong relation with the de-position of the self.[22]

Although we make the terminological choice to use the notion of *sociality*, this does not indicate a return to the sociological paradigm that Levinas so desperately wanted to avoid. It is not the intention, here, to discuss processes of socialization or the different sides of inter-human relations and interactions that are characteristic of our coexistence in society. The meaning that we seek to bring to sociality is very different from, for example, that which Georg Simmel sees as the "impulse to sociability in man," since this impulse is towards sociality as an association, a togetherness which tends to a "union with others."[23] Our approach does not represent a sociological perspective, even a phenomenologically-inspired one. Thus, this work is not intended as a contribution to the social phenomenology opened up by Alfred Schütz.[24] Rather, we are looking for a philosophical meaning of sociality that, instead of expressing an established association, disturbs the very bond of association, and at the same time gives sense to it. Nevertheless, this figure is not to be confused with a Kantian "unsociable sociability," thought as the antagonism between the "propensity to enter into society" and the "resistance that constantly threatens to break up this society."[25] The interruption characteristic of the notion of sociality that we propose does not threaten to break up a social link; it is, rather, this interruption that gives the very sense of

---

[21] EI 25–6.
[22] On Levinas's preference to phenomenology over a Durkheimian sociology, see Chapter 5.
[23] Georg Simmel, "The Sociology of Sociability," trans. Everett C. Hughes, in *American Journal of Sociology*, Vol. 55, No. 3 (1949): 254–261.
[24] See for example, Alfred Schütz, *The Phenomenology of the Social World* (1932), trans. G. Walsh and F. Lehnert, (Evanston: Northwestern University Press, 1967).
[25] Immanuel Kant, "Idea for a Universal History with a Cosmopolitan Aim" (1786), trans. Allen W. Wood, in *Kant's Idea for a Universal History with a Cosmopolitan Aim. A Critical Guide*, eds. Amélie Oksenberg Rorty and James Schmidt (Cambridge, United Kingdom: Cambridge University Press, 2009), 13.

any social link. The *un-commonness* of sociality, in our understanding, is not a threat, but a "without-common" as exception, in the Levinasian sense of exception (from ex-cipere), meaning to take out, a term which again suggests de-position. Due to its refusal of fusion and its interruptive character (aspects that will be clarified later on) sociality does not form an essence of the self or a common foundation for community, not even in the form of common resistance. Given the double meaning of the un-common (both 'without common' and 'ex-ception') and the etymological inheritance of the word 'sociality,'[26] in using the expression 'un-common sociality' we aim to articulate a deposition, a trembling of the common ground, which gives sense to the common, and in this way, is always already in the common. Through this approach, we open the Levinasian notion of sociality up to a dialogue with debates on community thought differently than a communion based on a shared common *something*. This provides a perspective on Levinas's work that makes us re-think the notion of sociality and its importance.

Now, after clarifying the reasons for developing the notion of sociality from Levinas's work, in other words, of thinking an un-common sociality with Levinas, let us present how this developing process is structured in this work. A first step in approaching the question of sociality consists in recognizing two dimensions through which the relation to the other is problematized in Levinas philosophy: the first is that which we will call the "inside-out" dimension, in which the relation to the other is approached from the hither side, and the second is an "outside" dimension, one which allows consideration of the relation itself, bringing it to the foreground. Recognizing this distinction is necessary in order to reveal a sociality that is thought in terms other than that of a dyad or the many. The first part of the thesis, entitled *Subjectivity and Multiplicity*, is dedicated to clarifying the meaning of these two dimensions. It brings forth the radical multiplicity at the heart of Levinasian subjectivity and its ambiguous intertwinement with multiplicity understood as the plurality of others. The "inside-out" dimension is shown to be different from subjectivism or an enclosed inside. Instead, it is an inside through an outside, conceived by way of Levinas's thinking of subjectivity as de-position. The self is de-posed, "turning itself inside out"[27] Levinas claims,

---

[26] Read via its etymology the meaning, sociality indicates that it is not merely a characteristic attached to the self. On the etymological meaning of sociality, see below, Chapter 5.
[27] OB 117, see also: "Substitution" (1968), trans. P. Atterton, S. Critchley, and G. Noctor, in BPW 91.

hence the name we are giving to this inside-out dimension. In this first part of the thesis we argue that the inside-out dimension is neither an inside nor an outside, but the very questioning of interiority and exteriority, of singularity and plurality. It is characterized by irreciprocity, asymmetry, 'bad' consciousness and 'bad' time, and a radicalized meaning of multiplicity thought differently than in terms of singular/plural or other/others. On the other hand, the outside dimension of the relation to the other is reflected in the question of justice and requires an outside perspective upon the relation itself. This opens up the possibility of comparison, calculation and judgement. Through the outside perspective, aspects such as reciprocity and symmetry find their way in Levinas's philosophy, along with thematizing consciousness, synthetical time-structure, and multiplicity thought in terms of singular and plural. Meanwhile, the paradoxical intertwinement of the two dimensions—inside-out and outside—will be brought forth in a way which shows that, although different (or rather non-indifferent), they are not to be considered separate realms.

The inside-out dimension and its ambiguous intertwinement with the outside dimension of the relation to the other, introduced in Part I, lays the groundwork for the discussion of sociality as it appears in Levinas's writings, and the possible directions of its development. This broadly constitutes the thematic of Part II and III. Part II, *Sociality*, investigates the ways in which both the word and the notion of sociality appear in Levinas's work, by analyzing the different ways in which Levinas approaches the question of sociality. Part II, on the one hand, seems to be the closest to Levinas; this is particularly the case when his understanding of sociality is being analyzed through close readings of his texts. There, we find sociality expressing interruption, fission and a refusal of fusion. On the other hand, it is in this section that we can begin to distance ourselves from some of Levinas's claims, in that a critique is articulated of his insistence on thinking sociality in terms of dyad. The critique of sociality as dyad leads to a problematizing of the importance that Levinas gives to the face-to-face relation. At the end of Part II we argue for our preference for an understanding of sociality expressed as "facing" instead of as face-to-face relation, an argument which is continued in Part III.

Part III, *Un-common Sociality*, develops further the notion of sociality, revealing new aspects by addressing the notion in relation to the question of community. This means that the third part of the thesis will partially turn away from Levinas's own texts, in order to address more closely the Nancy-Blanchot debate on community. Our attempt, here, will be to connect sociality, previously described as resistance to fusion and interruption, with community thought otherwise than based on *something* in common, in particular, with the "inoperative" and "unavowable" community introduced respectively by Nancy and Blanchot. It is this connection which will reveal the notion of sociality as the *un-common* at the core of any community, as well as introduce Levinas into a discussion where, until now, he has previously been underestimated. While remaining an irreciprocal relation viewed from the inside-out, sociality is revealed as the interruptive movement of facing. As such, it does not constitute a foundation for community, but rather signifies the very de-position, fission in foundation which is, however, necessary for any foundation. By thinking sociality with Levinas, we show the importance of problematizing an un-common, irreciprocal sociality that interrupts the foundation in a shared common ground, but at the same time is always presupposed by that shared common ground.

Reading about Levinas

Discussion of Levinas's philosophy has remained lively over the years. Studies on Levinas offer a wide variety of different kinds of readings, and in recent years it has become a custom to divide the Levinas scholarship into three waves chronologically following each other.[28] First, there is an "early wave" consisting mainly of exegetical works with reflections on *Totality and Infinity*. Soon after, a "second wave" followed, marked by Derrida's critique from *Violence and Metaphysics* (1964), which has inspired a critical approach and alternative interpretations. Although Derrida's work focuses on *Totality and Infinity*, interpretations that stem from this "second wave" often consider *Otherwise than Being* and Levinas's later work as well. Subsequently, a "third wave" has started to develop, and in fact is still continuing today, which is preoccupied with Levinas's relevance in dialogue

---

[28] This way of devidivng the Levinas scholarship can be found in an increasing number of recent works, e.g. Peter Atterton, "Editors' Introduction: The Third Wave of Levinas Scholarship" (with Matthew Calarco), in *Radicalizing Levinas*, eds. Peter Atterton and Matthew Calarco (Albany: SUNY Press, 2010), ix-xvii; John E Drabinski, *Levinas and the Postcolonial: Race, Nation, Other* (Edinburgh,: Edinburgh University Press, 2011) or Jeffrey W. Robbins, "Thinking Transcendence with Levinas: From the Ethico-Religious to the Political and Beyond," *Analecta Hermeneutica*, Vol 2 (2010).

with other thinkers and topics, and represents more than an exegetical or a critical account, reaching beyond Levinas's work itself.[29] According to this division, the present work inscribes itself in the third wave, not just chronologically, but also in its approach, since it relates the question of sociality developed out of Levinas's philosophy to contemporary debates on community, and opens up the notion in a way that reaches beyond Levinas's own writings as such. Nevertheless, this also implies a need to remain close to Levinas's texts, in order to grasp the meaning of sociality in his thinking, as well as a critical approach towards some of the turns his philosophy takes. This makes the thesis less of an exegesis and more a process of thinking the meaning of sociality, a process that also includes critical reflection on Levinas's philosophy.

Attempting to provide a comprehensive overview of the different readings of Levinas would be unfeasible here in terms of space, and also thematically too broad. Instead, we will sketch briefly, and in a preliminary way, those philosophical debates on Levinas that this endeavor, directly or indirectly, will engage. Thus we will be able to map out the position that will be taken up here in relation to the abundant scholarly work on Levinas by highlighting particular questions that it touches upon.

One of the problems that has opened up a number of questions in regard to Levinas's philosophy concerns the problem of the political. It is no sur-

---

[29] This last wave also includes attempts to address Levinas in a different context than the strict phenomenological or theological field, such as sociopolitical issues, feminism, postcolonialism, medical care, literature etc. A slightly different division comes from Jack Marsh (Jack Marsh, "Levinas en Amérique du Nord aujourd'hui. Trois vagues et deux écoles," *Cahiers d'Etudes Lévinassienes*, 11 [2012] : 193–211). Marsh, by referring specifically to the North American reception of Levinas, distinguishes between the phenomenological and the Derridian schools of research; the former is represented by those who consider Levinas as a phenomenologist and thus read him in close connection to Husserl' phenomenology, while the latter refers to those who employ a deconstructionist reading of Levinas, and thus follow a Derridian interpretation. Yet another partition of the secondary literature on Levinas comes from Robert Bernasconi and Stacy Keltner (See Robert Bernasconi and Stacy Keltner, "Emmanuel Levinas: The Phenomenology of Sociality and the Ethics of Alterity," in *Phenomenological Approaches to Moral Philosophy: A Handbook,* ed. John Drummond, [Dordrecht: Kluwer, 2002], 262.). In an essay attempting to introduce the reader to Levinas's philosophy, they differentiate among three dominant trends: firstly, scholars who consider Levinas to give a phenomenological description of the relation to the other; then, there are those who strongly emphasize Levinas's indebtedness to Judaism; and last but not least, those interpreters who approach Levinas from a Derridian perspective.

prise, then, that these questions have attracted the interest of various readers of Levinas. The general significance of the problem raised by the political in Levinas's work can be linked to his thoughts on justice.[30] The relations of symmetry and reciprocity that justice introduces are inherited by the political sphere, whereas the difference between the asymmetrical and symmetrical, between the irreciprocal and the reciprocal relation to the other marks a difference between the ethical and the political. This leads to the question regarding the compatibility of the ethical with the political, or, to put it bluntly: *how does Levinas solve the tension between uniqueness and equality, between asymmetry and symmetry?* Thus, scholars who discuss the question of the political in Levinas's philosophy deal in particular with the difficulty of reconciling Levinas's thoughts on the asymmetrical relation to *the other* with the symmetrical relation to a plurality of others, or even to *all others*. This difficulty has provoked critique from several scholars, pointing out a gap in Levinas's philosophy,[31] and at the same time has led to several attempts to elucidate the problem by emphasizing the importance of the political in Levinas's philosophy, and its fundamental interconnection with the ethical.[32] What these readings share, however, is that they consider the difference between the ethical and the political to be a matter of the other vs. others, singular and unique vs. plural and comparable. Thus, reconciliation between ethical asymmetry and political symmetry translates into the transition from a dual relation with the other to the plurality of more than just one other.

Although it is not the intention, here, to focus on the question of the political in Levinas's philosophy, we will take up, in Chapter 4, the discussion of the relation between ethics and justice. We will there find ourselves in agreement with the above-mentioned interpretation, which claims that

---

[30] It needs to be noted here that Levinas's conception of justice changes over time. In order to avoid any confusion, in our approach the term will carry the meaning given by Levinas in his later works (*Otherwise than Being* and after). There, justice concerns the necessity of measuring and comparing responsibilities. This is also the meaning closely associated by Levinas with the one represented by the state, institutions and law, but also with the political. For further details see Chapter 4.

[31] See for instance Slavoj Žižek, "Neighbors and Other Monsters: A Plea for Ethical Violence," in *The Neighbor: Three Inquiries in Political Theology*, eds. Slavoj Žižek, Eric L. Santner and Kenneth Reinhard (Chicago: University of Chicago Press, 2006), 134–190.

[32] See for example Simon Critchley, *The Ethics of Deconstruction: Derrida and Levinas* (West Lafayette, IN: Purdue University Press, 1992/1999).

the ethical is always in profound connection with the political. Yet, it is argued that to fully understand the significance of this interconnection, we need to distance ourselves from some of Levinas's comments in which he uses the other/others distinction as a way to differentiate between the ethical and the political. These comments actually contradict Levinas's own thoughts that point towards understanding sociality differently than as a dyad. Thus, we propose reading the notion of sociality beyond a binary relation between the self and the other, yet without identifying it with the society of the many. Instead, sociality will be seen to disrupt the very alternatives of singular/plural, other/others, which will bring forth not only the somewhat obvious idea that the other must be approached quite differently than as a simple numerable entity, but more radically, that the transition from a dyad to the many proves to be a false problem. This means that, through re-thinking sociality in different terms than as a relation of two, the problem of a gap between the political and the ethical also becomes a false problem; not because sociality would correspond to what Levinas has called "the third," and in this way fill in a gap, but because it disrupts thinking that limits itself to the alternative of singular vs. plural, the other vs. others. This deeper meaning of sociality, as something more than a mere dyad, instead of offering a solution to the transition from the other to the others, shows that there it is no need for such solution, there is no need for a reconciliation since it is not a matter of transition or intertwinement of two distinct *realms*, but of different dimensions in a paradoxical relation to each other.

The importance we place on paradox instead of on alternatives intersects with yet another ongoing discussion among Levinas scholars, one that advocates *the primacy of the Other and the Same/Other distinction in Levinas's philosophy.*[33] In his early work, Levinas indeed laid more emphasis on the Same/Other division; and certainly, he often evokes 'the other' (both

---

[33] As for example Badiou, Irigaray, Durfee or even Nancy do. See Alain Badiou, *Ethics: An Essay on the Understanding of Evil* (1998), trans. Peter Hallward (London and New York: Verso, 2001); Luce Irigaray, "Questions to Emmanuel Levinas. On the Divinity of Love," trans. Margaret Whitford, in *Re-reading Levinas*, eds. Robert Bernasconi and Simon Critchley (Bloomington: Indiana University Press, 1991), 109–119; Harold A. Durfee, "War, Politics and Radical Pluralism," *Philosophy for Phenomenological Research*, Vol. 35, no. 4 (1975): 549–558; Jean-Luc Nancy, trans. Robert D. Richardson and Anne E. O'Byrne, *Being Singular Plural* (Stanford, California: Stanford University Press, 2000).

as '*autrui*' and '*autre*') throughout his work, a move that could suggest its primacy as a notion. Nevertheless, in Part II and III we argue that reading Levinas through the notion of the Other and the Same/Other distinction is neither fruitful nor entirely faithful to Levinas's philosophy. On the one hand, the very meaning of an-archy, which is so important throughout Levinas's work, serves to disturb the order of originarity and primacy. On the other hand, but in a way that is related, Levinas makes strong efforts in his later work to break down dichotomies. The growing role given to interruption in Levinas later works shows the significance of disrupting thinking in terms of dualities and oppositions. In our view, this is the reason why the Same/Other opposition is mainly present in Levinas's early and middle-period work, while it fades away in *Otherwise than Being* and in later works.

Highlighting the importance of sociality as interruption, rather than the primacy of the other or the Same/Other distinction, opens up Levinas's philosophy towards the dialogue begun by Nancy and Blanchot on the subject *community*. While Blanchot was quite close to Levinas, both personally and philosophically, Nancy is thought to be more distant from Levinas's philosophical make-up due to his attachment to ontology and his apparent lack of interest in the question of the other. As a consequence, Levinas's philosophy is little discussed in connection with Nancy's thoughts on community without a shared common ground, despite the fact that both of them recognize the key significance of de-position. The handful of articles that involve Levinas in the discussion on re-thinking community without a common ground as proposed by the Blanchot-Nancy debate, are either representing a Levinasian perspective which brings out the shortcomings of Nancy's philosophy,[34] or they underline Nancy's critiques of Levinas.[35] Thus, these readings do not so much create a dialogue as take sides and, as a consequence, further accentuate the gap between Levinas and Nancy. By reconsidering the way in which they both criticize a totalitarian ontology as well as an undisturbed determinacy, we attempt to show the

---

[34] As does, for instance, Simon Critchley in "With Being-With? Notes on Jean-Luc Nancy's Rewriting of *Being and Time*," *Studies in Practical Philosophy*, 1, no. 1 (1999): 53–67.

[35] As seen in the works of Stella Gaon, "Communities in Question: Sociality and Solidarity in Nancy and Blanchot," *Journal of Cultural Research*, 9, no. 4 (October 2005): 387–403; or Christopher Watkins, "A Different Alterity: Jean-Luc Nancy's 'Singular Plural,'" *Paragraph* 30, 2 (2007): 50–64.

closeness between the notion of sociality as facing that we will develop from Levinas's thinking, and the notion of community thought as inoperative and unavowable, a closeness that enriches the meaning of sociality. Framing Levinas's philosophy around a notion of sociality that interrupts a thinking that insists on dichotomies shows its importance in the question of community without a common ground, carrying his philosophy towards regions so far little explored.

PART I
Subjectivity and Multiplicity

Sociality, considered in very general terms, usually denotes the relation we have with one-another. To be sure, much more specificity will be given to this notion in the course of this work, but for now let us say that, for Levinas, this general understanding of sociality can be translated as my relation to the other/others.[1] Levinas discusses the relation to the other/others, on the one hand, in terms of a responsibility for the other embedded in the self, a responsibility/responsiveness which makes the self itself emerge, and on the other hand, in terms of the social context of living with one-another, as a more general responsibility for others. In the first part of the thesis we will see that these two different approaches towards the relation to the other(s) are not determined by the other/others distinction as it might appear, but by two dimensions of the relation to the other. As has been already indicated, this approach proves to be somewhat different from mainstream Levinas scholarship which, whilst recognizing two different aspects of responsibility, tends to base this distinction (which corresponds to the distinction between ethics and justice) on whether responsibility involves the Other (singular) or others (plural). Here, we argue that the distinction is not a question of whether the other is considered to be singu-

---

[1] Although in Levinas's work we encounter both the expressions "rapport/relation avec l'autrui/l'autre" and "rapport à l'autrui/l'autre" referring to what we call "relation to the other," when discussing the question of sociality we have decided to use the expression "relation to..." instead of "relation with..." for at least two reasons: firstly, due to Levinas's critique of the "with" that would foreground the link of the relation itself (we will address this issue later on, especially in Chapter 6 and 11), and secondly because the expression "relation with the other/others" would imply, misleadingly, a social relation of having something in common with someone else, a relationship with someone; that is to say, a relation characteristic to a common society and not to an un-common sociality such as that which we would like to describe here (we will return to the difference between sociality and society in Chapter 7).

lar or plural, but has to do with the very thinking in terms of singular and plural.

In what follows we will introduce what will be referred to throughout as the "inside-out" and the "outside" dimensions of the relation to the other. The inside-out dimension is that which is opened up through the responsiveness of the self as *me*. Consequently the term is closely connected to Levinas's thoughts on subjectivity and the de-position of the self. Hence the notion of substitution, so important for those thoughts on subjectivity, needs to be addressed first, and Chapter 1 will be centered on subjectivity in the form of substitution. The inside-out dimension of the relation to the other reveals subjectivity on the hither side of time and consciousness, aspects that are taken up in Chapter 2. Then, in Chapter 3, the de-posed subjectivity of *Otherwise than Being* will be once more brought into the discussion, this time in order to re-think the meaning of radical multiplicity presented in *Totality and Infinity*. Radical multiplicity designates a radicalized notion of multiplicity that blurs the separation between the other (singular) and others (plural) in the very context of the inside-out dimension of responsibility—that is, without involving comparison and justice. The question of justice introduces the "outside" dimension of the relation to the other, which is discussed in Chapter 4, the last chapter of part one. To the outside dimension, we argue, corresponds a non-radicalized multiplicity, and thus multiplicity this time will be thought in terms of singular/plural. The great importance of considering that the inside-out and outside are *dimensions* and not two alternatives, is further underlined through their ambiguous intertwinement (different yet not separate realms).

CHAPTER 1

Substitution

Especially in the later works, Levinas's philosophy exhibits an increasing focus on the problem of subjectivity. Some might even argue that his (chronologically) second major work, *Otherwise than Being*, has at its very centre the question of subjectivity.[1] This focus on the subject might surprise us, since by the time Levinas entered the philosophical scene a serious questioning of the whole problematic of subjectivity was already underway. Particularly following the Heideggerian critique of metaphysics, one can notice a clear distancing from the essentialist view that argues for the subject as substratum. In this sense, it would be expected that Levinas would also renounce the concept of the subject and the focus on subjectivity. Yet he does not do so. Levinas is holding onto a concept that seems otherwise to disappear from the phenomenological discourse. Consequently, it seems justified to ask whether this represents a step backwards in the phenomenological tradition, with which he nonetheless affiliates himself.[2] This chapter examines this problem closely and shows that, instead of re-installing a concept of the subject that has already been overcome, Levinas re-thinks subjectivity in a way that not only corresponds with the tendency to destitute the subject as foundation, but attempts to strengthen this tendency.[3] The question of subjectivity means for Levinas a

---

[1] As for example Richard Cohen does in the foreword to the English translation of *Otherwise than Being*, or Jacques Rolland in his postscript to *God, Death and Time* (see "Postscript" [1975–6], in GDT 225–243).

[2] Here, we refer to the tradition of phenomenological thinking in a broader sense, to which Levinas is a self-confessed affiliate. Whether Levinas is faithful to Husserl, founder of phenomenology, remains disputable. In this sense, see also Chapter 2 where Levinas's relation to Husserl is discussed in the light of the problematic of consciousness.

[3] Levinas's refusal of a foundationalist view surfaces clearly in the last of his regular lecture courses taught at the University of Paris, Sorbonne, "God and Onto-theo-logy" in

questioning of subjectivity, that is to say, a questioning of the very positioning of the subject both in its relativity to the other, and as self-sufficient substratum. Above all in his later work, and in particular in *Otherwise than Being*, as Jacques Roland notes, the subject appears as already turned towards the other but never joining the other.[4] In other words, subjectivity for Levinas does not imply a foundation; on the contrary, as will become clear by the end of this chapter, Levinas in fact attempts to break down the subject-centered thinking.

Although the overall effort to decentralize the subject is evident throughout Levinas's work as a whole, there seems to be a change in the way he approaches the problem, especially when one compares his two major books *Totality and Infinity* and *Otherwise than Being*. Readers of Levinas have tended to share this view,[5] and indeed, one can observe several differences between the way *Totality and Infinity* and *Otherwise than Being* present subjectivity. In *Totality and Infinity*, Levinas makes the rather strong differentiation between the Same and the Other, and highlights the separateness of the self. In *Otherwise than Being*, however, a new terminology emerges: the Same and the Other distinction and the self separated in enjoyment are replaced by the emergence of the self that is already for the other, in *substitution*. The important role given to substitution in thinking subjectivity, something that is missing from *Totality and Infinity*, becomes fully developed in *Otherwise than Being*. For this reason, it is *Otherwise than Being* which will be the primary source of reference for this chapter.

The very last paragraph of the book summarizes Levinas's main task:

1975. There, Levinas shares the Heideggerian critique of onto-theology, and at the same time presents his own philosophical project of "beyond being." It is certainly not a coincidence that these lectures were held right after the publication of *Otherwise than Being*. See GDT, Part II. "God and Onto-theo-logy," especially the first two lectures.

[4] Rolland, "Postscript," GDT 234–5.

[5] As does for example Philip J. Maloney, "Levinas, substitution, and transcendental subjectivity," *Man and World*, 30 (1997): 49–64. There is a tendency among readers to find in the notion of substitution characteristic to *Otherwise than Being* (but not to *Totality and Infinity*), a response to Derrida's critique from *Violence and Metaphysics*, one of the first critical essays addressing Levinas's *Totality and Infinity*.

> In this work, which does not seek to restore any ruined concept, the destitution [destitution] and the desituating [dé-situation] of the subject do not remain without signification [.][6]

As the above quotation suggests, in *Otherwise than Being* Levinas is not looking to revive the concept of the subject as a foundation; on the contrary, he emphasizes its de-situating, or de-position.[7] The first part of the chapter attempts to unfold the meaning of this de-position. Based on this meaning, in the second part we will introduce the *inside-out dimension* of my relation to the other, as a first layout in terms of which the notion of sociality must be framed.

1.1. De-posed subject

Divorcing his thinking from the essentialist view of the subject holds great importance for Levinas, and is reflected in his general avoidance of giving a definition of the subject. Any straightforward definition would necessarily correspond to the question "Who/what is the subject?" This, for Levinas, is not the right question. For him, the subject does not appear as an answer to the question 'who' or 'what,' but is rather a response prior to any questioning. "Here is a problem preliminary to the questions 'who?' and 'what?'"[8] he writes. In order to provide a deeper insight into the meaning of the subject, he points towards the Latin form of the concept, *sub-jectum*.[9] The use of a hyphen demonstrates Levinas's intention of bringing forth the etymological roots of the concept, though nonetheless with a twist. Etymologically, *subjectum* is the Latin translation of the Greek *hypo-keimenon*, meaning 'that which is underneath' or 'thrown under,' expressing thus a foundation.[10] Levinas, though, understands this 'thrown under' in the sense of being 'subjected to.' This does not mean however that he

---

[6] OB 185, AE 283-4.
[7] Levinas often uses the two expressions ("de-situation" and "de-position") synonymously. See for instance OB 50, AE 86.
[8] OB 24. Regarding the inadequacy of the questions "who?" and "what?" see also Ibid., 27.
[9] "The self is a *sub-jectum*; it is under the weight of the universe, responsible for everything.," Ibid.,116.
[10] This way of understanding subjectivity is one of the reasons Heidegger refuses the use of the concept. See *Being and* Time, trans. by John Macquarrie and Edward Robinson (New York: Harper Collins Publishers, 1962) 72/46.

returns to a meaning conceived before the sovereign subject of modernity, to the subject as that which is subjected to something else (e.g. the subject of an experiment).[11] Levinas, following the spirit of his time, pulls away from the subject-object correlation, and thinks instead the 'subjected to' of *subjectum* as a calling into question, subjected to a question, or rather to a call (*appel*) without an actual questioning: "called into question prior to questioning, responsibility over and beyond the logos of response."[12] The subject is an answering or responding subject, yet paradoxically, the response comes before the possibility of formulating any specific question. The call for response is not a question *about* something; it does not search for information or knowledge. To consider the subject as response does not imply identifying it with a specific answer, as *something* that would fill in the lack put forth by the question and that would take up the role of essence through determination. The subject is not an established, determined response, nor is it a response thought relatively, as a re-action. Instead, it is the very *responsiveness* itself. The subject is always already subjected to a question, and it is in this way that Levinas turns the concept of *sub-jectum* around, avoiding its sedimentation.

Thought as responsiveness outside any particular question, instead of as representing a substratum or a fundamental layer, the subject becomes, in Levinas's work, the very lack of foundation, a null-site (non-place, non-lieu) or u-topia: "the locus or non-lieu, locus and non-lieu, the Utopia, of the human."[13] Here, the concept of utopia expresses precisely the lack of a

---

[11] The way in which Levinas re-thinks subjectivity is called by Simon Critchley "post-deconstructive," that is to say, a subject that is "[neither] metaphysical, nor naively pre-Heideggerian." Simon Critchley, "Post-Deconstructive Subjectivity," in *Ethics, Politics, Subjectivity: Essays on Derrida, Levinas and Contemporary French Thought* (London: Verso, 1999), 62.

[12] OB 102.

[13] Ibid., 45. Subjectivity as u-topia comes as a critique targeting the interpretation of the self as fundament for itself. Nonetheless, Levinas does not ignore the more common understanding of utopia, utopia as an ideal place or state, to which he gives a negative connotation, for instance in the early essay "Place and Utopia" (1950), re-published in the collection of essays entitled *Difficult Freedom* (1976). There, he considers utopian thinking to be useless and even dangerous: "Utopia seems not just vain in itself, it is also dangerous in its consequences. The man of utopia wishes unjustly. Instead of the difficult task of living an equitable life, he prefers the joy of the solitary salvation. He therefore refuses the very conditions in which his bad consciousness had set him up as a person," DF 101. Later on, in *Totality and Infinity*, Levinas starts to think utopia as openness. However, here the concept still indicates a sort of grounding in the form of

certain place and of a certain state through which the self would determine itself—a lack that, however, does not look for fulfillment. Utopia, understood as *non-lieu*, non-place, null-site or atopia, has nothing to do with ideality as an ideal place or state. On the contrary, the u-topia of the subject means freeing it from any kind of ideality. Subjectivity becomes the openness of the self without a previously established I.

> The openness of space as an openness of self without a world, without a place, Utopia, the not being walled in, inspiration to the end, even to expiration [.][14]

Utopia signifies an out of place, out of ground. This does not necessarily mean displacement, as displacement would already presuppose a place from

dwelling, where the self is at home with itself: "The primordial function of the home does not consist in orienting being by the architecture of the building and in discovering a site, but in breaking the plenum of the element, in opening in it the Utopia in which the "I" recollects itself in dwelling at home with itself.," TI 156. Thus, in *Totality and Infinity* the utopia of the self is both grounding and disturbance. Other times, as for example in the essay from 1986 "The Paradox of Morality," Levinas goes so far as to explicitly recognize a utopian move in his own philosophy, and seemingly this does not bother him: "There is a Utopian moment in what I say; it is the recognition of something which cannot be realized but which, ultimately, guides all moral action. This utopianism does not prohibit you from condemning certain factual states, nor from recognizing the relative progress that can be made. Utopianism is not a condemnation of everything else. There is no moral life without utopianism—utopianism in this exact sense that saintliness is goodness." "The Paradox of Morality: An Intervieew with Emmanuel Levina" (1986), interview conducted by Tamara Wright, Peter Hughes and Alison Ainley, in *The Provocation of Levinas. Rethinking the Other*, eds. Robert Bernasconi and David Wood, (London and New York: Routledge, 1988), 178. As we can see, evaluating Levinas's standpoint on utopianism is not so simple, especially since he is not consistent in his approach. According to John Drabinski, the encounter with Celan (1960) marked a turning point for Levinas regarding the thinking of utopia. From then on, the concept of utopia in Levinas's work distanced itself from the messianic, and got closer to spatiality, or rather to "asymmetrical spatiality" as Drabinski calls it. (John E. Drabinski, "Wealth and Justice in a U-topian Context," in *Addressing Levinas*, eds. Eric Sean Nelson, Antje Kapust, and Kent Still [Evanston IL: Northwestern University Press, 2005], 185-198). Nevertheless, we are interested here in the null site or non-place that characterizes subjectivity, and since that is developed in *Otherwise than Being*, we will follow Levinas's understanding of utopia as it is presented in his work from 1974.

[14] OB 182. We can also observe here the reference to inspiration and expiration. The metaphor of breathing often appears in Levinas's vocabulary as either an allusion to the self in substitution (as it is in the example above), or to diachrony, where it is sometimes accompanied by the metaphor of the heartbeat (for instance in Ibid., 109). We will discuss diachrony in the next chapter.

which the subject is dis-placed. Nor is it re-placement, as replacement would be a mere exchange of one place for another. Instead, the very placing of the self is disturbed. Since it is not a process of placement or displacement, the *out of place* of the self cannot be translated into any concrete event or state that happened, could happen, nor one that could/should be aspired to achieving. In this context, utopia is clearly not a matter of chasing an ideal state of being. The u-topia of the subject is the self always already out of place, and this out of place is already part of every event, without utopia being an event in itself.[15] Instead of a *dis-* or *re-*position, Levinas proposes a *de-*position. The sub-jectum, out of place, is presented in *Otherwise than Being* as a *de-posed* subject: "[t]he subject posited as deposed is me."[16] This de-position is further emphasized by Levinas through the notion of *exile*. Exile does not mean that the self disperses in a movement from here to there, but leads to a "hither side of the here," "a trembling of substantiality."[17] It is a disturbance, a "trembling" of the very foundation, the very grounding of the subject: "The exile or refuge in itself is without conditions or support."[18] The question of groundlessness that is involved here already points towards an interconnection with Nancy's and Blanchot's work, which underlines the importance of groundlessness and exile. We will discuss this problem in detail later on.[19] For now, let us focus on the meaning of deposition involved in the question of groundlessness, since it holds the key in understanding the need for the notion of substitution.

---

[15] "[W]hat took place humanly has never been able to remain closed up in its site. There is no need to refer to an event in which the non-site, becoming a site, would have exceptionally entered into the spaces of history." OB 184. In the next chapter we will return to this point by showing that the de-position characteristic of subjectivity cannot become an event in history for it is not conceived in terms of synthetical time structure.

[16] Ibid.,126. The "me" [moi] that the deposed subject expresses, constitutes an important element of our discussion on subjectivity. We will return to it in the following sections and give it the proper attention.

[17] "The restlessness of respiration, the exile in oneself, the in itself without rest, is not an impossibility of inhabiting that would already become a movement from here to yonder; it is a panting, a trembling of substantiality, a hither side of the here." Ibid.,180.

[18] Ibid.,105–6.

[19] This will be discussed in the third part of our thesis, which will be concerned with the question of the un-common and groundlessness, engaging Levinas in the debate between Jean-Luc Nancy and Maurice Blanchot on community without a common ground.

The de-posed subject becomes a part of Levinas's alternative conceptual reservoir introduced in *Otherwise than Being*; it goes beyond the dialectical[20] and descriptive ontological discourses,[21] and enters a theoretical framework where paradoxes are welcomed. Already the expression "deposed subject" (*sujet deposé*) proves to be somewhat paradoxical if we consider that the French verb *déposer*, just as in English, means both 'to deposit,' 'to keep' or 'to sediment,' and 'to destitute,' 'to dethrone.' Levinas's de-posed subjectivity reflects both of these seemingly contradictory meanings: the subject is out of place and in its place, in such a way that its place, its position is precisely its deposition. In other words, the very 'out of place' becomes the place of the subject. Through this de-position, the subject is "out of phase with itself,"[22] meaning that it does not posit itself as its own ground. In this way, for Levinas, the subject is not rooted in itself, it does not emerge from itself:

> Identity here takes form not by a self-confirmation, but, as a signification of the-one-for-the-other, by a deposing of oneself [.][23]

For the emergence of the self, there is a need for exteriority, outside the self itself. A double role is given to exteriority here: it both prevents subjectivity from becoming a totality in the form of an enclosed sphere of interiority,[24]

---

[20] When we refer to dialectics, we do so in the Hegelian sense, and not the later, Kierkegaardian re-thinking of dialectics as 'inverted dialectics.' The latter introduces an inversion which makes dialectics not the resolving of opposites by synthesis (as a Hegelian dialectic would), but, on the contrary, maintaining paradox itself. By this, we follow Levinas's own reference to dialectics. See "What one asks of oneself, one asks of a saint," 8.

[21] "It turns out, as we will see in the course of this study, that, even if one neglects the fact that cognition makes its way in it, the human sphere approached as an object among others takes on significations that link up and implicate one another in such a way as to lead to extreme and irreducible conceptual possibilities, possibilities that go beyond the limits of a description, even if it is dialectical, of order and being, lead to the extraordinary, to what is beyond the possible. Such conceptual possibilities are *substitution of one for another, the immemorable past that has not crossed the present, the positing of the self as a deposing of the ego, less than nothing as uniqueness, difference with respect to the other as non-indifference.*" OB 58, emphasis by Levinas.

[22] "This self is out of phase with itself, forgetful of itself, forgetful in biting in upon itself." Ibid., 115.

[23] Ibid., 79.

[24] This aspect is emphasized in Levinas's early- and middle-period writings in the form of the threat of the totalitarianism of the subject, and is expressed as the totality of the Same.

and also assures the above mentioned de-position characteristic of the subject as *sub-jectum*, where the subject is out of its place, and in this sense, outside itself as ground. The interplay between inside and outside that the de-posed self creates is best articulated in Levinas's notion of *substitution*. With the help of this notion, Levinas attempts to break down the relative determination of interiority and exteriority. In the next section we argue that through the substituting self that does not allow the relative determination of interiority and exteriority, subjectivity is approached from the hither side and the self is turned inside-out.

1.2. Inside-out

As we have seen, Levinas tackles the de-essentialization of the subject by means of the de-position of the self. There is a disturbance at the core of subjectivity that pushes the self "out of phase with itself," making its substantiality "tremble." Levinas's notion of substitution,[25] introduced later in his work, expresses precisely this "out of phase," as the self substitutes itself for the other. As we are about to see, this means that the self emerges as a self through the other, for the other. The purpose of this section, besides presenting Levinas's view on subjectivity by means of the notion of substitution, is to reveal a dimension of the relation to the other that is always approached from the hither side, without bringing the relation itself into the foreground; this we call the *inside-out dimension* of the relation to the other, due to the de-position of the self that turns it "inside-out." Although the *inside-out dimension* of the relation to the other is not articulated explicitly in Levinas's writings, it is certainly implicit, and its explicit problematizing will prove to be very important later on when we will show that this inside-out dimension is precisely where sociality inscribes itself. For now, though, we will elucidate the meaning of the inside-out dimension involved in subjectivity by exploring the texts in which Levinas discusses the meaning of substitution.

---

[25] Levinas's notion of substitution and its developemend have been linked to the work of Gabriel Marcel (see Robert B. Gibbs, "Substitution. Marcel and Levinas," *Philosophy & Theology* 4 [1989]: 171–85), and the works of Husself and Heidegger (see Bettina Bergo "'When I Opened He had Gone': Levinas's Substitution as a reading Husserl and Heidegger," *Discipline Filosofiche* 1 [2014]: 97–118).

Only briefly mentioned in a few previous essays,[26] substitution as a notion is developed for the first time in the essay "Substitution" from 1968. Then, in 1974 a revised version of this essay was included in *Otherwise than Being*, as its 4th chapter. The importance of the concept of substitution for Levinas's later work is clear, as he himself notes in a footnote placed at the very beginning of the chapter: "This chapter was the germ of the present work."[27] In *Otherwise than Being*, substitution reveals the emergence of the subject in a different way than by way of its determination. To show this, Levinas differentiates between the self *for itself* and the self *for the other*. Beyond engaging a philosophical reference to their previous use in Hegel and Sartre,[28] these expressions are also linked to two grammatical cases: the *for itself* to the nominative, and the *for the other* to the accusative. Nominative and accusative express both the grammatical form and the way in which the subject emerges: a nominative/nomination characterized by self-sufficiency, a determined self in enclosed interiority, and an accusative/accusation, which is always addressed through something other than itself, and in this way always refers to exteriority. Taken in purely grammatical terms, the nominative form would characterize the subject case, while the accusative would be the object case, and would relate back to the nominative (subject). However, Levinas proposes the subject as accusative, suggesting, in other words, that the accusative is not secondary to a nominative, nor does it refer back to one; instead it signifies the *subjectum* as responsiveness, as being subjected to a call, where the self is not found in itself, but rather finds itself in the loss of itself: "And it is the sense of the 'oneself,' that accusative that derives from no nominative; it is the very fact of finding oneself while losing oneself."[29]

In the context of the Levinasian subjectivity, the *for itself* designates the subjectivity of consciousness that refers to itself through itself in the form of a self-identification. The self is calling itself, in the nominative, by giving

---

[26] For example in the Talmudic readings "The Temptation of Temptation" from 1964 (NTR 30–50) and "As Old as the World?" from 1966 (NTR 70–88), which is relatively close in time to "Substitution." Although already there substitution is mentioned in the context of responsibility even for the other's sins (responsibility that leads to substitute myself for the other's death), the notion as such is not developed.
[27] OB 193, n1.
[28] The connection between Levinas's expression "for itself" and the way it was previously used by Hegel and Sartre becomes even more obvious through Levinas's problematization of the "for the other" in different terms than consciousness (See Chapter 2).
[29] OB 11.

itself determination. This is a process of detachment and reattachment of the self with itself in a self-coincidence: "being itself losing itself and finding itself again so as to possess itself by showing itself."[30] According to Levinas, in this detachment and reattachment of the self to itself, the self is not only the term but also the relation, because this very movement of auto-identification, which constitutes the relation, is what makes up the self (i.e. its identity). Although it can be seen as a movement, it is a movement in interiority; the self never departs from itself and, thus, remains in coincidence with itself. In this sense, the self is self only *for* the self itself, only *for itself*.[31] This is not much of an "adventure," Levinas claims, since it can only find what already was there: "[a]nything unknown that can occur to it is in advance disclosed."[32] For Levinas, this movement represents nothing more than a "detour of ideality."[33] At the same time, through the meaning of the *for itself*, Levinas presents a critique of thinking the self in its preoccupation with itself (with its own being, and hence its own death).[34] On several occasions, in terms borrowed from Spinoza, Levinas expresses

---

[30] Ibid., 99.

[31] In *Totality and Infinity*, enjoyment had a similar role of self-sufficiency and auto-referentiality, enjoyment enjoying, that was associated with the *for itself*, "It is for itself as in the expression 'each for himself'; for itself as the 'famished stomach that has no ears,' capable of killing for a crust of bread, is for itself; for itself as the surfeited one who does not understand the starving and approaches him as an alien species, as the philanthropist approaches the destitute. The self-sufficiency of *enjoying* measures the egoism or the ipseity of the Ego and the same." TI 118. Nevertheless, the two thoughts do not coincide perfectly, since Levinas still reserves a positive role for enjoyment in *Totality and Infinity*, while in *Otherwise than Being* the interested self is usually viewed in a critical light. We will return to the question of the enjoying self in Chapter 3.

[32] OB 99.

[33] Levinas's expression points towards his critique to the Hegelian dialectic. According to Levinas's reading, the dialectical auto-determination is just a detour of the self to find itself again by means of self-consciousness; it is a detour since it already starts from the self itself. "The detour of ideality leads to coinciding with oneself, that is, to certainty, which remains the guide and guarantee of the whole spiritual adventure of being. But this is why this adventure is no adventure. It is never dangerous; it is self-possession, sovereignty, ἀρχή. Anything unknown that can occur to it is in advance disclosed, open, manifest, is cast in the mould of the known, and cannot be a complete surprise. For the philosophical tradition of the West, all spirituality lies in consciousness, thematic exposition of being, knowing." Ibid.

[34] Later on we will return to discussing how Levinas re-thinks the importance of death in the light of sociality. See especially Chapters 7 and 10.

the insufficiency of *conatus essendi*.[35] By *conatus essendi* he means the persistence of the self in its own self, being's interest in its own being (or essence).[36] This is again a self-referential movement, although of a different kind than that provided by consciousness. Here, the self *for itself*, besides being self-identification, is also interest. *Interest* could be understood in two ways, and both interpretations accord with Levinas's thought. Firstly, inspired by the etymology of this composed word, *interest* can be understood as inter-esse, where 'inter' carries the meaning of 'between,' 'in the midst of,' or 'in relation to'—in this sense, *interest* means to be in close relation to Being. In the second sense, the meaning of *interest* approaches closer to its common understanding, as having something to gain and the possibility of exchange: "the persisting in being, interest, is maintained by the future compensation," says Levinas.[37] In this sense, interest expresses commerce and implies calculation and determination through reciprocity. Hence, both interpretations of the word "interest" bring us to positioning and determination. So, instead of the *for itself* of determination in interest, Levinas proposes to think subjectivity as the *for the other* of *dis-interestedness*, which disrupts the bond to Being and its positioning. In one of his later essays, Levinas explicitly points out the meaningfulness of *dis-interestedness*:

> So, as I say: *disinterestedness*. It is a good word because it contains the root esse, meaning "being." *Interestedness* means bound to being, and *disinterestedness* the self's withdrawal from being. I always say: *dis-inter-estedness*.[38]

As a consequence, when Levinas tries to avoid thinking in terms of "interested" subjectivity he uses the term "disinterestedness," which signifies at once the de-position of the subject from its determination through its own being, but also irreciprocity, since the disinterested subject denotes the asymmetrical responsive self.[39]

---

[35] Levinas's reading of *conatus essendi* is problematic in the sense that it links the persistence of self in itself with the persistence of Being in its own being. Nevertheless, our argument relies on Levinas's thoughts, and the discussion regarding whether his reading of Spinoza is just or not, does not constitute a central issue for our thesis.
[36] For Levinas, 'Being' and 'essence' often coincide in their meaning. See OB xlvii.
[37] See Ibid., 4.
[38] "Intention, Event and the Other" (1989), in IIRT 150, emphasis by Levinas.
[39] "The reverting of the ego into a self, the de-posing or de-situating of the ego, is the very modality of dis-interestedness." OB 50.

Nevertheless, Levinas's critique of self-referentiality and interest in Being is not meant to deny the importance of thinking Being. Instead, he tries to show that thinking the self in terms of *for itself* bears an insufficiency, and that it is therefore necessary to re-think it in terms of *for the other*.[40] Levinas lifts subjectivity out of its usual setting, revolving around consciousness, self-determinacy and coincidence. He searches, instead, for a self that is beyond, or more precisely on the hither side of identity, where subjectivity, rather than auto-proclaiming itself *for itself,* emerges as a subject *for the other*.[41] Emerging already as *for the other* does not mean that the self loses itself *in* an other. On the contrary, it is due to the other as exteriority that the subject is deposed from its position, from its *in*:

> I posit myself deposed of my sovereignty. Paradoxically it is qua *alienus*—foreigner and other—that man is not alienated.[42]

The deposition of the self, where the *for itself* is replaced by the *for the other*, marks the road that leads Levinas to introduce the notion of *substitution*: the self, which, according to the essentialist view stays at the core of its subjectivity, becomes a self in substitution. The self substitutes itself for the other, and this substitution is now at the core of its selfhood. We will turn now to discussing the meaning of substitution in the light of the de-posed subjectivity.

As we have seen, Levinas proposes to think subjectivity in the accusative, where the subject is not a result of a self-discovering (or self-uncovering), but an "accusation" that comes from the outside. The subject is convoked from the outside, "assigned as irreplaceable"[43] not for itself, but *for the other*. The *for the other* is not about altruism; it cannot be accounted for in the categories of egoism and altruism,[44] because it is not a matter of choice: I am

---

[40] Levinas does not try to set exclusive alternatives, but rather point out a necessary intertwinement of thinking the self for the other, and of thinking it in terms of consciousness. This creates an ambiguous relation between de-position and positioning, between indeterminacy and determination, which we will address in more detail in Chapter 4.

[41] OB 108.

[42] Ibid., 59.

[43] "In responsibility as one assigned or elected from the outside, assigned as irreplaceable, the subject is accused in its skin, too tight for its skin," OB 106.

[44] See OB 197, note 27. Levinas occasionally refers to the *for itself* or the "conatus" as egoism (See for example Ibid., 4 or "Dialogue on Thinking-of-the-Other" (1987), EN

not choosing myself into selfhood, nor can I choose to be chosen. This reveals subjectivity not only as subjectum (subjected to accusation, in accusative), but also in terms of *subjection*,[45] suggesting the incapacity to chose its own chosenness. The self can only become unique, and thus it can only gain its identity "by the other."[46] This assignation by the other is frequently called by Levinas "election."[47] Although the uniqueness through election gives unity to the self and a form of in-dividuation (both in the sense of singularity and indivisibility),[48] it is a pre-synthetic unity.[49] That is to say, it is a unity that does not offer a foundation, a resting place for the self. The elected self is not resting in itself, but it is "'more and more one,' to the point of breakup, fission, openness."[50] We find here a good example of the way Levinas uses superlatives and overemphasis in order to break with the traditional way of understanding concepts, in this case, the unity of the self. The overstressing or "outdoing" of unity, which Levinas calls the

---

201–2), but "egoism" has the role to strengthen the meaning of the self's persistence in itself, the self referring back to itself and its own essence and it does not denote a way of conduct.

[45] "More exactly, it is accusation which I cannot answer, but for which I cannot decline responsibility. Already the position of the subject is a deposition, not a *conatus essendi*. [...] We have to conceive in such terms the de-substantiation of the subject, its de-reification, its disinterestedness, its subjection, its subjectivity." OB 127.

[46] "It [identity] is not self-consciousness attaining itself in the present, but the extreme exposure to the assignation by the other, already realized behind consciousness and freedom.," Ibid., 145.

[47] "The identity aroused thus behind identification is an identity by pure election.," Ibid., 145. The notion of being chosen or elected certainly has a theological intonation to it. Nevertheless, in Levinas's case it is not about the chosen people, as in the biblical sense, but it expresses the uniqueness of the self, uniqueness which cannot originate from the self itself. Levinas is quite clear on this point in an interview from 1989: "I am chosen. To me this means, 'I am the chosen one': as 'myself' and not as a Jew. As a 'self'! The contrary of this is probably the meaning of chosenness in the theological sense.," "Intention, Event, and the Other" (1989), in IIRB 153.

[48] In *Otherwise than Being* Levinas calls it supraindividuation (*surindividuation*). See OB 118, AE 187.

[49] "These negative qualifications of the subject of the oneself do not consecrate some ineffable mystery, but confirm the presynthetic, pre-logical and in a certain sense atomic, that is, in-dividual, unity of the self, which prevents it from splitting, separating itself from itself so as to complete or express itself, and thus show itself, if only under a comic mask, to name itself otherwise than by a pro-noun." OB 107.

[50] OB 107.

recurrence of the self,[51] expresses a de-possession of the self until it loses itself;[52] it is a moment of contraction, an implosion of the self that instead of destroying the self, leads to the demolition of its place. This is where *substitution* enters the scene. The loss of self, the de-position and de-possession of the self does not lead to a point zero, Levinas explains, but to the substitution for the other. In substitution "I is an other" (*Je est un autre*),[53] says Levinas by following Rimbaud's famous claim. Nevertheless, he immediately adds that this is not to be understood in the Rimbaudian sense as a transformation into another. For Levinas, the de-possession of the self does not mean that the *I* becomes another.[54] The de-position of the self does not end up in a re-position. The unity of the self is not given by coincidence, but as "non-coincidence," as Levinas likes to call it, again using unusual formulations in an effort to break down concepts and dualities (in this case, that of coincidence/division).[55] Substitution is the-other-in-me[56] or the-other-in-the-same[57] without coincidence.[58] Through these expressions

---

[51] For recurrence as the "outdoing (*surenchère*) of unity" see OB 108, AE 170. In general on recurrence see especially OB 102–9.

[52] "Responsibility for the others has not been a return to oneself, but an exasperated contracting, which the limits of identity cannot retain. Recurrence becomes identity in breaking up the limits of identity, breaking up the *principle* of being in me, the intolerable rest in itself characteristic of definition." Ibid., 114.

[53] OB 118 (translation altered), AE 187.

[54] "In substitution my being that belongs to me and not to another is undone, and it is through this substitution that I am not 'another,' but me." OB 127.

[55] Another way in which Levinas underlines that he is not simply evoking a division based on the difference between me and the other is by the expression "non-indifference." We will return to this later on.

[56] See, for instance, OB 125.

[57] See, for example, OB 25.

[58] The-other-in-me or the-other-in-the-same, as Levinas sometimes describes substitution, brings about a comparison to maternity. (see especially OB Chapter III.5 and IV.2.) The example of maternity is interesting for at least two reasons. Firstly, it introduces an aspect of the feminine that has not been considered in *Totality and Infinity*, and by this, Levinas changes the father-son constellation associated with the notion of fraternity (the question of fraternity will be discussed in Chapter 9). Secondly, maternity has a metaphorical sense, illustrating the other-in-the-same of substitution, and at the same time it has more than just a metaphorical role. For example, in the following, Levinas refers to maternity as a pre-ontological past: "Subjectivity of flesh and blood in matter—signifyingness of sensibility, the one-for-the-other itself—is the pre-original signifyingness that gives sense, because it gives. Not because, as preoriginal, it would be more originary than origin, but because the diachrony of sensibility, which cannot be assembled in a representational present, refers to an irrecuperable pre-

Levinas undoes the Same/Other dichotomy, which is still present in his earlier works (for example in *Totality and Infinity*). This time, the self is not inter-ested (as it was in the case of the *for itself*), and so does not imply commerce and reciprocity.[59] Substitution is irreciprocal; that is, the self is

---

ontological past, that of maternity" (OB 78.) Unfortunately, Levinas does not develop sufficiently his thoughts on maternity. Perhaps he is overly cautious, so as not to mislead the reader into interpreting the self of substitution as an empirical self, which would go against his thought (see Ibid., 116). Although this issue is not in the focus of the present thesis, there are several other works preoccupied specifically with this topic, for example: Kathryn Bevis, "'Better than metaphors'? Dwelling and the Maternal Body in Emmanuel Levinas," *Literature and Theology* 21, no.3 (2007): 317–329, and Jennifer Rosato, "Woman as Vulnerable Self: The Trope of Maternity in Levinas's Otherwise Than Being," *Hypatia*, 27, no. 2, (2012): 348–365.

[59] As a consequence, death has meaning outside itself, outside the inter-esse of being. According to Levinas, by substitution it is possible to preserve the meaning of the self in a death *for the other*. This gives meaning to sacrifice and suffering. The only meaning of suffering could be found in the suffering for the other, according to Levinas. I can only suffer for the other because, again, there is no division inside oneself, there is nobody for whom I can suffer for, but the other. In this sense, suffering for the self itself could not have any meaning; it is useless. (See "Useless Suffering" [1982], in EN 91–102) When the self is thought in terms of *for the other* suffering and death are also thought in terms of *for the other*. In this sense, the possibility of suffering for the other comes from substitution. In the same way, pity, compassion, pardon can exist only because the substitution of the subject, without this being a causal relation. "For the condition for, or the unconditionality of, the self does not begin in the auto-affection of a sovereign ego that would be, after the event, 'compassionate' for another. Quite the contrary: the uniqueness of the responsible ego is possible only in being obsessed by another, in the trauma suffered prior to any auto-identification, in an unrepresentable before" (OB 123.). Or, in well-known words of Levinas: "It is through the condition of being hostage that there can be in the world pity, compassion, pardon and proximity—even the little there is, even a simple 'After you, sir.'" (Ibid., 117.) Only a subjectivity based on substitution could offer the possibility of sacrifice. "[T]he passage of the identical to the other in substitution which makes possible sacrifice," says Levinas. ("Substitution" [1968], in BPW 90) Levinas's remark inspires Bernasconi's essay, "What is the question to which 'substitution' is the answer?." He recognizes the importance of Levinas's claim and finds in sacrifice the question for which substitution could be an answer, thus a purpose for the concept as such. (see Robert Bernasconi, "What is the question to which 'substitution' is the answer?," in *The Cambridge Companion to Levinas*, eds. Simon Critchley and Robert Bernasconi [Cambridge: Cambridge University Press 2002], 234-251.). Concerning the problem of sacrifice, an interesting addition is Denis King Keenan's reading of Levinas's concept of sacrifice as "sacrificing sacrificing sacrificing." (see Denis King Keenan, *The Question of Sacrifice* [Bloomington: Indiana University Press, 2005], 74-88.) This rather awkward formulation is nevertheless meaningful for understanding Levinas's concept. Keenan's phrase on one hand, expresses the obsession characteristic

for the other, but this does not mean that the other is for the self. Substitution does not permit replacement or interchangeability.

It has become clear by now that substitution is understood very differently from the everyday use of the term (i.e. replacing, putting something in the place of something else). It is irreciprocal non-coincidence, and it makes the transference from the *through the other* (the self emerging through the other, as election) to the *for the other*.[60] The self emerges through the other, for the other—this is at the core of the subjectivity proposed by Levinas. Substitution, in this formulation, would be the comma that indicates the difference between, but also the congruence of the *through* and the *for* the other. The emergence of the self through the other and the responsiveness for the other are not two separate movements, but only different aspects of the same move. I am responding to the call with a "Here I am" (*me voici*),[61] which expresses the exposure to the other, and in the same move, the emerging *me*.[62] Understanding the self as *me* is very important to Levinas's thoughts on substitution, and needs to be highlighted, as it will become

---

to proximity and the non-reciprocal relation to the other (by obsessive repetition of the word "sacrificing"), but it could be as well understood as a rigorously constructed thought: the sacrificing act sacrificing itself as sacrificing. This leads us to an even deeper connection between sacrifice and substitution. Sacrificing as a volitional act (sacrificing as sacrificing) is sacrificed in a primordial sacrifice, which is not an act anymore. The self cannot sacrifice itself, but it can only be sacrificed. In this sense, substitution could be seen as the primordial sacrifice of the ego that "immolates itself" for the other (OB 108, 118), which makes any other sacrifice as such possible.

[60] "What can it be but a substitution of me for the others? [...] I exist through the other and for the other, but without this being alienation: I am inspired.," OB 114.

[61] There are at least two biblical references to the "here I am" as a response to the call of God: Exodus 3:4, where Moses is approached by God through a burning bush, God calls Moses's name and he responds with "here I am lord"; 1 Samuel 3:4, where God wakes up Samuel by calling his name, and Samuel responds "here I am." It is interesting to see that in both of these instances God calls the name of Moses, and respectively, Samuel, that is to say, the call is at the same time election into uniqueness (it is not anybody, but it is Moses, it is Samuel that God calls). Levinas seems to refer to the story from the Exodus, see "Enigma and Phenomenon" (1965), in BPW 72.

[62] "There is an assignation to an identity for the response of responsibility, where one cannot have oneself be replaced without fault. To this command continually put forth, only a 'here I am' *(me voici)* can answer, where the pronoun 'I' is in the accusative," OB 142. It is not a coincidence that the response is linked to speech, to saying "me voici." This introduces the problematic of the Saying and the Said, thematization and the unthematized. On the Saying and the Said, see Chapter 4.

crucial later on in the project of thinking sociality beyond a dyad/many distinction.

Although the English translation does not make this clear, the French original "me voici" calls attention to the "me," *me* which is different from the *I*. Perhaps it would be more appropriate to say "here's me," but even then, the English language constrains us to use the copula, and thus gives determination. The key to understanding this "me," which indicates the emergence of the self, is to think it as a refusal of determination. The self as *me* expresses the self that does not find itself at the bottom of itself, at its foundation. The "here" of the "here I am" does not designate a position for the *me*. On the contrary, it indicates *the hither side of identity*, which instead of enclosing it in a place opens up the self for the other. However, the indeterminacy of the *me* should not be confused with a loss of the particularity of the self into an undetermined generality. On the contrary, the self in terms of *me* resists turning into a general concept.[63] No abstraction is permitted here, either in the sense of generalization, or in the sense of avoidance: the self cannot avoid the election, for it is no previous self that would be capable of avoidance;[64] at the same time, the privilege of being called is always mine, without possession, and without being transformed into a universal principle.[65] It is "*my* substitution," and Levinas seems to insist on this: "*My* substitution—it is as *my own* that substitution for the neighbor is produced."[66]

---

[63] The assignation, the election by the other removes the self from generalization: "Election traverses the concept of the ego to summon me as me through the inordinateness of the other. It extracts me from the concept in which I continually take refuge" OB 145.

[64] "The self in a being is exactly the not-being-able-to-slip-away-from an assignation that does not aim at any generality" Ibid., 127.

[65] However, since Levinas does not want to create a universalized notion of the self even the use of the expression "the self" with a definite article is criticized by Levinas. This is one of the deep significations of the "accusation": that the self is not in a nominative, but always in the accusative form, even grammatically. In *Otherwise than Being*, for example he writes: "Everything is from the start in the accusative. Such is the exceptional condition or unconditionality of the self (*soi*), the signification of the pronoun *self* (*Se*) for which our Latin grammars themselves know no nominative form" Ibid., 112, AE 177, emphasis by Levinas.

[66] Ibid., 126, emphasis by Levinas.

Thus, in substitution, subjectivity is not anymore thought in terms of *ego* or *I*, but instead, in terms of *me*-ness.[67] This has nothing to do with subjectivism (i.e. a subjective point of view):

> It is not simply a passage to a subjective point of view. One can no longer say what the ego or I is. From now on one has to speak in the first person. I am a term irreducible to the relation, and yet in a recurrence which empties me of all consistency.[68]

The *me*-ness, brought forth through substitution, does not become a *mine*-ness, a self-possession leading to a closed-up interiority.[69] *Me* is an open interiority, without allowing an outside perspective upon the relation itself, yet preventing the self from enclosing upon itself. This is precisely what Levinas means to show through the notion of substitution: the interiority of the self is not its own, but is given through the other (substitution as through the other, for the other), and in this way, it is an opened-up interiority. Here, the relative determination between the inside and outside is disturbed. The inside is not determined by the boundaries of the outside,

---

[67] In order to make this point more clear, Levinas writes *Moi* with a capital letter to denote conceptualization, which was translated into English as *ego* (or generalized I), and *moi* without capitalization, which is usually translated as *me* (or I) and expresses the elected self that does not bear generalization nor is it the deduction of the particular from a general. Levinas is more specific on these differentiations in the lecture course from 1975-6, *God, Death, and Time*: "Indeed, in ethics, in responsibility for another, it is a question of the nearness of the other who obsesses me without measure, to the point of placing in question my in-itself and my for-itself. All the way to me, who am not only the singularized concept of I [*Moi*]. When I say 'I' [*je*], I am not the particular case of a concept of the I [*Moi*] to say 'me' ['*moi*'] is to escape this concept. In that first person, I am a hostage, a subjectivity supporting all the others, yet unique, without the possibility of having someone replace me, or in an impossibility of hiding before responsibility," GDT 140. A similar remark can be found in the later essay called "No identity" (1970): "[S]ubjectivity is not the ego (*Moi*), but me (*moi*)," in CPP 150, *Humanisme de l'autre homme*, (Montpellier: Fata Morgana, 1972 ; L.G.F., Le Livre de poche. Biblio essais, 1987), 111 . However, we cannot say that Levinas is overly consistent with the use of capitalized and non-capitalized forms. Here, we use the word 'me' as a correspondence to the meaning of the non-capitalized *moi* described above, although it does not bring out its full emphatic character (since *moi* without actually expressing nomination, can have an emphatic character, stressing the I, *je*).
[68] OB 82.
[69] Closed up interiority, or what Levinas in *Totality and Infinity* calls "the Same," is characterised by self-sufficiency. On interiority see "The I and the Totality" (1954), in EN 14-5.

but the self is from the start invaded by the outside, "backed up against oneself," without migrating somewhere else than its selfhood; yet, its selfhood is its very resistance to determination.[70] In substitution, the self is *inside-out*: "emptying itself of its being, turning itself inside out."[71] It is not about a transposition of the inside to the outside, or a transformation process where the inside becomes the outside and vice-versa. It is a turning *to* the other without turning *into* an other; a movement that does not lead us "outside-the-self," but rather goes "deeper-than-self."[72]

> Its [the subject's] being "turned to another" is this being turned inside out. A concave without a convex.[73]

In this sense, the self in exile does not find its *place (endroit)* outside itself. It is not an outside, but it is its very turning inside-out out "like a cloak" (*comme une veste*).[74] By stretching the meaning of the "inside-out," that in Levinas's work is characteristic to the de-posed subjectivity, we propose, here, an *inside-out dimension* that would designate the relation to the other from the inside-out, that is, from the open inside of the relation. In using the expression "inside-out dimension" we are far from trying to re-establish an inside-outside dichotomy, but on the contrary, we are claiming that the opened-up inside that Levinas is suggesting in the context of de-posed subjectivity has precisely the role of doing away with the inside-outside poles.[75]

Although Levinas never discusses it in terms of inside-out dimension of the relation to the other, he certainly calls attention, as we have seen, to the

---

[70] "To be in-oneself, backed up against oneself, to the extent of substituting oneself for all that pushes one into this null-place, is for the I to be in itself ," OB 116., "Etre en-soi, acculé à soi, au point de se substituer à tout ce qui vous pousse dans ce non-Lieu, c'est précisément cela être en-soi," AE 183.

[71] OB 117, "de se vider de son être, de se mettre «à l'envers»," AE 185. See also "Substitution" (1968), in BPP 91. Although here the English expression "inside-out" is a translation of the French expression "à l'envers," Levinas other times is using "en retournant" in order to express the same thing. See AE 82.

[72] "Hermeneutics and the beyond" (1977), in EN 65.

[73] OB 48–9, "Son «envers l'autre» est cette mise à l'envers même. Envers sans endroit.," AE 83.

[74] OB 48, AE 83.

[75] In this sense, the "inside-out" can even be formulated as "outside-in," with the same condition, that is to say, signifying the very disruption of the two poles "inside" and "outside," "in" and "out," without one becoming another.

self on the "hither side [*en deçà*] of my identity."[76] For the purpose of this thesis, it is important to bring forth this inside-out dimension of the relation to the other, so that later on, sociality cannot be confused with a notion of social relations focusing on the relation itself, or with a pure subjectivism representing a relative point of view.[77] At this point, what is important to underline is that the inside-out dimension, when articulated in terms of subjectivity as *me*, inherits the irreciprocity and the asymmetry characteristic of the relation to the other when approached from the hither side. Here, asymmetry is closely connected with the irreciprocity discussed earlier. Just as substitution does not permit interchangeablility between me and the other, it is not reducible to mirroring either. In other words, substitution as the other-in-the-same does not mean that the self sees itself through the eyes of the other, or, vice versa, that the other is constituted through me.

The question is, however, where the inside-out dimension, opened up by the de-posed subjectivity, takes us? It is rather clear that Levinas opens up a different plane of discussion than simply describing possible empirical situations. It is not about a concrete event of being called or accused by an empirical other. Just as u-topia does not designate an event in itself, so the emergence of the self cannot be translated into an empirical event.[78] Substitution never actually takes place, but in a sense, it has always already taken place; it belongs to a past that was never present, and can never become an object of consciousness; yet the present, and consciousness,

---

[76] See for instance OB 92 or OB 116.

[77] Perhaps the closest remark in this sense from Levinas's part comes some years later, in a text from 1982, *Useless Suffering*. There, he brings up the problem of the self for the other, which resists both generalization and a relative point of view, by evoking something called "interhuman perspective" in relation to suffering: "To envisage suffering, as I have just attempted to do, in the interhuman perspective—that is, as meaningful in me, useless in the Other—does not consist in adopting a relative point of view on it [...] The interhuman, properly speaking, lies in a non-indifference of one to another, in a responsibility of one for another," "Useless Suffering" (1982), in EN 100-1.

[78] "These [that the self is out of phase with itself] are not events that happen to an empirical ego, that is, to an ego already posited and fully identified, as a trial that would lead it to being more conscious of itself, and make it more apt to put itself in the place of others. What we are here calling oneself, or the other in the same, where inspiration arouses respiration, the very pneuma of the psyche, precedes this empirical order, which is a part of being, of the universe, of the State, and is already conditioned in a system. Here we are trying to express the unconditionality of the subject, which does not have the status of a principle.," OB 115–116.

carries its trace. The inside-out dimension of my relation to the other does not represent an alternative time and an alternative consciousness, but the hither side of time and consciousness. These aspects are to be discussed in the next chapter.

CHAPTER 2

Bad Consciousness and Bad Time

In the previous chapter we introduced the inside-out dimension of the relation to the other opened up by the de-position of the self, to prepare the terrain for the development of a notion of sociality. We have shown that the inside-out dimension corresponds to an approach from the hither side of the relation to the other, and that it does not allow for an outside perspective upon the relation itself. At the same time, however, it does not lead to subjectivism, in that the 'inside' is not a closed-up interiority, but is rather the openness of the subject turned inside-out. In this chapter we need to address more deeply the inside-out dimension, this 'hither side' that has so far remained only partially developed.

The hither side represents a form of what Levinas more generally calls 'otherwise,' 'beyond,' or 'transcendence' and, as such, it has a crucial role not only for the understanding of subjectivity but for Levinas's philosophy in general. Because of this general importance of the 'hither side,' the notions engaged in the discussions that follow are likely, to some extent, to be familiar to the experienced Levinas reader. However, the discussion here will be carried out through the prism of the inside-out dimension of the relation to the other, enabling us to re-think these familiar terms from this specific angle. As we shall see, an-archy disrupts thinking the hither side in terms of *when* and *where*; in other words, it makes us re-think consciousness, and with it, temporality. The de-position of the self, and the inside-out dimension that it opens cannot, in light of this re-thinking, be considered events in time or states of consciousness characteristic to specific circumstances (for example, according to this interpretation, it would be wrong to say that the moment I see another person the inside-out dimension suddenly opens up). We find in Levinas's work an inversion of intentionality, inverted through the inside-out of the de-posed self, which makes consciousness 'malfunction,' become non-intentional, a 'bad' consciousness, and transforms synthetical temporality into an interruptive temporalization of time, in the form of diachrony or 'bad' time. Consequently, this chapter focuses on the hither side as an-archy and the reformulation of consciousness and time in terms of non-intentionality and diachrony.

2.1. The an-archy of the hither side

As previously indicated, the meaning of the expression 'hither side' often coincides with that of 'otherwise' or 'beyond,'[1] and reflects Levinas's way of understanding transcendence. This already shows the importance of the hither side, since Levinas himself confessed to having more interest in transcendence than in ethics as such.[2] It is important to keep in mind, however, that transcendence expressed as otherwise, beyond or hither side does not constitute another world outside this one.[3] Searching for the "where" of the hither side, in this case, would be inappropriate. The hither side loses its meaning as soon as it receives determination, i.e. when it becomes *somewhere*, be it an empirical place or an ideal world (we can recognize here that this corresponds to the previously discussed notion of u-topia). Consequently, in searching for the meaning of the hither side, the question should not be "*where* this hither side is?" nor should it be "*what* is on the hither side?" Instead, Levinas poses the more phenomenological question of *how*: not a question about transcending something to arrive somewhere else (a *somewhere* on the hither side), but rather the question about the way of the hither side, its *how*. The *how* of the hither side is given as disruption, including disruption of the transcendence/immanence dichotomy itself. In this way, the transcendence that the hither side stands for becomes transcendence in immanence, without transcendence being reduced to im-

---

[1] See for instance OB 14.
[2] "It is the meaning of beyond, of transcendence, and not of ethics that our study seeks. It finds this meaning in ethics. We write *signification,* because ethics is structured as one-for-the-other; a signification of the beyond being, because outside of all finality in a responsibility that always increases: dis-interestedness where being rids itself of its being," in OGCM 200, n. 23. The significance, for Levinas, of transcendence over ethics has been pointed out, for instance, by Robert Bernasconi, see "Levinas's Ethical Critique of Levinasian Ethics," in *Totality and Infinity at 50*, eds. Scott Davidson and Diane Perpich (Pittsburgh PA: Duquesne University Press, 2012), 253–271.
[3] "[T]he *beyond* […] is not 'another world' behind the world," "The Trace of the Other" (1963), trans. by Alphonso Lingis, in *Deconstruction in Context*, ed. Marc C. Taylor (Chicago: University of Chicago Press, 1986), 354.

manence, or the two overlapping each other. [4] The disruption of dichotomies, embedded in the very meaning of the hither side, does not result in the annulling of the difference between the two sides of the dichotomy. Rather, the point is, precisely, to reveal their significance outside a relative determination. Due to its disruptive character, the hither side cannot be integrated into an order (e.g. the order of transcendence, the order of immanence, the order of dialectics, etc.). It represents, Levinas says, "a movement" that is "outside of order."[5] Outside of order, the hither side is *anarchy*: "On the hither side is expressed precisely in the term anarchy."[6] Anarchy designates the way Levinas formulates the disruption, or the *how* of the hither side that we are looking for. For this reason, we will now direct our focus to the meaning of anarchy.

In order to understand the meaning that Levinas gives to anarchy we need to return to the etymological roots of the word. Anarchy as *an-arche* means without origin and without ideal principle; as such, it encompasses Levinas's efforts to disrupt chronological and ontological order. 'Arche' is understood here as originarity and as principle itself, and hence becomes the building block of any kind of order. The privative tone of the 'without' (the 'an' from 'an-archy') does not have an annulling function that would transform the anarchical into the eternal, nor does it suggest some kind of primordiality (in the sense of the *first* order); instead it breaks down the very 'logic' of ordinarity and originarity itself.

> [P]reliminary, the pre-originary, the hither side, is not even equivalent to a beginning, does not have the status of a principle, but comes from the dimension of the anarchic, which has to be distinguished from the eternal. [7]

Thus, the anarchy of the hither side, without origin and outside principle, disrupts order without being against it (it escapes both negativity and relativity). Levinas's occasional use of a hyphen when discussing an-archy

---

[4] For a discussion on transcendence within immanence in Levinas see Bettina Bergo, *Levinas Between Ethics and Politics. For the Beauty that Adorns the Earth* (The Hague: Martinus Nijhoff Publishers, 1999), 156ff.
[5] OB 195, n. 11.
[6] Ibid., 196, n. 20.
[7] Ibid., 188, n. 2.

has the purpose of accentuating this meaning.⁸ In his note to Levinas's lectures from 1976, Jacques Rolland has suggested a double reading of anarchy, including the above mentioned, but also its "obvious sense" as "contesting the power of the State."⁹ Nevertheless, we argue that by engaging the notion of anarchy Levinas does not try to bring a political nuance to the 'hither side.'¹⁰ Thought in terms of revolt, anarchy would again be submitted to the rules of disorder, returning to dichotomies and relative definitions, and would thus convert it back to a form of order: revolt and disorder always refer back to the order against which they revolt (in other words, the contestation of power is also power): here, it is helpful to recall Levinas's often expressed agreement with Bergson's claim that, as disorder, anarchy is just another order.¹¹ However, he insists, equally that it is not the case that all anarchy turns necessarily into the order of disorder:

> Contrary to what is maintained in *Creative Evolution*, all disorder is not another order. The anarchy of the diachronic is not "assembled" into an order, except in the said. Bergson, distrustful as he is of language, is here a victim of the said.¹²

The form of anarchy that escapes both order and disorder is anarchy understood as without origin; in other words, anarchy thought not as a reversal of a previous order, but disruption of order altogether, of any order:

> But anarchy is not disorder as opposed to order [...]. Disorder is but another order, and what is diffuse is thematizable. Anarchy troubles being over and beyond these alternatives.¹³

Through its detachment from *arche,* an-archy disturbs not only order (as disorder, or the contestation of order would do), but the very thinking in terms of order. Reading Levinas's text in this way suggests that an-archy

---

⁸ For example, this is the way he discusses anarchy in his lecture from *God, Death, and Time* (1976). See especially GDT 172–5.
⁹ GDT 277, n. 1.
¹⁰ "The notion of anarchy we are introducing here has a meaning prior to the political (or antipolitical) meaning currently attributed to it. It would be self-contradictory to set it up as a principle (in the sense that anarchists understand it). Anarchy cannot be sovereign, like an arche.," OB 194, n. 3.
¹¹ See for instance OB 194, n. 3.
¹² OB 191, n. 6. We will explain what Levinas means by "the said" in Chapter 4.
¹³ See OB 101.

would represent the contestation of the power of the State (as Rolland proposed) *only* when we understand it as the interruption of order as such, not just the order imposed by the State, but any order.

Now, when we link the subjectivity that we discussed in Chapter 1 with the meaning of an-archy, we can see much more clearly that Levinas is not attempting to pinpoint an originary moment of the 'birth' of the subject.[14] As shown, one of the roles given to the notion of substitution is precisely to indicate that the subject lacks its own origin in itself, in other words, that it is an-archical.[15] This an-archy of the subject places its own origin outside of itself, yet does not invest it with eternity; hence it is an inside-out subjectivity. Nevertheless, Levinas does not intend to work out a formal structure of subjectivity, and even if he avoids turning his notions (such as substitution) into specific empirical events, this does not mean that they become idealities. We should keep in mind that an-archy also means 'without ideal principle.' The anarchy of the hither side liberates Levinas's notions from being translated into mere empirical events or into ideal principles, which makes his philosophy overcome the constraints of both description (i.e. a genetic of the subject and of sociality), and prescription (i.e. responsibility understood as acting responsively). By thinking in terms of anarchy, Levinas carries the phenomenological discussion beyond the frames given by the presence of perception. As expected, this has repercussions when it comes to the way Levinas re-thinks consciousness. We continue our discussion in this direction, by exploring the hither side of consciousness.

2.2. Non-intentional consciousness

At first site, it seems somewhat contradictory to speak about non-intentional consciousness, especially if we think it in Husserlian terms: for Husserl, consciousness is always consciousness *of*, and in that sense, it is

---

[14] "The 'birth' of being in the questioning where the cognitive subject stands would thus refer to a *before the questioning,* to the anarchy of responsibility, as it were on this side of all birth." OB 26.
[15] We find quite explicit references to this in Levinas's text, for example in his lecture dedicated to the topic subjectivity and an-archy, part of his course from 1976 entitled "God and Onto-theology": "It is as though there were here something before the beginning: an *an-archy.* And that means placing the subject as spontaneity into question: I am not my origin unto myself; I do not have my origin in myself." GDT 172.

always intentional. Levinas, though, employs this term to express a critique of considering consciousness exclusively in terms of thematization. In addition to his own ethical language, Levinas frames his thoughts by employing a Husserlian terminology in order to show more clearly, on the one hand, his rootedness in phenomenology, and on the other hand, his contribution to phenomenological thinking.

Although the extent to which Levinas remains faithful to the phenomenological method can be debated,[16] he does understand his own philosophy as phenomenology,[17] and from an early stage shows interest in Husserl's thinking, even though he chooses often to approach phenomenological problems from an angle different to that of Husserl: "I think that in spite of everything, what I do is phenomenology, even if there is no reduction, here, according to the rules required by Husserl; even if all the Husserlian methodology is not respected," he says in an interview from 1977.[18] Levinas sees his own approach as one that completes and, in a sense, improves Husserl's work by engaging in aspects that were recognized but never really developed by Husserl himself. One of these aspects regards consciousness in relation to the unthematized. According to Levinas, subjectivity, and with it, the relation to the other (the-other-in-the-same of substitution), are not phenomena of consciousness, meaning that they are not thematized, "a theme put before me":

> The same has to do with the other before the other appears in any way to a consciousness. Subjectivity is structured as the other in the same, but in a way different from that of consciousness. Consciousness is always correlative with a

---

[16] There are several opinions concerning the extent to which Levinas remains faithful to the phenomenological method, some even doubting that his thinking has any phenomenological value (see, for example Alain Badiou, *Ethics: An Essay on the Understanding of Evil* (1998), trans. Peter Hallward [London: Verso, 2001], Ch. 2 "Does the Other Exist?" 18–29). There are also attempts, elsewhere, to defend Levinas and to argue that his philosophy is indeed phenomenology and not merely theology or failed attempts at philosophy. This, in its turn, shows a supposable need for defending Levinas as a philosopher (See in this sense Formosa, Paul, "Levinas and the Definition of Philosophy: An Ethical Approach," in *Crossroads. An Interdisciplinary Journal for the Study of History, Philosophy, Religion and Classics* 1 (I), [2006]: 37–46). Others argue that Levinas's work remains faithful to the Husserlian phenomenological method (See John Drabinski, *Levinas and Postcolonialism* [2011], or *Sensibility and Singularity: The Problem of Phenomenology in Levinas* [2001]).
[17] See "Questions and answers" (1977), in OGCM 89–90.
[18] Ibid., 87.

theme, a present represented, a theme put before me, a being which is a phenomenon. The way subjectivity is structured as the other in the same differs from that of consciousness.[19]

Levinas's critique finds its target in the overpowering of theoretical or representational thinking, and he recognizes this threat in Husserl's conception of consciousness. This conception, Levinas considers, became too much dominated by theory, representation and knowing, and tends to enclose the self and the other in the totality of conceptualization.[20] To be clear, Levinas does not dismiss the importance of manifestation as such. His objection is to thinking the de-posed subject, the subject emerging in its relation to the other, in terms of showing; that is to say, Levinas rejects the determination of subjectivity and alterity through manifestation. Rather than refusing completely phenomenological thinking, he proposes instead to re-think phenomenology otherwise than from an emphasis on the phenomenon and thematizing consciousness.

When it comes to alterity, and to an understanding of the de-posed self, Levinas's insistence on a rejection of determinacy through manifestation suggests that he is interested in the non-phenomenon, in non-manifestation. He does not, however, advocate a negative approach—one that would only seek to disclose the phenomenon of the non-phenomenon or the manifestation of non-manifestation; he is not looking to build a phenomenology of dissimulation and concealment, which would still rely on the paradigm of showing and manifestation. According to Levinas, escaping determination does not necessarily create an indeterminate phenomenon in the form of the "indetermination of a noema,"[21] nor is it "the absence of a yet non-revealed," a lack waiting to be fulfilled, but it is

---

[19] OB 25.

[20] "However, in the phenomenological analysis of that concreteness of mind, there appears in Husserl—in conformity with a venerable Western tradition—a privilege of the theoretical, a privilege of representation, of knowing; and hence, of the ontological meaning of being. And this is the case despite all the opposing suggestions one can also get from his work: non-theoretical intentionality, a theory of *Lebenswelt* (the life world), the role of the lived body, the importance of which Merleau-Ponty has succeeded in demonstrating. That is the reason [...] why my reflection deviates from the last positions of Husserl's transcendental philosophy, or at least from its formulation.," "Nonintentional Consciousness" (1983), in EN 124.

[21] OB 94.

"the anarchy of what has never been present."²² Hence, he criticizes a specific way of thinking phenomenology: phenomenology understood in a descriptive sense, which, due to its disclosing character, "cannot leave the sphere of light."²³ Instead of a prevalence of light, Levinas underlines the importance of darkness, of the unknown and unthematized thought outside the relative or dialectical alternatives (i.e. darkness would not become a counterpart of light). Here, the point is not that there would be *something* unthematized, but that the thematized gains its meaning through unthematization.²⁴ It is the unthematized that gives direction, orientation, and thus sense to the thematized through an interruptive movement.²⁵ The phenomenon is disturbed by alterity, and phenomenology is interrupted by the unthematized.²⁶ Levinas seeks to approach the signification of the unthematized not by making it a separate object of study (which would still pose the problem in terms of manifestation), but by situating it with respect to the phenomenology it interrupts.²⁷ As a consequence, the phenomenological questioning remains important; even though there is no phenomenon of the unthematized, its phenomenality still needs to be addressed. In

---

[22] OB 97.
[23] He makes this clear from early on, in works such as *Existence and Existents*: "Phenomenological description, which by definition cannot leave the sphere of light, that is, man alone shut up in his solitude, anxiety and death as an end, whatever analyses of the relationship with the other, it may contribute, will not suffice. *Qua* phenomenology it remains within the world of light, the world of the solitary ego which has no relationship with the other *qua* other, for whom the other is another me, an alter ego known by sympathy, that is, by a return to oneself.," EE 85.
[24] The importance of unthematization for Levinas should not be confused with a Wittgesteinian attitude. He is rather clear on this point: "[I] do not see my own views at all in what Wittgenstein postulates: 'for doubt can exist only where a question exists, and an answer only where something can be *said*.' I do not believe that. In situations where nothing can be said, one must be silent, he says. The question of primary concern to me signifies much more and is not theoretical in content. The issue for me is the question: 'Is being legitimate? Do we have a right to exist?' In my thought, therefore, asking the question implicates conscience: it asks about the meaning of life, a meaning that always takes the form of a question. I am put in question, it appears. Asking this question, I have no firm ground under my feet but am put in question. And that 'being put in question' relates to the most natural of all things, namely the fact that I am.," "What one asks of oneself, one asks of a saint," 4.
[25] We will discuss the meaning of orientation and face as facing in the next two parts of our thesis.
[26] "Enigma and Phenomenon" (1965), BPW 71–5.
[27] "The Trace of the Other," in *Deconstruction in Context*, 356.

this sense, one can say that Levinas problematizes the *phenomenality* of the non-phenomenon, without entering a mode of thinking governed by the primacy of manifestation and determination.

Until quite late in his work, Levinas associates determination with consciousness in general since, by following Husserl, he seems to consider all consciousness to be intentional consciousness. Thus, he tries to approach the undetermined self and the other by going beyond consciousness, in the form of un-conscious or non-conscious.[28] In his later essays, though, this idea becomes more nuanced, and he begins to consider intentionality, rather than consciousness as such, to be that which gives determination, since intentionality is what makes consciousness always consciousness *of*. As a consequence, instead of doing away with the notion of consciousness altogether, Levinas tries in his later texts to re-invent intentionality by freeing it from determination—this is what he calls *non-intentionality*. Although the separation between intentionality and consciousness seems to be strange, and Levinas ends up with a term which is seemingly contradictory (i.e. non-intentional consciousness), it helps him to bring forth a form of consciousness that does not operate within the rules of presenting (showing, determination) and presencing (synchronic time, dominated by a gathering present).

The term "non-intentional consciousness,"[29] then, entered Levinas's vocabulary rather late. In its most explicit form, non-intentional conscious-

---

[28] See for instance OB 197, note 26. There Levinas talks in terms of non-conscious rather than of non-intentional consciousness, as he does in the later essays; nevertheless, it is a non-conscious of different kind than that of psychology: "But the non-conscious can be read in a different way—Levinas says—on the basis of its traces, and undo the categories of mechanism. The non-conscious is understood as the non-voluntary event of persecution, which qua persecution breaks off every justification, every apology, every logos," Ibid. Or, in another note Levinas clearly expresses that he does not refer to the unconscious in a negative sense, in its relation with consciousness, for in that way it would keep it in the structure of self-determination, "the structure of self-knowledge," thus originarity and arche. Again, Levinas tries to break dichotomies and orders, this time, the consciousness/unconscious interplay. "It is not a question here of descending toward the unconscious, which, defined in a purely negative way with reference to the conscious, preserves the structure of self-knowledge (whatever be the unexpected ramifications that would then complicate this structure), of a quest of self, though it be led astray on obstructed byways.," OB 194, note 6.

[29] It should be mentioned that the notion as such is not reserved only to a Levinasian vocabulary. It was used, for instance, by both Gurwitsch and Sartre to designate non-egological consciousness.

ness becomes the focus of his essay from 1981 entitled "The Bad Conscience and the Inexorable,"[30] which is the first version of a series of essays that capture in different forms the same underlying idea: consciousness is not reducible to determination, neither in the form of self-awareness, nor in the form of meaning provided through intentionality. Among the essays inspired by this first one, we should mention: "Nonintentional Consciousness" (1983),[31] "Ethics as First Philosophy" (1984),[32] "Philosophy and Transcendence" (1989),[33] "From the One to the Other: Transcendence and Time" (1983).[34] To a certain extent, all these works have incorporated the essay from 1981 ("The Bad Conscience and the Inexorable") in ways that differ slightly from one to another, according to the general topic of the respective collection in which they were published. It is not, however, our purpose here to analyze these differences. Instead, the focus will remain on bringing forth the meaning of non-intentional consciousness.

In appealing to the term "non-intentional consciousness" Levinas has chosen to frame his question in a Husserlian vocabulary, and thus needs to build up his argument in relation to Husserl's philosophy. Indeed, a common theme in the different versions of the essays is Levinas's starting point, which often takes the form of an overview of Husserl's theory of intentionality and the problem of pre-reflective consciousness. However, in

---

[30] "La mauvaise conscience et l'inexorable" was first published in *Exercises de la Patience* 2 (Paris: Editions Obsidiane, 1981). Subsequently, it was included in the collection *De Dieu qui vient à l'idée* (1986). (see DQVI 258–265), English translation by Bettina Bergo, "Bad Conscience and the Inexorable," in OGCM 172–178.

[31] "La conscience non-intentionnelle" was first published in *Philosophes critiques d'eux-mêmes*, vol. 10, (1983): 143–171, then included in *Entre Nous. Essais sur le penser-à-l'autre* (1991) (see ENEPA 132–142), translated by Barbara Harshav and Michael B. Smith, as "Nonintentional Consciousness," in EN 123–132.

[32] "Éthique comme philosophie première" was first published in *Justifications de l'éthique* (Bruxelles: Editions de l'Université de Bruxelles, 1984). It was translated in English as "Ethics as First Philosophy" in LR 75–87.

[33] "Philosophie et transcendance" was first published in *Encyclopédie philosophique universelle* (Presses Universitaires de France, 1989), after that being included in the first chapter of *Altérité et transcendance* (Montpellier: Fata Morgana, 1995), and translated in English by Michael B. Smith as "Philosophy and Transcendence," in AT 3–38.

[34] "De l'Un à l'Autre. Transcendance et temps," was first published in *Archivio di filosofia*, vol. 51, n°1-3, 1983; later on, the revised version of the same essay was published in the volume *Entre Nous. Essais sur le penser-à-l'autre*. Paris: Grasset, 1991. English translation by Michael B. Smith and Barbara Harshav as "From the One to the Other: Transcendence and Time," in EN 133–154.

reading these texts, one should keep in mind that Levinas aims for more than a mere commentary on Husserl's work.[35] Rather than a meticulous analysis of Husserl's text, he intends to develop his own ideas, and it is not unusual for him to sometimes exaggerate, as a tool in bringing forth new ideas. Since, here, our focus is not on a comparative account of Husserl's and Levinas's works, it is of less interest to this study whether Levinas is doing justice to Husserl.[36] Instead, our focus will be on Levinas's main critique, namely the critique of considering intentional consciousness to be the only source of meaning, in order to understand his thoughts on non-intentional consciousness.

In discussing intentional consciousness, Levinas lays emphasis on its active character. Intentional consciousness has always an active character to it, since it is a meaning-giving *act*. Although early phenomenology already seeks to abolish the subject/object dichotomy, in Levinas's view, the intentional act remains attached to the subject, since it is the act of an active subject. Nevertheless,—and this marks the beginning of Levinas's critique— the "I" of intentional consciousness, while constituting the world, is indirectly conscious of itself as part of the world it constitutes, yet is not necessarily turned towards itself through reflection. That is to say, the self is already in the midst of what it constitutes, even if there is no intentional directedness towards the "I" itself.

---

[35] We are referring here to the texts mentioned above, not to Levinas's work in general. There are indeed other texts by Levinas that focus specifically on Husserl' work, for example the essays from Levinas's early career that are gathered in the collection *En découvrant l'existence avec Husserl et Heidegger* (1949) (parts of which were translated in English by Richard A. Cohen and Michael B. Smith as *Discovering Existence with Husserl* [Evanston: Northwestern University Press, 1998]), or his first dissertation, *Théorie de l'intuition dans la phénoménologie de Husserl* (1930), translated by André Orinne as *The Theory of Intuition in Husserl's Phenomenology* (Evanston: Northwestern University Press, 1995).

[36] There are several works focusing on Levinas's reading of Husserl's theory of intentionality and representation. A few examples in this sense are Jeffrey Powell, "Levinas Representing Husserl on Representation," *Philosophy Today* 39, no 2 (1995): 185-97., Rudolf Bernet, "Levinas's Critique of Husserl," in *The Cambridge Companion to Levinas*, 82-99, Søren Overgaard, "On Levinas's Critique of Husserl," in *Metaphysics, Facticity, Interpretation: Phenomenology in the Nordic Countries*, eds. Dan Zahavi, Sara Heinamaa, and Hans Ruin (Netherlands: Springer, 2003), 115-138, and the list could continue.

> If the constituting "I" runs up against a sphere in which he finds himself bodily intertwined with what he constituted, he is there in the world as if in his skin, in accordance with the intimacy of the incarnation that no longer has the exteriority of the objective world.[37]

Here, Levinas points towards a pre-reflective self-consciousness to be found in Husserl's philosophy, which designates an immediate consciousness of the self and accompanies intentional consciousness without itself being intentional.[38] Yet arguing that Husserl's conception of consciousness might include an immediate, pre-reflective consciousness is still just an anchor for the critique that follows. Levinas remarks that this type of immediate consciousness, as accompanying consciousness lacking intentional directedness towards the I itself, tends to be considered by Husserl in its negativity, as "non-explicit knowledge," "confused consciousness," "pre-intentional" or "pre-reflective":

> What goes on in this nonreflexive consciousness which is taken as merely prereflexive, and which, implicitly, accompanies intentional consciousness as the latter intentionally focuses in reflection on its own self, as if the thinking self appeared in the world and belonged there?[39]
>
> [O]ne is forced, no doubt too quickly, to consider, in philosophy, all this immediate consciousness merely as a still confused representation to be duly brought to "light."[40]

Levinas wants to change the secondary character that seems to be attributed to the immediate form of consciousness, and to emphasize a non-intentional consciousness, one which does not just accompany, but gives meaning to intentional reflective consciousness. According to Levinas, it is not

---

[37] "Philosophy and Transcendence" (1989), in AT 17.

[38] This interpretation of Husserl's text is not unusual. In this sense, see for example the work of Dan Zahavi, who has also argued for the existence of a pre-reflected type of self-awareness in Husserl. He is suggesting that it is strongly related with the inner time consciousness. See especially "Inner Time-Consciousness and Pre-reflected Self-awareness" in *New Husserl: A Critical Reader*, ed. Donn Welton, (Bloomington,: Indiana University Press 2003), 157–180; or *Husserl's Phenomenology* (Stanford CA: Stanford University Press 2003).

[39] "Nonintentional consciousness," in EN 128.

[40] "Ethics as First Philosophy" (1984), in LR 79–80. See also "The Bad Conscience and the Inexorable" (1981), in OGCM 172–173, AT 16–17, or "Nonintentional Consciousness," in EN 133.

enough to merely acknowledge some form of pre-reflexive consciousness; it also needs to be thought independently from intentional consciousness. Thus, Levinas is not only addressing the question of non-reflective consciousness, but more importantly, he is trying to decentralize the role of intentionality in meaning-giving:

> It is not forbidden, nevertheless, to wonder whether—beneath the gaze of reflected consciousness taken for self-consciousness—the non-intentional, experienced in counterpoint to the intentional, preserves, and delivers its true meaning.[41]

The decentralization of intentionality goes hand in hand with Levinas's questioning of the philosophy of consciousness based on vision; hence the critique of the phenomenology of "light" that was previously discussed. The fundamental project of a philosophy centred on the "intentional consciousness of reflection" is, Levinas explains, that of "bringing to light" the hidden horizons.[42] When philosophy is preoccupied with showing, bringing to light through "the *gaze* of reflected consciousness," in other words, with thematization, it makes presentation and re-presentation the primary source of meaning, while the unthematized is considered a not-yet explicit knowledge, one which is waiting to be thematized and "brought to full light."[43] Linking Levinas's critique of intentionality to his critique of phenomenology as visibility suggests that he does not necessarily have a problem with intentional consciousness as such, but that the critique runs deeper, targeting the tendency to think consciousness *exclusively* in terms of vision, gaze, in other words, in terms of thematization. Levinas's critique of intentionality is then a critique of thematizing intentionality (not intentionality as such). This critique, in one form or another, is a recurrent argument in Levinas's work. We find it in very early works, such as *Existence and*

---

[41] "The Bad Conscience and the Inexorable," in OGCM 173.
[42] "The intentional consciousness of reflection, taking the transcendental *I*, its states and mental acts, as its object, can also thematize and seize or explicate all its of non-intentional lived experience, qualified as implicit. It is invited to do so by philosophy in its fundamental project, which consists in bringing to light the inevitable transcendental naivete of a consciousness forgetful of its horizons, of its implicit elements and the time it lasts" AT 18.
[43] AT 18.

Existents (1947),⁴⁴ as well as in his later works, such as *Otherwise than Being* (1974).

In *Otherwise than Being*, the work which, from the point of view of the discussion of subjectivity is of most interest to us here, that which is later articulated as non-intentional consciousness takes the form of an "inversion" of intentionality. Once again, this shows that Levinas does not seek a negation of intentionality, but rather its re-thinking. The inversion of intentionality is reflected in the way Levinas describes substitution: the subject is not an ego that aims, it is not a sovereign and active subject for itself, but, as we have seen in the previous chapter, it is for the other, turned inside-out.⁴⁵ The turning inside-out of subjectivity displaces intentionality as the meaning giving source of the self, and makes consciousness also turned inside-out. As substitution is revealed from the hither side, that is to say, in an-archy, the movement of inversion that displaces intentionality as thematization is also an-archical.⁴⁶ Anarchy, by disrupting order, also disrupts thinking in relative and negative terms. Continuing the same line of thought in the essays from the 1980's, Levinas proposes a more "positive" interpretation of pre-reflective consciousness,⁴⁷ one which has a deeper meaning than that of a mere preliminary stage for the reflective, intentional consciousness. So, even if Levinas starts out by calling the unthematizing consciousness "non-intentional," he knows that the name "non-intentional" remains a negative expression and is thus still being thought in relation to thematizing intentional consciousness. As a consequence, Levinas introduces the term "bad conscience/consciousness" (*mauvaise conscience*)⁴⁸ as a more positive expression of non-intentional consciousness:

---

⁴⁴ See especially *Existence and Existents* (1947), part 2: "The World."

⁴⁵ OB 47.

⁴⁶ "Obsession traverses consciousness countercurrentwise, is inscribed in consciousness as something foreign, a disequilibrium, a delirium. It undoes thematization, and escapes any *principle,* origin, will, or ἀρχή, which are put forth in every ray of consciousness. This movement is, in the original sense of the term, an-archical." OB 101.

⁴⁷ "What can that supposed confusion, that implication, signify positively in some sense?" See "Nonintentional consciousness," in EN 128.

⁴⁸ In the English translations, either the expression "bad conscience" is used (for example in "Non-intentional Consciousness" or "The Bad Conscience and the Inexorable") or else the French form is retained (as in "Ethics as First Philosophy"). Some commentators also refer to it as "unhappy consciousness," as does Seán Hand in the preface he wrote for the essay "Ethics as First Philosophy" when it was first translated. Although this suggests a connection with Hegel's "unhappy consciousness" (to which Hand makes reference in a footnote without, however, developing the connection), Levinas is actually

> In its non-intentionality, on the hither side of all will, before all wrong-doing, in its non-intentional identification, the identity draws back from the eventual insistence that may be involved in identification's return to self. Bad conscience or timidity: accused without culpability and responsible for its very presence.[49]
>
> 'Conscience' that, rather than signifying a knowledge of self, is a self-effacement or discretion of presence. Bad conscience: without intentions, without aims, without the protective mask of the character [*personnage*] contemplating himself in the mirror of the world, self-assured and affirming himself. Without name, position, or titles. A presence that fears presence, stripped bare of all attributes. A nakedness that is not that of unveiling or the exposure of truth.[50]

If non-intentional consciousness was introduced in direct reference to a Husserlian terminology, bad consciousness broadens the terminological field. Due to the double meaning of the French term *mauvaise conscience*, the expression *bad consciousness* constitutes a clever way to re-define the notion of non-intentional consciousness outside a Husserlian vocabulary. The French word "conscience" can be read both as conscience and as consciousness. Accordingly, there are two possible readings of *mauvaise conscience*, creating thereby a twofold concept: bad conscience and bad consciousness. However, the two readings do not imply two separate kinds of non-intentionality, but rather show the complexity of the notion. Thus, on the one hand, *mauvaise conscience* as *bad consciousness* expresses an out of order consciousness that has gone 'bad' because it is not functioning by means of thematizing intentionality. On the other hand, *mauvaise conscience* can be read as *bad conscience*, implying accusation or guilt.[51] Accusation refers to the self in the accusative, something which we have already discussed in the previous chapter. Both accusation and guilt must be understood here outside culpability, that is to say, without presupposing an active

---

using a different phrase when he mentions Hegel's term ("'malheur' de la conscience," ENEPA 144, or "conscience malheureuse", *Altérité et transcendance*, 32). For Hegel's "unhappy consciousness" the usual French translation of the term is *conscience malheureuse* (see Jean Hyppolite's translation from the 1930's), while for his nonintentional consciousness as "bad conscience" Levinas is using the term *mauvaise conscience*. Thus, besides their clearly different philosophical agenda, the fact that Levinas engages a different terminology from Hegel's, leads us to believe strongly that he does not intend to connect his notion of *bad conscience* with Hegel's *unhappy conscience*. As a result, we find no reason to insist on the possibility of such connection.

[49] "Nonintentional Consciousness," in EN 129.
[50] Ibid.
[51] See AT 21.

I that is conscious of its acts and *takes* responsibility. Even if I am responsible for the other, I do not *have* this responsibility properly speaking, since only due to this responsibility can there be "me."[52] Non-intentional consciousness is not consciousness of something, and thus guilt does not mean being guilty of *something*.[53] Levinas describes it as "fear for the other."[54] To have bad conscience in the sense of culpability, to be guilty of something, already requires a bad conscience as a "fear for the other."[55] Fear for the other signifies for Levinas the subjectivity under question, the questioning of the self, the self "having to answer"[56] not for itself but for the other. Once again, it is necessary to point out that non-intentional consciousness, now in the form of bad consciousness/conscience, is not a reflective movement: fear for the other, Levinas explains, is "my fear, but nowise fear *for* me."[57] The "fear" from the "fear for the other" cannot be converted into a fear for myself or into my being frightened. The emphasis is on the "for the other," an expression familiar to us from our discussion of subjectivity.[58] What is at stake here is consciousness beyond self-affirmation

---

[52] "[The transcendence of the one for the other] signifies neither intentionality nor a property of the 'me' (*moi*) that would be responsibility for the other. It is on the contrary, as responsibility and in responsibility that the "me" gains its uniqueness.," GDT 158.

[53] However, Levinas does not lose the term "guilt" altogether. He uses it for example when he speaks of proximity in "A Man God " (1968), in EN 51, or OB 109 and 112.

[54] "Nonintentional Consciousness," in EN 130.

[55] Not surprisingly, this resonates with Levinas's understanding of responsibility as responding for the other, responsiveness required for any kind of moral responsibility to be possible.

[56] "The very justice of being posited in being *is put in question*; being, that is affirmed with intentional thought, knowledge and the grasping of the now. Here we have being as bad conscience, in that putting in question; being-in-question, but also put before the question. Having to answer. [...] To have to answer for ones right to be, not in relation to the abstraction of some anonymous law, some legal entity, but in fear for the other.," "Philosophy and Transcendence," in AT 22–23.

[57] "Nonintentional Consciousness, " in EN 131.

[58] Bad consciousness as fear for the other implies a clear reference to Heidegger: the "good consciousness/conscience" (*bonne conscience*) of Being, which is disturbed by the bad consciousness/conscience (see AT 19–26). Good consciousness/conscience, presented in its attachment to Being, always curls back to itself, just as intentional consciousness, remaining explicitly (as thematizing self-consciousness) or implicitly (as being towards *my own* death) self-referential. In the essay "The Meaning of Meaning" (1980) Levinas argues that the ultimate question is not the one regarding the meaning of being—which he associates with the good conscience—but is the question "Is being just," the question that denotes the bad conscience (see OS 92–4).

and presentation. Non-intentional consciousness means both "discretion of presence,"⁵⁹ and where "identity recoils before its affirmation."⁶⁰ Along with the critique of thematization, goes a critique of the synthetic structure of temporality. Thus, as our next step we need to address the question of time.

2.3. Diachrony of Time

Levinas's critique of the predominance of vision, that is, of thinking consciousness exclusively in terms of thematizing intentionality, resonates with the way in which he re-thinks time. Unsurprisingly, the essay "Diachrony and Representation", which tackles the question of temporality, begins with a critique of the priority given to vision in the philosophical tradition.⁶¹ Once again, Levinas questions the ways of conceiving knowledge and intelligibility that belong to the Western philosophical tradition, which he considers to be dominated by thematization, a bringing to present, in a gathering, synchronous movement. By suggestively using the word "com-prehension" (*com-prendre*) to designate this knowledge,⁶² Levinas points towards its etymological meaning, 'to hold together,' in order to emphasize more strongly the unifying and appropriating (grasping) character of thematizing intentionality. Levinas is fully aware of the three-fold structure of Husserlian intentionality given by its temporal horizon (protention and retention). Thus, the critique of thematizing intentionality becomes a critique of its synthetical time structure. The primal impression, protention and retention are brought together in the same conscious act of the present, making it synthetical and determinative.⁶³ "[T]he presence of the present, as

---

⁵⁹"Nonintentional Consciousness," in EN 129.
⁶⁰ "Ethics as First Philosophy" (1984), in LR 81.
⁶¹ "The sphere of intelligibility –the reasonable– in which everyday life as well as the tradition of our philosophic and scientific thought maintains itself, is characterized by vision. The structure of *seeing* having the *seen* for its object or theme –the so-called intentional structure– is found in all the modes of sensibility having access to things. It is found in the *intellectual* accession to the state-of-things or to the relationships between things.," "Diachrony and Representation" (1985), in TO 97.
⁶² See for instance "Philosophy and Transcendence" (1989), in AT 13.
⁶³ Levinas's critique is nothing like the critique that associates Husserl's subjectivity with a pure self-presence, and which Zahavi rejects by invoking the temporal horizon of the intentional act. See Zahavi, *Husserl's Phenomenology*, 93–98.

temporality," says Levinas, "is the promise of a graspable, a solid."[64] Even something similar to the Husserlian Ur-impression, Levinas explains, finds its place in thematizing consciousness as retention, and is brought by this to presence in the present.[65] Levinas, again, plays on words to emphasize the grasping of the present through presence: he suggestively writes the French word for 'now' (*maintenance*) with a hyphen, as *main-tenance*, so that it means 'the present time,' if read together, and 'holding in hand,' 'grasping,' if considered as separated by the hyphen.[66] It thus becomes clear that, along with the problem of consciousness, at stake here is also that of temporality. The de-posed subject, without ground, is on the hither side of both consciousness and time. Consciousness becomes 'bad,' as we have seen in the previous section, since it does not function as proper intentional consciousness. In the following we are about to see that time turns into contra-time, or 'bad' time, as its synthetical structure is disturbed:

> No grounds (*non-lieu*), meanwhile [entre-temps] or contra-tempo time (or bad times (*mal-heur*)), it is on the hither side of being and of the nothingness.[67]

In developing his thoughts on temporality, Levinas acknowledges his debt to Bergson on several occasions.[68] Besides well-known ideas that Levinas clearly appreciates, such as Bergson's differentiation between chronological time and duration, or the critique of thinking time in spatial terms, most relevant for us is the emphasis on the non-coincidence of time. Bergson

---

[64] "Diachrony and Representation," in TO 98.

[65] "When it turns out that this consciousness in the living present, *originally* non-objectifying and not objectified, is thematizable and thematizing in retention, without thereby losing the 'temporal place' which gives 'individuation,' then we see the non-intentionality of the primal impression fitted back in the normal order, not leading to the hither side of the same or of the origin. [...] The thesis that the non-intentionality of the primal retention is not a loss of consciousness, that nothing can be produced in a clandestine way, what nothing can break the thread of consciousness, excludes from time the irreducible diachrony whose meaning the present study aims to bring to light, behind the *exhibiting* of being," OB 33-4.

[66] See for example "Diachrony and Representation," in TO 98.

[67] OB 109, AE 172.

[68] Levinas includes Bergson among the great figures of the history of philosophy, and considers *Time and Free Will* one of his most important works. (See EI 37) Levinas's preference for this particular writing suggests the significance of temporality, and as we will see in Chapter 3, the significance of qualitative multiplicity for his own thought, given that *Time and Free Will* extensively discusses these topics.

argues for the heterogeneity of duration (*dureé*) (non-chronological time); according to him, considering time in terms of a successive order (that is, in terms of a before and an after) would only reduce it to homogeneity, since, in order to recognize successiveness, a homogeneous medium is needed that allows the successive display; in other words, the successive moments need to be thought simultaneously, in relation with each-other, in order that their successiveness be considered. In this sense, time as succession presupposes homogeneity and simultaneity: it is already spatial. Duration, however, denotes temporality in heterogeneous terms, according to Bergson, without its being reduced to simultaneity or juxtaposition.[69] We can easily see why the heterogeneity of duration, in other words, its non-coincidence, is so appealing for Levinas: the refusal of unifying simultaneity corresponds to Levinas's critique of thematizing intentionality. However, he is not completely able to embrace Bergson's idea of duration. In Levinas's view, the idea of duration proposed by Bergson never fully overcomes the prevalence of thematizing consciousness, since it remains strongly connected to intuition.[70] The intuition of duration remains an act performed by the I, and, as such, it cancels the role of the other for the emerging self.[71] Indeed, as the most illustrative example of intuition, Bergson evokes the intuition of myself as the act of a sovereign "I," without the need for exteriority; that is to say, Bergson's duration suggests a posited self, differing from Levinas's deposed subjectivity.[72]

Levinas's version of duration is "absolutely outside the activity of the *I*."[73] It expresses passivity without the activity of self-reflective consciousness,

---

[69] Henri Bergson, *Essai sur les données immédiates de la conscience* [1889]. *Time and Free Will*, trans. F. L. Pogson (London: George Allen and Unwin, 1910).

[70] For Bergson there is a strong link between intuition and duration. We have access to duration through intuition. See H. Bergson, *The Creative Mind*, trans. Mabelle L. Andison (New York: Philosophical Library, 1946), especially chapter VI.

[71] Here is an example of Levinas's critique to the Bergsonian intuition: "Is not Bergsonian intuition as consciousness –be it prereflexive, as the spontaneous and immediate 'actually lived life' –confusion and coincidence and, thus, an experience still rediscovering its standards in a worked over alterity?," "The Old and the New" (1980), in TO 133.

[72] "There is at least one reality which we all seize from within, by intuition, and not by simple analysis. It is our own person in its flowing through time, the self which endures. With no other thing can we sympathise intellectually, or if you like, spiritually. But one thing is sure: we sympathize with ourselves." Bergson, *The Creative Mind*, 191.

[73] AT 20.

pure passivity, "prior to all passivity."[74] By "prior" Levinas is not suggesting some kind of chronological hierarchy or order of causality. To understand this we need to keep in mind the an-archical character of the hither side. Just as Levinas is not simply opposing non-intentionality with intentionality, he is not opposing passivity to activity; on the contrary, he continues to refuse dualities: "it is a passivity," he says, "inconvertible into an act, the hither side of the act-passivity alternative."[75] If we think passivity from within the passive-active duality, we are still approaching it in relation to activity, giving it a relative determination. We know by now that Levinas does not make us choose between alternatives, nor think in terms of alternatives. The point is precisely that pure passivity is beyond alternatives. By going beyond the dualities of passive-active, a move similar to the one observed in the case of an-archy and order, Levinas refuses what he considers to be a synthetical, unifying way of thinking.

The same attempt to escape dualities makes Levinas refer to passivity as "more passive than all passivity," as he does, for example, in *Otherwise than Being*:

> Subjectivity, locus and null-site of this breakup, comes to pass as a passivity more passive than all passivity.[76]

This context however, brings a new dimension to the meaning of passivity, a temporal dimension:

> To the diachronic past, which cannot be recuperated by representation effected by memory or history, that is, incommensurable with the present, corresponds or answers the un-assumable passivity of the self. *"Se passer"*—to come to pass— is for us a precious expression in which the *self (se)* figures as in a past that bypasses itself, as in ageing without "active synthesis."[77]

Passivity understood as "to come to pass", indicates a past without determination, without ever having been in the present, yet not outside time. It is on the hither side of past, "a past that bypasses itself." It belongs

---

[74] See, for instance, OB 196.
[75] Ibid. 117.
[76] Ibid. 14.
[77] Ibid., emphasis by Levinas.

to the undetermined hither side of time, which Levinas calls *diachrony*.[78] The indeterminacy of diachrony is articulated in the above quotation, when Levinas refers to the "diachronic past." The diachronic past is an immemorial past without origin (an-archy), like a "lapse of time" that can be neither presented nor represented. In this way, temporality escapes the initiative of the *I*:

> For the lapse of time is also something irrecuperable, refractory to the simultaneity of the present, something unrepresentable, immemorial, pre-historical [...] Through it time passes (*se passe*). The immemorial is not an effect of a weakness of memory, an incapacity to cross large intervals of time, to resuscitate pasts too deep. It is the impossibility of the dispersion of time to assemble itself in the present, the insurmountable diachrony of time[.][79]

> [...] This anarchy, this refusal to be assembled into a representation, has its own way to concern me: the *lapse*. But the lapse of time irrecuperable in the temporalization of time is not only negative like the immemorial. Temporalization as lapse, the loss of time, is neither an initiative of an ego, nor a movement toward some telos of action. The loss of time is not the work of a subject.[80]

Diachrony is Levinas's way of re-thinking the temporality of time without creating an alternative time, *another* time outside of time.[81] By opening up time itself, diachrony disrupts it from determination, from its synthetical structure.

The disruptive diachrony of time and the irrecuperable past reinforces the importance of an-archy: instead of the recollectable memory of origin we have an immemorial past, a lack of origin, one never presented or re-presented, "prior to every memory," "non-present par excellence."[82]

---

[78] Levinas's use of the term diachrony is not to be confused with diachrony as movement through time, like Saussure's diachrony from linguistics (in his *Course in General Linguistics* [1916]), which means the study of language through time considering its historical development (contrary to the more abstract study of language characteristic to a given moment in time). For Levinas, this way of understanding diachrony would still be synchronic, because it would gather time through synthesis when it approaches from a historical overview.
[79] OB 38.
[80] Ibid., 51.
[81] "The *otherwise than being* cannot be situated in any eternal order extracted from time that would somehow command the temporal series." Ibid., 9. Emphasis by Levinas.
[82] "A linear regressive movement, a retrospective back along the temporal series toward a very remote past, would never be able to reach the absolutely diachronous pre-original

Diachrony reveals this paradoxical character of the hither side, which is not *in* time, yet not *outside* of time either. Levinas compares it with the diastole of the heart, meaning both dilation (as the Greek etymology of the word suggests) and relaxation between two heartbeats (as the medical term in use since the 16th Century indicates). There can only be a heartbeat if there is a pause, an interruption. Diachrony becomes the expression of dilation or the pause that does not nest any particular event, but gives sense to all events. Through its disruption, diachrony implies "the impossible synthesis of I and the Other," as Levinas puts it in *God, Death and Time*:

> The always of time, the impossibility of the identification of I (*Moi*) and the Other, the impossible synthesis of I and the Other. Diachrony. Diastole or dilation. The impossibility of settling on the same terrain, of com-posing in the world, the impossibility in the form of a slippage of the earth beneath my feet.[83]

This remains the main idea behind Levinas's metaphor of the heartbeat, even when it does not signify the diastole, but rather time standing still (*le temps mort*), beyond the systole-diastole duality, as in *Otherwise than Being*:

> [T]he dead time (*le temps mort*) or the *meanwhile* (*l'entre-temps*) which separates inspiration and expiration, the diastole and systole of the heart beating dully against the walls of one's skin.[84]

Diachrony, both as the pause of the diastole and the "meanwhile" of time standing still, not only remains outside any dichotomy, but also gives sense to the parts of the dichotomy in a non-relative way—that is to say, it breaks with its synthetical structure. We find here a similar movement as in the case of substitution: the self emerges through its own disruption by the other (the call), while hindering a relative definition of the self and the other. When the metaphor of the heart is brought back in Levinas's lectures from 1976, it is used in connection to the-other-in-me (or the-other-in-the-same), the other at the heart of me "where disquiet disturbs the heart at

---

which cannot be recuperated by memory and history. [...] The unlimited responsibility in which I find myself comes from the hither side of my freedom, from a 'prior to every memory,' an 'ulterior to every accomplishment,' from the non-present par excellence, the non-original, the anarchical, prior to or beyond essence." OB 10.
[83] GDT 111.
[84] OB 109, AE 173. Emphasis by Levinas.

rest."[85] Here, the very de-position of subjectivity is expressed through diachrony.[86] This is also the case with Levinas's comments regarding the word "*in*" from "the other-*in*-the-same" (the "model" of subjectivity), which, according to him, illustrates diachrony.[87] In this way, diachrony not only disrupts synthetic time, but is also an expression of the ambiguous relation, outside relatedness, between the self and the other. We will dedicate the next chapter to a discussion of this ambiguity.

---

[85] GDT 110–111.

[86] Subjectivity as diachrony accords with the way diachrony is presented as "in two times" in *Otherwise than Being*: "Neither conjuncture in being, nor reflection of this conjuncture in the unity of transcendental apperception, the proximity of me with the other is in two times, and thus is a transcendence. It temporalizes itself, but with a diachronic temporality, outside, beyond or above, the time recuperable by reminiscence, in which consciousness abides and converses, and in which being and entities show themselves in experience." OB 85. Later on, in the third part of this thesis, we will see that this "in two times" also alludes to sociality as that which opens up time itself.

[87] GDT 19.

CHAPTER 3
Self and Multiplicity

Up to this point we have discussed the question of subjectivity in terms of deposition and the approach from the hither side. We have also analyzed the hither side in terms of an-archy in order to reveal its disruptive character, and have shown that it indicates an inside-out dimension of the relation to the other, a dimension opened up by substitution. In turn, this led us to rethink temporality and consciousness, as diachrony and bad consciousness. Levinas's critique regarding thematizing consciousness, which we discussed previously, and the synthetical time structure that goes with it, makes the relation to the other a paradoxical relation without a synthesis given by relatedness or by negativity. In this sense, the anarchical relation to the other is, as Levinas famously said, a "relation without relation."[1] The non-relatedness of this special kind of relation means that it is neither a matter of interchangeability, nor one of mirroring between me and the other. In this sense, we have already seen that the inside-out is characterized by irreciprocity and asymmetry: I am through the other and for the other in substitution, yet this does not mean that the other is for me and through me (irreciprocity), or that the other is defined as non-me, or as alter-ego, or that the self is determined as non-other (asymmetry). In this chapter, we attempt a closer inspection of this unthematized, irreciprocal and asymmetrical relation to the other and will show that it represents a paradoxical multiplicity that is not inscribed in the singular/plural distinction.

In the following pages we will particularly focus on Levinas's two major works, *Totality and Infinity* (1961) and *Otherwise than Being* (1974), as the comparative reading of these two works reveals the relation without relation to the other as an anarchical radical multiplicity. In both of these texts the subject is presented as the emergence of the unique self, yet the relation to

[1] TI 80.

the other through which the self becomes unique is described in different terms in the two books. As we are about to see, in *Totality and Infinity* Levinas describes it as a 'radical multiplicity,' which he carefully differentiates from homogeneous, numerical multiplicity, that is to say, from multiplicity thought with reference to unity, to a whole that it forms. In this chapter we argue that radical multiplicity has the role of breaking up singularity/multiplicity, singular/plural dichotomies. We attempt to show that, although in *Otherwise than Being* the expression 'radical multiplicity' appears to have been abandoned, its meaning does not fade away along with the actual term; instead it is expressed in the vocabulary corresponding to *Otherwise than Being* and hence heterogeneity beyond the singular/plural distinction remains important throughout Levinas's writings. Showing that the profound meaning of radical multiplicity is preserved in both of these books, offers an important link between the two works and it reveals the consistency in Levinas's work as a whole—that is to say, it has a methodological purpose for us, the readers. At the same time, investigating radical multiplicity has a more profound significance: by breaking up the singular/plural dichotomy radical multiplicity carries the relation to the other beyond the simple dyad of me and another, yet remaining on the hither side (it still reflects the inside-out dimension). The importance of this conclusion will show its full potential in the second part of the thesis, since it brings sociality outside a dual relation yet without the implication of the third. In this way, the chapter constitutes an important step regarding the general argument of the thesis.

3.1. The radicalization of multiplicity

In this section we will turn our focus to the meaning of 'radical multiplicity' presented in Levinas's work from 1961, *Totality and Infinity*.[2] Perhaps due

[2] The expression 'radical multiplicity' is introduced in *Totality and Infinity* in the chapter "Subjectivity and Pluralism." Although here the expression 'pluralism' leads to and eventually becomes synonymous with radical multiplicity, there seems to be no clear consistency regarding the term 'plurality' or 'pluralism' throughout Levinas's writings and they don't seem to be established as separate concepts. It is usually the context that plays the most important role in determining their meaning. For example, in a later text, Levinas uses 'plurality' in the context of the other's other, thus raising the question of justice and comparison (See "The Proximity of the Other" [1986], in IIRB 214), which certainly is not the case in the context of radical multiplicity from *Totality and Infinity*.

to the rather brief encounter of the expression as such throughout Levinas's writings the meaning of 'radical multiplicity' has remained somewhat unexplored in the Levinas scholarship. However, we do not seek to fill in this gap through examining the question of multiplicity for its own sake. The purpose here is not that of an exhaustive discussion of the possible interpretations of multiplicity in Levinas's work in general, nor that of analyzing the question of multiplicity in itself, but to show the important role that this particular, radicalized meaning of multiplicity has for the way we understand and interpret the other/others distinction in Levinas philosophy. In other words, we are interested in the 'radicality' of Levinas's 'radical multiplicity' that allows it to go beyond a singular/plural distinction. Nonetheless, in order to do so, first we need to examine the context of subjectivity from *Totality and Infinity*, where the notion of radical multiplicity is brought forth, context that, as we shall see, differs from that of *Otherwise than Being*.

3.1.1. Subjectivity in "*Totality and Infinity*"

For Levinas, both in *Otherwise than Being* and *Totality and Infinity*, the refusal of a relative definition of the self and the other hold great importance. While in *Otherwise than Being* Levinas expresses the emergence of the self as the relation to the other in the form of substitution, in *Totality and Infinity* the connection of the self to the other, or rather the connection of their disconnectedness (i.e. non-relativeness) is discussed in a different setting. Here, the break with thinking in dichotomies is expressed in the form of a break with totality, since an all-embracing, totalizing gaze is what makes the dichotomies function as they refer back to one another. This break with totality is presented in two different sequences: the first occurs in interiority, where the self breaks totality through its separateness, and a second rupture is created by the absolute exteriority of the other. Yet, as we will see later on, they are part of the same move.

From the start, it is quite clear that in *Totality and Infinity* Levinas describes the self and its relation to the other in a manner that is different than the discourse with which we have become familiar from Levinas's later

---

In order to avoid the possible confusions to which the word 'plurality' or 'pluralism' could lead, in this chapter we will remain consistent in using the term 'radical multiplicity' in the sense in which it occurs in *Totality and Infinity*.

work. Here, we do not find the self emerging as the-other-in-me (as in *Otherwise than Being*); instead, Levinas starts out by describing a self-sufficient, enjoying self:

> It [the ego] is an existence *for itself*—but not, initially, in view of its own existence. Nor is it a representation of the self by itself. It is for itself as in the expression "each for himself"; [...] The self-sufficiency of *enjoying* measures the egoism, or the Ipseity of the Ego and the same.[3]

As we can already see from the above quotation, in *Totality and Infinity* Levinas frames his question of subjectivity by starting from the self that is 'for itself.' However, this self 'for itself' does not have the reflective movement of the conscious self for itself that we find in *Otherwise than Being*. If, in the later text, the self 'for itself' carries the determinative effect of self-sufficiency—that is to say, the self determines itself—here, the self 'for itself' has the purpose of reinforcing non-relativity through self-sufficiency. Despite this distinction, Levinas seeks to emphasize in *Totality and Infinity* something similar to the refusal expressed in *Otherwise than Being* of an auto-identified and determined Ego. In this sense, we can recognize in the enjoying self for itself from *Totality and Infinity* a refusal of a thematization of the self.[4] This idea lies behind Levinas's emphasis on the *separateness* of the self.[5]

> The unicity of the I conveys separation. Separation in the strictest sense is solitude, and enjoyment—happiness or unhappiness—is isolation itself.[6]

---

[3] TI 118, emphasis by Levinas. It is important to bear in mind that all these words, 'egoism,' 'enjoyment,' 'for itself,' do not carry a moral connotation. They describe the sphere of interiority, a movement towards oneself, which Levinas suggestively calls Ipseity in order to emphasize even more the singularity or unicity of the self.

[4] "The upsurge of the self beginning in enjoyment, where the substantiality of the I is apperceived not as the subject of the verb to be but as implicated in happiness (not belonging to ontology, but to axiology) is the exaltation of the *existent* as such. [...]. When the I is identified with reason, taken as the power to thematization and objectification, it loses its very Ipseity." TI 119.

[5] According to Richard Cohen, the idea of separation is borrowed from Franz Rosenzweig's *Star of Redemption*. See translator's note 9 from TO 45.

[6] TI 117.

Levinas's choice of words might surprise us, as in everyday language the word 'separation' is used in a somewhat similar sense as a limitation between two parts that are exterior to each other. Limitation would engage a relativity of the parts that limit each other. This cannot be what Levinas means, since thematization through relativeness is exactly what he tries to overcome.[7] Instead of limitation, the separateness of the self implies autonomy, in the sense that it is separated in its own interiority and without reference to an exteriority that would limit it.[8] Yet the goal of stressing separateness is not that of establishing a self-generating self, but that of thinking it differently than in terms of individuality.[9] Individuality, for Levinas, remains related to a genus, to a totality, a whole, as if it would be the result of a division until reaching in-divisible elements (in-dividuals). This would make the self, as individual, only a sample or specimen of a unifying genus.[10] In both *Totality and Infinity*[11] and *Otherwise than Being*[12]

---

[7] Simon Lumsden emphasizes that the separateness of the self "reserves a place for the I outside the dialogue." See Simon Lumsden, "Absolute Difference and Social Ontology: Levinas Face to Face with Buber and Fichte" *Human studies* 23 (Kluwer Academic Publisher, 2000), 227–241. The priority of dialogue itself would destroy the very difference between me and the Other (uniting them under a common "we"), this being one of Levinas's main critique to Buber's "I-Thou" relation. We will return to Levinas's critique of the dialogical relation in Part II.

[8] "[Separation] does not result from a simple split, like a spatial removal. To be separated is to be at home with oneself," TI 147.

[9] Even the term "singularity" does not always seem suitable for Levinas, as in GDT he clearly goes against the "I" as singularity, which would be an Ego, and instead he opts for characterizing the self as unique: "The subject is not an opaque being equipped with the structure of egoity, as though it had an essential eidetic structure, for this would permit us to think of it as a concept whose realization would be the singular being. *Through substitution, it is not the singularity of the me that is asserted, it is its uniqueness*" GDT 182, emphasis by Levinas.

[10] "The I is not unique like the Eiffel Tower or the Mona Lisa. The unicity of the I does not merely consist in being found in one sample only, but in existing without having a genus, without being the individuation of a concept. The ipseity of the I consists in remaining outside the distinction between the individual and the general," TI 117–8.

[11] See, for instance, our previous note or the beginning of section IV from *Totality and Infinity*, TI 252.

[12] See OB note 9 Ch 4: "The singularity of the subject is not the uniqueness of an *hapax*. For it is not due to some distinctive quality, like fingerprints, that would make of it an incomparable *unicum*, and, as a principle of individuation, make this unity deserve a proper noun, and hence a place in discourse. The identity of the oneself is not the inertia of a quiddity individuated by an ultimate specific difference inherent in the body or in

Levinas thinks the self outside the individual/general dichotomy.[13] In this sense, through its separateness and thus its refusal to refer back to a genus, the self breaks from the totality of universal determination. Through the separated self, the break with totality is "concretely accomplished," says Levinas,[14] because the separated self cannot become nor belong to a universal I—in other words, the particularity of the self is not the result of abstraction.[15]

However, thinking the self in terms of autonomy runs the risk of the enjoying self forming its own totality, a "totality of contentment."[16] According to Levinas, this threat of totality is overcome by the exteriority of alterity—which brings us to the second sequence of the break with totality. Nevertheless, for the break to be successful alterity has to be the alterity of the absolute other. In *Totality and Infinity* there is a first acquaintance with alterity, which is similar to a relation to nourishment: the other is trans-

---

character, or by the uniqueness of a natural or historical conjuncture. It is in the uniqueness of someone summoned," OB 194.

[13] However, Levinas does not renounce the word "individual" altogether. Despite the fact that he explicitly states that Ipseity is "outside the distinction between individual and general," he still sometimes refers to the separated self as individual. See TI 118.

[14] "The I (*le moi*) is thus the mode in which the break-up of totality, which leads to the presence of the absolutely other, is concretely accomplished. It is solitude par excellence," TI 118, TeI 122.

[15] Levinas's preference for concretization, clearly expressed in *Totality and Infinity*, reveals his refusal of formalism: "The method practiced here does indeed consist in seeking the condition of empirical situations, but it leaves to the developments called empirical, in which the conditioning possibility is accomplished—it leaves to the *concretization*—an ontological role that specifies the meaning of the fundamental possibility, a meaning invisible in that condition," TI 173. While he stresses the importance of concreteness, Levinas's words are not simple praising the empirical. Instead, he rejects the use of a formalist method of thinking that gives a privileged position to the theoretical structures from which the concrete supposedly derives. The formalist way of theoretization is, unsurprisingly, very unappealing to the self-confessed phenomenologist Levinas. Seen in this light, it becomes clear that prioritizing concretization for Levinas has the purpose of escaping a pure abstraction and formalization of the self, the other, and the relation of the self to the other (i.e. sociality)—in other words, it serves the purpose of keeping them from becoming empty notions (TI 50). The threat of falling into formalization lies behind Levinas's analysis of the problematical character of "concepts" and the question of the unthematized, or of the unsaying of the said [*dedire*]—questions to which we will return later on, when we discuss the non-relative interplay between the unthematized and thematization in the form of the Saying and the Said (in Chapter 4 and 5).

[16] TI 179.

posed in the same, in the interiority of the self, (it is consumed)—this constitutes the very essence of enjoyment.[17] The alterity of the 'consumable' other can be appropriated, while the absolute exteriority remains alterity, it cannot become one with the self. In trying to emphasize even more the differentiation between the two kinds of alterity, in his early works Levinas introduces two kinds of transcendence, calling the transcendence through enjoyment the "transcendence of need."[18] Nevertheless, in *Totality and Infinity* he seems to be more cautious with his terminology and he does not consider anymore need in terms of transcendence properly speaking. Instead, Levinas carefully differentiates between the relation of transcendence (relation to the absolute other) and the relation *analogous* to transcendence in which the other is eventually subsumed into the same (as is the case of the self in its relation to nourishment).[19] Here we will not engage further in a discussion of the different meanings of transcendence, since for the sake of our argument it was sufficient to underline the difference between the relation to the subsumable other (where the other eventually is determined through the self, i.e. it is consumed) and the undeterminable other, the other that cannot be appropriated.[20]

The absolute other cannot bring satisfaction as enjoyment does, for it is not a relation of need but one of a (meta-physical) desire that cannot be fulfilled; it is "beyond satisfaction and nonsatisfaction,"[21] Levinas says. It is important to note that, here, the 'absolute' of the 'absolute other' regains its etymological meaning of ab-solute, as being without relation.[22] Nevertheless, 'relation' is understood in terms of a relatedness that permits synthesis (a putting together, unification) on the basis of the relation itself. For

---

[17] "Nourishment, as means of invigoration, is the transmutation of the other into the same, which is in the essence of enjoyment," TI 111.
[18] "Time and the Other" (1947), in TO 64–67.
[19] See TI 109.
[20] On the topic of transcendence and its different understanding throughout Levinas work see Bettina Bergo, "Ontology, Transcendence, and Immanence in Emmanuel Levinas's Philosophy," *Research in Phenomenology*, 35, no. 1 (2005): 141–180., Robert Bernasconi, "No Exit: Levinas's Aporetic Account of Transcendence," *Research in Phenomenology* 35, no. 1 (2005): 101–117.
[21] TI 179.
[22] "[A]bsolute in the etymological sense of that adjective, by virtue of its always separable from every relationship and synthesis," "Diachrony and Representation," in TO 107. Absolute has the same etymological roots as ab-solved, which is another word that Levinas plays on when describing the self disrupted from its own identity as origin in itself, i.e. the self without relativeness. See for instance OB 92, or ibid., 115.

Levinas, the 'without relation' of the absolute, does not place the other in an isolated realm; the bonds of the relation are not cut, yet "these bonds do not unite the same and the other into a whole."[23] In this sense, the ab-soluteness has the role of overcoming relatedness and not that of making the other some kind of separate untouchable entity. Instead, the 'absolute' goes against a thematized relation and thematization through the relation itself. The absolute other is not the other withdrawn from the world, but the other "withdrawn from the categories,"[24] that is to say, its absoluteness means resistance to determination. Here as well, as we have already observed, indeterminacy does not signify a lack (that can be fulfilled through anticipation as object of need), but rather an absence that cannot be anticipated: it remains in indeterminacy (it is not needed, but desired).[25] Thus, absolute alterity neither become a totality in itself, nor does it form a totality through a union with the self—or, in the language more typical to Levinas's later works—it is not subsumed by the all-embracing gaze of thematization.

Now, we have shown in brief the way Levinas discusses subjectivity in *Totality and Infinity*: on the one hand, the self is separated, i.e. the self is not incorporated into a totality of genus, and on the other hand, through absolute alterity, it does not become the totality of an enclosed interiority. However, there is a problem with the two moments of subjectivity from *Totality and Infinity*: it seems as if, at first there is no relation to the other (separateness comes from interiority itself, without having anything to do with absolute alterity), and *then* the separated self is interrupted by exteriority through its relation to the absolute alterity. Almost as if an enclosed self in its own autonomy and interiority suddenly opens up to the other. The descriptions regarding the self in relation to the world, and the way the book itself is structured, might suggest that *Totality and Infinity* recounts the story of the origin of the self and its relation to the other. Nevertheless, this is not the case. At this point, it is very important to consider some of Levinas's remarks that, we argue, bring the two sequences of the break with totality into the same move. Although the self seems to be closed up in itself, Levinas's text suggests that its closedness must not hinder the escape from interiority so that it permits the relation to the other.

---

[23] TI 48.
[24] Ibid., 71.
[25] In this sense, the difference between lack and absence corresponds to the difference between need and desire.

Interiority hides in itself an opening towards the other, making it at the same time open and closed:

> In the separated being the door to the outside must be hence at the same time open and closed.[26]

Closed interiority but still open towards exteriority—in this consists the paradox of the self in its ab-solute relation to the other. Levinas calls this openness in closedness "the idea of the infinite in the finite."[27] Here the "finite" designates the separateness of the self, the "infinite" the alterity that makes the other ungraspable, while the "in" signifies, as Levinas explains later on in 1975, the very questioning of the self as me, the trembling, the "disquietude (*l'inquiétude*) of time," in other words, diachrony:

> What does this *in* (*dans*) signify? It signifies the putting in question of me (*moi*) by the other (*l'autre*) that takes the form of an appeal to my responsibility, that

---

[26] TI 148.

[27] Inspired by Descartes's 3rd meditation, the importance of this idea never fades from Levinas's writings. In *Totality and Infinity* he introduces this thought already in the preface (see TI 26), and later on explains it in relation to Descartes's philosophy: "This relation of the same with the other, where the transcendence of the relation does not cut the bonds a relation implies, yet where these bonds do not unite the same and the other into a Whole, is in fact fixed in the situation described by Descartes in which the 'I think' maintains with the Infinite it can nowise contain and from which it is separated a relation called 'idea of infinity.'" TI 48–9. One should be careful not to consider the Infinite as *something* outside the realm of finitude. The overflow of the Infinite (that the "I think" "can nowise contain and form") shows that the Infinite is not *something* but the indeterminable otherness that always remains other, irreducible to knowledge. It is not an alternative for the realm of immanence, but the very openness of that same realm. The idea of the Infinite in the finite has a similar signification to the expression "the thought that thinks beyond what it thinks" (See for example "Philosophy and the Idea of the Infinite" [1957], in CPP 54.). The content (if one might dare to use this word) of this thought can never be fully thought of, it remains in indeterminacy. However, Levinas does not follow Descartes until the end (that is to say, the idea of Infinite put into us by God). Instead of "Idea" as principle, in his version of the expression "the idea of the Infinite in me" is thought in terms of desire: "In Descartes the idea of the Infinite remains a theoretical idea, a contemplation, a knowledge. For my part, I think that the relation to the Infinite is not a knowledge, but a Desire. I have tried to describe the difference by desire and need by the fact that Desire cannot be satisfied," EI 92. In this way, the idea of the Infinite does not lead to an Infinite that the idea would point to: "Infinity is then not the correlate to the idea of infinity," "The Trace of the Other" (1963), 354.

confers on me an identity. [...] A questioning in which the conscious subject is liberated from himself, in which it is split apart (*scinde*) but by excess, by transcendence: there we find the disquietude of time as awakening.[28]

Thus, in *Totality and Infinity*, through the open-closed self, we are presented with a different scenario than that of a temporal or logical order that begins with the closed self which only afterwards enters in relation to the other. If we lay emphasis on the open-closedness of the self, it becomes clear that Levinas tries to break the order that a descriptive account of events would imply and makes us think outside order as such. It is important to notice this move in *Totality and Infinity* for it indicates an earlier account of the disrupted temporality discussed in the previous chapter. This brings *Totality and Infinity* close to *Otherwise than Being*, a closeness which it is necessary to take note of if we want to discuss radical multiplicity in the context of Levinas's later work, as we intend to do shortly. For now, let us turn our attention toward the role that radical multiplicity plays in the context of *Totality and Infinity*.

3.1.2. Radical multiplicity

Due to some inconsistencies throughout Levinas's writings regarding the meaning of "multiplicity,"[29] it must be specified from the start that what we will be considering here is not the multiplicity of the third party, one which introduces the necessity of comparison and is at the same time a thematized relation. This kind of multiplicity will be explored in the next chapter. The radicalized multiplicity that we are problematizing in this chapter is that which is brought about by a relation without relation (i.e. an unthematized relation) to the other.

---

[28] GDT 110, *Dieu, la mort et le temps* (Paris: Grasset, 1993), 126. Or: "The *in* of infinity is not some sort of "non-," but its negation is the subjectivity of the subject, its subjectivity behind, or prior to, intentionality" GDT 219.

[29] Even though in *Totality and Infinity* Levinas clearly brings forth the term in its radicalized meaning, in other contexts, either multiplicity is not of special interest for Levinas, or else it has a very different meaning. In *Otherwise than Being*, for example, multiplicity is not at all radical, but rather, on the few occasions where it is mentioned, it indicates the plurality of equals—a clear reference to the order of justice. However, later on we will see that in the context of substitution Levinas makes an exception in this sense.

In the previous chapter we pointed already to a connection between Levinas's and Bergson's philosophy. We showed how Levinas's conception of temporality stays close to Bergson's thoughts on duration, although it does not coincide with them. Now we are about to see that the way in which *radical multiplicity* is described also bears a remarkable similarity to Bergson's notion of *qualitative multiplicity*, though also without coinciding with it. To begin with, Bergson distinguishes two kinds of multiplicity: qualitative and quantitative, linking quantitative multiplicity to space and qualitative multiplicity to duration. Space offers a homogeneous medium, where the elements are juxtaposed and countable. The operation of counting presupposes two important conditions: that the counted elements are of the same kind, and that they are given simultaneously. Even if the elements would be given in different moments of time, in order to count them one must have a perspectival view and consider them simultaneously, as if they were juxtaposed. Thus, homogeneity, juxtaposition, and simultaneity are characteristic to quantitative multiplicity. Qualitative multiplicity, on the other hand, is heterogeneous; its elements resist the abstraction into similar units that would permit counting and juxtaposition.[30] Homogeneous quantitative multiplicity and heterogeneous qualitative multiplicity are what elicit Bergson's distinction between difference in degree and difference in kind. Difference in degree, characteristic of quantitative multiplicity, is a measurable, quantitative difference between terms of the same kind. Qualitative multiplicity carries a difference in kind, which makes comparison impossible.[31] We can say that quantitative multiplicity is based on similarity, while qualitative multiplicity is based on difference. Just as Bergson's qualitative multiplicity, for Levinas, radical multiplicity entails the impossibility of a comparison, that is to say, radical multiplicity is not a result of a countable amount of multiple entities. Levinas clearly differentiates radical multiplicity from homogeneous numerical multiplicity:

---

[30] See especially Henri Bergson, *Time and Free Will* (1889), trans. F. L. Pogson (London: George Allen and Unwin 1910), 121–3.

[31] In *Matter and Memory,* Bergson shows how confusion between difference in kind and difference in degree generates false problems. Perhaps the most famous example, which appears also in *Time and Free Will,* is Zeno's paradox. This confusion is at the root of thinking time as a homogeneous medium, instead of heterogeneous duration. See Henri Bergson, *Matter and Memory* (1896), trans. Nancy Margaret Paul and W. Scott Palmer (London: George Allen and Unwin, 1911), Chapter IV.

> The dimension of height from which the Metaphysical comes to the Metaphysician indicates a sort of non-homogeneity of space, such that a radical multiplicity, distinct from numerical multiplicity, can here be produced.[32]

Levinas's refusal to inscribe the relation to the other in a numerical multiplicity is stated in *Totality and Infinity* before even mentioning 'radical multiplicity':

> The relation between the Other and me, which dawns forth in this expression, issues neither in number nor in concept.[33]

In a way, the relatively early emphasis on differentiating the relation to the other from numerical multiplicity should not surprise us. To consider the other as a mere number is certainly incompatible with the relation without relatedness to the ab-solute other that Levinas tries to bring forth in *Totality and Infinity*. However, this idea has a much deeper meaning than a simple refusal to consider the other as an element of a calculus: it also implies the very breaking of the singular/plural dichotomy itself. Here is where Levinas surpasses Bergson's qualitative multiplicity, and this is the point that we would like to highlight in the following.

Even though Bergson refuses a synthesis by juxtaposition, the qualitative multiplicity characteristic of duration still permits a kind of osmosis, a fusion of singularities one into the other.[34] For Levinas, any kind of fusion would erase the very alterity of the other, by forming a totality.[35] Thus, Bergson's notion of multiplicity, just as in the case of duration, is not satisfactory for Levinas.[36] As we have seen in the previous chapter, for

---

[32] TI 220.

[33] Ibid., 194.

[34] Similarly with the colours of a spectrum (one of Bergson's favourite examples). See "Introduction to Metaphysics" (1903), in *The Creative Mind*, trans. Mabelle L. Andison, (New York: Philosophical Library, 1946), 192.

[35] "I have precisely wanted to contest the idea that the relationship with the other is fusion." TO 90.

[36] Leonard Lawlor, while commenting on the differences between Levinas and Bergson, contrasts the Bergsonian movement of alteration, where in "the same [is] becoming-other" (Leonard Lawlor, *Challenge of Bergsonism* [London: Continuum International Publishing, 2003], 82), with Levinas's notion of alterity: "It seems to me that if one prioritizes language over intuition, then one has a philosophy of the other as you find in Levinas and now Derrida; but if one prioritizes intuition over language, then one ends up with a philosophy of alteration (not alterity) as I believe it is conceived by Bergson

Levinas, diachrony disrupts synthetical time; it does not become another time, but it marks the temporalization of time. One could say that, through diachrony, Levinas is radicalizing the Bergsonian duration, and with it qualitative multiplicity. The radicality implied here has a double meaning: as the 'root' of multiplicity in general, but also as the 'limit case' of multiplicity. Radical multiplicity (through the open-closedness of the self) makes possible any kind of multiplicity.[37] In this sense, radical multiplicity is the 'radix' (root) in which multiplicity itself is rooted. At the same time, radical multiplicity is radical also as an extreme, excess of multiplicity. There is an excess, on overflow of indeterminacy (an indeterminacy characteristic both of the self and of the other) due to the openness towards exteriority that is embedded in the self. This, instead of a lack of meaning, brings rather its excess. In the next section, when we discuss how the notion of radical multiplicity is reflected in Levinas's later work, we will be able to pinpoint more clearly the deeper meaning of this excess, in the form of the-other-in-me. For now, we need to underscore that the radicalization of

---

and now Deleuze.," Ibid., 62. Lawlor argues that the Bergsonian intuition in not "embedded in theoretism": it is not just another form of representation as Levinas would consider it, but is pure movement, variation and alteration. One can recognize in Lawlor's argument not only a re-consideration of the meaning of intuition in Bergson's philosophy and the critique directed at Levinas for being unjust to Bergson in this sense, but also a certain reproach concerning the inert alterity that, according to him, Levinas's thinking implies. On the one hand, to argue for the disparity between a movement of alteration and absolute alterity is well justified, since the self is not an active participant in bringing forth its own uniqueness; it needs the exteriority of the other to call it into selfhood—as we have seen, this is one of Levinas's critiques of Bergson. Still, should we conclude that for Levinas there is only a static notion of alterity? Is there no movement, no alteration involved? If we look closely at how Levinas thinks subjectivity, we can argue that there is indeed movement and with it a certain alteration, only that it is conceived in different terms than those of a self-initiated alteration. The outdoing of unity through the movement of recurrence of ipseity "without any rest in itself, 'more and more one,' to the point of breakup, fission, openness," (OB 107) already suggests a certain movement of alteration that transpires without becoming another. The de-position or exile of the self through the other could likewise be interpreted as the movement of alteration: "I is an other," yet not in the Rimbaudian sense. (Ibid., 118) Levinas himself notes that the election through which the *me* emerges is "an alteration without alienation." (Ibid., 141) In this sense, we could even say that substitution as the-other-in-me is this movement of alteration.

[37] Later on in this thesis (see especially Chapter 11) we will discuss in more details the meaning of such possibility in the context of the interplay between the Saying and the Said or the un-common and the common.

multiplicity in *Totality and Infinity* becomes more than a question of difference in kind characteristic to the Bergsonian qualitative multiplicity. In Levinas's case, neither the self, nor the other belongs to a genus, to a certain 'kind,' due to the resistance to determination of both the self and the other. In this sense, Levinas's radical multiplicity, instead of indicating a difference in kind, breaks up the dialectic of differentiation itself, yet without turning it in indifference.[38] The open-closed self remains separated without relativeness, yet in multiplicity with the other.[39] Just as the separated self is not defined through its opposition to the other, singularity is not thought in a dialectical couple with multiplicity.[40] In this way, the radicalization of multiplicity performed by Levinas in *Totality and Infinity* inscribes itself in the line of over-determined concepts such as the previously discussed bad consciousness and bad time. In their over-determination there is an overflow, an excess of meaning that cannot be shown directly, but can only be expressed through overemphasis and the embracing of paradoxes. In a similar way, by radicalizing the notion of multiplicity Levinas pushes it outside its reference to the one (as in one/multiple) or to singularity (as in singularity/multiplicity). Radical multiplicity is neither a yet-unrealised unity to come, nor an already dissembled one. Hence we find here, once again, the refusal of dichotomies, a gesture repeated by Levinas throughout his work. Levinas's radical multiplicity implies heterogeneity without allowing comparison,[41] but it also breaks the singular/plural distinction itself. One should not underestimate Levinas's efforts to refuse any numerical calculus when it comes to radical multiplicity, since he aims much further with these remarks than just the

---

[38] We are hinting here at Levinas's notion of non-indifference which we will discuss later on, in the context of sociality in *Totality and Infinity*. (See Chapter 6).

[39] One can observe that we refer here to the self being separated, and not the other as also separated. This is due to our care not to include any kind of reciprocity, and to remain on the hither side of the relation, the inside-out dimension of subjectivity.

[40] "Separation not being reducible to a simple counterpart of relation, the relationship with the other does not have the same status as the relations given to objectifying thought, where the distinction of terms also reflects their union. The relationship between me and the other does not have the structure formal logic finds in all relations. The terms remain absolute despite the relation in which they find themselves. The relation with the other is the only relation where such an overturning of formal logic can occur. […] The distance and interiority remain intact in the resumption of the relationship." TI 181.

[41] The difference between me and the other is not a result of comparison. "The alterity of the other is in him and is not relative to me," says Levinas (TI 221).

acknowledgment that the other should not be considered a mere number. Numerical multiplicity implies a unifying view from outside the relation, and it relies on the singular/plural dichotomy. With radical multiplicity and its disruption of the singular/plural dichotomy comes the impossibility of a view from the outside upon the relation itself; subsuming the self and the other under a third, uniting part, from which multiplicity could be looked upon, would end up in juxtaposition and homogeneity:

> This inequality [between me and the other] does not appear to the third party who would count us. It precisely signifies the absence of a third party capable of taking in me and the other, such that the primordial multiplicity is observed within the very face to face that constitutes it. It is produced in multiple singularities and not in a being exterior to this number who would count the multiples. The inequality *is* in this impossibility of the exterior point of view, which alone could abolish it.[42]

The refusal of an outside view means that radical multiplicity can be approached only from within the relation. This is an important remark and Levinas returns to it on several occasions.[43] It is not only a precautionary move, in order to prevent radical multiplicity for becoming a formalized relation, but points also towards the hither side, which seems to be involved not only in Levinas's way of thinking subjectivity, time and consciousness, but also multiplicity. In order to avoid forming a totality and cancelling both the separateness of the self and the unthematized relation to the other, multiplicity must be considered from this side of the relation, proceeding "from me to the other."[44] In light of this, radical multiplicity reflects the hither side, inside-out dimension of the relation to the other. Now, the importance of the hither side is certainly more fully developed in Levinas's

---

[42] TI 251, Levinas's emphasis.
[43] Here is yet another example: "Then multiplicity can be produced only if the individuals retain their secrecy, if the relation that unites them into a multiplicity is not visible from the outside, but proceeds from one to the other. If it were entirely visible from the outside, if the exterior point of view would open upon its ultimate reality, the multiplicity would form a totality in which the individuals would participate; the bond between persons would not have preserved the multiplicity from the addition. In order that multiplicity be maintained, the relation proceeding from me to the other—the attitude of one person with regard to another—must be stronger than the formal signification of conjunction, to which every relation risks being degraded. This greater force is concretely affirmed in the fact that the relation proceeding from me to the other cannot be included within a network of relations visible to a third party." Ibid., 120–121.
[44] TI 121.

later work. And yet, in these later works, radical multiplicity seems to disappear. The question we would like to ask is, thus: does the meaning of radical multiplicity, i.e. heterogeneity beyond the singular/plural distinction, remain important to Levinas by the time his thoughts on subjectivity have become more developed? If so, this will have significant repercussions regarding the relation between the two works, and, more importantly, would bring the relation to the other, and with it sociality, beyond the singular/plural distinction. Hence, as the next step, we return our focus to *Otherwise than Being*.

3.2. Radical multiplicity in "*Otherwise than Being*"

One of the most remarkable turning points that *Otherwise than Being* brings in Levinas's philosophy is the notion of substitution, which changes greatly the scenery set up in *Totality and Infinity*. In *Otherwise than Being* we find Levinas focusing on the self as *me*, de-posed from its foundation, instead of on the separated enjoying self of *Totality and Infinity*. The uniqueness of the self, outside any genus, is now brought forth through substitution, while its non-relativeness, previously emphasized through separateness, is given in *Otherwise than Being* by the paradoxical other-in-me. The pure interiority, "withdrawal into oneself"[45] characteristic to the enjoying self from *Totality and Infinity*, becomes in *Otherwise than Being* the movement of recurrence, where the overdrive of the "more and more one"[46] ruptures the very ground of the self. Thus, the self is not "at home with itself" anymore, as it is in *Totality and Infinity*;[47] and this is precisely the meaning of de-position in *Otherwise than Being*. These are but a few examples of the changes that Levinas's philosophy undergoes between his two major works. The author himself acknowledges that there are differences in the way his work from 1961 and the one from 1974 are displayed:

---

[45] Ibid., 118.
[46] OB 107.
[47] TI 147.

> In *Totality and Infinity*, the idea of enjoyment and of autonomy played a role of the first importance. In *Autrement qu'être*, however, the idea of election has central place.[48]

By the time of Levinas's second major work, as we have pointed out, the expression "radical multiplicity" disappears, and instead expressions such as "substitution," "the-other-in-me," "proximity" or "one-for-the-other" are prioritized. We can observe, here, a new terminology emerging, and alongside "substitution," other ethically charged words begin to enter Levinas's vocabulary. In a later interview, from 1986, Levinas discusses this change of terminology:

> *Totality and Infinity* was my first book. I find it very difficult to tell you, in a few words, in what way it is different from what I've said afterwards. There is the ontological terminology: I spoke of being. I have since tried to get away from that language. When I speak of being in *Totality and Infinity*, what remains valuable is that, above all, it indicates that the analyses should not be taken as psychological. What is described in these human states is not simply empirical, but it is an essential structure. And in the word "essential" there is the word "esse," being. It is as if it were an ontological structure.[49]

Despite these differences, in what follows, we argue that, although the term is not explicitly used, the meaning of radical multiplicity from *Totality and Infinity* is carried over into Levinas's later works.

---

[48] "What one asks of oneself, one asks of a saint", 23. Although not as strongly present as in *Totality and Infinity*, enjoyment does not disappear completely from *Otherwise than Being*. (On enjoyment in *Otherwise than Being* see especially OB 72-4) Yet, now it is implied through the notion of vulnerability. Vulnerability, Levinas tells us, expresses sensibility as "an exposure to wounding in enjoyment" (OB 64); thus, enjoyment, now part of vulnerability, remains necessary in order to prevent the co-determination of the self and the other (i.e. to prevent their relative determination).

[49] "The Paradox of Morality: An Interview with Emmanuel Levinas," in *The Provocation of Levinas*, 170-1. The citation continues by emphasizing the different understandings of "justice" in the two works, in *Totality and Infinity* as a synonym to ethics, while in *Otherwise than Being* with a meaning linked to calculation. We will return to this in the next chapter.

3.2.1. The continuity in thinking subjectivity

Having discussed, in our first chapter the way Levinas presents subjectivity in *Otherwise than Being*, and now that we have seen how he frames the question in his earlier work, *Totality and Infinity*, it becomes quite apparent that the mode of problematization and the terminology differs in the two works. This makes us wonder whether these disparities are signs of a radical turn in Levinas's thought, and whether he re-thinks subjectivity in his later writings in a way incompatible with his earlier thoughts. At first glance it appears that Levinas makes a shift from an approach of subjectivity in terms of originarity (in *Totality and Infinity*) to one in terms of an-archy (in *Otherwise than Being*). "Subjectivity *originates* in the independence and sovereignty of enjoyment," says Levinas in *Totality and Infinity*.[50] Indeed, in *Totality and Infinity* the self is "at home" as the pure enjoying self in interiority, and 'home' means grounding, originarity, while in *Otherwise than Being*, as we have seen in the previous chapters, subjectivity interrupts originarity itself, it is an-archical; the self is in exile.

However, despite the apparent disparity between the two works, Levinas's understanding of subjectivity might not after all turn out to differ as much as all that. In *Totality and Infinity*, as shown earlier, the self in pure enjoyment (i.e. at home with itself) is interrupted in its enjoyment, through exteriority (its ground is shattered). This interruption (or break with totality) through exteriority makes the self open-closed. It seems to us that this open-closedness of subjectivity from *Totality and Infinity* is the very expression of an-archy, the break with originarity, since it disrupts the self from enclosing upon itself, from grounding itself in itself. In this way, the an-archy of subjectivity from *Otherwise than Being* already shows itself in *Totality and Infinity*. In a sense, the open-closedness from *Totality and Infinity* seems to correspond to the other-in-me from *Otherwise than Being*, as it expresses the instability of the self in itself; its very essence is its de-essentialization, and its very closedness (interiority) is its openness. Moreover, the importance of the hither side, or of what we have called the inside-out dimension of subjectivity, something that Levinas develops in his later work, transpires rather clearly in *Totality and Infinity*. We have argued that it is precisely the heterogeneity of radical multiplicity that implies an approach from the hither side of the relation. An outside view upon the

---

[50] TI 114 (emphasis added).

relation would presuppose a juxtaposition of the self and the other, in order to bring forth the relation itself. This juxtaposition would replace heterogeneity, characteristic to radical multiplicity, with homogeneity (homogeneity, necessary to juxtapose). In this sense, the hither side, the inside-out dimension of the relation to the other, which in *Otherwise than Being* is opened up by substitution, is in *Totality and Infinity* brought forth through the meaning of radical multiplicity. The self, instead of an enclosed singularity, becomes the paradoxical open-closedness.

The continuities between *Totality and Infinity* and *Otherwise than Being* regarding the importance of the hither side (the inside out dimension of the relation to the other) and resistance to determination indicates that, even if there is a noticeable difference in terminology, the meaning of radical multiplicity is still alive in Levinas's later work. In *Otherwise than Being*, the meaning of radical multiplicity is reflected through the resistance to determination of the self, hindering it from forming a totality in itself. "The Mind is a multiplicity of individuals,"[51] says Levinas when he speaks about substitution (i.e. the other-in-me). Here, we are not trying to rehabilitate the term 'multiplicity' for its own sake.[52] Rather, we find the radicalization of multiplicity a helpful means of pointing to the disruption of the singular/plural dichotomy.

3.2.2. For the other(s)

In the first part of this chapter we showed that radical multiplicity in *Totality and Infinity* displaces the notion of multiplicity from the singularity/multiplicity duality; radical multiplicity has the role of assuring resistance to the determination both of the self and of the other in their relation without relation, and as such, it goes beyond the singular/plural dichotomy. Relying on the continuity of thought throughout Levinas's work that we have established, we will, in the following, bring forth the signi-

---

[51] OB 186. This is however, perhaps the only occasion in *Otherwise than Being* when the actual expression "multiplicity" is used in its radicalized meaning.
[52] If we look at the word 'multiplicity,' we can certainly see that it has shortcomings that might have led Levinas to refrain from using it in his later writings. It is indeed rather hard to displace completely the word 'multiplicity' from its mathematical or logical references, and consider it outside its relation to singularities (i.e. as multiplicity formed by units). Although Levinas does not provide us with any specific reason for abandoning this particular expression, we can safely assume that the leaving aside of the term is a result of his change to a more ethical vocabulary.

ficance of the disrupting of the singular/plural dichotomy in the context of Levinas's later work.

As we recall, in *Otherwise than Being* the unthematized relation to the other is presented in its connection with subjectivity, in the form of substitution, the-other-in-me—conception of subjectivity which is maintained in Levinas's later work. Now, this unthematized relation is of interest to us, as it implicates both the self and the other, and in this sense, is already multiplicity; however, it does not express a multiplicity of determined singularities, since neither the self nor the other are defined (me and the other remain undetermined)—it is *radical* multiplicity. Thought in terms of radical multiplicity, the relation to the other that is revealed through substitution carries a meaning beyond the singular/plural distinction; it can be translated as an unthematized relation not just to the other (singular), but to the other(s): a relation, in other words, where the distinction between singular and plural is overcome.

It is no mere coincidence that, in his later work, Levinas chose the word 'proximity' in order to describe the unthematized relation to the other approached from the hither side. The choice of the word 'proximity' proves to be quite fortuitous, since even in its everyday sense it has the advantage of not specifying anything regarding the number of those involved. Proximity does not mean simply being close to another, or to find oneself among others; it is no mere spatial contiguity. Instead, it is described by Levinas as the "closer and closer,"[53] yet never coinciding. The closeness of proximity is never close enough to subsume the other in the self or vice-versa. In this sense, it expresses multiplicity outside the singularity/multiplicity alternatives. Through Levinas's notion of proximity, we again find an expression of radical multiplicity that disrupts thinking in terms of singular and plural, where the relation to the other has a deeper meaning than a relation between two:

> It is then not enough to speak of proximity as a relationship between two terms, and as a relationship assured of the simultaneity of these terms. It is necessary to emphasize the breakup of this synchrony, of this whole, by the difference between the same and the other in the non-indifference of the obsession exercised by the other over the same.[54]

---

[53] OB 82.
[54] Ibid., 85.

Proximity exceeds the limits of a one-to-one relation, yet without becoming the plurality of the many (thought in relation to the singular).[55] The relation to the other, when revealed as *radical* multiplicity, gives a deeper meaning to multiplicity in the context of the unthematized relation to the other. It is neither the relation to a singular other (creating a dyad), nor a relation to a plurality of others (introduced by Levinas's notion of the third).[56]

Going beyond a numerical barrier, and breaking with the singular/plural counterparts seem to lie behind Levinas's occasional references to "responsibility for others" (note the plural), in the context of the de-posed self. As an example we can evoke a few lines from his discussion on subjectivity as "hostage" from *Otherwise than Being*:

> The word *I* means *here I am*, answering for everything and for everyone. Responsibility for the others (pour les autres) has not been a return to oneself, but an exasperated contracting, breaking up the limits of identity.[57]

Key here is to recognize that Levinas is still referring to the inside-out dimension of *my* relation to the other. The *me* of the *here I am* (*me voici*) is, from the start, through the other(s), for the other(s); that is to say, the election of the self by the other does not refer to the election by one singular other or by many others: the other is not considered in terms of singular or plural. This recognition leads us to the important conclusion that, in their unthematized relation, *the self (as me) and the other do not form a couple;* the primordial response to the other, through which the self emerges, escapes a dual relation. Hence, our insistence on the notion of radical multiplicity throughout this chapter is due to the importance of its role regarding the unthematized relation to the other: by thinking it as a radicalized form of multiplicity, the unthematized relation to the other becomes no longer reducible to the relation to one singular other (a one-to-one type dualistic relation), nor to the relation to many others. Approached from the hither side, responsiveness/responsibility permits neither comparison nor calculation, nor even a counting to two (you and me).

However, when the question of justice is raised, the distinction between singular and plural is made. Multiplicity changes its meaning, and becomes

---

[55] We will return to discussing the meaning of proximity in more details in the context of sociality (Part II).
[56] For a discussion on the meaning of the third see Chapter 4.
[57] OB 114, AE 180–1. Emphasis by Levinas.

a multiplicity of persons and the society of many; the incomparable subject "revert[s] into a member of society."[58] It is a change that marks the distinction between the unthematized relation to other(s) and the thematized relation to a plurality of others (a multiplicity of persons), one which cannot be simply translated into the distinction between the other (singular) and the others (plural). Instead, it implies a change in the mode of thinking: from the relation to other(s), beyond the singular/plural distinction, to a relation to the other or others in which singularity and plurality are reintroduced. This approach opens up an outside dimension of the relation to the other. This outside dimension, as well as its relation to the inside-out dimension, will be the topic of the next chapter.

---

[58] OB 158.

CHAPTER 4

The Question of Justice

In our quest to develop a Levinasian notion of sociality, we have been examining the different meanings that the relation to the other receives in Levinas's work, starting with the unthematized relation at the core of subjectivity. This is presented in *Otherwise than Being* in the form of substitution, the paradoxical other-in-me, which reflects what we have called the *inside-out dimension* of the relation to the other. In the previous chapter we explored the notion of *radical multiplicity* from *Totality and Infinity*, and have shown that this radicalized meaning of multiplicity remains important for Levinas's later work, as it breaks up thinking in terms of singular/plural. The point is precisely that radical multiplicity remains connected with the unthematized relation to the other that we have found emphasized throughout Levinas's work. Hence, the inside-out dimension characteristic of the unthematized relation does not depend on whether it is a relation with the other (singular) or the others (plural). The importance of this consideration will show itself more clearly in the present chapter when we discuss another dimension of the relation to the other, which we call *the outside dimension*, where the relation itself comes into focus and the difference between singular/plural, other/others is re-established. In what follows we argue that the two dimensions of the relation to the other, inside-out and outside, are intertwined in an essential ambiguity. Levinas's famous words from *Totality and Infinity*, "The third party looks at me in the eyes of the Other,"[1] is often seen as a direct reference to this intertwinement. Yet, as radical multiplicity is different from the plurality of others (i.e. a numerical multiplicity), we will argue in the final section of the chapter that the difference between the two dimensions is not translatable to the difference between the relation to the other (singular) and the

---

[1] TI 213.

relation to others (plural). Instead, they represent two modes of thinking (hence the word 'dimension'): one mode that breaks up the singular/plural differentiation, and another that makes us think in terms of singular and plural, other and others. This has important repercussions when it comes to addressing the problem of justice and politics in Levinas's work: it means that the necessity of justice is not simply the result of the constraint given by the fact of sharing the world with many people and thus encountering many others at once, as some of Levinas's comments might suggest. To put it roughly: we argue instead that the problem with which we are faced in the intersection between ethics and justice is not that of the question: 'for *how many* am I responsible?' but rather concerns numericality itself, or, more precisely, the very thinking in terms of singular/plural alternatives.

4.1. An outside dimension

Up until now, we have been discussing what we call the *inside-out dimension* of my relation to the other, where the relation is approached from the hither side, and is characterized by non-relatedness, i.e. the relation as such remains unthematized. However, Levinas's writings disclose another way of approaching the relation to the other, one that places the focus on the relation as such and thus thematizes it. Now we need to turn our attention to this other dimension, where the self has a perspective on the relation itself, as if viewed from the outside. From now on we will call this *the outside dimension* of the relation to the other.

In order to shed light on what this outside dimension means, let us start with the way in which Levinas differentiates between two orders, one that refers to *my* relation to the other revealed through the de-posed subject, and another that implies the necessity of justice:

> That is the principal idea: I pass from the order of responsibility, from mercy, where even that which should not concern me concerns me, to justice, which limits that initial precedence of the other from which we started.[2]

We will return shortly to the problematic character of the 'limitation' that justice seemingly imposes on *my* responsibility, but first we need to clarify

---

[2] "The Proximity of the Other" (1986), in IIRB 214.

the meaning behind the two 'orders' that Levinas evokes.[3] Clearly, the order of responsibility "where even that which should not concern me concerns me" reflects what was previously presented as the unthematized relation, always approached from the hither side, opening up an inside-out dimension of the relation to the other. That is to say, everything concerns *me* since there is no position from which there can be an outlook upon the other's concern (the self as me is de-posed). The order of justice, on the other hand, represents a different dimension of the relation to the other. It problematizes the relation from the *outside* (the third person's perspective), and places the focus on the relation itself, thus thematizing it. We now have two dimensions, an inside-out and an outside dimension, corresponding to two ways of approaching the relation to the other. While the inside-out dimension is opened up by the de-posed self, the outside dimension is reflected in the notion of justice.

There is no explicit definition of justice to be found in Levinas's writings. Moreover, we can find a shift in its meaning throughout his work.[4] Levinas himself, in an interview from 1986, notes the change in his use of this term:

---

[3] When we read this or similar quotations, we need to be careful how we interpret the word "order," as it carries a double meaning. On the one hand, in relation to justice, "order" takes on a meaning familiar to us, in the form of the previously discussed understanding of order to which even disorder belongs (see Chapter 2). Later on we will see that justice, through the necessity of comparing, is thought in terms of synthesis and thematization, and as such, a synthetical time structure and a thematizing intentional consciousness are required. This means that, when it comes to justice, we will no longer think in terms of an-archy but in terms of arche. Thus, in this case, "order" will come to mean originarity and principle. On the other hand, as responsibility that concerns *me*, "order" denotes Levinas's reference to ordering, expressed in *Otherwise than Being* as "the order ordering me towards the other." (OB 162.) This ordering does not designate any law or abstract set of rules (such as a moral code): it is not, here, a matter of principle, but rather it concerns the accusative that marks the de-posed subjectivity. In the case of the responsibility that "concerns *me*," "order" denotes paradoxically, the an-archy characteristic of the hither side of the relation to the other; an-archy as without origin and principle, without initiation from the self itself, and ordering as responsiveness outside intentional consciousness and will.

[4] Others had also pointed out the instability of the notion of justice in Levinas's work. For example, Simon Critchley emphasizes the shift in Levinas's thinking of justice: if in *Totality and Inifnity*—Critchley explains—justice has an ethical meaning (as Levinas points out in the preface to the German translation [See TeI, pt. II]), in *Otherwise than Being*, justice is clearly differentiated from the ethical and is connected, rather, with politics. In this sense see Critchley, *The Ethics of Deconstruction*, 274 and *Ethics, Politics, Subjectivity*, 99–100.

> In *Totality and Infinity* I used the word 'justice' for ethics, for the relationship between two people. I spoke of 'justice,' although now 'justice' is for me something which is a calculation, which is knowledge, and which supposes politics; it is inseparable from the political.[5]

For our purpose, we have chosen to adopt the conception of justice typical of Levinas's later work, partly because we have so far been discussing the notion of subjectivity in relation to its meaning in that later work, but also because Levinas seemed, there, to have settled on the meaning of justice that involves equality, calculation and knowledge. When asked, during a conversation at the University of Leyden, just one year after the publication of *Otherwise than Being*, about the different meaning of justice throughout his work, Levinas appears quite confident in his choice:

> The word 'justice' is in effect much more in its place, there, where equity is necessary and not my 'subordination' to the other. If equity is necessary, we must have comparison and equality: equality between those who cannot be compared.[6]

In order to think in terms of justice a change of scenery is needed from the hither side of the relation to an outside perspective, from a de-posed subjectivity to a positioning of the self. This position is precisely the position from which the self has the perspective upon the relation itself, and upon its own position in this relation—it makes synthesis and thematization possible. The self, now posited, is the *I* (the Ego). The difference between the positioned *I* and the de-posed *me* is well illustrated by Levinas's discussion of the biblical story, from Genesis, of the brothers Cain and Abel. Levinas's remark concerns the passage in which God asked Cain about his brother's, Abel's whereabouts and Cain, who has killed his brother, responds: "Am I my brother's keeper?"[7] Levinas sees in Cain's response not a revolt against God, but a positioning of the self towards itself and towards the other. The self is determined as *I*:

---

[5] "The Paradox of Morality: An Interview with Emmanuel Levinas" (1986), in *The Provocation of Levinas*, 171. Here, besides the notion of justice, there are revealed two other notions that need clarification: ethics and politics. We will return to these notions in a moment, but for now let us keep our focus on clarifying the meaning of justice.
[6] "Questions and Answers" (1975/1977), in OGCM 82.
[7] See Genesis 4:17.

> We must not take Cain's answer as if he were mocking God or as if he were answering as a little boy: "It isn't me, it's the other one." Cain's answer is sincere. Ethics is the only thing lacking in his answer; there is only ontology: I am I, and he is he. We are separate ontological beings.[8]

Through its positioning, it is not only the self that becomes a determined I, but equally it is the other who also receives determination ("I am I, and he is he"). It is now that the symmetry of the relation shows itself. Judging requires a totalizing view from which to decide, as well as calculation and measuring (i.e. the evaluation of a certain situation or relation), and as such it presupposes a symmetrical relation and a shared equality that makes it possible to compare and compute. In the order of justice, responsiveness/responsibility is not *only* mine; not in the sense of sharing *my* responsibility, but in the sense that the responsiveness/responsibility of the others is also to be considered. When discussing the question of justice it is necessary to consider the relation between others (the neighbor's neighbors) who are now seen as equals, just as I am one among the equals. Justice brings into play symmetry and reciprocity, both of which are possible only through the view upon the relation as such, through thematization. Along with thematization comes the synthetical time structure and contemporaneousness necessary for presentation (bringing forth a theme):

> Justice requires contemporaneousness of representation. It is thus that the neighbor becomes visible, and, looked at, presents himself, and there is also justice for me.[9]

We have seen that, according to Levinas, thinking in terms of presentation and synthetical time also means thinking in terms of showing, of light, thinking in terms of thematizing intentional consciousness, and of knowledge. The order of justice opens up the possibility of judging, of making judgements, assertions, the possibility of knowing and determination. We can see how the elements that Levinas presented at first negatively now fall into their place and receive their positivity through the order of justice. Justice introduces symmetry, reciprocity, calculation, synthetical time and thematizing consciousness, but in a positive way. The I can now make decisions (it is positioned, it has will) and needs to decide:

---

[8] "Philosophy, Justice, and Love" (1982), in EN 110.
[9] OB 159.

> Who, in this plurality, comes first? Here is the hour and birthplace of the question: of a demand for justice! Here is the obligation to compare unique and incomparable others; this is the moment of *knowledge*.[10]

Justice answers the question "Who comes first?" which makes comparison necessary. This question is nothing like the de-posed self as questioning; this time it is a question posed by the self. It concerns the very capacity of the self to engage in an enquiring.[11] We can say that while the self in question marks the de-position of the *me*, the *I* takes up the position of questioning, and through it, the self becomes posited.

The difficulty is, however, to decide whether there are repercussions that the positioning of the *I* has for the de-position of the self. Does the order of justice annul de-posed subjectivity? In the following we shall discuss the ambiguous relation between de-position and position, between inside-out and outside.

4.2. "Inside-out" and "outside" intertwined

4.2.1. Ethics and justice

Since Levinas often discusses the question of justice through its relation to ethics, we need, at this stage of our argument, to introduce into our terminology the Levinasian notion of 'ethics' or the 'ethical.'[12] So far, we have preferred to use a different terminology as the terms 'ethical' or 'ethics' can seem problematic for at least two reasons: firstly, due to their association with moral theory, something that Levinas clearly does not have in mind,[13] and secondly, because of the tendency to read Levinas's ethics as a reinforcement of the ethics/ontology opposition, a move that in our view is

---

[10] "Diachrony and Representation" (1985), in TO 106–7.

[11] "The first question in the interhuman is the question of justice. Henceforth it is necessary to know, to become conscious," "Peace and Proximity" (1984), trans. by Simon Critchley, Peter Atterton and Graham Noctor, in BPW 168.

[12] There is no explicit distinction made by Levinas between the ethical and ethics. The way he uses the two words makes us conclude that he does not intend any conceptual differentiation between them, but rather applies the appropriate grammatical form, i.e. ethics as a subject, and ethical (relation) as attribute.

[13] While presenting our general reading of Levinas (see Introduction), we have already shown that for him ethics does not designate a moral way of conduct.

not justified.[14] Despite our reservations regarding the use of the words 'ethical' and 'ethics,' we need to temporarily adopt them in the context of the intertwinement between *my* relation to the other(s) and justice, if we want successfully to follow Levinas's text.

Without entering into a detailed analysis (this not being the purpose of our argument), we need to mention that Levinas denotes the "ethical self" as the "priority of the for-the-other."[15] This denotation, which comes rather late in Levinas's career (in 1987), proves to be more helpful for the purpose of this chapter than the quasi-definition of ethics from *Totality and Infinity*, where ethics is described as the "calling into question of the same by the other."[16] Ethics, as the "priority of the for the other" points towards the an-archical, interruptive character of the de-posed self: not for itself but for the other, that is to say, the very de-position of the self from having its origin in itself. In this sense ethics, or the ethical aspect of the relation to the other, reflects the inside-out dimension, and our question regarding the relation between the two dimensions, inside-out and outside, now becomes a question regarding the relation between ethics and justice.

Readings of Levinas that concern the relation between ethics and justice have been growing in popularity over the past years. One of the most controversial incidents, and one which gave birth to a critical reaction from Levinas's readers, concerns Levinas's comments on a particular political event, the massacre of the Palestinian refugees at Sabra and Shatila from 1982. In a radio interview with Shlomo Malka, shortly after the massacre, Levinas refuses to identify "the Palestinian" with "the other," as the interviewer would like him to do.[17] Unsurprisingly, this became the source of a

---

[14] We will develop this issue in the last part of the thesis.
[15] "Dialogue on Thinking-of-the-Other" (1987), in EN 202.
[16] TI 43.
[17] The following fragment contains some of the remarks considered controversial: "S.M.: Emmanuel Levinas, you are the philosopher of the 'other.' Isn't history, isn't politics the very site of the encounter with the 'other,' and for the Israeli, isn't the 'other' above all the Palestinian? E.L.: My definition of the other is completely different. The other is the neighbour, who is not necessarily kin, but who can be. And in that sense, if you're for the other, you're for the neighbour. But if your neighbour attacks another neighbour or treats him unjustly, what can you do? Then alterity takes on another character, in alterity we can find an enemy, or at least then we are faced with the problem of knowing who is right and who is wrong, who is just and who is unjust. There are people who are wrong.," "Ethics and Politics" (1982), radio interview with Shlomo Malka on Radio Communauté, 28 September 1982, trans. Jonathan Romney, in LR 294.

series of harsh critiques, which reproached Levinas for considering as the other only the neighbor, the close one, instead of the Palestinians, and for evading a straightforward answer regarding the responsibility for the Palestinians in this concrete situation.[18] In our view, these critiques are the result of confusing the two dimensions of the relation to the other, inside-out and outside, reflected by the "order" of ethics and, respectively, the "order" of justice. Nevertheless, our point here is not so much to offer an in-depth reply to such critiques; others have already adequately done that,[19] but rather to underline the importance of differentiating between the two dimensions of the relation to the other, inside-out and outside. In other words, Levinas's refusal to consider the Palestinians as such in terms of alterity, discloses the difference between two ways of approach, and the importance of considering this difference. To Malka's question: "Isn't the 'other' above all the Palestinian?" Levinas responds: "My definition of the other is completely different."[20] In our view, by his response, Levinas is trying to say that the meaning of the relation to the determined other (that is, the Palestinian as a member of an ethnic, national or political group) differs significantly from the hither side of the de-posed self, where the self is indeed infinitely responsible/responsive for the other(s), and where the other(s) is not determined by specific characteristics. When the other or others belong to a group, and is/are determined through their belonging to that group, the relation requires a determining outside perspective—it reflects the outside dimension of the relation to the others.[21] Thus, to say

---

[18] Howard Caygill provides an example of this critique, and is much preoccupied by Levinas's reaction, or rather his lack of a strong reaction to the events from 1982. Howard Caygill, *Levinas and the Political* (New York: Routledge, 2002), 190-4. One can easily find similar critiques throughout the extensive literature preoccupied by the question of politics in Levinas's philosophy: see for instance Martin Jay, "Hostage Philosophy: Levinas's Ethical Thought," *Tikkun* 5, 6 (1990): 85-87, or the more recent work of Judith Butler, *Parting Ways: Jewishness and the Critique of Zionism* (New York: Columbia University Press, 2012), esp. p.23.

[19] For a reply to such critiques combined with an overview of their development see, for instance, Oona Eisenstadt and Claire Elise Katz, "The Faceless Palestinian: A History of an Error," *Telos* 174 (Spring 2016): 9-32.

[20] "Ethics and Politics" (1982), in LR 294.

[21] It is interesting to see that here determination also carries a certain "anonymity" of the other, as it becomes a mere part of a group, an in-dividual. This is the reason why the "face" [visage], which corresponds to the other approached from the hither side of the relation, has to remain undetermined ("not even to notice the color of his eyes," says

that the other is the Palestinians, or even to regard the other as a Palestinian per se, would miss Levinas's point of considering the other's resistance to determination. To put it roughly, the interviewer's question is posed in a wrong way. Levinas's response brings forth the importance of understanding the difference between the two ways of approaching the relation to the other, that is to say, between the two dimensions that we have also been emphasizing.[22] There is no point in us entering more deeply this discussion. What remains important for our argument is already clear: that neglecting the difference between the inside-out and outside dimension of the relation to the other could lead to serious misunderstandings and even misreadings of Levinas's text. In a similar way, if the asymmetrical relation to the other, characteristic of the de-posed self, is interpreted without consideration of the inside-out dimension of responsibility, then one might read some of Levinas's statements as highly controversial; as for example, his claim—inspired by Dostoyevsky's *The Brothers Karamazov*—that "the I always has one responsibility *more* than all the others,"[23] or his insistence that "the persecuted one is liable to answer for the persecutor."[24] When the inside-out dimension of responsibility is not considered, these statements seem to reflect a demand for an impossible or even perverted ethical practice. However, if we look at it from the inside-out, where I cannot consider the other in its responsibility since I am always on the hither of the relation, it becomes clear that, from this hither side, nothing can be claimed about the

---

Levinas in EI 85) yet it does not fall into a generalized anonymity. We will discuss the importance of the face in the next part of our thesis.

[22] Another, similar example occurs when Levinas is asked whether the executioner has a "face"—this being a typical way in which he is confronted, in interviews, about the relation between ethics and justice. Here is an example of the typical answer from Levinas: "the whole problematic of the executioner is opened here; in terms of justice and the defence of the other, my fellow, and not at all in terms of the threat that concerns me. If there were no order of Justice, there would be no limit to my responsibility. There is a certain measure of violence necessary in terms of justice; but if one speaks of justice, it is necessary to allow judges, it is necessary to allow institutions and the state; to live in a world of citizens, and not only in the order of the Face-to-Face.," "Philosophy, Justice, and Love" (1982), remarks recorded by R. Fornet and A. Gómez, in EN 105.

[23] EI 99.

[24] OB 111.

other's responsibility; it remains "his affair,"[25] while the only one who is responsible/responsive is *me*.[26]

Although, as we have seen, it becomes extremely important in certain contexts to differentiate between the two dimensions of the relation to the other, inside-out and outside, Levinas also points to their intertwinement. We are facing a paradox, where separation and interconnection need to be thought together. This paradoxical intertwinement of the two dimensions is often presented by Levinas through the relation between ethics and justice, and described as an "essential ambiguity":

> How, in effect, can one be answerable for all? Who comes first among all? This is the essential ambiguity of the relation between the ethical order of the responsibility for the other and the juridical order, to which the ethical nevertheless appeals.[27]

The two dimensions of the relation to the other, represented here by ethics and justice, are very close, yet they do not coincide. Levinas often uses the notion of *the third* in order to explain the ambiguous intertwinement between ethics and justice. What makes the relation between ethics and justice "extremely narrow," Levinas claims, is the presence of the third

---

[25] EI 98.

[26] In a text written in the same year as the essay "Substitution" Levinas provides a clue to the inspirational origin of his seemingly controversial claims, and at the same time, refers to what we call the inside-out dimension of responsibility, on the hither side of identity: "According to Lamentations 4:30, 'He giveth his cheek to him that smiteth him; he is filled full with reproach.' Not because suffering has any supernatural power whatever; but because it is still I who am responsible for the persecution I undergo. The self is the passivity on the *hither side of identity*, that of the hostage.," "A Man-God" (1968), in EN 59 (emphasis added). Or: "In the trauma of persecution it is to pass from the outrage undergone to the responsibility for the persecutor, and, in this sense from suffering to expiation for the other. Persecution is not something added to the subjectivity of the subject and his vulnerability; it is the very movement of recurrence." OB 111. We can observe that here, "persecution" receives another, deeper meaning that concerns subjectivity. Persecution also signifies the persecution of the other that calls *me* in question. Or, another example in this sense "When this relation is really thought through, it signifies the wound that cannot heal over of the self in the ego accused by the other to the point of persecution, and responsible for its persecutor." OB 126.

[27] "Responsibility and Substitution" (1996), interview with Levinas conducted by Augusto Ponzio, trans. Maureen Gedney, in IIRB 230. Here, by the "juridical order" Levinas refers to the order of justice, since it brings the need for comparison: "Who comes first among all?."

already in my responsibility for the other.²⁸ What makes it even more difficult to express the meaning of *the third* in Levinas's work is the lack of clarity surrounding the notion. Different kinds of "thirdness" can be found in Levinas's writings: the third party (*le tiers*), the third person (*la troisième personne*), the third man (*le troisième homme*) and even illeity (*illéité*) or "he-ness" (the grammatical third person).²⁹ The difference between these kinds of thirdness, however, is not always obvious.³⁰ In this chapter we are

---

²⁸ "Questions and Answers, " in OGCM 82.

²⁹ According to Robert Bernasconi, there are three notions in Levinas's work which designate the third, each reflecting different aspects of it: the third party (*le tiers*), the third person (*la troisième personne*) and illeity (*illéité*). (See Robert Bernasconi, "The Third Party. Levinas on the Intersection of the Ethical and the Political," *Journal of the British Society for Phenomenology,* 30, no. 1, [1999]: 67–87.). In his view, the third party (or "the third man") would be the passage between the ethical and the political, the third person designates a neutral observer's standpoint, while illeity, which although addresses the same problem as the third party, reveals the "conflict" between the ethical and political "that arose from the location of the third party in the face of the Other," ibid., 82. Others, such as William Paul Simmons, identify the third with "the appearance of another person," which helps to "extend" the responsibility for the other. (See William Paul Simmons, "The Third. Levinas's theoretical move from an-archical ethics to the realm of justice and politics," *Philosophy and Social Criticism,* 25, no. 6 [1999]: 93). We shall show that Simmons's and similar interpretations carry the risk of reducing radical multiplicity to a dyad and of an empirical interpretation of the third. Although Simmons acknowledges that the appearance of the third is "not necessarily an empirical fact," he still sees somehow the face-to-face relation as a dualistic, empirical relation: "it is impossible to have a face-to-face relationship with each member of humanity. Those far away can only be reached indirectly. Thus, the appearance of the Third extends the anarchical responsibility for the Other into the realm of the said," ibid., 93.

³⁰ An example in this sense comes from *Otherwise than Being*, where "illeity" seems to correspond to the "third person," while the "third party" with the "third man": "It is in prophecy that the Infinite escapes the objectification of thematization and of dialogue, and signifies as illeity, in the third person (*la troisième personne*). This 'thirdness' is different from that of the third man (*troisième homme*), from the third party (*tiers*) that interrupts the face to face of a welcome of the other man, interrupts the proximity or approach of the neighbor, the third man with which justice begins," OB 150, AE 234 (translation altered). Although here we do not intend to enter the question of illeity, it seems reasonable to think that its "thirdness" is due to its escape from thinking in exclusive alternatives (in this sense, see for instance, the section called "Subject and illeity" from an essay from 1965 entitled "Enigma and Phenomenon" [1965], BPW 73–76). It is in this sense, that in *Otherwise than Being* illeity is referred to as the "excluded middle" and its absence is the absence of the never having been present, anarchical infinite that can only be revealed through the trace in the face: "The trace of a past in a face is not the absence of a yet non-revealed, but the anarchy of what has never been present, of an infinite which commands in the face of the other, and which, like an

interested only in one of these aspects, that which Levinas's calls "le tiers," which can be translated as "the third party," or, just simply "the third." This is the thirdness that is quite consistently used in introducing the problematic of justice in its interconnection with ethics. The third, in this sense, offers a response to the question why it is necessary to problematize justice. Levinas makes this clear already at the beginning of *Otherwise than Being*, when he writes:

> The act of consciousness is motivated by the presence of a third party (*tiers*) alongside of the neighbor approached. A third party is also approached; and the relationship between the neighbor and the third party cannot be indifferent to me when I approach. There must be a justice among incomparable ones. There must then be a comparison between incomparables and a synopsis, a togetherness and contemporaneousness; there must be thematization, thought, history and inscription.[31]

The third introduces the problematic of the other's other, or the neighbor's neighbor, indicating a plurality that needs contemporaneousness, simultaneity ("a synopsis"), and that presupposes a view from the outside and the possibility of comparison. Thus, the third refers to a non-radicalized multiplicity and the outside dimension represented by justice. Here we should emphasize the simple but very important point that the third party, although in its name indicating an ordinal number, does not mean a physical person that would be added as the third companion in a supposedly dual relation that I had, until then, with one other person. The notion of the third does not indicate an empirical third person:

> [I]t is not that the entry of the third party would be an empirical fact, and that my responsibility for the other finds itself constrained to a calculus by the force of things.[32]

A strong emphasis on the non-empirical character of the third is necessary, as some of Levinas's texts do appear to allow for an empirical interpretation.

---

excluded middle (*comme un tiers exclu*), could not be aimed at (*ne saurait être visé*)." OB 97, AE 153.
[31] OB 16, AE 33.
[32] OB 158. The same idea is already present in Levinas's earlier work: "Thus the multiplicity in which the relation with the third party is placed does not constitute a contingent fact, a simple empirical multiplicity," "The *I* and the Totality" (1954), in EN 22.

Later on in this chapter we will address the highly problematic character of these interpretations. For now, though, let it suffice to keep in mind that Levinas introduces the third in order to address the question of justice. Yet the third is neither an epitome nor the representation of the intertwinement between ethics and justice. Instead, it fully belongs to the order of justice because it always implies a non-radicalized multiplicity, where the singular/plural alternatives are re-introduced. Although the third is not a representation of the intertwinement between ethics and justice, it is however reasonable to say that, through this notion, a change of emphasis takes place, from ethics to justice.

This change of emphasis from ethics to justice makes us wonder whether the order of justice comes as a replacement of the order of ethics. In other words, does the outside dimension replace the inside-out dimension of my responsibility for the other, which would now have to be viewed through the need for justice? We have arrived at the core of the problem, namely, the essential ambiguity of the intertwinement between ethics and justice. The dimension, introduced by the third and corresponding to justice, does not simply annul the ethical, inside-out dimension. Ethics and justice enter into contradiction *only* when thought as extremes, which, as we shall see, is not Levinas's way to think them:

> I think that there is a direct contradiction between ethics and politics, if both these demands are taken to the extreme. It's a contradiction which is usually an abstract problem.[33]

We should not be dazzled by Levinas's sudden change of terminology from "justice" to '"politics" in the above quotation. The meaning of justice and politics often overlaps in Levinas's writings. In *Totality and Infinity*, the political appears as an early version of what Levinas later discusses under the problematic of justice.[34] In Levinas's later work, for which the meaning of justice had already changed, this becomes "inseparable from the

---

[33] "Ethics and Politics" (1982), in LR 292.
[34] For instance, the following fragment from *Totality and Infinity* presents reciprocity and equality as being characteristic to politics; in Levinas's later work, these are associated with the notion of justice: "Politics tends toward reciprocal recognition, that is, toward equality; it ensures happiness. And political law concludes and sanctions the struggle for recognition," TI 64.

political."³⁵ Justice implies the necessity of law, the public realm and the State. As a consequence, Levinas's discussions of justice often intersect with issues concerning organized society, and thus, in his later work, justice becomes a political question.³⁶ This correlation between justice and organized society might suggest that the intertwinement between ethics and justice is simply given by the necessary compromise that comes from living in a society; in other words, their intertwinement would be the simple result of co-habitation. This however, would be to give an empirical interpretation of the whole problematic of the relation between ethics and justice, as if it were one that could be constrained "by the force of things." No matter how tempting it might be to adopt this straightforward interpretation, we need to look deeper.

When we consider Levinas's general way of thinking, his tendency for disrupting dichotomies and embracing paradoxes, it becomes clear that we need to interpret the relation between ethics and justice accordingly. In this sense, to think ethics and justice as a contradiction to be solved, would indeed lead to an abstract problem, as it would introduce relatedness and co-definition. This, in turn, would be a mere conceptual play of abstract notions, co-defining each other. In our view, Levinas has something different in mind. Through his embracing of paradoxes, instead of conceptual interplays and reconciliation, he urges us to re-think the relation between ethics and justice, "comparing the incomparables" through the importance of sustaining the paradox, and not by dissolving it and making justice take over ethics, or vice-versa. Ethics and justice are "inseparable and simultaneous," as Levinas's notes in an interview from 1982:

---

[35] "The Paradox of Morality: An Interview with Emmanuel Levinas," in *The Provocation of Levinas*, 171.

[36] Regarding the distinction between "the political" and "politics" we find no explicit clarification on Levinas's part. This is probably because, on the one hand, he was not extensively preoccupied with the problem of the political or politics as such, and, on the other, due to the fact that the increasing interest in problematizing "the political" (*le politique*) as different from "politics" (*la politique*) in the French philosophical context came too late to influence Levinas in a meaningful way in this sense (emerging as a full blown philosophical problem through the discussions at the *Centre for Philosophical Research on the Political* [1980–19849] established by Jean-Luc Nancy and Philippe Lacoue-Labarthe).

Justice itself is born of charity. They can seem alien when they are presented as successive stages; in reality, they are inseparable and simultaneous.[37]

I think rather, as I said at the beginning, that charity is impossible without justice, and that justice is warped without charity (*se déforme sans la charité*).[38]

The "outside" of the third person's view does not mean that the self steps out from its approach from the hither side; *I* can never escape *my* responsibility for the other. The self is not just suddenly relieved of infinite responsibility as soon as it faces a situation requiring justice, since that would mean that the order of justice simply erases the order of ethics, and the very de-position of the subject. It is not about a replacement, but rather a change in focus: in justice, the other's other, and their relation is at stake. I need to make a judgement. The third assures a view upon the relation between other and another other—this is the only way that the "I" can consider an other as the other's other, and this is the place where a need for justice, comparison, calculation, reasoning and judgement has to be addressed; and it is why Levinas so often links the birth of consciousness to the third party.[39]

---

[37] "Philosophy, Justice, and Love" (1982), remarks recorded by R. Fornet and A. Gómez, in EN 107.

[38] Ibid., 121, ENEPA 131. Here, where we would expect the word "ethics," or infinite responsibility, we actually find the word "charity." In fact, "charity" is the biblical correspondent for the word "Agape," which means "selfless love," and in Christianity is associated with God's love. Love and charity are often interchangeable in Levinas works, probably because of the above-mentioned translation. The similarity of love without lust and charity is visible already in Levinas's words from the very beginning of same interview from 1982: "From the start, the encounter with the Other is my responsibility for him. That is the responsibility for my neighbor, which is, no doubt, the harsh name for what we call love of one's neighbor; love without Eros, charity, love in which the ethical aspect dominates the passionate aspect, love without concupiscence." (Ibid.,103), and becomes even more clear when he reclaims the priority of charity, just a few lines bellow, as the priority of love, so as the sentence: "Justice itself is born of charity" (Ibid.,107), becomes "Justice comes from love." (Ibid.,108). Love and charity in Levinas's later work often express the relation without relation to absolute alterity, which is a role that in his early writings was occupied by Eros. In this sense, charity reflects the inside-out dimension inscribed in the ethical relation. Keeping this in mind, the above citation, while claiming the priority of charity, it actually refers to the priority of the ethical. However, this priority is not a chronological one: justice is "born of" charity, yet they are not presented as separated stages. We will return to the question of love in Levinas's work later on.

[39] "The act of consciousness is motivated by the presence of a third party," OB 16.

In engaging justice, in measuring and comparing others, there is always a risk of a certain violence against the uniqueness of the other, in the sense that the other, as incomparable, must be compared.[40] And there is a risk that this violence, which makes the incomparable comparable, will translate into a totalitarian politics. Levinas, as one would expect, recognizes this threat.[41] Precisely to combat the threat of totalitarianism, the differentiation between ethics and justice needs to be maintained in its paradoxicality; instead of taking over (governing) politics (or vice-versa), ethics brings a different approach than that of the objective law that justice requires.[42] Ethics is not another *kind* of relation than justice, but comes in the form of interruption of totality (in this case, the universality of the law). When asked about his political philosophy, Levinas explains that casuistry (taking into account the concrete situation of each case) is involved in balancing politics by ethics—otherwise politics could easily turn into a totality and forget the uniqueness of the other. Although casuistry has a bad reputation, Levinas explains, due to its abuse in the justification of acting in one's own interest, it has an important role in politics for it stands against a mechanization of the law.[43]

---

[40] "Comparison is superimposed onto my relation with the *unique* and incomparable, and, in view of equity and equality, a weighting, a thinking, a calculation, the comparison of incomparables [...] and through this, finally, the extreme importance in human multiplicity of the political structure of society, subject to laws and thereby to institutions where the *for-the-other* of subjectivity –or the ego—enters with the dignity of a citizen into the perfect reciprocity of political laws which are essentially egalitarian or held to become so.," "Peace and Proximity" (1984), in BPW 168.

[41] In *Totality and Infinity*, Levinas's critical words on the state and the tyranny in which it can turn by objectification and totalization show quite clearly his concerns. See for example TI 300.

[42] In this context, it becomes even more important that ethics not stand for a normative demand—it doesn't say what we *should* do. That would only transform the particularity, the uniqueness proper to *my* relation to the other into a norm, a rule, and thus would lead to generalization, tearing out the very core of what an interruption of the totality means.

[43] "Where proximity is concerned, however, every instance, each particular case prevails. In casuistry this is the method. The importance of casuistry lies in the fact that it constantly takes into account the person who is opposite me, the concrete situation of each 'case'," "What one asks of oneself, one asks of a saint," 29. Still, this will not lead to a pragmatic understanding of Levinas's ethics. When asked whether he pleads for a political pragmatism, Levinas replies: "That depends on what is meant by pragmatism. Pragmatism assumes that there is uncertainty, that in each particular situation one must grope and search for what is practical and suitable, I would rather say that one should pay attention to each individual human." *Ibid.* For the same reason Levinas insists on the

Without the disruptive movement of the ethical, without the anarchy interrupting synthesis, justice can easily end up in totality[44] and politics in totalitarianism. Justice needs ethics as its critical tool—critique not in the sense of theoretical exercise, but interruption of the pure conceptual system created by an abstract justice, the need for the judge in justice.[45]

> [J]ustice is not a legality regulating human masses, from which a technique of social equilibrium is drawn, harmonizing antagonistic forces. That would be a justification of the State delivered over to its own necessities. Justice is impossible without the one that renders it finding himself in proximity. His function is not limited to the "function of judgment," the subsuming of particular cases under a general rule. The judge is not outside the conflict, but the law is in the midst of proximity. Justice, society, the State and its institutions, exchanges and work are comprehensible out of proximity.[46]

In *Adieu to Emmanuel Levinas*, examining the "enigmatic relationship," as he calls it, between Levinas's ethics and politics, Derrida implies that politics cannot be left without ethics; without the ethical order politics would judge in absence—Derrida says—in abstraction, without facing the other.[47] Simon Critchley also emphasizes the necessity of ethics for politics in Levinas's philosophy. He suggests that ethics makes every political decision a particular, distinctive one, and re-introduces uniqueness in a decision provoked by the objectivity of the law. Critchley goes even further, claiming that

---

importance of being a person who stands between the law and the one who is judged, thus the importance of judges (persons who judge). The judge impersonates the ambiguous simultaneity of justice and my responsibility for the other. "Judgment should not be exercised by a neutral mechanism, but by persons, by judges. It is absolutely essential that a judge, a thinking individual, stands between the law and the person to whom it is applied, in other words someone who can have unique relationship with someone else." Ibid., 30.

[44] "It is necessary that the institutions required by justice be overseen by charity, from which justice itself issues.," "Who Shall Not Prophesy" (1985), in IIRB 223.

[45] Justice has "bad conscience," Levinas says, and this makes it adjustable, allowing the possibility of changing the law. See "The Other, Utopia, and Justice" (1988), in IIRB 206. As we have seen, this "bad conscience" or "bad consciousness" signifies precisely the anarchical and hither side of the relation. Thus, Levinas, here again, stresses the necessary intertwinement between the two dimensions of the relation to the other.

[46] OB 159.

[47] Jacques Derrida, Adieu to Emmanuel Levinas, 97.

ethics is for the sake of politics.[48] It has to be for the sake of something else than itself, since ethics just for the sake of itself would create the ethereal environment that Levinas tries to avoid, the "sociality of angels"[49] which is just a misleading abstraction. We partially agree with these interpretations, since, as we have seen, Levinas himself insists on the importance of a constant review of politics through the critique provided by the ethical. However, our agreement remains only partial because "for the sake of" indicates a form of utility which is not appropriate in this context, as it tends to treat ethics and justice as two different realms, even if interconnected; whilst in our interpretation, ethics and justice are not separate realms, but rather represent two different dimensions, two ways of approaching the same relation to the other. Although it is about different dimensions of the same relation, this does not imply that the meaning of our everyday relation to the other is brought forth as a totality formed by combining together these two dimensions. The inside-out and outside dimensions do not reflect two realms that would characterize the relation "at the same time." "At the same time," Levinas says, "would not be enough for the breakup of order."[50] Their intertwinement is a paradox and should remain as such. In order to make our point even more clear, in the following we discuss the paradoxical intertwinement of ethics and justice by

---

[48] "On my view, ethics is ethics for the sake of politics. Better stated perhaps, ethics is the metapolitical disturbance of politics for the sake of politics, that is, for the sake of politics that does not close over itself, becoming what Levinas would call totality, becoming a whole," Simon Critchley, "Five problems in Levinas's View of Politics and the Sketch of a Solution to Them," *Political Today*, 32, no. 2 (2004): 182. See also Critchley, *The Ethics of Deconstruction*, Chapter 5 "A Question of Politics: The Future of Deconstruction," 188–218.

[49] The following fragment appears in the context of Levinas's critique to Buber' *I-Thou* relation, and here the ethereal sociality of angels would mean thinking ethics as abstraction: "But is not the *for the other* itself of sociality concrete in *giving*, and does it not presuppose *things*, without which, empty-handed, the responsibility for others would be but the ethereal sociality of angels?" "Apropos of Buber: Some Notes" (1982), in OS 47. Emphasis by Levinas. Other times, (for example in OB 6.) angelic or ancillary would have the meaning of a mediator. Whereas nor the other, nor the face can be thought as a mediator (it is not a simple sign of something higher). We suspect that Levinas's expression "ethereal sociality of angels" might stay at the roots of the name "angelic reading" given by Simon Critchley for the readings that isolate the ethical from its intertwinement with the political. See Simon Critchley, *The Ethics of Deconstruction*, 230 or "Five problems in Levinas's View of Politics and the Sketch of a Solution to Them," 182.

[50] "Enigma and Phenomenon" (1965), in BPW 72.

considering the larger context of the ambiguous relation between the unthematized and thematization.

4.2.2. The saying and the said

We have seen that justice requires positioning, determinacy, thematization, while ethics, understood as the "priority of the for the other," keeps the self in its relation to the other unthematized (not constrained to *something* determined). Viewed in this way, our question regarding the relation between ethics and justice, between the inside-out and outside dimension of the relation to the other, translates into the deeper question regarding the relation between indeterminacy and determinacy, the unthematized and thematization. We will turn our attention now to this deeper dilemma, in order to attain a better understanding of the ambiguity characteristic to the relation between the two dimensions.

In Levinas's thought, the problem regarding the relation between the unthematized and thematization is reflected by his re-definition of the relation between the *Saying* (*le dire*) and the *Said* (*le dit*).[51] The notions of Saying and the Said are developed quite late in Levinas's work,[52] even if Levinas is concerned from early on with underlying questions regarding thematization and language. The complex problematic opened up by the notions of the Saying and the Said (e.g. the question of language, the difference between speech and writing) would require a study of its own. For our purpose it will suffice to explore the ambiguity of the relation between the unthematized Saying and the thematizing Said, inasmuch as it reflects the ambiguous intertwinement between the two dimensions of the relation to the other.

Levinas introduces the notions of the Saying and the Said in an effort to redefine their relation given by a denominating language. In a denominating language, the Saying becomes the theme of the Said; it is a subject-

---

[51] Although Levinas is not consistent in his capitalization of Saying, Said or Unsaying (throughout his work he uses both forms) we have opted to use capitalized forms in order to emphasize their special meaning.

[52] It has been argued that the differentiation between the Saying and the Said was inspired from Rosenzweig's *Star of Redemption*. In this sense see Robert Gibbs, *Correlations in Rosenzweig and Levinas* (Princeton, New Jersey: Princeton University Press, 1994), 30; or David Michael Levin, *The Philosopher's Gaze: Modernity in the Shadows of Enlightenment* (Berkeley: University of California Press, 1999), 471, n. 82.

object relation. The Said thematizes a recovered time, it narrates history (it tells what the Saying once was). When re-defining this relation, Levinas breaks down the subject-object structure, in a way that the unthematized Saying does not end up as the Said. By tearing away the Saying from its resting place in the Said, Levinas is not against thematization as such, but rather the understanding of thematizing language as the *only* meaning-giving system. From a Levinasian point of view, thematization needs to be interrupted, and through this interruption prevented from becoming a totality. It is, once again, the openness, the exposure to the other that obstructs the coagulation of the self into a determined and essentialized identity. The Saying signifies the exposure of the exposedness of self to the other, it is Saying without saying *something*, but the simple "here I am" or "here's me" (*me voici*) of the emerging self. "Saying saying itself, without thematizing it, but exposing it again."[53] In his attempt to emphasize the escape from a totalizing system of thematization, Levinas considers the Saying a communication that is also the condition to all communication:

> Saying is communication, to be sure, but as a condition for all communication, as exposure. [...]The unblocking of communication, irreducible to the circulation of information which presupposes it, is accomplished in saying.[54]

The Saying is communication without the communicating of anything specific. Here, communication does not designate the transmission of *something* that we share, but it is rather an exposing to that which cannot be Said, where subjectivity is understood as "exciding and dispossession."[55] In this way, the exposure of the Saying, its communication, is very different from thematization. It does not *show* anything (in the way the Said shows this *as* that), but it is contact without contracting, without transmission, holding nothing in common, but an opening in a response. The Saying means responding to the other. In other words, the responsibility for the

---

[53] OB 143, "Dire disant le dire même, sans le thématiser, mais en l'exposant encore," AE 223. And then he continues: "it [Saying] is to expose the exposure instead of remaining in it as an act of exposing." OB 143.
[54] OB 48.
[55] "It is with subjectivity understood as self, with the exciding and dispossession, the contraction, in which the ego does not appear, but immolates itself, that the relationship with the other can be communication and transcendence, and not always another way of seeking certainty, or the coinciding with oneself." OB 118.

other is the Saying otherwise than Said, Saying that transgresses thematization and resists totalization. The exposure, which Levinas calls signifyingness, does not mean showing something that was previously hidden, it is not an unveiling. Instead of denomination, it opens up towards alterity and refers back to an irrecuperable past (the an-archical past of the responsiveness/ responsibility for the other). In this sense, exposure can be be read as ex-posure, as out of place, and it refers to the de-cored self and to the inside-out dimension that it implies.[56] The passivity that characterizes the hither side is now characteristic of the Saying:

> The saying signifies this passivity [the passivity of the exposure]; in the saying this passivity signifies, becomes signifyingness, exposure in response to ... being at the question before any interrogation[57]

Through re-defining the Saying, Levinas manages to save alterity and the self from thematization, and to place meaning outside a meaning-giving *system*. At the same time, this does not imply that the Saying would be of a higher order than the Said, and that the Said would be a degradation of the Saying. Such considerations would be fed by a dialectical thinking that considers the thematized/unthematized to be alternatives. This is very much against Levinas's intentions, and to make his point clear he introduces the notion of "Unsaying" (*dedire*).

The Unsaying has the role of disrupting the way of thinking in alternatives, by constantly rescuing the Saying from being a mere correlate of the Said, through an interruption, a protest.

---

[56] While discussing the question of signifyingness in Levinas's work, Didier Frank argues that it is precisely the exposure of Saying that obstructs the self from solidifying into the "position" of the "here I am": "Does this 'here I am' which is self-showing (*exposition*) to others, 'extradition of the self to neighbor,' not always imply an act, a 'position' and thereby the return of the unbreachable nucleus of the unity of apperception? Probably, but this return will not be definitive if the 'here I am' is itself, as an inspired saying, passivity and exposition of the exposition (*passivité et exposition de l'exposition*), the self-showing of self-showing" Didier Frank, "The Sincerity of the Saying," in *Between Levinas and Heidegger*, eds. John E. Drabinski and Eric S. Nelson (Albany: SUNY Press, 2014), 79, *L'un -pour-l'autre. Levinas et la signification* (Paris: PUF, 2008), 195–6.

[57] OB 49. Or: "Saying is this passivity of passivity and this dedication to the other, this sincerity. Not the communication of a said, which would immediately cover over and extinguish or absorb the said, but saying holding open its openness, without excuses, evasions or alibis, delivering itself without saying anything said." Ibid., 143.

> As I speak, I inevitably make use of the language of ontology. This is precisely the reason why one must unsay and resay (*dedire*). Unsaying does not counter what one wanted to say; it is always a protest against what one has already-said.[58]

The Unsaying has a double function dictated by the double risk of the Saying: first, the Saying carries the risk of being absorbed in the Said as its coagulation, and secondly the risk of becoming the *realm* of Saying, and receiving determination as that *realm*, which again would mean becoming the Said. Hence, the Unsaying has the role of approaching the Saying not in itself (making it a separate realm), but through the constant questioning of the Said. Just as it would be a misunderstanding to consider the Saying a correlative or an alternative to the Said, so would it be inappropriate to think the signification of Saying on its own, and that it only afterwards would somehow be infused in the Said. The movement is the other way around. The constant Unsaying of the Said is what leads back to the signification of the Saying, which in itself remains undetermined.

> But one can go back to this signification of the saying, this responsibility and substitution, only from the said and from the question: "What is it about…?" a question already within the said in which everything shows itself.[59]

> One has to go back to that hither side, starting from the trace retained by the said, in which everything shows itself.[60]

The unthematized relation of the Saying is signaled; not shown, nor indicated, but referred to indirectly, yet without mediation. Levinas describes this signaling like a trace or an echo[61] that does not lead to *something* behind the trace, or to a *determinate* voice behind the echo. The trace is not some kind of "residue" left by a past present,[62] an imprint of *something determinate*; in other words it does not lead to another realm. Instead, Levinas remains faithful to thinking the hither side, to which the unthematized Saying belongs, in terms of an-archy. In this way, the trace is untraceable, it is not a lead anywhere, but instead it disturbs, "striating with

---

[58] "What one asks of oneself, one asks of a saint" (1980–81), 5.
[59] OB 44.
[60] Ibid., 53.
[61] Ibid., 44.
[62] "The infinite then cannot be tracked down like game by a hunter. The trace left by the infinite is not the residue of a presence; its very glow is ambiguous. Otherwise, its positivity would not preserve the infinity of the infinite any more than negativity would." Ibid., 12.

its furrows the clarity of the ostensible (*la clarté de l' ostensible*)."[63] Without entering more deeply the complex problematic of the trace,[64] for us what is important is to retain the backwards movement of the trace without destination, towards the hither side, which, instead of leading somewhere, has a disruptive function.[65]

The interruptive, backwards movement, leading nowhere, of Unsaying is also a reductive movement,[66] yet a reduction that expresses a "positive phase," that of showing "the signification proper to the saying on the hither side of the thematization of the said."[67] This reduction leads back to the hither side, without thematizing it—the hither side, through its anarchical character, escapes determination in the form of something original. Hence, it does not lead to another world to a world that is better or more authentic then the world of thematization (manifestation), but instead dismantles thinking in alternatives.[68] This also means that the Saying is not deduced from the Said, despite the importance of the reductive move of the Unsaying. The Unsaying unsays the Said in an interruptive movement and not by stabilizing it into determination.

---

[63] "This way of passing, disturbing the present without allowing itself to be invested by the ἀρχή of consciousness, striating with its furrows the clarity of the ostensible, is what we have called a trace." says Levinas in OB 100, AE 158.

[64] For more on the trace see Levinas's essay from 1963 "The Trace of the Other," in *Deconstruction in Context*, 345–359. Originally published as "La trace de l'autre," *Tijdschrift voor Filosofie*, 3, (1963): 605–623. The text was later integrated in the volume *Humanism of the Other* (1972), trans. Nidra Poller (Urbana and Chicago: University of Illinois Press, 2003).

[65] This aspect we will revisit during our discussion regarding the face [visage], which in its turn has a crucial role in the question of sociality as facing.

[66] "The movement back to the saying is the phenomenological reduction. In it the indescribable is described. The subject is described as a self, from the first in the accusative form, (or under accusation!), already presupposed by 'the infinite freedom of the equal' with which Hegel characterizes the return to self involved in consciousness and time. This is produced already in a tale, in the said," OB 53.

[67] Ibid., 43.

[68] "The reduction, the going back to the hither side of being, to the hither side of the said, in which being shows itself, in which the eon is hypostatized, could nowise mean a rectification of one ontology by another, the passage from some apparent world to a more real world. It is only in the order of being that rectification, truth and error have meaning, and that the betrayal is the lack of a fidelity. The hither side of or the beyond being is not an entity on the hither side of or beyond being; but it also does not signify an exercise of being, an essence, that is truer or more authentic that the being of entities." Ibid., 45.

Instead of putting to rest the unthematized by incorporating it into a theme, in the Unsaying there is always a movement of questioning, a critical movement, but also a movement that, through its questioning, brings forth the meaning of that which it questions. There is a necessary movement of "alternation," as Levinas puts it, between the two moments: that of questioning, and the questioning of the very mode of questioning itself.[69] Levinas performs a de-thematization of thematization from within thematization itself. We can observe here a somewhat parallel movement to that of the deposed self, where the self does not find itself either in itself or in the other. Here, in a similar way, the meaning of the thematized is found neither in itself, nor outside itself. Instead it is brought forth through the unthematized, through interruption, without however identifying its meaning with the unthematized as such: the meaning (sense) of thematization is de-posed from thematization itself.[70] This movement between the unthematized and thematization expresses the ambiguous relation between the two dimensions, inside-out and outside of the relation to the other.

To make the point still clearer, let us return to the previously emphasized distinction between radical and non-radical multiplicity, characteristic of the two dimensions of the relation to the other.[71] In *Totality and Infinity* we find Levinas criticizing the tendency of Western philosophy to treat pluralism[72] solely as a plurality of subjects that exist, and to depict it as a countable, numerical plurality revealed through a synthetical view:

---

[69] "The meaning that philosophy lets us see with the aid of these forms [the ontological forms] frees itself from the theoretical forms which help it to see and express itself as if these forms were not precisely encrusted in that which they allow to be seen and said. In an inevitable alternation, thinking comes and goes between these two possibilities. It is this alternation that the enigma of philosophy resides, relative to ontological dogmatism and to its unilateral lucidity. But it is there also that the permanence of philosophy's crisis resides. This signifies, concretely, that for philosophy the ontological proposition remains open to a certain reduction, disposed to unsaying itself and to wanting itself wholly otherwise said.," "Manner of Speaking" (1980), in OGCM 180.

[70] Identifying the unthematized with the very meaning of thematization would lead to unwanted consequences: on the one hand, it would give determination to the unthematized, thus annulling its very resistance to thematization, and on the other hand, it would create a separate realm to which the unthematized belongs to which is, again, against Levinas's intention.

[71] See Chapter 3.

[72] We should remind ourselves that in *Totality and Infinity* "pluralism" is interchangeable with "radical multiplicity," as we have explained in Chapter 3.

> Pluralism appears in Western philosophy only as a plurality of subjects that exist. Never has it appeared in the existing of those existents. The plural, exterior to the existence of beings, is given as a number; to a subject that counts it is already subordinated to the synthesis of the 'I think.'[73]

Despite his harsh critique of Western philosophy, a critique the importance of which we have previously addressed,[74] we would now like to emphasize another, perhaps more subtle point discernible in the above quotation: Levinas's critique is not targeting numerical plurality as such, but merely the tendency to consider it the *only way* of approaching the question of multiplicity. In other words, Levinas's goal is not that of criticizing the thematizing character of non-radicalized multiplicity as such, but to disrupt the correlative thinking of the unthematized and thematized relation to the other. In this way, it is important to say that radical multiplicity, like Saying, is not a separate realm of multiplicity. We cannot have, for example, a politics of radical multiplicity, a society of radical multiplicity, etc., just as we cannot have a politics or society of the unthematized. In a sense, all politics, all society is radical multiplicity since the unthematized echoes in the thematized. Or, more precisely, thematization carries in itself the trace of the unthematized. Through the Unsaying, through questioning and critique, one can follow the trace of radical multiplicity in non-radical multiplicity, without however actually reaching it and ever bringing it to the surface.

At this point, together with Levinas, we ask why is it even necessary for thematization to carry the trace of something that is beyond thematization:

> Why would proximity, the pure signification of saying, the anarchic one-for-the-other of beyond being, revert to being or fall into being, into a conjunction of entities, into essence showing itself in the said? Why have we gone to seek essence on its empyrean? Why know? Why is there a problem? Why philosophy?[75]

The answer to this question comes from Levinas's considerations of the space of contiguity. Contiguity, Levinas says, "already presupposes both thematizing thought and a locus and the cutting up of the contiguity of

---

[73] TI 274.
[74] See Chapter 2.
[75] OB 157.

space into discrete terms and the whole—out of justice."⁷⁶ We are led here towards the self in the quotidian and in its everyday relation with a multiplicity of others, a non-radicalized multiplicity, where the equality and the measuring required by justice would not be possible without thematization. We have previously seen that justice requires contemporaneousness, and contemporaneousness means that an outside dimension of the relation to the other needs to be considered. The disclosure of thematization is necessary for justice and the political sphere.

> This reverting of contact into consciousness and into a discourse that states and that is logical, in which the communicated theme is more important than the contact of communication, is not due to chance or the clumsiness of a behavior. It is due to the relationship between the neighbor and a third party, before whom he may be guilty. It is due to the justice that is nascent in the very abnegation before the neighbor.⁷⁷

In this way, multiplicity thought in terms of singular and plural, numerical multiplicity, finds its own importance in Levinas's philosophy through the problematic of justice. Justice demands the possibility of comparison. We need plurality in order to compare, and thus we need an un-radicalized multiplicity that would reflect the outside dimension of the relation to the other. This multiplicity is numerical not in the sense that the other becomes a mere numerical entity, but in the sense that justice implies the necessity of thinking in terms of singular and plural. The inside-out dimension does not exclude the outside dimension of the relation to the other; it is not morally better or more authentic; it does not signify an attitude or a perspective that we have the ability to adopt. The two dimensions, inside-out and outside, as well as the two kinds of multiplicities (reflected in ethics and in justice, respectively), are different, and yet do not form separate realms; instead, they maintain an ambiguous relation characterized by an interruptive movement, one in which separateness and intertwinement are not opposites.

---

[76] Ibid.
[77] OB 193, n. 29.

4.3. Singular and plural

The discussion of the paradoxical relation between the inside-out and outside dimensions, and with it, the intertwined yet different ways to think multiplicity, has prepared us to address some problems that are fuelled by Levinas's own words. In the following we are about to show a rather problematic aspect regarding some of Levinas's description of the relation between ethics and justice: the possibility of reading the third as some kind of limitation of the infinite responsibility for the other, or as an extension of an ethical relation between two; in other words, we are confronted with the risk of reading the inside-out dimension of my relation to the other as a dyad that is "disturbed" by justice.

Our problems start with Levinas's occasional reference to the third, and with it, justice as a limitation to ethics. Justice "limits that initial precedence of the other from which we started,"[78] Levinas says in 1986; or again, in 1982: "If there were no order of Justice, there would be no limit to my responsibility."[79] Occasionally, in both early and later writings, Levinas also refers to a "disturbance" in *my* relation to the other by the third[80]—as if the "entry" of the third changed the setting from a relation between two to a relation between three or more.[81] Here is a fairly typical example:

> If there were only the two of us in the world, you and I, then there would be no question, then my system would work perfectly. I am responsible for the other in

---

[78] "The Proximity of the Other" (1986), in IIRB 214.

[79] "Philosophy, Justice, and Love" (1982), in EN 105. Another example is in the interview from 1984: "Now, there is the appearance of the third who is a limitation on this measureless *hesed*. Because the other for whom I am responsible can be the executioner of the third who is also my other. Thus the necessity of justice," in IIRB 100; We need to note briefly here that *hesed* means gratuitous charity. (For more on this term, see in Chapter 6, section "Sociality and Love").

[80] See for example "The *I* and The totality," from 1954: "The third man disturbs this intimacy (the intimacy of the I-thou relation) essentially: my wrong with regard to you, which I can recognize entirely in terms of my intentions, is objectively falsified through your relations with *him*, which remain secret to me, since I, in turn, am excluded from the unique privilege of your intimacy." in EN 19; or the interview conducted by Anne-Catherine Benchelah from 1986: "Yet this apparent simplicity of the I-Thou relation, in its very asymmetry, is again disturbed by the appearance of the third man who places himself beside the other, the Thou.," "The Proximity of the Other" (1986), in IIRB 214.

[81] "One should then also recall that proximity is not from the first a judgment of a tribunal of justice, but first a responsibility for the other which turns into judgment only with the entry of the third party," OB 190, n. 35.

everything. [...] But we are not only two, we are at least three. Now we are a threesome; we are a humanity. The question then arises—the political question: who is the neighbor?[82]

The above fragment, and similar moments that can be encountered from time to time in Levinas's work[83] create the impression that the third might disturb an idyllic setting of the ethical space which up to that point was inhabited by me and the other alone—as if the third party would force some kind of re-adjustment of the ethical couple, since now the self has to deal with others (plural) and not just the other (singular). The risk of this sort of interpretation is high as it leads to an empirical understanding of the third, and more importantly, because it reduces *my* relation to the other(s) to a mere dyad. In other words, the singular/plural distinction is introduced in the inside-out dimension and hence the radicality of multiplicity is lost; consequently, reconciliation is brought to the paradoxical intertwinement between ethics and justice. Although the majority of these comments were given in interviews, hastiness cannot be considered an excuse for Levinas since, occasionally, similar remarks can be found in works that were carefully thought through, such as *Otherwise than Being*.[84]

When we consider the third as a disturbance of the couple, or the limitation of something that would be considered the ethical,[85] in other words, if we fail to see that ethics and justice represent two *dimensions* and not two *realms* of the relation to the other, the relation between ethics and justice becomes a problem: there is a need for finding a "passage" from ethics to justice. It gives birth to a "gap" between ethics and justice and the

[82] "Being-Towards-Death and <Thou Shall Not Kill>" (1987), interview conducted by Florian Rötzer, translated by Andrew Schmitz, in IIRB 133.
[83] Another example would be in "Philosophy, Justice, and Love" (1982), in EN 107.
[84] "If proximity ordered to me only the other alone, there would have not been any problem, in even the most general sense of the term. A question would not have been born, nor consciousness, nor self-consciousness. The responsibility for the other is an immediacy antecedent to questions, it is proximity. It is troubled and becomes a problem when a third party enters," OB 157. In "Peace and Proximity" (1984) he reformulates his explanation from *Otherwise than Being* to a more radical and dualistic understanding of the ethical relation: "Doubtless, responsibility for the other human being is, in its immediacy, anterior to every question. But how does responsibility obligate if the third party troubles this exteriority of two where my subjection of the subject is subjection of the neighbor?" BPW 168.
[85] As does, for example, Simmons (See "The Third. Levinas's theoretical move from an-archical ethics to the realm of justice and politics," 93).

necessity of overcoming this gap. This is the case in Žižek's reading, which claims that "[f]ar from preaching an easy grounding of politics in the ethics of the respect and responsibility for the Other, Levinas rather insists on their absolute incompatibility, on the gap separating the two dimensions."[86] A similar reading, evoking a "gap" or "hiatus" between ethics and politics comes from Drabinski[87] and even from Critchley (who, though, as we have seen, solves this problem in a manner inspired by Derrida).[88] Keeping in mind that the intertwinement between ethics and justice refers back to the paradoxical relation between the unthematized and thematization, it seems just as ridiculous to consider that the nature of the relation would somehow shift, or flip from ethics to justice and vice-versa, depending on whether the self faces one (singular) other or a plurality of others, as if thinking the necessity of addressing justice is only imposed by a social reality (i.e. by the fact that we are more than two in the world). We know that Levinas refuses to identify the self and the other in relative or dialogical terms, and hence we can safely assume that he would also reject thinking *my* responsibility to the other in terms of a duo. *My* responsibility for the other is approached from the hither side and thus indicates an inside-out dimension of the relation to the other(s), where multiplicity is radicalized and does not permit thinking in terms of singular/plural. Our examination shows that the interplay between ethics and justice takes an interruptive form, yet without them designating two separate (although intersecting) realms. The anarchical, radicalized relation to the other interrupts the tendency of determination and positioning that the third and justice convey in the form of will, knowledge, thematizing consciousness or originarity. This means that there cannot be any limitation to ethics, any obstruction—interruption itself cannot be limited or interrupted. Interpreting the third as a necessary completion of a duo (me and the other) is far too simplistic and misleading. As we have seen, the term "third" points towards a different *dimension* of the relation to the other and not towards a different *kind* of relation, even if

---

[86] Slavoj Žižek, "Neighbors and Other Monsters," in *The Neighbor: Three Inquiries in Political Theology*, 149.

[87] John Drabinski, "The Possibility of an Ethical Politics" (2000), in *Emmanuel Levinas. Critical Assessments of Leading Philosophers*, Vol 4, *Beyond Levinas*, eds. Claire Katz and Lara Trout (New York: Routledge, 2005), 188–212.

[88] Critchley is rather clear on this view, where he claims: "So the relation of ethics to politics is that there is a gap or hiatus between these two domains," Critchley, "Five problems in Levinas's View of Politics and the Sketch of a Solution to Them," 179.

this other kind of relation would somehow coexist with the "previous" ethical relation. In our view, Levinas's claim from *Totality and Infinity* that "the third party looks at me in the eyes of the Other,"[89] should not indicate a "passage" through the gap between ethics and justice by simply acknowledging that we are never alone with an other (that there are always other others around us). The great significance of the third is neither that I exit an unrealistic dual relation to the other (in which only myself and a singular other were included), nor that a dual relation is simply extended to a relation between at least three (myself and more than one other). The inside-out dimension that is reflected in ethics is not about a dual relation to the other in the first place. The different setting introduced by the third is not given by first considering a singular other and then a plurality of others; that is to say, the difference between ethics and justice is not given by the other/others distinction; instead, it is due to thinking in different terms, in terms that now allow the singular/plural, other/others distinctions. To put it simply, it is not that there would be more than one person for whom I am responsible, but rather it is a different dimension of the relation that is emphasized. This outside dimension concerns the relation of the other to another, between the neighbor and the neighbor's neighbor; that is to say that here, an outside perspective upon the relation itself is considered. Seen in this way, the entry of the third does not disrupt my infinite responsibility, simply because it does not concern *my* responsibility anymore. This idea transpires rather clearly in *Otherwise than Being*:

> The third party is other than my neighbor, but also another neighbor, and also a neighbor of the other, and not simply his fellow. What then are the other and the third party for one another? What have they done to one another? Which passes before the other? The other stands in a relationship with the third party, for whom I cannot entirely answer, even if I alone answer, before any question, for my neighbor. The other and the third party, my neighbors, contemporaries of one another, put distance between me and the other and the third party.[90]

The distance that the relation between the other and the other's other places between them and me (the self) is the distance that a perspective upon them, upon their relation, requires. It is also the distance that gives position to the self, now considered as *I*. This distance also assures simultaneity

[89] TI 213.
[90] OB 157.

given by a perspectival view upon the relation itself, and with it comes thematization, comparing and calculation. What is most important here is not necessarily that the I (the posited self) and the other are countable terms of the relation, but that the I is capable of counting from the outside. In a sense, *I* is the third person, or at least has the third person's view. This reading, which we consider more consistent with Levinas's thoughts on ethics and justice, makes the problem of a gap between ethics and justice a false problem. The problem regarding the difference between ethics and justice is not about a "gap" in need of a "passage," but it reflects an ambiguity, and carries the necessity of thinking differently than in terms of the simple division between dyad and triad, that is to say, in terms different than that of other/others and singular/plural.

We will not go any further with this argument, as the question of singular/plural, other/others distinction will be revisited shortly. If, here, our point was to emphasize the intertwinement of the two dimensions of the relation to the other, in the next part the focus will be on the question of sociality and the importance of thinking it outside the singular/plural distinction.

PART II
Sociality

We began our exploration by approaching sociality in a general way, as the relation to the other. Subsequently, we examined two dimensions of the relation to the other that transpire in Levinas's work, the inside-out and the outside dimension, corresponding first to the unthematized relation, approached from the hither side, and beyond the singular/plural, other/others alternative, and secondly, to the thematization of the relation as such, where measuring, comparison and thinking in terms of singular/plural is required. In this part of the thesis, we propose a closer scrutiny of the meaning of sociality according to Levinas, while adopting a critical approach towards some of his considerations. In this way, we attempt to go beyond mere exegetical work. We are not looking for a precise 'definition' of sociality; instead we intend to develop a meaning that in our view is in accordance with Levinas's philosophy, even if Levinas himself did not express this meaning in a clear and consistent manner.

Searching for the meaning of sociality in Levinas's work becomes more complicated insofar as he only seldom uses the actual expression 'sociality,' and yet explicitly places sociality at the centre of his philosophical project. In this sense, we find that sociality is at once present and absent in Levinas's work, and in Chapter 6 and 7 we examine Levinas's philosophy, from the early to the late writings, in the light of how he discusses sociality in the different phases of his work. During this scrutiny we will revisit some questions regarding the consistency of Levinas's work, questions already raised in the previous section in relation to certain problematic comments made by Levinas himself. Now, in respect of sociality, we will be confronted with a similar problem, in that some of Levinas's text might allow an interpretation of sociality in purely dyadic terms, an interpretation that we will refute in Chapter 8. There, certain expressions that are used as synonyms for sociality will be put into question, such as 'one-to-one' relation, or even 'face-to-face,' as they leave room for neglecting the inside-out dimension of my relation to the other. Instead, 'facing,' will be proposed as a more appropriate expression of sociality.

We start our itinerary, in Chapter 5, with a deeper look at the meaning of the actual word 'sociality,' and address some problems that might emerge in considering sociality as a notion.

Sociality: the Word and the Notion

When thinking sociality with Levinas, we need to take into consideration that sociality as a notion can become problematic insofar as it implies some sort of determination—this would be quite clearly against Levinas's overall intentions of keeping the relation to the other unthematized. Then, the question is how we can speak in terms of *notion*, which usually means at least some degree of determination, when we, along with Levinas, need to sustain a resistance to the determination of the relation to the other. In other words, how can one disclose the resistance to disclosure, without damaging it? Why and how can we thematize the very impossibility of thematization? These are questions that had preoccupied Levinas himself, and by relying on his own answers, in the first part of this chapter we attempt to explore the way in which sociality can be adopted as a notion while remaining close to Levinas.

When questioning the meaning of the notion of sociality, we should take note that Levinas himself does not make any explicit differentiation between 'sociality' (*socialité*) the word (i.e. the actual linguistic unit), and sociality the notion.[1] Despite Levinas's silence on this issue, in the second part of this chapter we propose to examine more deeply the meaning of sociality by studying the etymological roots of the actual word. This exploration will enable us to show that, through its etymological meaning, sociality can be read as an 'already' relation to the other, that is to say, not a mere characteristic added to an established subject.

---

[1] From now on, whenever we refer to sociality the word, we will use quotation marks ('sociality').

5.1. Sociality – the notion

In his general philosophical development and, more specifically, in his thoughts on sociality, Levinas, as one would expect, was clearly influenced by some of the thinkers of his time. When his philosophical thinking started to develop, that is, during his studies in Strasbourg, the teaching of Durkheimian sociology was widespread. Maurice Halbwachs, one of Levinas's teachers, and someone to whom he attaches "an incomparable prestige,"[2] was a Durkheim follower, and introduced Levinas to the sociological spirit of the time:

> But it was Durkheim and Bergson who seemed to me especially alive in the instruction and attention of the students. It was they whom one cited, and they whom one opposed. They had incontestably been the professors of our masters.[3]

In these circumstances, one would expect to find a philosopher preoccupied with the relation to the other, such as Levinas, to engage in, or at least actively react to the leading sociological ideas. Nonetheless, Levinas never really took the path opened by the Durkheimian thinking. Instead, he remained reserved in his reactions to sociological theories, and from early on he clearly stated his task to be different from a sociological study.[4] Although Levinas acknowledges the novelty and the importance of Durkheim's ideas—suggesting that "the social does not reduce to the sum of individual psychologies"[5] and that the other "is not simply a part of a Whole, nor a singular instance of a concept"[6]—generally speaking, he considers that Durkheim's theory of the social has the tendency to remain in a structure of "collective representation."[7] Instead of choosing to pursue a study with sociological inspiration Levinas, as references throughout his work clearly show, is much more attached to the phenomenological tradition represented by Husserl and Heidegger:

---

[2] EI 25.
[3] Ibid., 25–6.
[4] "This thesis is in no way sociological.," TO 39.
[5] EI 26–27.
[6] TI 68.
[7] Ibid., 68.

> In Durkheim there is, in a sense a theory of "levels of being," of the irreducibility of these levels to one another, an idea which acquires its full meaning within the Husserlian and Heideggerian context.[8]

Levinas was always open about his appreciation of and great indebtedness to phenomenology. The influence of the early phenomenological approach, especially that represented by Husserl and Heidegger, becomes clear not only when considering Levinas's biography,[9] but also in his own early works, and in the numerous implicit and explicit references throughout his writings.[10] Despite acknowledging the important change they have brought to philosophy (the phenomenological method, or the ontological difference), Levinas remains unsatisfied with both Husserl's and Heidegger's account on the relation to the other. As previously shown, Levinas's remained unsatisfied with the way in which Husserl approaches the problem of the unthematized relation to the other by means of intentionality, which makes Levinas re-think time and consciousness.[11] Although Heidegger distances himself from the Husserlian notion of intentionality, and makes being-with-one-another (*Miteinandersein*) an important component of the ontological structure of *Dasein*, ultimately, according to Levinas, by prioritizing *Dasein*'s own death, Heidegger's sociality remains founded on solitude.[12] In both Husserl's and Heidegger's case Levinas finds

---

[8] EI 26–7.

[9] Levinas studies with Husserl in Freiburg and attends Heidegger's seminars in 1928–1929.

[10] Levinas (in collaboration with Gabrielle Peiffer) translated Husserl's, *Cartesian Meditations* and by this introducing it to the French speaking philosophical circles; he wrote his doctoral dissertation on Husserl's philosophy, *The Theory of Intuition in Husserl's Phenomenology* (1930), and from early on, engaged in discussions of both Heidegger and Husserl's philosophy in *En découvrant l'existence avec Husserl et Heidegger* (1949).

[11] See Chapter 2

[12] See for example Levinas's critique from EE 95, or his later essay "Dying for…"(1978) in EN 205–218. Nevertheless, in his interpretation of Heidegger, Levinas sometimes seem to overstate or "deform" Heidegger's thoughts in order to make his own point more visible. As Levinas himself confesses in a footnote from *Otherwise than Being*: "These lines, and those that follow, owe much to Heidegger. Deformed and ill-understood? Perhaps. At least this deformation will not have been a way to deny the debt. Nor is debt a reason to forget…," OB 189, n. 28. Our purpose is not that of doing justice to Heidegger, since the focus of this thesis is not on the Heidegger-Levinas debate. However, we will return to the question of death and solitude in Chapter 6, and in Part III, where we discuss it in the larger context of ontology and being-with.

an underdevelopment of the problematic of the unthematized relation to the other and its important role for the self. Gabriel Marcel's approach is getting closer to problematizing the unthematized relation that concerns Levinas, since Marcel considers the relation to the other to be different from a relation of knowledge.[13] Attending Marcel's seminars (or "salons") from the 30s is likely to have been a formative experience for the young Levinas. Nevertheless, it is Martin Buber's I-Thou relation that, according to Levinas, for the first time makes the important point that the I-Thou relation cannot be understood in the same terms as the I-It, which is an appropriation through consciousness and knowledge of the "It"—in other words, Buber recognizes that the relation to the other is irreducible to determination.[14] Although one might think that Buber directly influenced Levinas, this is not the case. As Levinas indicates in an interview with François Poirié:

> I do not refuse this [allegiance and gratitude] to Martin Buber, even if, in fact, it is not by starting out from the Buberian oeuvre that I was led to the reflection on the alterity of the other, to which my modest writings are consecrated.[15]

Yet neither Buber's nor Marcel's thoughts were fully accepted by Levinas. He criticizes Marcel for continuing "the high Western tradition for which the supreme characterization of the Divine amounts to identifying it with being."[16] Buber remained perhaps the closest, although in the later essays Levinas begins to become more outspoken in his criticism.[17] He mainly reproaches Buber for conceiving the relation to the other (Thou) in terms of reciprocity and symmetry, and keeping it somewhat isolated from the world. We will discuss this critique in detail later on, as it also reveals some

---

[13] For Levinas's comparative reading of Marcel's and Buber's conception of sociality see "Martin Buber, Gabriel Marcel and Philosophy" (1978), in OS 20–39.

[14] In *Totality and Infinity* Levinas clearly expresses his appreciation of both Marcel's and Buber's thought: "Because of a current of ideas appearing independently in Gabriel Marcel's *Metaphysical Journal* and Martin Buber's *I and Thou*, the relationship with the Other as irreducible to objective knowledge has lost its unwonted character, whatever be the attitude one adopts with regard to the accompanying systematic expositions," TI 68. Regarding Levinas's acknowledgment to Buber see also "The Proximity of the Other," in AT 100.

[15] "Interview with François Poirié," (1986), in IIRB 72.

[16] "Martin Buber, Gabriel Marcel and Philosophy," in OS 23.

[17] As for example in ibid., 20–39.

important aspects of Levinas's account of sociality.[18] For now, though, we confine ourselves to observing that, regardless whether or not they had a direct influence on Levinas, and despite the criticism, the philosophies of Husserl, Heidegger, Marcel and Buber helped Levinas greatly to refine his notion of sociality. Taking into account his attitudes towards these different problematizations of sociality we can already make the claim that one of Levinas's major concerns is that of thinking sociality in terms of the unthematized relation to the other.

Levinas's emphasis on the importance of addressing the question of the unthematized relation to the other goes hand in hand with distancing his philosophy from a mere conceptual system, which in his view represents a framework of thought constructed through relatedness and co-determination. Such a framework would have its well-defined rules for the creation of new concepts and the establishment of their relations, similar to a game in which one is armed with a set of rules of playing.[19] Here, we can already see developing Levinas's view of what a 'concept' entails, a view which is very different from, for instance, an analytical or a Deleuzian approach. From Levinas's perspective (a perspective that we need to adopt if we want to problematize sociality with Levinas), a concept is part of a formal system of thought, and as such, it presupposes a certain degree of abstraction, which in its turn implies a unifying ideal principle. It is clear then, that to make a formal concept out of the unthematized relation to the other would go against its very an-archical character.[20] This brings up a difficulty, one which concerns not only our own investigation, but also Levinas's text itself: the problem of thematizing the very refusal of thematization. Any theoretical discourse, and thus Levinas's as well, needs thematization, which in itself is a form of unifying under an abstract idea: a theme. Levinas, even with his ethical terminology from the later works, still needs concepts in order to pursue a theoretical investigation. However, in a

---

[18] See Chapter 7.
[19] "Concepts are ordered and unfold in truth (whose presuppositions, like conventions, make the combinations of concepts like a game), according to the logical possibilities of thought and the dialectical structures of being." OB 57.
[20] 'An-archy' besides indicating an-originarity, without origin, it also becomes an expression of the refusal of a unifying principle, the refusal of a formal universalized system: an-arche as without-ideality. "Proximity is thus *anarchically* a relationship with a singularity without the mediation of any principle, any ideality," OB 100, emphasis by Levinas. See also Ibid., Ch. IV. 1. Principle and anarchy.

philosophical text, a full escape from the theoretical is impossible, and Levinas knows this well; hence, addressing the unthematized relation to the other without compromising its very unthematized character becomes a problem. From the point of view of our thesis, this translates into the question: how is it possible to develop a *notion* of sociality in such a way that we remain faithful to Levinas and avoid reducing the unthematized relation to thematization when enveloping it in *a theme* of investigation?

Here, we need to remind ourselves of our discussion of the ambiguous relation between the unthematized and thematization that was addressed in the context of the intertwinement of ethics and justice.[21] There we had already noted that Levinas is not against thematization as such, nor is he against the objectivity that language can convey; rather, he objects to considering it *the only way* of approaching the relation to the other. In other words, Levinas argues against the understanding of denominative language as the *only* meaning-giving system. If meaning would come through denomination alone, the unthematized would be integrated into a theme, and alterity would be designated *as something*—it would give determination to alterity, thus annulling it.[22] Just as politics needs ethics, to prevent its becoming totalitarianism, Levinas argues that the language of thematization cannot function by itself. Thematizing language needs the an-archical unthematized as its source (yet not origin) of meaning.

Nevertheless, to actually take up in the form of writing the question of the very refusal of thematization, as Levinas does and as we do here, inevitably means that it needs to become, at least to some extent, part of a theme. Now we have reached the core of the problem: the difficulty of thematizing the very impossibility of thematization. The unthematized Saying, the an-archical relation to the other, the subject of substitution, they all constitute themes when we discuss them. Is the entire investigation of all of these problems betraying itself by inscribing itself in the very thing that is against? Levinas is well aware of this problem, and he evokes it several times throughout his writings.[23] However, he also points out that thematizing the

---

[21] See Chapter 4.
[22] "A word is a nomination, as much as a denomination, a consecrating of the 'this as this' or 'this as that,'" OB 36.
[23] Here is an example from *Otherwise than Being*: "The very discussion which we are at this moment elaborating about signification, diachrony and the transcendence of the approach beyond being, a discussion that means to be philosophy, is a thematizing, a synchronizing of terms, a recourse to a systematic language, a constant use of the verb

refusal of thematization becomes a problem only if one continues to think in the logic of thematization, by applying the rules of unifying coherence applicable to a thematizing language.[24] What Levinas is trying to underline is precisely the necessity of interrupting thematization and its rules of coherence, in order to resist its totalizing logic.[25] A critique from the perspective of thematization would miss the whole point of his project. Instead, he aims at interrupting thematization from within, by breaking its logic. Saying is outside the 'game' of concepts, it is outside the 'logic' of the Said.[26] The unthematized refers to an otherwise than thematization and not to its alternative (it is not about thematized vs. unthematized). As such, problematizing its thematization through the "logic" dictated by thematization itself is not an adequate way of posing the problem. Instead, Levinas recognizes the otherwise of thematization not in a different *realm* than the thematized, the Said, but as an interruptive movement in the Said—a movement which, although it does not lead to the Saying (this would make the unthematized a separate realm), nevertheless creates an opening towards its signifyingness. This interruptive movement, in a sense, is a backwards movement, a "reduction" that, as we have previously pointed out, Levinas calls the Unsaying of the Said.[27] In *Otherwise than Being*, he associates the movement of Unsaying with skepticism, because skepticism

---

being, a bringing back into the bosom of being all signification allegedly conceived beyond being. But are we being duped by this subreption? [...] What about our discussion, narrating, as though they were fixed in themes, the anarchy and the non-finality of the subject in which the Infinite would pass?" OB 155.

[24] "But does the coherence that would be lacking in this discussion consist in the immobility of the instant of truth, in its possibility of synchrony? The objection would then presuppose what is in question: the reference of all signification to essence. But our whole purpose was to ask if subjectivity, despite its foreignness to the said, is not stated by an abuse of language through which in the indiscretion of the said everything is shown." OB 155-6.

[25] In this sense, see also Derrida's discussion about the double meaning of the expression "at this very moment," which, Derrida argues, works as an interruptive element in Levinas's text. Jacques Derrida. (1980), "At This Very Moment In This Work Here I Am," trans. Ruben Berezdivin, in *Re-reading Levinas*, eds. Robert Bernasconi and Simon Critchley (Bloomington: Indiana University Press, 1991), 11-48.

[26] "Saying is not a game. Antecedent to the verbal signs it conjugates, to the linguistic systems and the semantic glimmerings, a foreword preceding languages it is the proximity of one to the other, the commitment of an approach, the one for the other, the very signifyingness of signification." OB 5.

[27] See Chapter 4.

would not only problematize its target for doubt, but also its own problematization, its own skepticism.[28] Here skepticism represents a "model" of thinking, the interruption itself, never letting it rest in itself, never in accordance with itself.[29]

> Skepticism then contests the thesis that between the saying and the said the relationship that connects in synchrony a condition with the conditioned is repeated. It is as though skepticism were sensitive to the difference between my exposure without reserve to the other, which is saying, and the exposition or statement of the said in its equilibrium and justice.[30]

Hence, when we discuss sociality in terms of the unthematized relation to the other, an important aspect to keep in mind is that although we indeed problematize sociality, we do not seek to describe a specific realm of existence (or supra-existence). Our analysis is neither descriptive nor prescriptive. By developing the *notion* of sociality we do not intend to create a universal model of sociality (i.e. a universal model of the relation to the other), nor to fall into ideality (i.e. a universal model of how the relation to the other should be). Having acknowledged the problems that result from

---

[28] "As the truth of what does not enter into a theme, it is produced out of time or in two times without entering into either of them, as an endless critique, or skepticism, which in a spiraling movement makes possible the boldness of philosophy, destroying the conjunction into which its saying and its said continually enter. The said, contesting the abdication of the saying that everywhere occurs in this said, thus maintains the diachrony in which, holding its breath, the spirit hears the echo of the *otherwise*.," OB 44; or "The skeptical discourse, which states the rupture, failure, impotence or impossibility of disclosure, would be self-contradictory if the saying and the said were only correlative," Ibid., 168.

[29] In this special potential of skepticism Levinas finds the meaning of philosophy: "Philosophy is not separable from skepticism, which follows it like a shadow it drives off by refuting it again at once on its footsteps. Does not the last word belong to philosophy? Yes, in a certain sense, since for Western philosophy the saying is exhausted in things said. But skepticism in fact makes a difference, and puts an interval between saying and the said. Skepticism is refutable, but it returns.," OB 168. Or, elsewhere: "the philosopher, while thematizing the problematic quality of the *question* as if it were being, can search for its proper original meaning, even if it had to go back, as we have suggested, to the bad conscience of being. The refutation of skepticism, which we have evoked as a model, also operates at the heart of a rationality proper to the knowledge of being, proper to ontology whose regime is already established," "Manner of Speaking" (1980), in OGCM 179. For a discussion on the topic of Levinas and skepticism see for instance Robert Bernasconi, "Skepticism in the face of philosophy," in *Re-reading Levinas*, 149–161.

[30] OB 168.

the universalization and idealization of sociality, we can only use 'concept' or 'notion' in relation to it so long as we strip their meaning from the thematization and universalization that they usually imply. If we look at the etymology of the two words 'concept' and 'notion' and compare them from that perspective, they both seem to carry, in one way or another, what Levinas would consider an imprint of thematization. 'Notion' comes from the Latin 'notionem,' which itself has its roots in the Greek 'ennoias,' meaning 'thought.'[31] 'Concept' derives from the Latin 'conceptum,' from 'concepiere,' meaning 'to hold, grasp together,' expressing quite clearly an appropriative and movement characteristic to thematization. Levinas did not evoke the etymology of these words; neither did he state explicitly whether he has a preference regarding one or another. However, by taking into account the way he uses these two words, we suspect that he prefers 'notion' over 'concept' when referring to his own terminology. In *Otherwise than Being*, for example, he has no problems referring to *the notion* of substitution (*la notion de la Substitution*)[32] or to *the notion* of anarchy (*la notion d'anarchie*),[33] while we know that he thinks both anarchy and substitution in terms outside thematization. On the other hand, and still in the context of substitution, he uses the word 'concept' in order to indicate universality and the outside perspective required by thematization.[34] Taking

---

[31] "Ennoias [...] points immediately to the problem of translating the Hermetic vocabulary of perception, cognition and intuition; especially problematic is the large family of words cognate with the noun nous or 'mind': e.g., noeō, noēma, noēsis, noētos, ennoia, dianoia, pronoia, etc.; and with the noun gnōsis or 'knowledge': e.g., gignōskō, gnōrizō, prognōsis, diagnōsis, etc. The first section of the first discourse, for example, contains four of these words: 'thought' (ennoias), 'thinking' (dianoias), 'know' (gnōnai) and 'understanding' (noēsas). To the materialist Stoics, who influenced Middle Platonists such as Antiochus of Ascalon, ennoia meant a concept derived from sensation, but to other contemporaries of the Hermetic writers, the Valentinian Gnostics, Ennoia was an hypostasis, one member of the first pair (suzugia) of thirty Aeons. The Hermetica treat ennoia as an abstraction, though not in the sense of Stoicism." Brian P. Copenhaver, *Hermetica: The Greek Corpus Hermeticum and the Latin Asclepius* (Cambridge: Cambridge University Press 2002), 96. We would like to note here, that the 'hypostasis' referred above is not understood in the sense in which Levinas uses the word 'hypostasis' (as "the upsurge of an existent in existence," EE 36. We will return to explaining the meaning of 'hypostasis' for Levinas in the next chapter).
[32] OB 113, AE 179.
[33] OB 194, n. 3, AE 160, n. 1.
[34] "The self without a concept (*soi sans concept*), unequal in identity, signifies itself in the first person, setting forth the plane of saying, pro-ducing itself in saying as an ego or as me, that is utterly different from any other ego," OB 115, AE 182.

into consideration Levinas's preference, we are opting to refer to sociality as *notion* (instead of *concept*), while keeping in mind that the core problem does not lie in using one word versus another, but rather in understanding the inescapable necessity of thematization that comes along with language, and that this thematization does not necessarily imply cancelling the unthematized. Levinas explains this necessity early on. He does, however, retain the deeper meaning of the notions he uses, beyond their formal structure:

> The conceptualization of this last refusal of conceptualization is not contemporaneous with this refusal; it transcends this conceptualization.[35]

5.2. The word 'sociality'

There is a tendency evident in Levinas's work to return to the etymological roots of his terminology. A good indication of this tendency is Levinas's quite frequent use of hyphenation to emphasize the original meaning of a word.[36] The etymological reference often carries an instrumental relevance for Levinas in his efforts to provide for his terminology a more refined meaning, and achieve the over-determination engaged by his ethical language.[37] By referring to the etymological roots of his terms, Levinas does

---

[35] OB 127. Nonetheless, we need to keep in mind that this "transcendence" does not elevate the unthematized relation to the other in to a higher realm, replacing the philosophical discourse with a theological or mystical approach. This is pointed out early on in Levinas's writings, for example in his essay from 1951, "Is Ontology Fundamental?": "No theology, no mysticism is concealed behind the analysis I have just given of the meeting with the other" "Is Ontology Fundamental?" (1951), in EN 8.

[36] Among such terms we can find: 'ex-ception' (coming from the Latin 'ex' + 'cipere' and meaning 'to take out'), 'an-archic' (from the Greek 'an'+ 'arche' and meaning 'without-origin' or 'without-principle'), 'diachrony' (from the Greek 'dia'+ 'chronos,' meaning throughout time), 'inter-ested' and 'dis-inter-ested' (from the Latin 'inter' + 'esse' and meaning 'in relation to being' or 'among essence/being'), 'ab-solute' (from the Latin 'ab-solutus' and meaning without relation, 'loosen from'), or, as we have seen, 'sub-ject' (from the Latin 'sub-jectus' and meaning 'thrown beneath' or 'placed beneath') and the list could continue at length.

[37] The turn towards an ethical terminology evolves gradually in Levinas's writings. *Totality and Infinity* already shows clear signs of his intentions in this sense, however, he does not manage to fully accomplish his project. In *Otherwise than Being* we already encounter a much more pronounced refusal to think in terms of negation and relative determinations. This is how he explains what he means by the 'ethical language' in

not dismissively cancel their everyday meaning; rather, he seeks to add new dimensions to them in order to emphasize an overflow of meaning, an excess that cannot be shown directly. Levinas redefines terms through over-determination, but at the same time he is playing on the everyday meaning of the words. His goal is to break with a specific way of thinking that is directed towards determination and presentation. This cannot be attained by one specific break at a specific discursive moment, since this would mean still integrating itself in an order of time, history, and thus, the order of thinking in terms of orders. So, the break that Levinas attempts to make has to be in the form of a constant interruption (the Unsaying of the Said), which on a terminological level shows itself through the slow introduction into the phenomenological discourse inherited from Husserl and Heidegger, of a terminology invested with new, refined meaning. The etymological roots of words contribute to this refinement of meanings, even when their everyday meanings do not completely vanish.[38]

In following Levinas's way of thinking, we need to look at the origins of the meaning of the word 'sociality' we are engaging. Examined from an etymological point of view, the word 'sociality' (*socialité*) comes from the Latin 'socius,' meaning 'companion'[39] in the sense of 'that which goes with'

Otherwise than Being: "The ethical language we have resorted to does not arise out of a special moral experience, independent of the description hitherto elaborated. The ethical situation of responsibility is not comprehensible on the basis of ethics. [...] the tropes of ethical language are found to be adequate for certain structures of the description: for the sense of the approach in its contrast with knowing, the face in its contrast with a phenomenon." OB 120.

[38] As an illustration, we can take the notion expressed by the word 'interest.' As a concept, interest reflects in some sense the usual meaning of the word: being interested in something, or having certain interest in something, receiving profit (any kind of profit). Understood as such, it implies commerce and reciprocity. Then again, through its Latin roots, 'interest' also signifies relatedness to being and essence, inter-esse as 'among being.' Accordingly, Levinas uses it to characterize the subject as it is defined through being (the etymological meaning) and among other subjects (reciprocity). The subject also *is*, it implies being in relation to being– it is what Levinas calls "ego" or "I" (*Moi*)—and at the same time it is together with a multiplicity of egos, in symmetrical and reciprocal relation with each other. (See OB 4.) For the question of dis-interestedness in relation to subjectivity see Chapter 1.

[39] "Socius, -a, -um: qui accompagne; associé avec. Souvent. substantivé: socius, social: compagnon, compagne, associé (e). Dans 1a 1. Du droit public 'allié,' employé surtout au pl. Socio- usité de tout temps.," A. Ernour and A. Meillet, *Dictionnire Etymologique de la Langue Latine* (Paris: Librairie C. Klincksieck, 1951), 1114.

(different from 'that which follows').[40] This etymological root of 'sociality' is shared with a range of other words, such as 'social,' 'sociable' or 'sociableness,' which are closely related, but nonetheless different from 'sociality.' If we decompose the word 'sociality' into 'social"+"ity,' we will have the adjective 'social,' which can also be used as an adverb, and thus expresses the possession of the characteristic of companionship.[41] The suffix '-ity' (or in French '-ité,' or Latin '-itas') found in 'sociality,' indicates not so much a potentiality or 'being capable of,' like the suffix '-able' from 'sociable,'[42] nor the nominalized form of having a capacity, as in, for example, the suffix '-ability' from 'sociability,'[43] but rather an 'already' state,[44] where the moment of origin has passed. In this sense, it is quite different both from an added characteristic, as an adjective would indicate (like in the case of 'social'), and from a certain aptitude (as 'sociable' or 'sociability' would suggest).

As we can see etymologically, the word 'sociality' indicates an already found companionship rather than an added characteristic or a possessed capacity. In this sense, sociality should be differentiated from a specific attribute or certain ability, both of which presuppose a previous subject or verb to which the attribute or ability would be attached. This understanding

---

[40] The latin 'socius' has no relationship with 'sequor': "Les Latins n'on jamais songé à établir une parenté entre sequor et socius. Socius n'est pas 'celui qui suit' mais 'celui qui va avec,' cf. Cic. Font. 17, 39 uitae social uirtus, mortis comes gloria," Ibid.,1115.

[41] In time it gained the more specific meaning of characterizing living together in society and nowadays it is clearly associated with society. This is reflected by the way it is defined for instance in the Oxford Dictionary, where the first entry is "connected with society," *Oxford Dictionary,* ed. Sally Wehmeier, Oxford University Press, 2005 [seventh edition]), 1452.

[42] "- able *also* -ible *adj suffix* [ME, fr. OF. fr. L *-abilis, -ibilis,* fr. -a-, -i- (thematic vowels of various conjugations of verbs) + *-bilis* capable or worthy of (being acted upon)] 1: capable of, fit for, or worthy of (being so acted upon or towards)—chiefly in adjectives derived from verbs <break*able*> <connect*ible*> <eat*able*> <lov*able*> 2 : tending to, given to, favoring, causing, able to, or liable to <agree*able*> <change*able*> <knowledge*able*> <peace*able*> <perish*able*>—-ableness *n suffix* -ES—*ably also* -ibly *adv suffix.*," *A Dictionary of Prefixes, Suffixes, and Combining Forms from Webster's Third New International Dictionary, Unabridged,* (Springfield: Merriam-Webster, 2002), 1.

[43] "-ability also -ibility n suffix -ES [ME, -ablete, -abilite, -iblete, -ibilite, fr. MF -ableté, -abilité, -ibleté, -ibilité, fr. L -abilitas, -ibilitas, fr. -abilis, -ibilis + tas -ty] : capacity, fitness, or tendency to act or be acted on in a (specified) way <ensil*ability*> <wash*ability*>," ibid.,1.

[44] "- ity *n suffix* -ES [ME -*ite,* fr. OF or L; OF -*ité,* fr. L -*itat-, -itas,* fr. -*i*- (thematic or, rarely, connective vowel) + *-tat-, -tas -ty*] : quality : state : degree <asinin*ity*> <theatrical*ity*>," ibid., 29.

of sociality indeed coincides well with the meaning of the unthematized relation to the other and its major role in thinking subjectivity that were examined in previous chapters. According to that discussion, the unthematized relation, just as the etymological meaning of sociality suggests, does not represent something taken on by an already constituted subject. We can say that, according to its etymological meaning, sociality needs to be thought in terms of an-archy, without being grounded in a pre-established subject. We reinforce this an-archical aspect of sociality in the next chapters, when discussing the presence and absence of sociality in Levinas's work.

The Presence and Absence of Sociality in Levinas's Early- and Middle-period Works

In several of his later essays, Levinas claims that his philosophical project is guided by the question of sociality.[1] Despite these rather general claims, the somewhat basic but at the same time necessary question regarding what he actually means by sociality remains problematic. Levinas has worked with his very specific terminology, where the word 'sociality' is less prominent—most probably due to his intention of distancing his philosophical discourse from sociological theories, as seen in the previous chapter. As a consequence, throughout his writings, Levinas often pursues his self-proclaimed principle project (i.e. the question of sociality) by means of other notions; one can say that Levinas emphasizes sociality without addressing directly its meaning. Thus, the meaning that a notion of sociality might carry is somehow always in sight, yet not directly brought forth; the notion of sociality is at once present and yet surprisingly absent from Levinas's writings.

Readings of Levinas usually do not try to compensate for Levinas's deficient elucidation of what he means by sociality. Despite the abundant discussion of different topics of Levinas's philosophy, works dedicated exclusively to explaining what sociality means are hard to find, and only a few studies focus explicitly on its importance for Levinas's philosophy in general.[2] Undoubtedly, the fact that Levinas's writings offer no systematic or

---

[1] See for example "From the One to the Other" (1983), in EN 148. "Diachrony and representation" (1985), in TO 109, and an interview from 1985 conducted by Anne-Catherine Benchelah, "The Proximity of the Other" (1986), in IIRB 215.

[2] Studies emphasizing the notion of sociality in particular include, for example Harold A. Durfee, "War, Politics and Radical Pluralism," *Philosophy for Phenomenological Research*, 35, no. 4 (1975): 549–558, Paul Formosa, "Levinas and the Definition of Philosophy: An Ethical Approach," *Crossroads* 1, no.1 (2006): 36–45, or Robert Bernasconi and Stacy

consistent account in this respect contributes to this lack in the secondary literature.[3] This not only leaves the meaning of the notion open to divergent interpretations, but also diverts the readers' focus towards other notions, much more frequent in Levinas's texts, such as the notion of the other, of ethics, of alterity, of transcendence, etc. No wonder, then, that these are the notions that have become more dominant in the Levinas scholarship, leaving sociality misleadingly marginal.

The following two chapters address the question: what then, is it that we can understand by 'sociality' if we want to stay close to Levinas's thought? The discussion will be guided by the actual occurrences of the word 'sociality' in Levinas's writings,[4] without however limiting our investigation only to examining these occurrences. We will explore the different contexts in which Levinas discusses sociality, in an attempt to reveal the different ways sociality as a complex notion appears in Levinas's work, beyond 'sociality' as a mere word.

From early on it becomes clear that the contexts in which Levinas discusses sociality are highly influenced by the different temporal periods of his work. In this chapter we start by focusing on Levinas's early and mid-period works. We argue that Levinas, in his early works, approaches sociality through the topics of time and death (here we will focus on *Existence and Existents* [1947] and *Time and the Other* [1947]), while in the mid-period works, sociality is connected to the welcoming of the face and to radical multiplicity (as in *Totality and Infinity* [1961]). Although already at this stage Levinas problematizes the de-position of the subject, he does this in an underdeveloped manner, hence the quest opened up by this chapter will continue into the next, where we take a closer look at Levinas's later work.

Keltner, "Emmanuel Levinas: The Phenomenology of Sociality and the Ethics of Alterity," in *Phenomenological Approaches to Moral Philosophy: A Handbook*, ed. John Drummond (Dordrecht: Kluwer, 2002) 249–268. Nevertheless, neither of them have as their goal the undertaking of a thorough analysis of the notion as such.

[3] For example, at some occasions, Levinas refers to 'multiple sociality' belonging to justice (See "The Other, Utopia and Justice" [1988], in EN 227, 230) while most of the time, as we will see, sociality expresses an unthematized relation.

[4] In identifying these occurrences we have consulted Cristian Ciocan and Georges Hansel, *Levinas Concordance* (Dordrecht: Springer, 2005).

6.1. "Existence and Existents" and "Time and the Other"

Existence and Existents (1947) is perhaps the earliest work in which Levinas engages the topic of sociality, although it does not appear to constitute the main focus of the book. *Existence and Existents* is framed around the question of existence without existents—a neutral and anonymous form of Being that Levinas calls *il y a* (there is)[5]—and around the particular event by which *il y a* turns into the Being of a being,[6] the event of *hypostasis*.[7] Levinas wants to emphasize from the start the adherence of the existent to existence, whilst keeping the difference between existence and existents, and thus without turning their relation into a tautology. In the discussions of fatigue, insomnia, lassitude, and indolence that run through the book, Levinas describes different states in which adherence to the existence of the existent, in a paradoxical way, appears like a "cleaving."[8] These states are exceptional

---

[5] Here, it is important to note that the Levinasian *il y a* (or "there is" in the English translation) should not be confused with the Heideggerian *es gibt*. For Heidegger, *es gibt* does not mean generality, and Levinas knows this very well. He is quite explicit about making this differentiation between the *il y a* and Heidegger's *es gibt* in an interview from 1986. (see "Interview with François Poirié" [1986], in IIRB 45.) Richard Cohen argues that *il y a* has been called the "elemental" in *Totality and Infinity* (see TO 46, translator's note 15.) However, we can only partly agree with this interpretation since in *Totality and Infinity*, *il y a* appears as the neutrality in a prolongation of the elemental, and not as its synonym (See TI 142). On the topic of the *il y a* and the elemental see also John Sallis article, "Levinas and the Elemental," in *Radicalizing Levinas*, eds. Peter Atterton and Matthew Calarco (Albany: SUNY Press, 2010), 87–95.

[6] Here we follow the classic translation in English of the Heideggerian differentiation between the verb 'Sein' and 'Seiende' with 'Being' and respectively 'being.' In French this corresponds to 'être' and 'étant.' However, sometimes in Levinas's vocabulary the Heideggerian ontological difference appears as the difference between 'existence' and 'existent,' without any added existential meaning (see for example TO 44).

[7] Hypostasis marks the position of the self, its ground in its existence. "An existent must be in act, even when it is inactive. This activity of inactivity is not a paradox; it is the act of positing oneself on ground, it is rest inasmuch as rest is not a pure negation but this very tension of a position, the bringing about of a *here*. The fundamental activity of rest, foundation, conditioning, thus appears to be the very relationship with being, the upsurge of an existent into existence, a hypostasis. This entire essay intends only to draw out the implications of this fundamental situation," EE 36. Due to the positioning that it implies, Levinas connects the hypostasis with light, knowledge and consciousness: "Light, knowing and consciousness appeared to constitute the very event of a hypostasis," EE 51.

[8] EE 22. This cleaving is sometime described by Levinas as an "abyss," or "void" (ibid., 71), where the self has no position, and everything becomes indistinguishable. One can

in the way that they bring to the surface the separation between existence and existent, and, at the same time, the impossibility for the existent of escaping its existence; in this sense, they break down the oppositions brought by thinking in terms of contradicting counterparts.

The topic of sociality is introduced only towards the end of the book, and at first glance, it does not seem to be a central topic. Nonetheless, it occupies an important role in relation to Levinas's overall project, of which he never really loses sight. In this sense, it is important to consider the preface to *Existence and Existents*, in which the author outlines not only the more specific topic of this particular book, but also his general project: the emphasis on otherwise than Being[9]—the same "otherwise" that ultimately leads Levinas to formulate a de-posed subjectivity, which, as we have seen in the earlier chapters, opens up an inside-out dimension in thinking my relation (without relation) to the other. Later on, in 1978, when Levinas writes the preface to the second edition of *Existence and Existents*, he makes it even clearer that the overall importance given to sociality transpires already in this early book.[10] As Levinas explains in this second preface, the Ego (*le Moi*) only reveals itself in the proximity of the other, in the asymmetry of the relation to the other.[11] In this sense, the hypostasis, as the

---

easily recognize in this description many similarities with the way Blanchot describes "the other night," which can be interpreted as the indeterminacy that does not have sense in itself, yet gives sense to determination. (See Maurice Blanchot, *The Space of Literature* [1955], trans. Ann Smock [Lincoln, London: University of Nebraska Press, 1982], 163–4). Although this leads our thoughts towards Levinas's notion of de-position, the "no position" of the *il y a* from *Existence and Existents* is more a dispersion (everywhere becomes the position) rather than a de-position.

[9] "The Platonic formula that situates the Good beyond Being serves as the general guideline for this research — but does not make up its content. It signifies that the movement which leads an existent toward the Good is not a transcendence by which that existent raises itself up to a higher existence, but a departure from Being and from the categories which describes it: an ex-cendence. But excendence and the Good necessarily have a foothold in Being, and that is why Being is better than non-Being. The theme of the present work is limited to this position in Being. Our exposition cannot, however, hide the perspectives within which it is situated, and it constantly anticipates developments reserved for a subsequent work.," EE 15, translation slightly altered (DEE 9)

[10] "Préface à la deuxième édition" (1978), in DEE 11–12.

[11] Although in this short preface we find "proximity" involved in the discussion of Levinas's early works, proximity is actually a concept that is predominantly found in Levinas's later works (we will return to it in the next section). It is interesting to see that he also turns to proximity, or "distance-proximity" as he calls it, in his second preface written in 1979 for *Time and the Other* (1947) (see "Preface" [1979], in TO 32.). For us,

upsurge of existent into existence, already makes "social exteriority," by which Levinas designates "the exteriority of the other," an "original form of exteriority."[12] That is to say, the very de-neutralization of the neutral *il y a* in hypostasis, the singularity of the ego, is given through the relation to the other.[13] This relation to alterity, and with it the "original sociality" that shows its significance through the de-neutralization of the hypostasis, is approached in *Existence and Existents* in connection to temporality.[14]

To engage the topic of sociality via the question of temporality is characteristic of Levinas's early work, and indeed this is exactly how he approaches sociality in *Time and the Other* (1947), originally published the same year as *Existence and Existent*. Here, the discussion that began in *Existence and Existents* deepens and, in this sense, it seems reasonable to consider, from now on, the two works together. Levinas, like many others of that period, criticizes the conception of time as equivalent instants linked up together by a stable *I*; according to him, this kind of conception would represent only the time of "economic life."[15] Time is not a movement in the sense of a fusion of instants, and it is not duration either, for duration starts

---

this reinforces the argument of the next chapter according to which Levinas's approach to sociality changes in time, becoming more and more connected to proximity as his work matures.

[12] "Social exteriority is an original form of exteriority and takes us beyond the categories of unity and multiplicity which are valid for things, that is, are valid in the world of an isolated subject, a solitary mind." EE 95. We observe here that Levinas frames the question of "social exteriority" in terms of origin. On the one hand, this is due to the very character of hypostasis: it is an "upsurge" and positioning, it designates originarity. Thus, the exteriority that it refers to is also stated in terms of origin, as it is viewed through the problematic of the hypostasis (thought in terms of origin). On the other hand, *Existence and Existents* is one of Levinas's early works where he was not preoccupied with the problem of an-archy. As we have seen in a previous footnote, regarding *Existence and Existents* Levinas himself stated: "The theme of the present work is limited to this position in Being." EE 15.

[13] In Levinas's later work, this idea is revealed in terms of non-place or null-side of subjectivity (discussed already in Chapter 1): "Our inquiry concerned with the *otherwise than being* catches sight, in the very hypostasis of a subject, its subjectification, of an exception; a null-site on the hither side of the negativity which is always speculatively recuperable, an *outside* of the absolute which can no longer be stated in terms of being." OB 17–8.

[14] "Préface à la deuxième édition" (1978), in DEE 12.

[15] EE 92.

from the self and remains within the self.[16] The subject is not a substratum carried through time, but is rather the very becoming in time, "the *subject* of its own becoming."[17] This is something that Husserl and Heidegger would have easily agreed with; yet, what Levinas reproaches in their manner of thinking time and subjectivity is their emphasis on solitude and that they consider the instant of indeterminacy (the renewal and indefiniteness of time) in terms of a nothingness that, according to Levinas, remains connected to the subject and to Being.[18] Levinas argues for thinking nothingness (here understood as the undisclosed indeterminacy of time) in a way that does not refer back to Being and the subject. The nothingness of the subject's time cannot be produced in the subject, not even as negativity;[19] it cannot have the subject as its own source. Time implies a renewal, it implies hope; it entails a non-determination of the future, and a re-birth of the *I* "the exigency for the non-definitive."[20] This is where the importance of sociality comes in. The other (*autrui*), outside myself, gives the alterity of the future; it assures the mystery of the future and my constant re-birth as a subject; "the relationship to the other is a relationship with Mystery," says Levinas.[21] Here "mystery" does not designate an unknown entity, but the unknowable, that is to say, the non-definitive and the non-definable, resistance to determination. In this way, the question of time becomes the question of the relation to the other, and temporality turns out to be directly connected with sociality.[22] Through

---

[16] We can recall here how for Bergson there was an *intuition* of duration tightly linked to the self. (see Part I).

[17] EE 97. Later on, in *Totality and Infinity,* Levinas suggests, possibly referring to Bergson's philosophy, that a philosophy of becoming goes beyond Being because in it manages to "envisage being outside the existent," TI 275.

[18] In this sense, Levinas makes an explicit reference to Heidegger in EE 94–95, and an implicit one to both Heidegger and Husserl, in TO 74–5.

[19] "[N]othingness necessary to time, which the subject cannot produce," Levinas says, "comes from the social relationship." EE 94. Here, "social relationship" expresses the same as sociality. This synonym is reoccurring in *Totality and Infinity* (where sometimes sociality carries the name "plurality" or "radical multiplicity," an aspect that we will discuss later on).

[20] EE 93.

[21] TO 75.

[22] EE 94.

time, Levinas explains in *Existence and Existents,* the self "recommences as other (*autre*)."[23]

We find a similar link between time and sociality in *Time and the Other*, with the difference that there Levinas reframes the problematic of the nothingness of the unknowable, or the indeterminacy of time, and relates it to the question of death. Instead of alterity in the form of hope, birth and renewal, as it appears in *Existence and Existents*, in *Time and the Other* we find alterity as the mystery of death. Resisting Heidegger's approach to death as Dasein's utmost possibility, Levinas instead understands death as a relation with the absolute other, an inassimilable alterity.[24] In this way, for Levinas, death breaks solitude, and existence is from the very start pluralist, not as a plurality of existents, but as the mystery of death, which introduces alterity in solitude.[25] Thus, sociality is approached here as the pluralism that interrupts solitude, through the problematic of death. We should mention that, here, solitude does not mean singularity, but is the bond, the chain that ties the self to itself; the "definite character of my very existence," that "I am forever stuck with myself."[26] Solitude can be seen as synonymous with the uninterrupted inwardness that forms a totality; it is a totality, on the one hand, on account of its uninterruptedness, and, on the other hand, on account of its "definite character," its determinacy.[27] This inwardness or

---

[23] EE 93. We find the idea of the mystery of the future as alterity, the renewal or re-birth of the subject, to be developed by Levinas in *Totality and Infinity* in the form of fecundity (to be discussed in Part III).

[24] In this sense, for Levinas, death is not a possibility, but precisely the "moment where we are no longer *able to be able* (*nous ne 'pouvons plus pouvoir'*)" (TO 74.), the impossibility of possibility. Regarding a comparison between Heidegger's and Levinas's approach on death and possibility see Tina Chanter, "Levinas and Impossible Possibility: Thinking Ethics with Rosenzweig and Heidegger in the Wake of the Shoah," *Research in Phenomenology* 28 (1998): 91–110. Later on, as his work matures, Levinas shifts the emphasis from death as such to the death of the other, an approach very similar to that which we find in Blanchot's thought, and which we will address in Part III. This shift goes hand in hand with the development of thinking the de-posed subjectivity: my death becomes less important as the very core of the self is not the I, but *me* in relation without relation to the other.

[25] TO 74–5.

[26] EE 84.

[27] In *Totality and Infinity*, Levinas designates this totality as "the Same," whereas solitude, as we have seen, takes the more positive meaning of resistance to relativeness (through separateness). Later on, solitude takes the form of "self folding back upon itself" (see for example OB 25.), meant to express the attachment of the self to itself,

solitude that Levinas describes is very different from the inside-out dimension of the relation to the other. The hither side, which becomes more and more emphasized in Levinas's later work, does not enclose the self in solitude, because it is an open inside, an inside-out; it "hollows out the dimension of inwardness."[28] The inside-out dimension denotes precisely the interruption of solitude and brings forth the interrupted self as "*me.*" This movement of interruption, which is not defined in temporal terms but as the very temporalization of time,[29] is indicated already in Levinas's early work, where sociality as the interruption of solitude is not only connected to the problematic of death and time, but becomes a key element in thinking time. Levinas goes so far as to say that sociality is time itself, time as precisely the "out of time" of diachrony:

> Is not sociality something more than the source of our representation of time: is it not time itself? If time is constituted by my relationship with the other, it is exterior to my instant, but it is also something else than an object given to contemplation.[30]

Through its connection to temporality, which we find in both *Existence and Existents* and *Time and the Other*, sociality represents not just a mere component in the structure of subjectivity, but the very core of the subject; only through sociality can we think temporality, and thus, subjectivity.[31] This is a very important point, one that indicates that already at this early stage Levinas is presenting ideas similar to those that, more than twenty years later, he will develop in terms of substitution and the other-in-the-same.

Towards the very end of both *Time and the Other* and *Existence and Existents*, Levinas engages more deeply the topic of sociality. There, he emphasizes a sociality that is characterized by immediacy and the refusal of fusion. These two characteristics are closely related to one another. The alterity of the other is mysterious, it has nothing to share, and the relation has no mediator. In this way, sociality is an *immediate* relation, refusing any kind of mediation that would ultimately unite the self and the other under a

---

without interruption; where the self is self *for itself*. (Earlier, in Chapter 1, we have explained the meaning of the *for itself* and *for the other*.)
[28] "Enigma and Phenomenon" (1965), in BPW 74.
[29] See Chapter 2.
[30] EE 93–4.
[31] Or, in Levinas's words, "The 'personality' of a being is its very need for time," EE 93.

common mediator that would lead to fusion. Sociality refuses any kind of unifying principle: "It is neither struggle, nor fusion, or knowledge,"[32] says Levinas. The importance of the immediacy of sociality becomes clear in the critique of Heidegger's *Miteinandersein* that is found in both *Existence and Existents*[33] and *Time and the Other*.[34] Levinas identifies Heidegger's version of sociality with *Miteinandersein*, or being-with-one-another, and argues that it is "completely found in the solitary subject" (solitary, in the above-mentioned sense). Moreover, according to Levinas, in using the word "with" Heidegger introduces a shared, common element into sociality and turns it into a mediated relation.

> One thinks that my relationship with the other tends to identify me with him by immersing me in a collective representation, a common ideal or a common action. It is the collectivity which says "we" that feels the other to be alongside of oneself, and not facing one. And a collectivity is necessarily set up around a third term which serves as intermediary, which supplies what is common in the communion. Heidegger's *Miteinandersein* also remains a collectivity of the with, and it is around truth that its authentic form is found. It is a collectivity formed around something common. And like in all philosophies of communion, in Heidegger sociality is completely found in the solitary subject. The analysis of Dasein, in its authentic form, is carried out in terms of solitude.[35]

Besides the explicit critique of Heidegger, two further important and interrelated points can be seen in the above quotation: on the one hand, the critique of the "collectivity which says 'we,'" or "collectivity of the with," exhibits Levinas's problem with thinking sociality in terms of 'being-with'; and on the other hand, through this critique, Levinas opens up the problematic of the face-to-face relation.

Regarding the first of these points, the question of sociality in terms of 'being-with,' we need to consider Levinas's argument that the 'with' takes up the role of a mediator and a third term. This implies fusion, which is only possible through a perspective from outside the relation; fusion annuls

---

[32] TO 88.
[33] EE 94–96.
[34] TO 93.
[35] EE 94–5. In *Totality and Infinity*, Levinas appears to engage again in criticizing Heidegger's *Miteinandersein*, only this time he views it as a coexistence in the form of "we" prior to the I and the other. "[F]or Heidegger intersubjectivity is a coexistence, a we prior to the I and the other, a neutral intersubjectivity. The face-to-face both announces a society, and permits the maintaining of a separated I." TI 68.

alterity and is a consequence of the shared third term.[36] According to Levinas, thinking sociality as a "with" would only solidify solitude instead of (dis)solving it. Although he never had the chance to discuss Nancy's version of "being-with" (which also has its starting point in Heidegger's Miteinandersein),[37] Levinas's critique of the "with" invites us to investigate the way in which it might apply to Nancy's philosophy. Would Levinas's comments on sociality as "being-with" go against Nancy's way of thinking community? Or, on the contrary, could it be that Nancy's community *without* a shared common is in line with Levinas's thoughts on sociality resisting fusion? We will return to this question later on. For now, let it suffice to keep in mind Levinas's refusal to think sociality as a common in communion, a collectivity with another that is 'alongside of oneself.'

This leads us to the second point that comes into focus in the above quotation: the critique of the "collectivity of the with" makes Levinas propose the face-to-face relation as an alternative to being side by side of one another. Just a few lines later, Levinas introduces the face-to-face encounter:

> To this collectivity of comrades we contrast the I-you collectivity which precedes it. It is not a participation in a third term — intermediate person, truth, dogma, work, profession, interest, dwelling, or meal; that is, it is not a communion. It is the fearful face-to-face situation of a relationship without intermediary, without mediations.[38]

At this point, both in *Existence and Existents* and *Time and the Other*,[39] the meaning of sociality is getting closer to the meaning of the face-to-face

---

[36] Further comments on his critique of the "with" from *Time and the Other* are given by Levinas during his conversation with Philip Nemo: "What is formulated here [Time and the Other] is the putting into question of this *with*, as a possibility of escaping solitude. Does "existing with" represents a veritable sharing of existence? How is this sharing realized? Or again (for the word "sharing" would signify that existence is of the order of having): Is there a participation in being which makes us escape from solitude?" EI 58.

[37] See for example Jean-Luc Nancy, *Being Singular Plural* (1996), trans. Robert D. Richardson and Anne E. O'Byrne (Stanford: Stanford University Press, 2000).

[38] EE 95.

[39] There is a similar passage in *Time and the Other*, where Levinas describes the relationship with the future as the face-to-face: "Relationship with the future, the presence of the future in the presence, seems all the same accomplished in the face-to-face with the Other. The situation of the face-to-face would be the very accomplishment of time." TO 79.

relation, which Levinas develops in *Totality and Infinity*. Thus, now we need to continue our investigation with this work, which dates from 1961.

6.2. "Totality and Infinity"

By now, we can see that in *Time and the Other* and *Existence and Existents* Levinas frequently approached sociality in negative terms: it is *not* fusion, it is *not* mediated, it is *not* a shared collectivity. Levinas himself notices that the question of sociality in his early works is dominated by negative terms, and he struggled to find a solution to this problem.[40] If he really wants to avoid relativeness, Levinas needs to change the negative definitions, he needs to change his vocabulary.[41] Eventually, as his work matures, he manages to change his terminology in a way that approaches sociality positively. As we are about to see, starting with his mid-period work, *Totality and Infinity* (1961), sociality begins to appear in a somewhat different formulation. Levinas himself, in his 1982 interview with Philip Nemo, claims that *Totality and Infinity* is the turning point towards a more positive approach of sociality:

> Totality and Infinity is my first book that goes in that direction. It aims to pose the problem of intersubjective relationship's content. For what we have said up to now is only negative. What positively does this "sociality" different from total and additive sociality consist in?[42]

---

[40] In *Existence and Existents* Levinas already tries to give positivity to sociality through its very negativity: its "the failure of communication," he says, "constitutes the positive character of the relationship." EE 95. Nevertheless, one might wonder whether "failure" manages to express something positive, as long as it refers to a loss (the loss of the capacity to communicate). Is this truly the escape from the relativity given by negation? Levinas himself does not seem to be satisfied by this solution either, as he gradually changes the "failure" of communication to the "overflow" or "surplus" of meaning that, as we will see becomes characteristic to sociality in *Totality and Infinity*.
[41] For Levinas's comments about his terminological change see "The Paradox of Morality: An Interview with Emmanuel Levinas" (1986), in *The Provocation of Levinas*, 170–1.
[42] EI 79–80. The "total and additive" sociality to which Levinas refers in the quotation signifies the understanding of sociality, on the one hand, as fusion and ultimately forming a totality, and on the other hand, as collective formed through addition. We have already seen from Levinas's early works that he wants to depart from both of these

Instead of constantly showing us that which sociality resists, Levinas now brings forth sociality as an overflow of meaning, as a "surplus," a formulation that clearly carries more positivity.[43] The word "surplus," expresses an overflow without being a missed containment. This overflow of meaning and the positivity it carries are characteristic of Levinas's terminological over-determination that we have already discussed. The over-determination is well illustrated by two ways of approaching sociality in *Totality and Infinity*: *radical multiplicity* and the *welcome of the face* (*l'accueil du visage*).

We are already familiar with the expression *radical multiplicity* from Chapter 3. There, we showed that, by radicalizing the notion of multiplicity, Levinas is attempting to overcome a thinking of multiplicity exclusively in simple terms of quantifiable plurality. Radical multiplicity breaks up relatedness by going beyond the singular/plural and other/others alternatives. In this way, it is not a mere opposition to singularity; it seeks neither to reach a supreme union, nor to dissolve separateness. In other words, radical multiplicity manages to express the resistance to fusion and the refusal to think multiplicity merely in terms of additive collectivity, aspects which described sociality in Levinas's early works. Thus, the resistance to fusion that characterized sociality in *Existence and Existents*, finds its correspondence in *Totality and Infinity* in the notion of radical multiplicity. However now, through the positivity that radical multiplicity introduces on a terminological level, sociality is no longer thought in negative terms, and in this way it escapes co-determination and thinking in alternatives. This is a very important step in thinking sociality, one which reveals the great change brought by Levinas's radicalization of multiplicity: it breaks down thinking multiplicity (and thus sociality) in terms of singular and plural alternatives. Just as radical multiplicity cannot be reduced to a dyad, so sociality is not between two. Sociality is neither limited to a dyad, nor is it a

ways of understanding sociality. Here, it is also noteworthy that Levinas uses the words 'intersubjective relationship' and 'sociality' as synonyms. This can be quite confusing, since intersubjectvity, through its "inter," seems to imply reciprocity, something that Levinas would like to exclude from the relation without relation of sociality. We encounter similar confusions in terminology in the case of 'pluralism,' 'radical multiplicity,' or 'social relationship'—all of them occasionally being used interchangeably with the word 'sociality.' Regardless of the different ways of expression, the contexts themselves suggest quite clearly that Levinas refers to the same notion, that of sociality.

[43] "The impossibility of total reflection must not be posited negatively [...] but rather as the surplus of the social relation," TI 221.

triad, tetrad and so on. Instead, sociality as radical multiplicity is outside the very alternatives of dyad, triad, tetrad, etc.

By going beyond singular/plural alternatives, sociality is not part of a dialectical couple of multiplicity/singularity. Singularity is retained, despite multiplicity, in the form of uniqueness. Moreover, this very uniqueness emerges as multiplicity without being confused with it. This strange setting sounds familiar for us from *Time and the Other*, where we saw that alterity introduces plurality in temporality, which, in its turn, is the very becoming of the subject in the form of the subject as becoming. Ultimately, one can say that in Levinas's work from both early- and mid-period, the singularity of the subject takes the form of uniqueness, which is given through sociality. Multiplicity and singularity, instead of being counterparts, are thought together in the form of sociality and uniqueness. In our discussions of subjectivity and radical multiplicity we showed that this paradox of uniqueness and multiplicity reflects the inside-out dimension of the relation to the other. This means that sociality needs to be approached from the hither side, and in *Totality and Infinity* Levinas indeed addresses this hither side through the face-to-face (*face à face*) relation.[44] We have seen that towards the end of *Existence and Existents* Levinas equates sociality with the face-to-face encounter. In *Totality and Infinity* this tendency is strengthened. In the latter, the face-to-face relation is presented as a relation "in which the interlocutor presents himself as absolute being (that is, as being withdrawn from the categories)."[45] We have seen already how Levinas emphasizes the etymological reading of ab-solute, with its literal sense of 'without relatedness.' When we apply this etymological meaning to the above quotation, we find that Levinas is considering 'categorization' as the relational link that would mediate between the 'interlocutors' of the face-to-face. For Levinas, mediation goes against the very meaning of the face-to-face relation, which needs to remain immediate: "The immediate is the face to face," he says,[46] just a few pages later describing the face-to-face as "straightforwardness itself."[47] Sociality as the face-to-face relation, in *Totality and Infinity* just as in *Existence and Existents*, has the role of replacing the collectivity of sharing *something* as the only way of approaching the relation to the other;

---

[44] TI 251.
[45] Ibid., 71.
[46] Ibid., 52.
[47] Ibid., 78.

that is to say, it replaces the 'side by side one another,' with a being directed 'face to face.' In this way, we discover the face-to-face relation to be an expression of the hither side, what we have called the inside-out dimension, the unthematized relation that corresponds to sociality.

We acknowledge Levinas's intention of bringing forth the unthematized relation through the face-to-face, and the asymmetry that it implies. In this sense it seems reasonable to understand sociality as the face-to-face relation. However, the expression itself, 'face to face' raises suspicions on our part for at least two reasons: on the one hand, if we look at the context, we can read this association as a mere reaction to thinking sociality as additive 'side by side 'collectivity. On the other hand, the face-to-face relation seems to remain compromised by a thinking in dualities, since the expression itself suggests the face-to-face meeting of two persons. To think sociality as a dyad, as the face-to-face relation seems to suggest, goes against the inside-out dimension that the hither side stands for, by bringing in an outside perspective upon the relation itself, and with it the differentiation between singular/plural, other/others.[48] We will return to this argument in more detail in the next chapter. In a similar vein, we cannot agree with those commentators who place too much emphasis on sociality as the face-to-face. Examples of such readings are easy to find: it will suffice simply to recall the suggestive title of one of the first collections of essays that interpreted Levinas's writings: "Face to Face with Levinas" (1985).[49] In the following, we will show that in *Totality and Infinity*, although the face-to-face relation is still strongly present, sociality is also connected with the 'welcome of the face.' We favor this latter expression, instead of the face-to-

---

[48] Levinas risks thinking in terms of duality not only when he emphasizes sociality as the face-to-face relation, but also when he describes the other in opposition with the self, as he does, surprisingly, in *Existence and Existent* ("The other as other is not only an alter ego. He is what I am not," EE 95), repeating the same gesture in *Time and the Other* ("The Other as Other is not only an alter ego: the Other is what myself am not," TO 83), or even when he over-emphasizes the Same/Other distinction, as he does in *Totality and Infinity*. We will return to this problem in Part III.

[49] *Face to Face with Levinas*, ed. Richard A. Cohen (Albany: SUNY Press, 1985). Although sociality as such is not very often discussed in the literature, the face-to-face relation is prioritized from early on in the interpretative writings. Other examples where sociality is explicitly thought in terms of face-to-face relation are to be found in John Drabinski, "The Possibility of an Ethical Politics" [2000], in *Emmanuel Levinas. Critical Assessments of Leading Philosophers*, Vol 4: *Beyond Levinas*, edited by Claire Katz and Lara Trout. (New York: Routledge, 2005), 188–212, or Seán Hand, *Emmanuel Levinas. Routledge Critical Thinkers* (London: Routledge, 2009).

face relation, since in our view it points more clearly in the direction of an an-archical openness towards the other.

Our suspicions regarding the face-to-face relation do not imply that we wish to give less importance to the face, as Dermot Moran does, for example. Moran provides quite a harsh critique of the 'face' in Levinas's philosophy, a critique that leads him to the dismissal of a philosophy that would be based on the 'face.'[50] Contrary to Moran's view, we would like to insist here that placing less emphasis on the face-to-face relation does not automatically imply doubting the importance of 'the face.' We might speculate, indeed, that Levinas himself, in time, became uncertain in regard to the expression 'face-to-face,' and that this is the reason behind the seldom use of it in *Otherwise than Being*, for example. Nonetheless, the notion of the face as such remains important for him throughout the years. Therefore, if we are attempting to understand and place emphasis on 'the welcome of the face,' we will need first of all to understand the meaning of 'the face.'

First, let us note that Levinas discusses *the face* (*le visage*) in more than physical terms. The face does not represent the agglomeration of physical features. Indeterminacy, crucial for Levinas's conception of alterity, remains important when it comes to the problem of the face. The face is not a disclosure, but rather an exposure, says Levinas, it is nudity.[51] The face is denuded not only of its physical characteristics, but also from its cultural or other contextual determination. In this sense, nudity has similar meaning to the sense of the ab-solute that Levinas has developed.[52] The face as nudity,

---

[50] Here is an excerpt of his argument: "Does a fish have a face, or an amoeba? Does a human embryo in the womb have a face? Levinas admits he is not able to give an account or set limits to the ascription of face: 'I cannot say at what moment you have the right to be called face.' But surely this is an extraordinarily serious admission. For Levinas, morality is a response to the face. If I don't see something as having a face, it has no call on me and I have no responsibility towards it. Then, surely, how one accords face is crucial. If there is no account of this, it is hardly a philosophy of the face at all," Dermot Moran, *Introduction to Phenomenology* (London and New York: Routledge, 2000), 350.

[51] "Peace and Proximity" (1984), in BPW 167.

[52] "The nudity of the face is a destitution without any cultural ornament, an absolution—a detaching in the midst of its very production. A face enters our world from an absolutely alien sphere—that is, precisely out of an absoluteness, which in fact is the name for fundamental strangeness." "The Trace of the Other" (1963), 352.

nakedness, denuded, is a re-occurring theme in Levinas's work. We find this thought already in *Totality and Infinity*:

> The nakedness of the face is not what is presented to me because I disclose it, what would therefore be presented to me, to my powers, to my eyes, to my perceptions, in a light exterior to it. The face has turned to me—and this is its very nudity. It *is* by itself and not by reference to a system.[53]

Levinas remains faithful to the indeterminacy of the face throughout the years. At the same time, he clarifies that this indeterminacy is not that of *a* phenomenon, but rather the indeterminacy of a 'trace' that marks the exposure to the Saying, without bringing it to manifestation.[54] In this sense, we can say that the face is exposure without exposition. In an interview from 1982 Levinas repeats his earlier thought of de-nuding from *Totality and Infinity*, this time even more clearly expressing the stripping bare from categories, from determination:

> The best way of encountering the Other is not even to notice the colour of his eyes! […] Ordinarily one is a "character": a professor at the Sorbonne, a Supreme Court justice, son of so-and-so, everything that is in one's passport, the manner of dressing, of presenting oneself. And all signification in the usual sense of the term is relative to such a context: the meaning of something is in its relation to another thing. Here, to the contrary, the face is meaning all by itself. You are you.[55]

This stripping bare from categories brings the meaning of 'the face' closer to the meaning of 'look'; not 'look' in the sense of an image, as in the way someone looks from the outside, but rather in the sense of the look expressed by someone which coincides with that someone's very expressive-

---

[53] TI 74–5. The same idea appears in *Ethics and Infinity* (1982): "The skin of the face is that which stays most naked, most destitute. It is the most naked, though with a decent nudity. It is the most destitute also: there is an essential poverty in the face; the proof of this is that one tries to mask this poverty by putting on a pose, by taking on a countenance." EI 86.

[54] "A face as a trace, trace of itself, trace expelled in a trace, does not signify an indeterminate phenomenon; its ambiguity is not an indetermination of a noema, but an invitation to the fine risk of approach qua approach, to the exposure of one to the other, to the exposure of this exposedness, the expression of exposure, saying." OB 94.

[55] EI 85–6.

ness.⁵⁶ Through the face, the other and its expressiveness coincide. The face does not lead to anything beyond it; it is neither an indication, nor a sign. To make this idea clear, Levinas often describes the face as an epiphany. The *epiphany of the face* means that the face is both appearance and otherwise than appearance.⁵⁷ It is not the manifestation of *something*, but signifies concealing itself, the very impossibility of manifestation, without becoming a sign or an indication of *something*. Instead of affirming *something*, the face is an accusation.⁵⁸

Yet, we have previously said that the face is *more than* a physical face. This 'more than' means that, although not exclusively, but at least to some degree, the face is also the physical face. Epiphany, as both appearance and beyond appearance, means that the face as embodiment coincides with its de-nuding. In this sense, it becomes a trace of itself, signification signifying itself, but without determination. The embodiment of the face is not reducible to the face as a part of the body. The whole body becomes a face (*visage*).

> [T]he signification of the face is due to an essential coinciding of the existent and the signifier. Signification is not added to the existent. To signify is not equivalent to presenting oneself as a sign, but to expressing oneself, that is, presenting oneself in person. The symbolism of the sign already presupposes the signification of expression, the face. In the face the existent par excellence

---

⁵⁶ Here it becomes important the difference between the two French words, 'visage' and 'face,' both of which are translated in English as 'face.' Nevertheless, when Levinas evokes the face, he employs the word 'visage.' Meanwhile, the 'face-to-face' relation remains 'face-à-face,' although at occasions it is used intercheangeable with 'vis-à-vis,' where 'vis' has the same etymological roots as 'visage.' We will return to this in Chapter 8.

⁵⁷ We need to note here that the face as epiphany becomes also a way of describing the ambiguous intertwinement between the two dimensions of the relation to the other, inside-out and outside. Reference to this can be found in *Totality and Infinity* (for example, in the previously discussed phrase: "the third party looks at me in the eyes of the Other," TI 213) as well as in *Otherwise than Being*: "and it is because the third party does not come empirically to trouble proximity, but the face is both the neighbor and the face of faces, visage and visible, that, between the order of being and of proximity the bond is unexceptionable," OB 160.

⁵⁸ "And yet as a destitution, a trace or shadow of itself and an accusation, a face makes itself an apparition and an epiphany," OB 154.

presents itself. And the whole body—a hand or a curve of the shoulder—can express as the face.[59]

The face is "presenting oneself in person," which is, on the one hand, an allusion to the phenomenality of the face, the face as manifestation (although, again, not as a phenomenon, but as a manifestation that carries the trace of the very impossibility of showing itself), and, on the other hand, it points towards the concreteness of the face.

Levinas's emphasis on the concreteness of the face is strongly connected with his general effort to resist formalism. Just as in the case of the notion of the other or the notion of sociality, the face would lose its meaning as soon as it becomes a mere formal conceptual construct. This point is so important for Levinas that he chooses to introduce the notion of the face in *Totality and Infinity* in the context of highlighting the significance of deformalization:

> The way in which the other presents himself, exceeding *the idea of the other in me,* we here name face. This *mode* does not consist in figuring as a theme under my gaze, in spreading itself forth as a set of qualities forming an image. The face of the Other at each moment destroys and overflows the plastic image it leaves me, the idea existing to my own measure and to the measure of its *ideatum*—the adequate idea. It does not manifest itself by these qualities, but καθ' αὐτό. It *expresses itself.* The face brings a notion of truth which, in contradistinction to contemporary ontology, is not the disclosure of an impersonal Neuter, but *expression*: the existent breaks through all the envelopings and generalities of Being to spread out in its "form" the totality of its "content," finally abolishing the distinction between form and content. This is not achieved by some sort of

---

[59] TI 262. In this sense, see also *Ethics and Infinity* (1982), where Levinas says: "the whole human body is in this sense more or less face," EI 97. A similar idea is expressed in "Peace and Proximity" (1984]) "The face is thus not exclusively a human face. In Vassili Grossman's *Life and Fate* the story is of the families, wives and parents of political detainees traveling to the Lubyanka in Moscow for the latest news. A line is formed at the counter, a line where one can see only the backs of others. A woman awaits her turn: ' [She] had never thought that the human back could be so expressive, and could convey states of mind in such a penetrating way. Persons approaching the counter had a particular way of craning their neck and their back, their raised shoulders with shoulder blades tense like springs, which seems to cry, sob, and scream.' The face as the extreme precariousness of the other," "Peace and Proximity" (1984), in BPW 167.

modification of the knowledge that thematizes, but precisely by "thematization" turning into conversation.[60]

Here, the phrase "at each moment destroys and overflows the plastic image it leaves me" signifies the "surplus" that disrupts thematization. The face cannot be shown; it has no determination, no characteristics. The shown face becomes a mere mask, it is the cadaver:

> The dead face becomes a form, a mortuary mask; it is shown instead of letting see—but precisely thus no longer appears as a face.[61]

Thus, the face opens up a different approach towards the question of the other, an approach different from showing, or knowledge, yet without divesting the other from its concreteness, without creating an abstract, formal or universal concept of the Other.[62] As we have previously shown, knowledge, showing and determination, in which formalization and generalization are included, are rooted in a positioned self, an established I. For Levinas, however, the face is an exteriority that is not approached and conquered by the I through appropriative knowledge, but it remains exterior to the self who "welcomes" it (*le moi qui l'accueille*).[63] This welcome, or welcoming of the face, proves to be an interesting notion in the context of this study, as it constitutes an alternative expression to the immediate relation to the other that was designated previously by the face-to-face relation.

We suspect that the reason why Levinas introduces the "welcoming" and, as we will see later, "facing,"[64] is precisely to combat the symmetry and

---

[60] TI 50–1, emphasis by Levinas. One can notice here in the notion of "conversation" an early account of what in *Otherwise than Being*, we have seen, Levinas calls "communication"; that is to say, here, conversation, just as communication in *Otherwise than Being*, gives sense to thematization.

[61] TI 262.

[62] Here, we have used capitalized 'Other' in order to designate the other as an abstract concept. Since this is neither Levinas's, nor our own intention in this thesis, throughout our text we are not using capital letter for 'the other.' This is for reasons of de-formalization in order to suggest, even through writing, that Levinas does not want to create a concept of 'the Other' that would somehow offer a generalized notion of otherness.

[63] TI 50, TeI 44.

[64] We will return to discussing 'facing' in Chapter 8.

dyadic thinking that could raise suspicions regarding the face-to-face relation. Most certainly, Levinas has no intention of introducing symmetry into the face-to-face relation, and thus he emphasized its asymmetry through the asymmetrical position of a relation of welcome: "The conjuncture of the same and the other" says Levinas, using a vocabulary typical of *Totality and Infinity*, "is the *direct* and *full face* welcome of the other by me."[65] Through its tight connection with the face-to-face relation, the 'welcome of the face' becomes another expression of sociality.[66] Despite their clear connection, in our view there is a significant difference between the welcoming of the face and the face-to-face relation. The face-to-face relation is sometimes described by Levinas in terms of directedness, similar to the directedness of an encounter.[67] Welcoming, on the other hand, is in a way both more and less than an encounter. We can observe that in *Totality and Infinity* Levinas describes the welcome of the face in terms of overflowing, surplus, linking it back to the earlier mentioned surplus of sociality:

> The idea of infinity, the overflowing of finite thought by its content, effectuates the relation of thought with what exceeds its capacity, with what at each moment it learns without suffering shock. This is the situation we call welcome of the face. The idea of infinity is produced in the opposition of conversation, in sociality.[68]

A few pages later, Levinas makes another explicit connection between welcoming and sociality, and identifies the "the welcoming of the being that appears in the face" with "the ethical event of sociality."[69] This *welcoming* resonates well with Levinas's words towards the end of the book, where he announces his main thesis as the "priority of orientation":

---

[65] TI 80, emphasis by Levinas.
[66] From early on, Derrida observed the importance of the welcoming for Levinas's philosophy, and found it to be the core of Levinas's work. (See Jacques Derrida, "A Word of Welcome," in *Adieu to Emmanuel Levinas* [1997], trans. Pascale-Anne Brault, and Michael Naas (Stanford: Stanford University Press, 1999). At the same time he developed his own idea of welcoming in term of hospitality. See for instance *Anne Dufourmantelle invite Jacques Derrida à répondre : De l'hospitalité*, Calmann-Levy. *Of Hospitality. Anne Dufourmantelle Invites Jacques Derrida to Respond* (1997), trans. Rachel Bowlby (Stanford, CA: Stanford University Press, 2000).
[67] See for example AT 93.
[68] TI 197.
[69] Ibid., 207.

> The priority of this orientation over the terms that are placed in it (and which cannot arise without this orientation) summarizes the theses of the present work.[70]

If we connect the above claim to Levinas's account of his own project as being led by the question of sociality, then, the meaning of sociality would coincide with orientation itself (i.e. openness, welcoming). While examining the relation between Buber's and Levinas's philosophy, Robert Bernasconi also notices a similarity between Levinas's emphasis on *the priority of orientation* and Buber's claims regarding the importance of *the primacy of relation*.[71] *Primacy*, Bernasconi argues, is not a relation, and thus for Buber, in the beginning there was not the I-Thou relation as such, but the *primacy* of relation. Similarly, Levinas does not prioritize the subject or the other, or the relation as such. Instead, the other-in-the-same, the *orientation* and openness towards the other become central.[72]

Orientation is not a *relation* based on difference, in the sense that the self and the other are self-standing entities which then enter into a relation with each-other; nor is it indifference, formed by the fusion between the self and the other. Instead, it is non-indifference, where the double negation is not the same as affirmation, but serves the purpose of precisely decomposing the difference/indifference contraries. Through Levinas's ingenious play on words, or rather over-determination, non-indifference becomes a key aspect of sociality.[73] Beyond simply expressing a double negation cancelling each other ('non' and 'in'), which would leave us with 'difference,' 'non-indifference' can be read in a twofold sense. Firstly, by understanding 'indifference' in its everyday use (as not caring for something) 'non-in-difference' would suggest on the contrary, a preoccupation. In this case, 'non-in-difference' highlights the self as already 'for the other.' Secondly, we can read 'in-difference'—perhaps in keeping closer to its etymological roots[74]—

---

[70] Ibid., 215.
[71] Bernasconi, Robert, "'Failure of communication' as a Surplus: Dialogue and Lack of Dialogue between Buber and Levinas," in *The Provocation of Levinas*, 100–135.
[72] Although we agree with Bernasconi's approach, in Chapter 8 we will take this idea even further, and argue for orientation or welcome expressed through a gerundive form of fac*ing*. This will prove to be more appropriate for designating sociality than a simple and static face-to-face relation.
[73] See for example in OS 124.
[74] From Latin 'indifferens,' which from the late 14c up until the early 16c was used to designate impartiality, and only after that gained its contemporary meaning.

as a non-partiality or neutrality expressing the third person perspective. Then, 'non-in-difference' would also mean the negation of a view from the outside, in other words it signals an involvement. Thus, orientation, through its non-indifference at once leads the meaning of sociality beyond a unifying common ground (in indifference), yet also beyond a separation that would be simply based on the difference between individuals. Hence welcoming, or orientation, bears a deeper meaning than a face-to-face *encounter*. Later on, the very notion of encounter becomes problematic for Levinas. In an interview with François Poirié (1986), when he is asked how to encounter the other, Levinas answers:

> To encounter, what does that mean? From the very start you are not indifferent to the other. From the very start you are not alone! Even if you adopt an attitude of indifference you are obliged to adopt it! The other counts for you; you answer him as much as he addresses himself to you; he concerns you![75]

Let us underline once again the meaning of sociality as it is presented in Levinas's early- and middle-period works: sociality expresses the refusal of fusion; it is a non-additive plurality which opens up time itself. In positive terms, sociality, on the one hand, takes the form of radical multiplicity, which interrupts thinking in terms of singular/plural; on the other hand, it signifies the 'welcoming of the face,' which, through its non-indifference, goes beyond a mere encounter. These aspects characteristic of sociality involve an approach from the hither side of the (unthematized) relation to the other, that is to say, they direct us towards what we have previously designated as the inside-out dimension given by de-posed subjectivity. Thus, the way Levinas thinks sociality in his early and middle-period work already announces his approach to subjectivity as the other-in-me characteristic of his later writings. We continue our search in the next chapter by addressing Levinas's later writings, where sociality becomes more and more related to substitution, the one-for-the-other, and proximity.

---

[75] "Interview with François Poirié" (1986), in IIRB 50.

CHAPTER 7
The Presence and Absence of Sociality in Levinas's Later Works

In an effort to bring forth a deeper meaning of sociality, we have shown that, already in Levinas's early texts, the question of sociality reflects what we have called the inside-out dimension of the relation to the other, which becomes fully developed through Levinas's understanding of the de-posed subjectivity, characteristic of his later works. Thus, Levinas's approach to the question of sociality in his early writings already shows signs of his mature thoughts on subjectivity.

In this chapter, we continue our discussion with Levinas's critique of the reciprocal model of sociality, reflected in his reproach of Buber's 'I-Thou' relation. The polemical relation between Buber and Levinas will be at the centre of the first part of this chapter. These polemical texts, not only represent the context in which Levinas most often engages the actual word 'sociality,' but they are also highly focused on developing the meaning of a notion of sociality. Although we find Levinas criticizing Buber already in his mid-period work, these critiques become more straightforward in his later texts. This is the reason behind the strategic decision of discussing the meaning of sociality revealed by Levinas's encounter with Buber in the context of his later works. As we already know, *Otherwise than Being* and the later essays mark the maturation of Levinas's understanding of subjectivity, and with it, the increased importance of the inside-out dimension that the de-essentialized notion of subjectivity puts into play. There, Levinas's notion of proximity develops and we find the meaning of sociality to be closely connected to it. Nevertheless, this connection is not completely clear, and our task in the second part of this chapter will be to clarify the relation between sociality and proximity. The aim is to see in what way the notion of proximity can help us understand the notion of sociality in Levinas's work. Finally, in the third and fourth parts of this chapter we will address the questions of love and society, in their connection to sociality. As we will see, these two notions start out by being very close to sociality in their meaning. In the later stages of Levinas's work however, the distinctions between love and sociality, and respectively, society and sociality become more accentuated. Tracing these lines of development helps us refine the meaning of the notion of sociality.

7.1. The 'correction' of the I-Thou

A recurring context in which Levinas refers to sociality is given by his critical writings on Buber's I-Thou relation. This is the context in which Levinas comes closest to formulating what we might call a notion of sociality. There is even a noticeable increase in the incidence of the word 'sociality,' a word that otherwise remains rather marginalized. Levinas's repeated insistence on enhancing the meaning of what he considers to be Buber's notion of sociality (i.e. the I-Thou relation) reveals the importance of these critical remarks for Levinas's own philosophy. Hence, they have the potential for pinpointing those aspects of sociality that Levinas finds most significant, and, in this sense, prove to be of great importance for our study.

Levinas wrote several essays dedicated to Buber's philosophy,[1] along with some comments dispersed throughout other texts.[2] Buber, in his turn, gave some short but meaningful responses to Levinas's critiques.[3] The polemical discussion between Levinas and Buber gave rise to a range of commentaries and comparative readings: some defending Buber against Levinas's critique,[4] others showing a rather straightforward distinction between the

---

[1] See "Martin Buber and the Theory of Knowledge" (1958/1963), "Dialogue with Martin Buber" (1965), "Martin Buber's Thought and Contemporary Judaism"(1968), "Utopia and Socialism" (1977), "The Word I, the Word You, the Word God" (1978), "Apropos of Buber: Some Notes" (1982), or "Martin Buber, Gabriel Marcel and Philosophy" (1978).
[2] For example in his two major works, *Otherwise than Being* and *Totality and Infinity*. We will discuss some of these comments later in this section.
[3] See Martin Buber, "Replies to My Critics," in *The Library of Living Philosophers*, Volume XII, *The Philosophy of Martin Buber*, eds. Paul A. Schlipp and Maurice Friedman (La Salle, IL: Open Court, 1967), or "Dialogue with Martin Buber" (1965), PN 36–39. The two texts share a common part.
[4] See for example Andrew Kelley, "Reciprocity and the Height of God: A Defense of Buber against Levinas" (1995), in *Levinas and Buber—Dialogue and Difference*, eds.

two philosophers,⁵ and then others emphasizing the similarities between Levinas's and Buber's thought, some of which remained unrecognized by the two philosophers themselves.⁶ The aim here is not that of analyzing the fairness of Levinas's critique against Buber, or that of a detailed comparison between the philosophies of the two. Rather the focus will remain on those critical remarks that we find relevant in formulating the meaning that Levinas gives to sociality in his later work.

Despite the fact that in *Totality and Infinity* Levinas insists on not having the "ridiculous pretention of correcting Buber,"⁷ his notion of sociality is often revealed in reaction to Buber's I-Thou relation. Levinas agrees with Buber's starting point of protecting the I-Thou relation from coincidence and the Thou from being an object of knowledge.⁸ On several occasions he acknowledges Buber's important contribution to thinking sociality without appropriation (attributing a determined identity to the other). In this way, the relation to the other that Buber calls 'I-Thou' manages to maintain alterity and difference. Levinas shows, both in his earlier works and in later texts, his appreciation for the merits of Buber's work.⁹ Yet he remains

---

Peter Atterton, Matthew Calarco and Maurice S. Friedman (Pittsburgh, PA: Duquesne University Press, 2004), 226–232.

⁵ See for instance Stephan Strasser, "Buber and Levinas: Philosophical Reflections on an Opposition," in *Levinas and Buber—Dialogue and Difference*, 37–48. or Damien Casey, "Levinas and Buber: Transcendence and Society," *Sophia* 38, no. 2 (1999): 69–92.

⁶ See for example Robert Bernasconi, "'Failure of communication' as a Surplus: Dialogue and Lack of Dialogue between Buber and Levinas," in *The Provocation of Levinas,* 100–35, or Lisbeth Lipari, "Listening for the Other: Ethical Implications of the Buber-Levinas Encounter," *Communication Theory*, 14, no. 2 (May 2004): 122–141.

⁷ TI 69.

⁸ Levinas summarizes Buber's philosophy in the following way: "Buber's project consists in maintaining in the I-Thou relation the radical alterity of the Thou, specifically in liaison. The I does not absorb the Thou as an object, nor is it absorbed by the Thou ecstatically. The I-Thou relation is a relation with what remain absolute despite the relation.," "Martin Buber and the Theory of Knowledge" (1958/1963), in PN 26.

⁹ See, for instance, the following passages: "Buber distinguished the relation with Objects, which would be guided by the practical, from the dialogic relation, which reaches the other as Thou, as partner and friend. This idea, central in his work, he modestly claims to have found in Feuerbach. In reality it acquires all its force only in Buber's analyses, and it is in them that it figures as an essential contribution to contemporary thought." TI 68. "Martin Buber was, in effect, the first to conceive the distinction between a thing that is and a thing that is for me, an 'it,' an object that I can know. He then opposes to the 'it' the relation to the other who is not an object, and who is one to whom I say 'thou.' Buber consequently opposes the I-Thou relation to the I-It

unsatisfied with the way Buber develops his project, mainly because of the dialogical symmetry that he finds characteristic of the I–Thou relation and the formalism that it involves. In Levinas's 'improved' version of the I-Thou, in other words, in his notion of sociality, as we are about to show, reciprocity is replaced by asymmetry and irreciprocity, while the focus shifts from the relation itself to the impossibility of fusion, in an effort to evade formalism. Let us elaborate on these critiques while focusing on the notion of sociality they reveal.

As early as 1958, in the essay, "Martin Buber and the Theory of Knowledge" (1958/1963), Levinas criticizes Buber's conception of the I-Thou relation.[10] From the start, the main criticism targets the reciprocity that, according to Levinas, Buber's *I-Thou* implies. Levinas provides as alternative an *irreciprocal and asymmetrical sociality*, for which my relation to the other is a relation without relatedness, and where the emphasis is not on the relation as such. That is to say, through asymmetry and irreciprocity, sociality reflects the inside-out dimension of the relation to the other, while symmetry and reciprocity entails an outside perspective upon the relation itself:

> We shall direct our main criticism to the reciprocity of the I-Thou relation. [...] We wonder whether the relation with alterity of others which appears in the form of dialogue, of question and answer, can be described without introducing a paradoxical difference of level between the I and the Thou. The originality of the I-Thou comes from the fact that relation is known not from the outside, but from the I that brings it about. Its place is therefore not interchangeable with the place occupied by the Thou. [...] If the I becomes I by saying Thou, I have obtained this position from my correlate, and the I-Thou relation is like all other relations[11]

---

relation. He thought that the I-Thou relation was irreducible to the I-It relation that the social relation to the other presented a total autonomy in regard to the establishment of things and in regard to knowledge.," "The Proximity of the Other" (1986), in AT 100.

[10] One can find earlier critical references to Buber, but these are rather sporadic. See for example the following excerpt from *Time and the Other* (1947): "Against this collectivity of the side-by-side [Levinas refers here to Heidegger's Miteinandersien] I have tried to oppose the "I-you" collectivity, taking this not in Buber's sense, where reciprocity remains the tie between two separated freedoms, and the ineluctable character of isolated subjectivity is underestimated," TO 94.

[11] "Martin Buber and the Theory of Knowledge, " in PN 32.

Here Levinas refers to the *I-Thou* relation throughout the whole quotation, which might suggest that he is referring to Buber's notion of sociality all along. Nevertheless, it becomes clear from the context that Levinas's real aim is not just to address Buber, but rather to change the meaning of the I-Thou, turning it into his own understanding of sociality by introducing "the paradoxical difference of level between the I and the Thou"; in other words, by introducing asymmetry and irreciprocity.

The more specific critique of Buber's I-Thou brings into focus Levinas's objection to thinking sociality as a dialogical relation. Although Levinas could be seen as a thinker of dialogue (due to the primordiality of the relation to the other and the importance he confers on Saying), this is not the case. Firstly, because Levinas distances himself from understanding the Saying as simply dialogue, and secondly, because a dialogical relation is considered by Levinas to be reciprocal (in the form of question-answer).[12] Accordingly, from a Levinasian perspective, sociality could not designate a dialogical relation, nor could the relation to the other correspond to a dialogical couple. It is reciprocity, and the third person's perspective that reciprocity entails, that turns the I-Thou into the formal schema of the dialogical couple—hence, Levinas's critique becomes two-sided. The third person's perspective (which corresponds to the outside dimension of the relation to the other) brings objectivity and formalism, ultimately reducing sociality to what Levinas calls an "angelic spiritualism," or "spiritual friendship."[13] Here, the expression "spiritual" bears no theological meaning to it, but indicates a formal structure susceptible to universalization. As for the expression "friendship," here it places the 'I' and the 'Thou' of the I-Thou relation in the same position and thus indicates symmetry and reciprocity. In other words, Levinas is criticizing Buber for a formalized understanding of the relation to the other as a dyad.[14]

The critique of formalism reflects Levinas's efforts to maintain the approach from the hither side, assuring thereby a *non-formalized* meaning of sociality, that is, to avoid turning sociality into a universal concept. In his

---

[12] "This responsibility [proper to Saying] is prior to dialogue, to the exchange of questions and answers," OB 111.

[13] "Martin Buber and the Theory of Knowledge," in PN 33.

[14] Not surprisingly this critique is formulated by Levinas around the time that he changed his mind regarding the loving couple as an original sociality, since by now, that would have fallen under his own critique of the dialogical couple. We will return to this issue later on in this chapter.

dialogue with Buber, Levinas finds a solution to escaping a formal determination of sociality by emphasizing the particularity of the other. Within this particularity, the other becomes the hungry, the widow, the one without shelter, etc., while the self is never empty handed and is capable of giving "the bread from one's mouth";[15] hence Levinas's famous phrase: "no face can be approached with empty hands and closed home."[16] The critique of reciprocity and of formalism are linked to one another, and both are repeated in *Totality and Infinity*[17] and in the later essay on Buber, "Apropos of Buber: Some Notes" (1982). There again, Levinas reads Buber's I-Thou as an abstract idea, a pure formal relation to the other, which he calls an "ethereal" or "angelic" sociality; and yet again, in order to gain a non-formalized meaning Levinas insists on the importance of giving.[18] This opens up the question of solicitude on which Levinas seemingly relies while formulating his version of sociality in relation to Buber's I-Thou, and we will return to this shortly. For now, let us insist on the "ethereal" that,

---

[15] This expression appears repeatedly throughout Levinas's texts, and not always linked to his critique to Buber. See for example, OB Chapter III, "Sensibility and Proximity."
[16] TI 172.
[17] Yet in *Totality and Infinity*, besides the critique of a generalized I-Thou relation, Levinas also criticizes the generality of the Thou as such. According to Levinas, Buber's Thou can be human-thou but also thing-thou. This is unacceptable for Levinas, for whom sociality always refers to the human other (autrui): "One may, however, ask if the thou-saying [tutoiement] does not place the other in a reciprocal relation, and if this reciprocity is primordial. On the other hand, the I-Thou relation in Buber retains a formal character: it can unite man to things as much as man to man. The I-Thou formalism does not determine any concrete structure. The I-Thou is an event (*Geschehen*), a shock, a comprehension, but does not enable us to account for (except as an aberration, a fall, or a sickness) a life other than friendship: economy, the search for happiness, the representational relation with things." TI 68–9. Levinas's preference for considering the other exclusively in terms of human other certainly makes his philosophy susceptible to charges of anthropocentrism. There is an ongoing discussion regarding a Levinasian reading of the question of the animal or environment. See for example: Peter Atterton, "Levinas and Our Moral Responsibility Toward Other Animals," Inquiry: *An Interdisciplinary Journal of Philosophy* 54, no. 6 (2011): 633–649, or Aphonso Lingis, *The Community of Those Who Have Nothing in Common* (Bloomington: Indiana University Press, 1994).
[18] "But is not the *for the other* itself of sociality concrete in *giving*, and does it not presuppose *things*, without which, empty-handed, the responsibility for others would be but the ethereal sociality of angels?" "Apropos of Buber: Some Notes" (1982), in OS 47, emphasis by Levinas.

according to Levinas, threatens to take over the meaning of Buber's sociality (as the I-Thou).

Derrida, in his early essay on Levinas's philosophy, *Violence and Metaphysics* (1964), divides Levinas's critique of Buber's I-Thou into three main points, similar to those highlighted above.[19] He sees Levinas's third party as that which assures a connection to the "universe," and in a sense, saves Levinas from thinking sociality as a pure formal relation; at the same time, however, Derrida points out that the third also carries a certain neutrality (he calls it "universal witness," or "the face of the world").[20] Regarding Derrida's comments, our previous interpretation of the third party[21] suggests that it could keep the I-Thou from abstraction only as far as the outside dimension that it opens is intertwined with the inside-out dimension of my relation to the other. However, if we read the 'universe' assured by the third as if the third would enlarge our perspective, which until now was limited to the couple of the two (me and thou), to include the world, this reading would lead us straight back to the dialogical thinking that Levinas criticizes. Does Derrida fall into the trap of reading Levinas's sociality as a dyad? This particular comment would suggest so, although we should keep in mind that his essay is based on Levinas's early and mid-period work and Levinas's early comments on Buber. In any case, it seems that Derrida wishes to do more, here, than just make an inventory of Levinas's critique. He goes so far as to defend Buber against Levinas's critique of formalism, by saying that Buber's relation, instead of being "referential or exclusive," is an "opening-up, on the contrary, the possibility of every relationship to Others."[22]

It is interesting to see that Derrida responds to Levinas in a way that is similar to that of Buber himself, in his letter published just a year after

---

[19] Derrida notes the following reproaches from Levinas to Buber: the I-Thou relation is reciprocal and symmetrical, it is formal, and it is a relation of the couple "forgetful of the universe" (meaning that Levinas's "third party" has no place in it). See Derrida, "Violence and Metaphysics," in *Writing and Difference*, 401–2, n. 37.

[20] "For there is also in Levinas's thought, despite his protests against neutrality, a summoning of the third party, the universal witness, the face of the world which keeps us from the 'disdainful spiritualism' of the I-Thou." Ibid.

[21] For a more detailed discussion on the question of the third party, see Chapter 4.

[22] Derrida, "Violence and Metaphysics, " in *Writing and Difference,* 401–2, n. 37.

Derrida's text.[23] Buber's response rejects Levinas's reading of his I-Thou by saying that on the contrary, the I-Thou is a more fundamental comradeship which maintains itself despite solicitude,[24] yet without transforming it into a formal relation.

> Levinas errs in a strange way when he supposes that I see in the *amitié toute spirituelle* the peak of the I-Thou relation. On the contrary, this relationship seems to me to win its true greatness and powerfulness precisely there where two men without a strong spiritual ground in common, even of very different kinds of spirit, yes of opposite dispositions, still stand over against each other so that each of the two knows and means, recognizes and acknowledges, accepts and confirms the other, even in the severest conflict, as this particular person. [...] This is no friendship, this is only the comradeship of the human creature, a comradeship that has reached fulfillment. No "ether," as Levinas thinks, but the hard human earth, the common in the uncommon.[25]

In a way that resembles Derrida's objections to Levinas's critique, Buber argues that the I-Thou is not a formal model of relation; on the contrary, it expresses the refusal of fusion ("without a strong spiritual ground in common") and highlights the importance of de-formalizing the relation to the other, without reducing it to 'something' determined. Yet Buber's answer exceeds that of a mere reply to a critique. It is, in its turn, also a critique. Just a few lines below, his counter-argument to Levinas's emphasis on the other as someone in need (the widow, the orphan, the hungry, etc.) appears clearly:

> Levinas, in opposition to me, praises solicitude as the access to the otherness of the other. The truth of experience seems to me to be that he who has this access apart from solicitude will also find it in the solicitude practiced by him—but he who does not have it without this, he may clothe the naked and feed the hungry

---

[23] Buber's letter, although published only in 1965 is originally dated 1963, that is a year previous to the publication of Derrida's essay. Thus, this leaves open the possibility that Derrida had read Buber's letter before its publication.

[24] The English word "solicitude" is the translation for the German word "Fürsorge," used by Buber, which can also be translated as caring for the other, or caring for the other's need. However, here it does not seem to have the connotation given to this word by Heidegger. We find that the translation solicitude fits well in this context, since Buber's critique, as we are about to see, targets Levinas's repeated use of the same context when discussing the relation to the other: a context which pictures the other always in need (the orphan, the widow, the hungry, etc.).

[25] Buber, "Replies to My Critics," in *The Library of Living Philosophers*, 723.

all day and it will remain difficult for him to say a true Thou. If all were well clothed and well nourished, then the real ethical problem would become wholly visible for the first time.[26]

Levinas's recourse to solicitude is, as we have seen, his way of avoiding the "ethereal sociality of angels," i.e. he wants to insist that the other is not just any other, it is a particular, unique other, and sociality is not a universal, generalizing concept. Nonetheless, Buber underlines powerfully that the same solicitude carries the danger of conditioning sociality—that is to say, without solicitude, without the need to help the widow, the poor, the hungry etc., sociality would lose its meaning. Keeping in mind Levinas's description of sociality from the early stages of his work, in which it means the interruption of solitude, and his continual efforts to think the relation to the other without relatedness, we can conclude that Levinas would have agreed with Buber's objection. When we consider Levinas's reply to Buber, it indeed suggests that solicitude in itself is not as important for Levinas as one might think. Instead, what is important for him is the rejection of fusion in the form of a generalizing abstract concept. The asymmetry that solicitude brings forth does not designate a social condition,[27] but rather the interruption, the resistance to fusion and unifying symmetry:

> In this defeatism, in this timidity that does not dare to dare, through this asking that does not have the impudence to ask and that is non-audacity itself, through this solicitation of the beggar, and of the homeless without a place to lay his head—at the mercy of the bidding of the one who welcomes—the humiliated person disturbs absolutely; he is not of the world. Humility and poverty are a bearing within being—an ontological (or meontological) mode—and not a social condition. To present oneself in this poverty of the exile is to interrupt the coherence of the universe. To pierce immanence without thereby taking one's place within it.[28]

Thus, we find here once again Levinas's emphasis on sociality as the very *interruption* that puts the self in exile. Exile, as shown in our discussion on subjectivity, marks, precisely, the de-posing the self from grounding itself in

---

[26] M. Buber, Replies to My Critics," in *The Library of Living Philosophers*, 723.
[27] This is however, not to argue that poverty as such does not refer to a social condition as well, but that here the emphasis is not on poverty as social condition, but as asymmetry.
[28] "The Man-God" (1968), in EN 55.

itself (the self emerging through the responsiveness/responsibility to the other), and it reflects the inside-out dimension of thinking the relation to the other. It breaks down referentiality, that is, the dialogical relation between me and the other. It cannot be formalized, since it interrupts thematization and it does not bring the relation into the foreground in a way that would provide the objectivity required by formalism. Interruption brings together the two aspects by which Levinas 'improves' Buber's I-Thou: irreciprocity and non-formalism.

As we can see, there is lot to be gained from exploring Levinas's encounter with Buber regarding the notion of sociality. The critical dispute between the two philosophers shows us the importance that de-formalizing the notion of sociality has for Levinas. Once again, Levinas highlights the need to think sociality otherwise than as a dialogical couple, and the risks brought by neglecting asymmetry and irreciprocity. His need to repeatedly emphasize these thoughts proves to us their general importance in thinking sociality. At the same time, in his conversations with Buber, interruption becomes for Levinas a succinct way to express the meaning of sociality, keeping it beyond formalism and beyond reciprocity.

Later on, Levinas continued to write *on* Buber and *to* Buber, and published two more essays detailing his critique.[29] In these later writings addressed to Buber, Levinas maintains his earlier critiques, but at the same time, his emphasis on the *otherwise than Being* becomes more and more pronounced. In one of these essays, "Martin Buber, Gabriel Marcel and Philosophy" (1978), while discussing Buber together with Marcel, he criticizes the use of an ontological language, and accuses both thinkers for their failure to detach from thinking in terms of Being.[30] We see emerging, one by one, notions typical of Levinas's later work, such as proximity, or approach.[31] In the following, we will attempt to grasp the meaning of sociality as it is revealed in the context of these notions.

---

[29] We refer here especially to "Martin Buber, Gabriel Marcel and Philosophy" (1978) and "Apropos of Buber: Some Notes" (1982).

[30] "Martin Buber, Gabriel Marcel and Philosophy," in OS 23. This additional critique is not surprising considering that the essay was written just about the time when Levinas started to change his vocabulary, from an ontological to an ethical. In the same year the essay "The Word I, the Word You, the Word God" (1978) was published, which also discusses Buber's thought. However, it is a relatively short essay with its main ideas having been more developed elsewhere, thus we are not engaging it directly in our discussion.

[31] See for instance "Apropos of Buber: Some Notes," (1982), in OS 44–46.

7.2. Sociality and proximity

We have already mentioned the notion of proximity in Chapter 3 in showing how radical multiplicity remains important for Levinas's later work. There, we argued that it illustrates well the disruption of the singular/plural dichotomy brought forth by the meaning of radical multiplicity. Given the connection established between Levinas's notion of proximity and the unthematized relation reflected by radical multiplicity, let us return to this notion for a deeper scrutiny, this time, in the light of its connections to sociality.

Approaching sociality through the notion of proximity is characteristic of Levinas's later work, when the notion of proximity became well integrated into his vocabulary.[32] However, this does not necessarily imply that the relation between proximity and sociality is clear and consistent. In some of these texts, sociality is used as if it might be synonymous with proximity,[33] while at other times proximity appears to be primordial to sociality.[34] Nevertheless, considering the lack of terminological clarifications in Levinas's work in general, and Levinas's indirect approach towards the question of sociality we should be very careful about relying solely on the actual use of the word 'sociality.' As we are about to show, there are, generally speaking, many common traits between the notion of proximity and that of sociality, and our task here is to see how these common traits contribute to tracing the meaning of sociality throughout Levinas's work.

The word proximity, in an everyday sense, carries a strong meaning of closeness, even spatial closeness. Indeed, one can observe that the increased

---

[32] Although reference to proximity can be found already in *Totality and Infinity*, and sporadically even in earlier texts, it is not emphasized as a notion, as it is in *Otherwise than Being* and later essays.

[33] This is the case for example in the essay "Sociality and Money" from 1987: "Proximity of the stranger—which is not a failure of coincidence, or immanence, but sociality.," "Sociality and money" (1987), trans. François Bouchetoux and Campbell Jones, *Business Ethics: A European Review*, 16, no. 3 (2007): 205. Another example comes from the essay "Everyday Language and Rhetoric without Eloquence" (1981): "The proximity that declares itself in this way is not a simple failure of the coinciding of minds that truth would bring with. It is all the surplus of sociality." OS 142; and from *Otherwise than Being*: "It [alterity] figures as what is near in a proximity that counts as sociality, which 'excites' by its pure and simple proximity," OB 16.

[34] For example in a work from 1984, sociality is presented as to be founded on proximity "the proximity of the Infinite and the sociality that it founds and commands can be better than the coincidence of unity," "Transcendence and Intelligibility," in BPW 159.

involvement of the notion of proximity in the late Levinasian discourse coincides with the occasional replacement of the word 'other' with 'neighbor' (*prochain*) which, among other meanings, can also indicate spatial proximity. However, when we look carefully at the way in which Levinas tackles the question of proximity we find that the spatial meaning of proximity would be insufficient and even misleading. Let us evoke, in this sense, Levinas's words from his conversation with Philip Nemo, referring to the way proximity appears in *Otherwise than Being*:

> In the book [Otherwise than Being], the proximity of the Other is presented as the fact that the Other is not simply close to me in space.[35]

For Levinas, the notion of proximity does not refer to spatial contiguity. Instead, it expresses the closeness of the other, close to the point of almost indistinguishability (indifference) without any mediator, yet with an unbridgeable abyss between myself and the other (difference)—this is the paradoxical relation of non-indifference which implies no possibility of fusion, where closeness and absolute difference are thought together. As we have already noted, the expression of 'non-indifference' serves the purpose of disrupting thinking in terms of terminological contraries: difference/indifference. We have previously seen, in discussing Levinas's early and mid-period work, that it is its double negation ('non' and 'in') that makes 'non-indifference' remarkable. In the terminology of Levinas's later work, we can read this double negation as a way of expressing the ambiguity of closeness to the point of substitution, yet also involving separateness and refusal of fusion; this is characteristic of the inside-out dimension of the relation to the other where synthetical time and thematizing consciousness are disturbed:

> The proximity does not enter into the common time of clocks, which makes meetings possible. It is a disturbance. Proximity as a suppression of distance suppresses the distance of consciousness of... The neighbor excludes himself from the thought that seeks him, and this exclusion has a positive side to it: my exposure to him, antecedent to his appearing, my delay behind him, my undergoing, undo the core of what is identity in me. Proximity, suppression of the distance that consciousness of... involves, opens the distance of a diachrony without a common present, where difference is the past that cannot be caught up with, an unimaginable future, the non-representable status of the neighbor

---

[35] EI 96.

behind which I am late and obsessed by the neighbor. This difference is my non-indifference to the other. Proximity is a disturbance of the remembrable time.

One can call that apocalyptically the break-up of time. But it is a matter of an effaced but untameable diachrony of non-historical, non-said time, which cannot be synchronized in a present by memory and historiography, where the present is but the trace of an immemorial past.[36]

While, in the context of Levinas's mid-period work, non-indifference takes the form of *orientation* and *welcome* (as it appears in *Totality and Infinity*), now, the same non-indifference is reflected in proximity as *approach*. Besides describing proximity as non-contiguity or non-fusion (that is, in negative terms), Levinas emphasizes it in a more positive way through the notion of approach.

[the Other] approaches me essentially insofar as I feel myself—insofar as I am—responsible for him.[37]

The word 'approach,' although it appears to suggest an action, can be read as Levinas's way of indicating an 'otherwise,'[38] that is to say, a disruption of the logical link that presupposes one active part that approaches and one passive part that is approached. Throughout his text, Levinas remains unclear about who is approaching whom: sometimes, as in the quote above, the self is approaching the other; other times the 'I' is approached, or *in* the approach.[39] This indeterminacy suggests that 'approach' is thought differently than a simple action leading to a higher degree of proximity (closer than before). It goes beyond the active-passive duality. It indicates a disruption in thinking passivity and activity as counterparts, and it is this that lies behind Levinas's apparent carelessness when it comes to attributing the

---

[36] OB 89, AE 142.
[37] EI 96.
[38] Here, in using the word "otherwise" we follow Levinas's general preference for this word in his effort of trying to escape dialectical dualities. We propose to use simply 'otherwise' instead of 'otherwise than….' The latter would keep the relative definition, while simply 'otherwise' expresses a different way of approaching something—changing the perspective. In our case, this is the change from the outside, spatial perspective that allows fusion, to the inside-out dimension of the relation to the other.
[39] In *Otherwise than Being*, although Levinas often speaks about me (the I) approaching the other (e.g. OB 84), in describing substitution he also evokes the I being approached in responsibility (e.g. OB 138).

approach to an initiator. Just as in the case of non-indifference, where we have a breakdown of the difference/indifference opposition, in the case of approach we witness the active/passive duality falling apart. This blurredness of priorities indicates the an-archical character of the approach, that it does not have a specific origin. Thus, the interruption of the active-passive dialectic goes together with an interruption of thinking in terms of origin and leads to *the an-archy of proximity*. In other words, proximity does not characterize a recollectable event that occurs to someone at some point, and neither does it have a clear starting point. The approach is nobody's initiative; neither I nor the other initiates approach; this is not because there would be an anonymity of approach which would endow approach with an abstract character (abstract in the same sense as the formalism that we have already seen Levinas criticizing), but because it cannot be associated with a starting point, an origin. In this way, approach coincides with proximity and is not just a mere effort to attain proximity. The approach in proximity, just as orientation and welcome, is the openness, or rather, the exposure to the other; and, just as in the case of orientation and welcome, proximity and approach are ways of expressing sociality. In Levinas's later works, proximity implies the refusal of fusion,[40] while in the context of Levinas's early- and mid-period works we find the same refusal of fusion to be characteristic of sociality.[41] Sociality, just as orientation, welcome or approach, needs to be thought in terms of an-archy, and in this sense it does not belong to a recollectable event, or to a specific experience. "[S]ociality is irreducible to the experience of sociality," says Levinas,[42] because the *experience* of sociality plays out in a different temporal modality then the an-archy corresponding to the notion of sociality that he proposes. According to Levinas, experience is the mode of presence, a modality of arche and originarity, while the anarchy of sociality expresses both its an-originarity and its refusal of formalism (given by "an-

---

[40] At one point, Levinas describes proximity as "better than fusion." See the interview conducted by Richard Kearney, "Dialogue with Emmanuel Levinas" (1984), in *Face to Face with Levinas*, 22.

[41] This idea is strengthened in Levinas later work. For instance, in "Diachrony and representation" (1985) (in the section entitled "Time and sociality"), sociality, again, is expressed in terms other than coincidence: "Sociality is not to be confused with some lapse or privation that would have taken place in the unity of the One, where 'perfection' and the unity of the coincidence, having fallen into separation, would aspire to their integrity.," "Diachrony and representation" (1985), in TO 111.

[42] "Martin Buber, Gabriel Marcel and Philosophy" (1978), in OS 24.

arche" as without-ideality). All these suggest a deep connection between proximity as approach and sociality.[43]

Levinas is, in his early- and mid-period works, as we have emphasized in the previous chapter, already critical of a model of sociality for which the self and the other are side-by-side one another. With that in mind, we need to ask whether proximity suggests a "being side-by-side"? Although Levinas specifies that the notion does not express spatial contiguity, the meaning that proximity inherits from its everyday use as nearness, must make us wonder what kind of closeness or nearness could be meant by this term. In this sense, the suspicion that Levinas might be expressing some kind of side-by-side is legitimate. However this suspicion, instead of challenging the notion of proximity, reveals the ingenuity of thinking proximity in terms of an-archical approach: approaching without an initiator would also mean that there cannot be a "side-by-side," since the sides themselves are not established (the non-indifference characteristic to proximity also means indeterminacy). Levinas describes the approach as the very fissibility (*fissibilité*) of the self; this is not a mere characteristic that is added to the self; rather, the self itself is its very fissibility.[44] As is suggested by the etymological meaning of sociality, the Levinasian notion of sociality as approach is not a characteristic added to the self. I am in the approach from the start, as soon as I can say 'me' (or, in Levinas's expression '*me voici*').[45] The fission or, more precisely, the fissibility of the self is always already, without happening, without representing a specific event or constituting an experience—we have already seen, after all, that a Levinasian notion of sociality cannot be thought in terms of experience. In an-archy (i.e. not a mere event at a specific moment in the life of the self, not even the birth—

---

[43] The connection of sociality to non-indifference, showing again the link between sociality and proximity, appears in an even more direct manner in "Notes on Meaning" (1879/81): "My non-indifference to the other has the irreducible signification of sociality.," in OGCM 163. For similar references see also for instance OS 124.

[44] The word 'fission' is used in biology to indicate the division of the cell and the non-sexual reproduction of simple organisms. From the context, it seems that Levinas is well aware of this meaning of fission (besides the more general meaning of split), since he refers to the self as a nucleus, which again has a biological connotation to it (in the form of the nucleus of the cell where the cell-division starts). See OB 180.

[45] According to Levinas, proximity is contact with the other, where the other, and not the self, is always "the first one on the scene" (OB 86) and the self finds itself already for the other.

understood here as origin—of the self) the approach signifies the constant interruption of the solidification of the self into an ego-core:

> The approach of the neighbor is a fission of the subject beyond lungs, in the resistant nucleus of the ego, in the undividedness of its individuality. It is a fission of the self, or the self as fissibility a passivity more passive still than the passivity of matter. To open oneself as space, to free oneself by breathing from closure in oneself already presupposes this beyond: my responsibility for the other and my aspiration by the other, the crushing charge, the beyond, of alterity.[46]

Hence approach, and with it sociality, thought in terms of fissibility, connects back to the meaning of sociality discussed earlier, on the occasion of Levinas's critiques of Buber, where it also played an interruptive role. At the same time, fissibility at the core of the self brings into play Levinas's deposed subjectivity. Its correlation with the de-position of the self reveals the importance of sociality for Levinas for the re-thinking of time and consciousness. If, in the context of his early work, we find sociality to be a key element for re-thinking time,[47] now sociality plays a crucial role in re-thinking spatiality. The notion of proximity signifies the way in which spatiality itself needs to be reconsidered in relation to sociality. Instead of spatiality thought of as the side-by-side, proximity marks spatiality as approach, not as coming closer, but as exposure, the opening up of spatiality itself. Just as in the case of time we had a critique of time as instants gathered by a constant 'I,' in the case of proximity we have a critique of space as contiguity. In this sense, we can say that the connection between Levinas's early and later thoughts on sociality also shows us how he re-thinks temporality and spatiality through the question of sociality. Just as diachrony in itself is not conceived in terms of time, but opens up temporality, so proximity in itself is not conceived in spatial terms, yet opens up spatiality. Revealed in Levinas's early works as the 'out of time' of diachrony which opens-up time itself, and now as proximity which opens-up space, we find sociality as the interruptive movement necessary for thinking both time and space.

The connection between sociality and subjectivity, with its re-thought time and spatial structure, again, leads us back to the inside-out dimension of the relation to the other. Now, through the notion of proximity, the

---

[46] OB 180f.
[47] EE 93–4.

importance of the inside-out dimension in thinking sociality is more directly expressed by Levinas. In *Otherwise than Being* he often employs the notion of proximity to underline that the relation between me and the other permits only an approach from within the relation, excluding any representation of the relation itself.

> Proximity is the subject that approaches and consequently constitutes a relationship in which I participate as a term, but where I am more, or less, than a term. This surplus or this lack throws me outside of the objectivity characteristic of relations.[48]

It seems that in his later works, Levinas becomes more and more aware of the need to escape thinking in terms of determination, given his more successful attempt to change his vocabulary. He manages to change the negative way of describing sociality that is predominant in his early works, into a positive terminology, a process that had begun already in *Totality and Infinity*, becoming even more pronounced later on, when sociality is expressed as proximity, approach and fissibility.

7.3. Sociality and love

As we have seen so far, the way in which sociality is approached varies in the different phases of Levinas's work. We need to note, however, that these phases are strongly marked by the change shown in Levinas's understanding of love. While in his early writings Levinas gives privilege to Eros, and considers the beloved to be the ab-solute other, as his work matures he turns away from thinking erotic love as a relation with ab-solute alterity, and directs his attention towards love without concupiscence. This shift makes its imprint on the way Levinas thinks sociality since, as he shows in an essay from 1983, the two notions are strongly related:

> A responsibility that is not the deprivation of comprehension-knowledge and grasping knowledge, but the excellence of ethical proximity in its sociality, in its love without concupiscence. [...] A responsibility which no doubt preserves the

---

[48] OB 82.

secret of sociality, whose total gratuitousness, even if completely vain, is called love of neighbor, love without concupiscence, but as irrefragable as death.[49]

Both the closeness between sociality and love, and also the turn that the meaning of love takes throughout Levinas's work make it relevant for us to address the question of love in Levinas's philosophy.[50] We dedicate the present section to this question.

Even though the meaning of the word 'love' appears to be worn out nowadays, either because it is often limited to the Christian doctrine or to romantic feelings, or because it gets dismissed as just another emotion among others, Levinas is not afraid of using it, as he claims in an interview from 1989.[51] Instead, he tries to revive the deeper meaning of love. As it is

---

[49] "From the One to the Other" (1983), in EN 148-9. Levinas repeats the same idea in 1985: "It is a responsibility that, without doubt, keeps the secret of sociality, whose total gravity — be it in vain to the limit — is called 'love of the neighbor' — that is, the very possibility of the unicity of the unique one (beyond the particularity of the individual in a genus). It is a love without concupiscence, but as irrefragable as death.," "Diachrony and Representation" (1985), in TO 110.

[50] The importance that Levinas accords to love is revealed also by its role in philosophy itself. Philosophy, instead of "love of wisdom," for Levinas, becomes "wisdom of love." This way, "love" has a privileged position in relation to wisdom, which is understood by Levinas as questioning. Questioning (as discussed in Chapter 4) is born when the outside perspective is brought into play. Philosophy thematizes, yet its thematization comes from the unthematized. This is why Levinas in *Otherwise than Being* says: "Philosophy is this measure brought to the infinity of the being-for-the-other of proximity, and is like the wisdom of love [...].Philosophy is called upon to conceive ambivalence, to conceive it in several times. Even if it is called to thought by justice, it still synchronizes in the said the diachrony of the difference between the one and the other, and remains the servant of the saying that signifies the difference between the one and the other as the one for the other, as non-indifference to the other. Philosophy is the wisdom of love at the service of love," OB 161-2. The same idea appears some years later, in the preface for the German edition of *Totality and Infinity* from 1987: "He [the author, Levinas himself] then asked himself whether all that was dear to the love of 'the love-of-wisdom,' or the love that is the philosophy of the Greeks, was the certainty of fields of knowledge directed toward the object, or the even greater certainty of reflection on these fields of knowledge; or whether knowledge beloved of and expected from philosophers was not, beyond the wisdom of such knowledge, the wisdom of love, or wisdom in the guise of love. Philosophy as love of love. A wisdom taught by the face of the other man!," "*Totality and Infinity*. Preface to the German Edition" (1987), in EN 200.

[51] "'I would say this quite plainly: what is truly human is—and don't be afraid of this word—love. And I mean it even with everything that burdens love or, I could say it better, responsibility. And responsibility is actually love, as Pascal said: 'without concupiscence.'" "Intention, Event, and the Other" (1989), in IIRB 143. Levinas refers to

the case with many of his terminological choices, Levinas is well aware of the complexity of the word 'love,' and the different meanings it can express.[52] In bringing forth these meanings, he resorts to the Greek and Hebrew roots of the word, and prioritizes two of these terms: *Eros*, in his early work, and *Agape*, or its Hebrew equivalent, *Hesed*, in his later writings.

In his early works Levinas approaches the question of love in terms of Eros. There, he considers the erotic relation a relation with absolute alterity. This is expressed both in *Time and the Other* and *Existence and Existents*. In *Time and the Other* Levinas explains that the privilege of the erotic relation resides in the impossibility of its being translated into a power relation. "It is neither a struggle, nor a fusion, nor a knowledge," Levinas says.[53] In the erotic relation the absolute other is unknowable and remains unknown while the self is invaded by love (Eros), yet there is no fusion with the other: "[Love] invades and wounds us, and nevertheless the I survives in it."[54] A similar idea is presented in *Existence and Existents*, where the relation to the other as Eros resists fusion.[55] At the same time, erotic love is clearly considered by Levinas as a relation 'between two,' that is to say, between the self and one singular other.[56] We can observe that thinking erotic love as a privileged dyadic relation to the other, a relation that refuses fusion and knowledge, goes hand in hand with Levinas's conception of sociality in his early works, and for now, it even seems as if the meaning of sociality coincides with the meaning of Eros: we find the unthematized relation to the other emphasized both in sociality and Eros. Nevertheless, Levinas's intentions with the notion of love as Eros do not end here. Although not fully developed in his early works, Levinas already anticipates there the importance of fecundity that is implied in Eros. We will return shortly to

---

Pascal's *Pensées*, and, besides the reference to Pascal being repeated several times when mentioning love without concupiscence, we find Pascal's words cited as motto at the beginning of *Otherwise than Being*. See OB VII.

[52] There are four forms of love in Ancient Greeks: *Eros*, which means love as passion, often synonymous with romantic love, *Storge*, designating love in kinship, *Phileo*, which means love as friendship, and *Agape*, meaning selfless love.

[53] TO 87-8.

[54] Ibid., 89.

[55] "Intersubjectivity is not simply the application of the category of multiplicity to the domain of the mind. It is brought about by Eros, where in the proximity of another the distance is wholly maintained, a distance whose pathos is made up of this proximity and this duality of beings." EE 95.

[56] "The pathos of voluptuousness lies in the fact of being two." TO 86.

the discussion of the questions of fecundity and the problems that it entails, but for now we will continue to focus on the meaning of love in its connection with sociality.

The privileged position accorded to Eros, as shown in Levinas's early work, has some problematic implications regarding Levinas thoughts on the difference between the masculine and the feminine. The sexual difference, according to Levinas, is not alike any other differentiation. "Sex is not something specific," he says in *Time and the Other*, "It is situated beside the logical division into genera and species."[57] The difference between the sexes neither represents a contradiction, nor a complementary relation. This understanding is consistent with the non-unifying character of the erotic relation, its resistance to fusing the self and the other into an *us*. Instead of constituting a complementary relation or a contradiction, the erotic relation, now emphasized in terms of sexual difference, is presented by Levinas as a mystery—a mystery due to the unknowable otherness of the feminine.[58] Hence, along with the priority of the erotic, in Levinas's early works we find absolute alterity portrayed as the feminine. In *Time and the Other*, for example, the feminine is described as "not merely the unknowable, but a mode of being that consists in slipping away from light,"[59] or in *Existence and Existents* the feminine is "the other par excellence."[60] This thought is carried into his mid-period work and is still to be found in *Totality and Infinity*.[61] Under these circumstances, it is not surprising that Levinas has faced some serious feminist critique. Views on the masculine language that Levinas employs, and on his thoughts regarding the feminine are divided between those who confront him with quite harsh critique,[62] those who find it inspiring for feminist theory,[63] and then again, those who do not find anything substantial that a feminist theory could gain from it.[64] Although

---

[57] TO 85.
[58] Ibid., 86.
[59] Ibid., 87.
[60] EE 85.
[61] See especially TI 154–6, 256–66.
[62] See for example Irigaray, "Questions to Emmanuel Levinas. On the Divinity of Love," in *Re-reading Levinas*, 109–118.
[63] See for example, Catherine Chalier, "Ethics and the Feminine," in *Re-reading Levinas*, 119–129.
[64] See for example Stella Sandford, "Levinas, feminism and the feminine," in *The Cambridge Companion to Levinas*, 139–160. Or Stella Villarmea, "The Provocation of

we acknowledge the importance of raising the question of the feminine and the problematic of sexual difference in Levinas's philosophy, we will not engage in this dispute here. Such a complex problematic requires a study of its own, and has already been addressed at length elsewhere.[65] What our examination of sociality is to gain through its connection with *Eros*, consists in underscoring that thinking sociality as a dyad remains typical for Levinas's early work.

Although the alterity of the feminine still bears importance by the time of *Totality and Infinity*, there Levinas gives priority to love without concupiscence over erotic love. Now, *Eros* is placed somewhere between desire and need:[66] the beloved has a 'face' (it is unique), yet the love offered to the lover involves reciprocity in the relation. Eroticism does not represent a figure of sociality anymore; instead, it becomes the "non-sociality of voluptuousness"[67] and the "non-sociality of the society of lovers."[68] On the one hand, this re-formulation is due to Levinas's realization of the problematic character of thinking sociality as a dyad. Through the duality of the erotic relation, sociality becomes closed up upon itself (it lacks 'the world'). On the other hand, Levinas recognizes that there is a reciprocity that concupiscence implies, where I love the love of my beloved.[69] As a

---

Levinas for Feminism," *The European Journal for of Women's Studies* 6, no. 3 (1996): 291–304.

[65] See, for example, Tina Chanter, ed., *Feminist Interpretations of Emmanuel Levinas* (University Park, PA: The Pennsylvania State University Press, 2001).; Claire Elise Katz, *Levinas, Judaism, and the Feminine: The Silent Footsteps of Rebecca* (Bloomington IN: Indiana University Press, 2003), or Stella Sandford, *The Metaphysics of Love: Gender and Transcendence in Levinas* (New Brunswick: Athlone Press, 2000).

[66] "The possibility of the Other appearing as an object of a need while retaining his alterity, or again, the possibility of enjoying the Other, of placing oneself at the same time beneath and beyond discourse—this position with regard to the interlocutor which at the same time reaches him and goes beyond him, this simultaneity of need and desire, of concupiscence and transcendence, tangency of the avowable and unavowable, constitutes the originality of the erotic," TI 255. See also Ibid., 271.

[67] TI 265.

[68] Ibid., 264.

[69] "I love fully only if the Other loves me, not because I need the recognition of the Other, but because my voluptuosity delights in his voluptuosity, and because in this unparalleled conjuncture of identification, in this *trans-substantiation*, the same and the other are not united but precisely—beyond every possible project, beyond every meaningful and intelligent power—engender the child. If to love is to love the love the Beloved bears me, to love is also to love oneself in love, and thus to return to oneself.

consequence, in *Totality and Infinity*, the erotic relation seems to lose significance when considered in its own, and instead it gains its importance through fecundity:

> Like need, *eros* is bound up with a subject identical with himself, in the logical sense. But the inevitable reference of the erotic to the future in fecundity reveals a radically different structure[70]

Thus, we encounter once again *Totality and Infinity,* mid-way through the development of Levinas's oeuvre. Although Eros remains important through the notion of fecundity that is connected to it, it is love as *Agape* that starts to becomes the model of responsibility in *Totality and Infinity*. This shift is explained retrospectively by Levinas in an interview from 1982:

> In *Totalité et infini* (*Totality and Infinity*) there is a chapter on Eros, which is described as love that becomes enjoyment, whereas I have a grave view of Agape in terms of responsibility for the other.[71]

We have to note here, however, that terminologically speaking Agape is not yet introduced in *Totality and Infinity*. It is only later, as his work matures, that Levinas seems to perform a complete break with the previously privileged position given to Eros, and introduces Agape as his new terminological tool for expressing the meaning of love. The break with prioritizing Eros shows itself, at times, in extremes; at one point, Levinas claims that the relation to the other is "the anti-erotic relationship par excellence."[72] Nevertheless, he usually does not go to these extremes, more typically confining himself to making explicit declaration of his change of view regarding love and the feminine: "I don't think that *Agape* comes from *Eros*. But I don't deny that sexuality is also an important philosophical problem. [...] I used to think that alterity begins with the feminine,"[73] says Levinas in the same interview from 1982, and then continues:

> Love does not transcend unequivocably—it is complacent, it is pleasure and dual egoism." TI 266.

[70] TI 272.
[71] "Philosophy, Justice, and Love" (1982), in EN 113.
[72] GDT 174.
[73] "Philosophy, Justice, and Love" (1982), in EN 113. Another example is from 1981: "My current view is that the face is prior to eros and libido. I was involved with this question in the foreword of the second edition of *Le temps et l'autre*. The other is other man,

I can say no more about it now; I think in any case that Eros is definitely not Agape, that Agape is neither a derivative nor the extinction of love-Eros. Before Eros there was the Face; Eros itself is possible only between Faces.[74]

Although a theological meaning of *Agape* would translate to God's love, in Levinas's work the term is stripped from its theological connotations.[75] Instead, Levinas focuses on the Greek roots of the word, and considers Agape to be selfless love, love without lust. The word 'Agape' is not mentioned very often, yet its meaning, love without concupiscence, remains emphasized throughout Levinas's later work. In *Otherwise than Being*, for example, Levinas never evokes the word 'Agape' as such. Nevertheless, by using a reference from *The Song of Songs,* he describes the I in the accusative as me "sick with love,"[76] while continuing to emphasize the importance of differentiating this kind of love from *Eros*:

> Beneath the erotic alterity there is the alterity of the-one-for-the-other, responsibility before eros.[77]

We have seen that in his early writings, Levinas relates, if not superimposes, the meaning of love as Eros and as sociality. Now we find him once again establishing a direct link between love and sociality; this time, however, it is

---

whether feminine or male, but the subject itself has to be understood as a 'pair.' I assign a totally different meaning to the term than the civic one of a form of living in which two partners complete each other. Incidentally, what this ought to mean: 'completing each other,' is not clear. The fact of the matter is that the unity of the subject cannot be understood as one in number.," "What one asks of oneself, one asks of a saint" (1980–81), 19.

[74] "Philosophy, Justice, and Love" (1982), in EN 113. Here, Levinas seems to suggest that instead of a radical distinction between Agape and Eros, Agape is already presupposed by Eros. Hence, one can say that Agape is more than Eros, and not simply an alternative to it.

[75] "Love is originary. I'm not speaking theologically at all; I myself don't use it much, the word love, it is a worn-out and ambiguous word.," "Philosophy, Justice, and Love" (1982), in EN 108. Although Levinas here claims that he do not use the word "love" very often, in fact—and we will see this below—there are plenty of places where he associates responsibility and the ethical order with love.

[76] "To this command continually put forth only a 'here I am' (me voici) can answer, where the pronoun 'I' is in the accusative, declined before any declension, possessed by the other, sick, identical." (OB 142), and then adds in the footnote the citation from *The Song of Songs.* 6:8: "I am sick with love," OB 198.

[77] OB 192.

love without concupiscence (i.e. love as *Agape*) that signifies the asymmetrical and irreciprocal relation to the other that sociality stands for:

> Love, or responsibility, is instead that which gives meaning to singularity. The relation is always non-reciprocal; love exists without worrying about being loved. That is my concept of dissymmetry. The other is, in this moment, the beloved, singular. And I am singular in another sense, as chosen, as being chosen for responsibility.[78]

In correspondence with the Greek *Agape*,[79] Levinas also refers to the Hebrew expression *Hesed*, meaning "gratuitous charity" without reciprocity.[80] In this context, it is interesting to see how Levinas overemphasizes the meaning of love through the Hebrew expression "ahavath hesed" (loving love), in one of his late interviews, in "In the Name of the Other," from 1990.

> But let me return to the Hebrew, to this complex expression from Micah 6:8, ahavath hesed. How does one translate it when both words have a very close literal meaning? Ahavath means "love," or "love of," and hesed, likewise, means "love." Does this result in "love of love"? It would, unless one remembers that the latter term can also be used as an adverb. This would give us "love loving."[81]

Although Levinas usually prefers the simpler meaning as "love without concupiscence," the expression "love loving" removes the meaning of love from its negative definition (love as irreciprocal and asymmetrical). The positive description of love, is given as an over-determination, as a surplus. We find here many similarities with the way sociality is approached in Levinas's later work, and later on we will see that the gerundive form "-ing" from "lov*ing*" finds its correspondence in the gerundive "fac*ing*," which we assign to the notion of sociality.[82] It is not accidental then, that in 1983

---

[78] "Intention, Event, and the Other" (1989), in IIRB 143. Although Levinas is uses the word "dissymmetry" here, its sense is clearly that of asymmetry.

[79] On the correspondence between "Agape" and "Hesed" see Bernard V. Brady, *Christian Love* (Washington DC: Georgetown University Press, 2003), 53.

[80] "I gladly use here the Hebrew term, hesed. This is an ancient word, since it appears in a particularly suggestive fashion in the Hebrew Bible, in what is termed (by Christians) the 'Old Testament.' It means charity in its absolute gratuity. The responsibility for the other, of which I am speaking, does not expect reciprocity.," "In the Name of the Other" (1990), in IIRB 193.

[81] "In the Name of the Other" (1990), in IIRB 193.

[82] See Chapter 8 and 11.

Levinas designates love without concupiscence as "the secret of sociality."[83] Love as *Agape*, or as *Hesed* does not carry the emphasis on the relation of love itself. Love is not a bond, but it is lov*ing*. This is very different from loving the other's love for me, as was the case with Eros. Here, it is not about me loving someone else's love, but loving without a previously determined *I* that enjoys the love received. When the meaning of love takes the form of love without concupiscence, the uniqueness of the other occupies a more important place than his/her love. "Only the unique is absolutely other. But the uniqueness of the unique is the uniqueness of the beloved. The uniqueness of the unique *signifies* in love," says Levinas in 1986.[84] The other is the unique loved one, beyond the particularity of the genus.

The close connection between sociality and love, both in Levinas's early and in his later work makes us wonder whether the two notions are the same. Undoubtedly, Levinas is unclear regarding the relation between sociality and love. One of the few occasions in which he directly addresses these problems is in his interview from 1986 with François Poirié. Here it would appear that, according to Levinas, love is not the precondition of sociality, but the other way around, the unthematized relation to the other is needed for there to be love:

> Q: How to go towards the other? Is it love that brings me to him?
>
> E. L.: Love goes further; it is the relation to the unique. It is proper to the principle of love that the other, loved, is for me unique in the world. Not because in being in love I have the illusion that the other is unique. It is because there is the possibility of thinking someone as unique that there is love.[85]

This suggests a subtle, yet significant difference between sociality and love, where sociality becomes the source of love. The same idea is strengthened in the essay "Sociality and Money," where Levinas refers to sociality as "conveying love."[86] Due to the character of Levinas's text (lacking conceptual

---

[83] "From the One to the Other" (1983), in EN 149. See also "Nonintentional Consciousness" (1983), in EN 131.
[84] "Uniqueness" (1986), in EN. 194, or "The 'unique one' means the *loved one*, love being the condition of the very possibility of uniqueness.," "Diachrony and Representation" (1985), in TO 108.
[85] "Interview with François Poirié" (1986), in IIRB 50.
[86] "Recognition of the Other by the way of responsibility, sociality in its irreducible excellence conveying love.," "Sociality and Money," 205.

systematization), it often remains difficult to distinguish between sociality and love. This is also our reason for avoiding a meticulous scrutiny that would try to measure the precise differences between the two notions, whilst bearing in mind that, when directly asked, Levinas himself gave priority to sociality. This makes us conclude that, even if in his early works Levinas equates sociality with *Eros*, as his work matures, the meaning of sociality departs from the meaning of *Eros* but remains close to that of love without concupiscence. However, the unthematized relation to the other, the resistance to determination of both the other and the relation itself, i.e. the way Levinas described sociality, is above all what is most important for Levinas.

7.4. Sociality and society

The notions of love and society have almost simultaneous phases of development. Just as the meaning of *Eros* was progressively separated from sociality in Levinas's work in order to combat a reciprocal and dualist understanding of sociality, so too the way in which Levinas perceives the difference between *society* and sociality also varies considerably depending on the period of his work. Hence, the distinction between sociality and society is not at all clear-cut in Levinas's early work. When *Eros* played an important role for Levinas, the original model of society was considered by him to be the society of lovers. By the time the emphasis on *Eros* was replaced by an emphasis on love without concupiscence, the notion of society becomes more clearly separated from the notion of sociality, and it receives its own place in Levinas's philosophy.

In the early stages of his writings, Levinas considers the loving couple as a kind of prototype for society. During that period, sociality was considered to be the society of the couple, described as a dyadic relation, a relation between two. A good example in this sense comes from the essay "The *I* and Totality" (1954). There, the "intimate society" coincides with the notion of sociality, while society as a structure is referred to as "real society."[87] The society of two expresses the society of love, which at the time of "The *I* and

---

[87] "The intimate society that makes forgiveness possible frees the will from the weight of acts that both escape and commit it—acts through which, in a real society, every will risks becoming alien to itself.," "The I and Totality" (1954), in EN 20.

Totality" had been thought by Levinas to be the erotic relation with the absolute other, thought in terms of a dyad.[88] This understanding of society seems to gain empirical emphasis when it is called 'social reality' or 'real society.' Here, then, the context becomes crucial in order to understand the exact meaning to which Levinas refers. The actual word 'society' carries both meanings of un-thematized, radical multiplicity characteristic to the ethical relation, and the un-radicalized multiplicity of justice. The apparent confusion between the two meanings of the word 'society' might be a way to suggest that the original society cannot be thought in isolation from the 'real' society, that is, from the rest of the world. One can easily recognize here an early version of the intertwinement of the ethical and the political.[89]

However, the difference between the notion of sociality and the notion of society has sharpened over time, and in *Totality and infinity*, Levinas starts to show signs of a clearer differentiation. There, he presents society as community, community that needs to be re-thought as 'fraternal community'[90] in which "the face presents itself to my welcome."[91] Levinas's formulation brings to mind that, in *Totality and Infinity*, 'orientation' and

---

[88] "In fact, such a society [the intimate society in truth] consists of two people, I and thou. We are among ourselves. Third parties are excluded. The third man disturbs this intimacy essentially: my wrong with regard to you, which I can recognize entirely in terms of my intentions, is objectively falsified through your relations with *him,* which remain secret to me, since I, in turn, am excluded from the unique privilege of your intimacy.[…]Violence in intimate society offends, but does not wound. It is either beyond or on the hither side of justice and injustice […] The society of love is a society of two, a society of solitudes, resisting universality. Its universality can be constructed only in time, by successive infidelities, by the change of friends. This is the love of one's neighbor, determined by chance proximity, and, consequently, a love of one being to the detriment of another; always privilege, even if it is not preference.," "The I and Totality" (1954), in EN 19-21.

[89] Nevertheless, this intertwinement should not lead to confusing a philosophy of sociality with a sociological analysis of society. Certainly, this is not Levinas's intention. "What guides our research, which is seeking out ways to elaborate nonpositive concepts, are human relationships, ethical relationships— improperly called ethical if ethics, as *ethos,* means habit and second nature. Outside of their dense material aspect, which only sociology retains, human relationships are structured according to another model than that of being. They signify the otherwise than being," GDT 185.

[90] In this sense, it becomes worthwhile to address the question of fraternity and to see how exactly the 'fraternal community' differs from sociality. However, these questions need to wait until the next part of our thesis, where we consider sociality in relation to community and community without a common.

[91] TI 214.

'welcome' are expressions of sociality. We can observe, here, the way in which Levinas changes the meaning invested in the word 'society,' from the society of the couple, signifying sociality, to the society of sharing, which carries in itself the an-archical interruption by sociality. Although in *Totality and Infinity* society already starts to be revealed as reciprocity and sharing, it is not as strongly related to the political, justice, institutions and the State, as it seems to be in *Otherwise than Being*. This is probably due to another change in Levinas conceptual vocabulary, this time regarding the notion of justice. Between the publication of his two major works (*Totality and Infinity* and *Otherwise than Being*) the meaning of justice slowly comes closer to the implication of the third, and begins to bring into play the question of the political.[92]

By the time of the publication of *Otherwise than Being*, it has become clear that sociality and society have very different meanings.[93] Levinas goes so far as to label society as a "superstructure,"[94] highlighting its reciprocity and symmetry, and clearly connecting it with justice, law, and the third party.[95] Society becomes the realm of measurement and comparison, where the self and the other are considered equals. Here, the equality that society implies is not to be understood as a utopian vision of society, with all its members living in equality; it does not represent an equality of rights, but the equality brought by the reciprocity between the members of society that makes possible judgment. Society understood in this way, implies the reciprocity and symmetry needed for measuring and categorization, where I become also an other for the other; it represents the equality provided by the outside dimension of the relation to the other.[96] In other words, now we have the notion of society as an un-radicalized multiplicity, a plurality of others amongst which the self also has a place. It is the society of *I* and all

---

[92] In this regard see Chapter 4.
[93] This distinction is also recognized by Pierre Hayat, in *Emmanuel Levinas, éthique et société* (Paris: Édition Kimé, 1995).
[94] See for example OB 127.
[95] "The extraordinary commitment of the other to the third party calls for control, a search for justice, society and the State, comparison and possession, thought and science, commerce and philosophy, and outside of anarchy, the search for a principle," OB 161.
[96] The association of society with the third, justice, measuring, or law appears quite explicitly in the following footnote from *Otherwise than Being*: "The description of proximity as a hagiography of the-one-for-the-other subtends society, which begins with the entry of the third man. […]. It then calls for comparison, measure, knowing, laws, institutions-justice," OB 193, n. 33.

the others, different from the sociality of me and the other(s). This way of understanding society seems to be maintained throughout Levinas's later work.

We have seen, then, that the meaning of "society" varies in Levinas's writings, depending on the time-period. As we have previously objected to considering the notion of sociality as a relation between two, we will not follow Levinas's understanding of society as the intimate society of the couple. Instead, just as we have followed Levinas's understanding of subjectivity and justice in his later period, here too we opt to borrow the meaning of society from Levinas's later works, where it is presented in a way that brings it closer to justice and to the possibility of measuring, state and the political.

Adopting the above-mentioned interpretation entails, though, additional clarification: does the meaning of society for Levinas, then, coincide with the meaning of the State and its political power? To answer this question we need to turn to the essay from 1977, "Utopia and Socialism," written as a preface to Buber's *Path in Utopia*. There we find Levinas highlighting the distinction between State and society in Buber's work (expressed also as the political and the social): the political (the state) reflects the idea of domination, while the social signifies the common life of man with man.[97] Levinas recognizes in Buber's dialectic of state-society that both state and society are collective bodies.[98] In this dialectic, society signifies the I-Thou relation. As such, it inherits the reciprocity of the I-Thou, since Levinas reads Buber's I-Thou as a reciprocal relation. Levinas acknowledges the importance of the distinction introduced by Buber between society that represents a collectivity, a *we*, and state power.[99] The notion of society, thought in this way, designates what Levinas on another occasion called "the collectivity which says 'we' that feels the other to be alongside of

---

[97] "Utopia and Socialism" (1977), in AT 113–4. Other times, however, it seems that this differentiation has no significant meaning, and the third necessarily brings the implication of the State: "If I heed the second person to the end, if I accede absolutely to his request, I risk, by this very fact, doing disservice to the third one, who is also my other. But if I listen to the third, I run the risk of wronging the second one. This is where the State steps in. The State begins as soon as three are present. It is inevitable.," "In the Name of the Other" (1990), in IIRB 194.
[98] "Utopia and Socialism" (1977), in AT 115.
[99] "The 'I-Thou' model allows us to conceptualize a firm distinction between society and the State, and to conceive of a society without 'power,'" "Utopia and Socialism" (1977), in AT 117.

oneself."[100] Nonetheless, if we read the essay while bearing in mind Levinas's critique of the I-Thou relation that we addressed earlier we can easily discern that the distinction between society and power is not enough for Levinas. There is also a need to think the notion of sociality as something different from the collectivity of a *we*, sociality based on non-indifference and irreciprocity, an-archical, without fusion, representing the inside-out dimension of the relation to the other.[101] To confuse sociality with society would lead to an approach to sociality by way of an outside view upon the relation, which would thematize the relation as such. In this sense, there is an essential difference between sociality and society, yet they are not contradictories; they do not annul each other. Society reflects the outside dimension (even if it is distinct from the state and its power) and it needs the interruption by sociality. Here again, we need to embrace the paradoxical relation between sociality and society: neither contradicting each other, nor overlapping in their meaning. Sociality is an-archical and it cannot enter in contradiction with society. Instead, it interrupts society from becoming a totality.

During our discussion of the presence and absence of sociality in Levinas's work, we argued that, despite the evident developments and changes in Levinas's thought throughout the years, changes that clearly affected the meaning of sociality, there are also consistencies in the way sociality is described. There is a strong and steady emphasis of the irreciprocal, asymmetrical and interruptive character of sociality. Along with this comes the importance of thinking sociality in terms of unthematized relation, reflecting the inside-out dimension of the relation to the other. This clearly transpires already in Levinas's early works, even though the thought itself is fully developed only in his later writings. Nonetheless, due to a certain lack of clarity and some inconsistencies in Levinas's thought we are forced to make some interpretational choices, and distance ourselves from Levinas's early emphasis on the face-to-face relation, and from his insinuations of considering sociality as a dyadic relation. We develop this argument in the chapter that follows, where we also propose to think sociality in terms of *facing* rather than face-to-face.

---

[100] EE 94.

[101] In this way, the interplay between sociality and society—distinct yet intertwined notions - opens up another sight, where the question of community, "we," and shared common are problematized in the light of sociality. The discussion from the third part of our thesis sets out precisely in this direction.

CHAPTER 8
Thinking Sociality with Levinas Against Levinas

The previous two chapters have served to depict the way sociality is presented in Levinas's work. We have shown, there, that the notion of sociality is absent in the sense that the meaning of this expression is seldom discussed directly, and yet at the same time very present in Levinas's oeuvre, in that it is always in sight when it comes to Levinas's overall project. Despite the elements that give continuity to Levinas's description of sociality throughout the different phases of his writings, there are, undoubtedly, elements that lack clarity, even inconsistencies in Levinas's texts. We argue that, in order to remain faithful to Levinas's more consistent thoughts on the meaning of sociality, we need to abandon some of the choices he makes in describing the notion. Hence, in a way, we are turning Levinas against himself.

In the following we will evoke some of Levinas's comments that seem to suggest a dyadic form of sociality (sociality between me and a singular other). Against these comments we maintain that, in order to remain in the spirit of Levinas's thought, sociality can neither be reduced to a dyad nor confused with the realm of the third. We begin by showing that our refusal of a dyadic reading is not bound to the necessary intertwinement between ethics and justice (i.e. the dyad leaves out the rest of the world). Rather, the problem goes deeper, and involves the connection between sociality and radical multiplicity. Then, we argue that the face-to-face relation remains susceptible to a dyadic reading of sociality, and owing to this risk, we choose to avoid this expression in our terminological vocabulary. Instead, we propose sociality as *facing* and, in the second part of this chapter, we discuss the advantages of opting for this expression.

8.1. The critique of the dyad

In discussing the intertwinement between ethics and justice,[1] we have expressed concerns regarding some of Levinas's comments that seem to depict the ethical relation in the form of a dyad. We argued subsequently that these comments carry the possibility of reading the ethical as being "disturbed" by justice, or the third as a limitation of the infinite responsibility for the other, both of which would disregard the radicality of multiplicity characteristic of the inside-out dimension of the relation to the other. Our examination has shown that the differentiation between ethics and justice is not given by the distinction between my relation to a singular other and the relation to a plurality of others, but rather depends on whether the relation to the other is considered beyond the constraints of a singular/plural alternative. With this in mind, we need to inspect once again Levinas's misleading comments that suggest a dyadic relation to the other, since they have serious repercussions for the way we read sociality in his work. Thus, this time, we need to analyze these comments in the light of the question of sociality.

When examining Levinas's early works, we have already come across a description of sociality as the loving couple, thoughts that Levinas developed in relation to Eros. Taking into account that later on Levinas appeared to change his mind and place an increasing emphasis on love without concupiscence, we will not be preoccupied with these early comments. In his later works, however, where sociality is approached in terms of Agape (instead of Eros) we find puzzling Levinas's allusion to sociality in terms of a dyad. In these later work, there are direct references to sociality as "the two of us,"[2] as well as indirect references to sociality thought as a duo. An illustrative example of the latter is given by an interview from 1987 when Levinas's interviewer formulates his question by explicitly stating that the relation between "two people" is the most important for Levinas.[3] Strikingly enough, Levinas does not show any objection to this way of formulating sociality. Instead, he invokes the intertwinement of ethics and

---

[1] See Chapter 4.
[2] See for example, "Philosophy, Justice and Love" (1982), in EN 106.
[3] "[C]an we be content with an abstract discourse on the ethical, when in fact the relation between two people—to which you [Levinas] give the greatest importance, and in which forgiving, forgetting, and unlimited self giving are possible—is not the real social situation?," "Dialogue on Thinking-of-the Other" (1987), in EN 201.

justice and the necessity of taking into account "humanity in its multiplicity," which in this context carries the meaning of the third party.[4] There are other, still more explicit accounts in which Levinas describes *my* relation to the other (that is, the inside-out dimension that sociality carries) in terms of a dyad. If the other and I were to be alone in the world, he explains, there would be no need for justice.[5] At other times, Levinas makes a strange division between two and three (between me and one other, and between me, one other and another other).[6] As we can see, there are plenty examples that can be evoked in order to show Levinas's troubling attitude towards a dyadic notion of sociality. In our view, there are at least two problems that such a dyadic notion raises: one regarding formalism (a problem that is recognized and solved by Levinas himself) and, another, regarding the overcoming of singular/plural, other/others dichotomies.

The first problem when considering sociality as a dyad is *the risk of creating a formal ethical structure*. We have seen Levinas's constant efforts to de-formalize the relation to the other. In order to avoid the same mistake that he described in Buber's I-Thou, in order, in other words, to avoid a merely "ethereal" sociality abstracted from the world, Levinas needs the third to be already implicated in sociality. Indeed, whenever Levinas makes a direct and explicit argument against thinking sociality as a relation between two, he always resorts to the necessity of justice, as always already implication of the third. Due to their intertwinement, the relation between ethics and justice is not exclusive, meaning that sociality (belonging to ethics) remains a dyad only as long as we abstract it from its necessary intertwinement with justice. This is a well-supported idea that occurs at

---

[4] "But then what about humanity in its multiplicity? What about the one next to the other—the third, and along with him all the others? Can that responsibility toward the other who faces me, that response to the face of my fellow man ignore the third party who is also my other? Does he not also concern me?," "Dialogue on Thinking-of-the Other" (1987), in EN 202.

[5] "it is the fact of the multiplicity of men and the presence of someone else next to the Other, which condition the *laws* and establish justice. If I am alone with the Other, I owe him everything; but there is someone else. The interpersonal relation I establish with the Other (autrui), I must also establish with other men (*les autres hommes*); there is thus a necessity to moderate this privilege of the Other; from whence comes justice." EI 89–90. See also OB. 157.

[6] "There lies a new difficulty, which invites us to a new development. We are not a pair, alone in the world, but at least three. Two plus a third.," "In the Name of the Other" (1990), in IIRB 193–4.

several occasions in Levinas's work, and is also taken up in different readings of Levinas.[7] Seen in the light of the question of sociality, this translates, on the one hand, into a designation on Levinas's part of sociality in terms of a dyad, and on the other hand, shows that there is never just a dyad, never just sociality, since there is never an exclusively ethical relation to the other. By this, Levinas offers a solution to the problem of thinking sociality in dyadic terms.

Taken in themselves, the intertwinement between ethics and justice and the refusal of a formal notion of sociality are indeed very important. Nevertheless, Levinas's argument suggests that he has no problem interpreting sociality as the relation between two people (me and *an* other), as long as we don't forget about the intertwinement between ethics and justice. At this point, the second problem with thinking sociality as a dyad shows itself: arguing against the framing of sociality in terms of a dyad solely on the basis of the always already need for justice, in our view, *fails to bring out the overcoming of the singular/plural, other/others distinction* that sociality implies. In other words, dismissing sociality as a dyadic relation simply on the basis of the intertwinement between ethics and justice, as seemingly Levinas does, deprives sociality from the more profound meaning given to it by Levinas's own radicalized way of thinking multiplicity. This seems like an inconsistency in Levinas's thought; an inconsistency that, if we are not careful enough, can easily lead to the simplification of a more complex meaning of sociality. Let us explain further.

As we have seen, one way of approaching the question of sociality in *Totality and Infinity* was through the expression "radical multiplicity." Sociality as radical multiplicity means that it cannot be considered in terms of singular/plural, other/others alternatives. On the contrary, it disrupts these alternatives, which already imply measuring and calculation. Thus, as radical multiplicity, sociality cannot represent a dyadic relation, a relation between two, for that would inscribe it in the singular/plural alternative. This also means that no account could be made regarding the number of persons involved in sociality, as the other/others alternative is disturbed as

---

[7] We have previously seen an example of such reading in Simmons, "The Third. Levinas's theoretical move from an-archical ethics to the realm of justice and politics," *Philosophy and Social Criticism* 25, no. 6 (1999): 83–104. Nevertheless, this reading appears from early on in different interpretations of Levinas's philosophy; one can find it already in Derrida's "Violence and Metaphysics" (see for instance *Writing and Difference*, 401–2.)

well. In this sense, sociality can neither be considered a relation to a singular other, nor a relation to a plurality of others, and as a consequence, the notion of sociality designates a relation to the other(s) where the resistance to the determination of the other(s) remains important. Understanding sociality as a dyadic relation and not as a radical multiplicity, and thus, thinking it in terms of a relation between the self and one singular other, would remain highly problematic. On the one hand, omitting the recognition of sociality as radical multiplicity could lead to differentiating between ethics and justice, and also between sociality and society according to number—which would be a rather absurd idea. On the other hand, if not considered in terms of radical multiplicity, sociality would lose the inside-out dimension of my relation to the other. Without the inside-out, an approach from the hither side of *my* relation to the other, sociality would be thematized and cease to remain a relation without relation.

As seen earlier, Levinas's own texts, on occasion, defy the crucial aspect of sociality, that it goes beyond the singular/plural, other/others alternatives. His confusing comments could easily mislead the reader into taking the notion of sociality as a simple relation between two. Such readings would a lack a consideration for the inside-out dimension that sociality holds, and thus greatly neglect that even thinking in terms of two (which already entails a differentiation between the other (singular) and others (plural)), turns sociality into a relation that allows for an outside perspective upon the relation itself—thus, thematizing the relation as such.[8] Richard Cohen's reading of sociality in Levinas's work is a good example in this respect, as it gives a dyadic reading of sociality. Although he uses expressions such as "social relation" or "intersubjectivity" (understandably, if we consider Levinas's unstable terminology), Cohen clearly refers to sociality and thinks it as a relation between two.[9] First, he gives a negative description of sociality as not interchangeable, not dialectical, and not representing a universal structure. We can easily agree with these claims, since we have also argued for irreciprocity, the refusal of relativeness and refusal of formalization to be important aspects of sociality. It is when he turns to a

---

[8] Levinas's use of the word *autrui*, which makes no distinction between singular and plural, indicates an indifference regarding how many others I am facing. It seems that the English translation of "*autrui*" as "other" or "Other," always in singular, contributes to this problem.

[9] See Richard A. Cohen, *Levinasian Meditations. Ethics, Philosophy and Religion* (Pittsburgh: Duquesne University Press, 2010).

more positive terminology, explicitly describing sociality as "dyadic,"[10] that we need to take a stand against Cohen's interpretation.

Unfortunately, the inconsistency of Levinas's text and his strange comments leave open the possibility of such readings. Nevertheless, we have shown that they fail to express the deeper meaning of sociality as radical multiplicity beyond the singular/plural, other/others distinction, and they neglect the inside-out dimension that sociality implies. Thus, it seems more valuable to remain in accord with Levinas's later thoughts on the de-posed subjectivity that, as we have seen, opens up the inside-out dimension. In the next part of the thesis, we reveal that our preference for following this aspect of Levinas's philosophy rather than considering the ethical relation as being between the 'two of us' opens up the notion of sociality towards the more complex context of community without a shared common. For now, however, we need to turn our attention to another expression often used in *Totality and Infinity*, the 'face-to-face' relation. Does not "face-to-face" also suggest a dyad? Me face-to-face with a singular other?

8.2. Sociality as Facing

The critique of thinking sociality in the form of a dyad relates to our previous objection regarding the face-to-face relation, presented in the context of sociality in Levinas's early and mid-period works.[11] Now, as we have shown the high risks brought by thinking sociality in terms of a duo, we need to return and discuss in more detail our objections to Levinas's expression 'face-to-face,' especially since it appears to be an expression of sociality.

We have seen that Levinas introduces the face-to-face relation while trying to find an alternative for the 'side-by-side' each other, that is to say, an alternative that would be outside the calculation and reciprocity that the 'side-by-side' type of relation implies. We can only agree with Levinas on the necessity of an approach from the hither side of the relation, which would challenge thinking exclusively in terms of reciprocity. At the same time, however, we are concerned about the risks that the expression 'face-

---

[10] "Intersubjectivity for both Levinas and Sartre is a relation that remains irreducibly dyadic and asymmetrical," Cohen, *Levinasian Meditations. Ethics, Philosophy and Religion*. 136.

[11] See Chapter 6.

to-face' carries. At occasions, the face-to-face relation is associated by Levinas with a relation "between individuals,"[12] a formulation which reinforces our concerns: the face-to-face relation seems to place the self and the other in comparable positions (me and the other are both individuals), despite the fact that this would contradict the immediacy implied by Levinas elsewhere.[13] Similar problems occur when Levinas depicts sociality as a "unique-to-unique," or "one-to-one" relation.[14] Expressing sociality in the form of 'face-to-face,' 'unique-to-unique,' or 'one-to-one' relations very much resembles a dyad, a relation 'between-the-two,' and thus suggests symmetry and reciprocity. At times, Levinas openly refers to the one-to-one relation as the "two of us."[15] We have seen however that, in the case of Buber, Levinas himself criticized the I-Thou relation for being a relation between the 'two of us,' a dialogical relation of reciprocity and symmetry. Now it starts to seem as if Levinas is making the same move that he criticized in Buber. Even if Buber specified that the I-Thou relation maintains the absoluteness of the other,[16] there is, according to Levinas's argument, symmetry and reciprocity implied by the I-Thou on account of their dialogical relation. When we apply the same critique to Levinas himself, it seems that although he insists on the immediacy of the face-to-face relation, this relation still carries the risk of introducing symmetry and

---

[12] "In the Name of the Other" (1990), in IIRB 194
[13] See for example TI 52.
[14] See for instance "Uniqueness" (1986), in EN 189–196 or "The Other, Utopia and Justice" (1988), in IIRB 200–210.
[15] The quotation that follows represents his answer to the question of whether there is a risk in exaggerating difference, for instance the risk of racism, anti-feminism etc., nevertheless it also serves to illustrate nicely Levinas's inconsistency regarding the "one-to-one" relation. "[T]here is a philosophy of human nature from the moment that there are two of us. And in fact there are three of us (laughter); and there is a sense in which my relationship with another is in conflict with my relationship with a third party. Consequently, I cannot live in society on the basis of this *one-to-one* responsibility alone. There is no calculation in this responsibility: there is no pre-responsible knowledge. The face carries everything, so in my view it is in the relationship to a third party that knowledge comes.," Interview with Emmanuel Levinas conducted by Raoul Mortley, in *French Philosophers in Conversation*, ed. Raoul Mortley (London: Routledge, 1991), 18; http://epublications.bond.edu.au/french_philosophers/2 (emphasis added). Clearly, in these contexts, we do not read "the third party" as an indicator of an empirical third (we have shown earlier that this is not the case for Levinas). Instead, what concerns us is the way Levinas seemingly identifies the one-to-one relation with the 'two of us.'
[16] "Martin Buber and the Theory of Knowledge" (1958/1963), in PN 26.

reciprocity into the meaning of sociality as long as it is described as a relation 'between two.'

We have previously seen that the de-posed self is not identifying itself to the other in a mirroring manner, nor does it hold out the possibility of changing positions to the other (it neither allows symmetry nor reciprocity). Nevertheless, the expression 'face-to-face' suggests that both the self and the other have a face (a symmetry), and that the self and the other are standing in front of, or in the face of *each other* (reciprocity). In order to keep the asymmetry and irreciprocity of the inside-out dimension of my relation to the other, the face (*visage*) needs to refer to the face of the other, and not to *my* face. Sociality, as an unthematized relation approached from the hither side, implies that the self as me is *the only one* responding/responsible. The other's responsibility should not be of concern in this context. Levinas openly agrees with this, by saying that the other's responsebility "is his [the other's] affair" and not mine.[17] Now, using Levinas's own words against himself, we can say regarding the face-to-face relation that only the other has a face, or rather that only the other is face (*visage*). My face, me being faced, cannot be of concern at this (inside-out) dimension of thinking the relation to the other; instead, this is "[the other's] affair." Evidently, by this argument we are not denying in a general way that the self (that I) has a face. The self also has a face, but in a different sense: if we describe the self in terms of face and of being faced by the other, we are already referring to the established, posited I; that is to say, this description already implies an outside dimension, where the posited I is an other for the other, and the question of the other's other is introduced; in this context, however, the relation becomes a 'side-by-side' type of relation.[18] Thus, we need to keep in mind that the irreciprocal and asymmetrical relation with the face of the other is problematized from the hither side, i.e. the inside-out dimension of the relation to the other. But in this sense, the self cannot be referred to in terms of face, and therefore the face-to-face relation as the expression of sociality (which we have seen represents the inside-out dimension) becomes unsuitable.

At this point, one might object that Levinas evokes the face-to-face relation using the French term '*face*,' and not '*visage*,' and thus that the two

---

[17] EI 98.
[18] We have seen earlier (Chapter 4) that this question brings up the problem of the third and justice in Levinas's philosophy.

expressions (face as *visage* and face as *face*) have different connotations. This would mean that by referring to the face-to-face relation Levinas does not imply that the self also has a face (*visage*) when its relation to the other is approached from the hither side, which would invalidate our previous critique. Unfortunately, Levinas does not explicitly problematize this question. Although, as we have already seen, there is a general difference between 'face' and 'visage' (the first one referring more to the physical face, while the latter is concerned with the epiphany of the face), we cannot find any indication in Levinas's text that there would be a significant difference between face as *face* from the face-to-face (*face-à-face*) relation and face as *visage*. At the same time, we also notice that occasionally he uses the expression 'face-to-face' interchangeably with '*vis-à-vis*,'[19] where 'vis' shares its etymological meaning with 'visage.'[20] These clues indicate that Levinas, as we suspected, refers to the 'face' from the face-to-face relation in terms of *visage*. His terminological choice to use *face-à-face* instead of *visage-à-visage* (both of which would be translated in English as 'face-to-face') seems to have only an operative role on the level of discursive flow (*face-à-face* being often used in the French language, in contrast to *visage-à-visage*, which would be a rather strange expression). Now, merely for the sake of argument, if we replace face-à-face with visage-à-visage our point regarding the risks of symmetry and reciprocity involved in the expression 'face-to-face' become even clearer: the face-to-face relation as visage-à-visage presupposes that I am also a face (*visage*) for the other, that I am also an other for the other—which, as shown above, is already the situation in need of an outside perspective upon the relation itself.

A second objection to our critique could be that Levinas is well aware of the duality that the face-to-face implies, and by using this expression he aims to endorse a dyadic description of sociality by relying on an empirical face-to-face situation. In such an empirical situation, one can look only into a single person's eyes, and it is impossible to look into the eyes of two or more persons at once. Thus, on a purely empirical level, this would indicate an impossibility of addressing more than a singular other (more than one). Hence, sociality as a face-to-face relation would need to be thought in dyadic terms, as the comments of Levinas that we have criticized seem to suggest. The problem with adopting this analogy is that it radically alters the

---

[19] See for example TeI 79.
[20] Both *visage* and *vis* (from *vis-à-vis*) originates from the Latin 'videre,' meaning 'to see.'

meaning of the 'face' by considering it in terms of the singular/plural alternative, and confuses it with a physical face. Rather than indicating a mere physical presence, we have previously shown that the face signifies concealment itself, the absolute alterity and mystery of the other—a mystery that loses all its meaning when we try to determine it.[21] Thus, if Levinas's intention with the face-to-face relation was to specifically endorse a dyadic reading of sociality through its empirical denotation (which we doubt is the case), this would only reinforce the need for critique.

Considering the discussion above, it seems a reasonable move to maintain the emphasis on the importance of the *face* while setting aside expressions such as 'face-to-face,' 'unique-to-unique' or 'one-to-one' as expressions of sociality.[22] Thus, instead of the face-to-face we propose sociality as *facing*, as me *facing* the other, which remains very different from the *facing each-other* that a face-to-face relation might suggest. *Facing each-other* would evidently imply reciprocity and symmetry. Sociality as *facing*, however, manages to keep the resistance to determination of the other (by considering the other in terms of face), while it maintains the relation's irreciprocity and asymmetry. Levinas's later work comes to support our proposal. In his preface from 1979 to *Time and the Other*, twenty years after the book was written, and fifteen years after the publication of *Totality and Infinity*, instead of presenting sociality as the face-to-face relation, Levinas refers sociality as "facing."[23] Just a few years later, in the essay "The Bad Conscience and the Inexorable" (1981), he calls facing, or "facing-up," "the secret of sociality":

> Even though, facing death, where the very rectitude of the face that calls me finally reveals fully both its defenseless exposure and its very facing-up [faire-face]; even though, in the last ultimate extreme the not-to-leave-the-other-man-

---

[21] See Chapter 6.
[22] Rejecting the unique-to-unique relation does not challenge the uniqueness of the self, but rather underscores that *my* uniqueness is brought by *my* election, as *me* (i.e. as the de-posed subject). The self is also unique, yet its uniqueness, *my* uniqueness is thought in terms of election and irreplaceability: the other is unique because alterity, while I am unique, Levinas explains, because I am the one called for response/responsibility for the other. Here is an illustrative quotation in this regard: "Q: The other man is unique. But I am too... E.L.: Where is my uniqueness? At the moment when I am responsible for the other I am unique. I am unique inasmuch as I am irreplaceable, inasmuch as I am chosen to answer to him," "Interview with François Poirié" (1986), in IIRB 66. In this sense, see also "The Vocation of the Other" (1988), in IIRB 108.
[23] TO 31.

alone consisted, in this confrontation and this powerless af-fronting [affrontement], in responding "here I am" to the demand that summons me. This is, doubtless, the secret of sociality.[24]

Even in *Totality and Infinity*, where Levinas indeed preferred the expression 'face-to-face,' we find reference to facing:

> [the surplus of the social relation] where the subjectivity remains in face of [en face de]..., in the straightforwardness of this welcome, and is not measured by truth."[25]

These developments in Levinas's writings strengthen our previously formulated argument that in order to grasp the meaning of sociality we need to shift our focus from the face-to-face as such, and approach sociality in terms of facing. Although the English word *facing* could also have the meaning of "turning my face towards something," this is not the meaning that we would like to propose. The French expression most often used by Levinas is '*en face de*,' which is sometimes translated in English as 'facing' other times as 'facing up' and it literary means 'in the face of....' Thus, instead of meaning '*me* turning *my face* towards something,' here, facing places the emphasis on the face of the other, as in *me facing* (me in the face of) *the other*. Read in this way, sociality as facing preserves the importance of the face by leaving it undetermined through the mystery of alterity. In order to emphasize this indeterminacy, we take advantage of the resources offered by the English language and, instead of the more literal translation of 'in the face of,' which would have a static and positioning character, we propose fac*ing* in its gerundive form.[26] The movement that the English word

---

[24] "The Bad Conscience and the Inexorable" (1981), in OGCM 175-6, DQVI 263. We should note here, although for now only in passing, that the expression Levinas introduces in the above quotation, "affronting" (affrontement), brings to our mind Nancy's affronted community [la communauté affrontée], (although the usual English translation is "the confronted community," (2001). Considering this resemblance of expression, it would be interesting to see how the two concepts relate. We will discuss this in Chapter 11.

[25] TI 221,"le surplus de la relation sociale où la subjectivité demeure en face de ... dans la droiture de cet accueil, et ne se mesure pas par la vérité.," TeI 244.

[26] The advantages of the gerundive form is highlighted in a recent conversation between Jean-Luc Nancy and Marcia Sá Cavalcante Schuback (see Jean-Luc Nancy and Marcia Sá Cavalcante Schuback, *Being With the Without* [Stockholm: Axl Books, 2013], 66-7.).

expresses is a movement without synchrony; it is not traced through the synchronous gesture of an overview. Through its mobile character, however, the gerundive of facing manages to express a de-positioning and maintains its resistance to determination. In this way, facing remains anarchical, an-original, without a place of departure in an established I.[27] The movement has no direction from a 'here' to a 'there,' but it has sense. Its sense is interruption itself, the disruption of totality and communion. Although, here, we call it movement, this interruption does not mark an action. Instead, it expresses precisely the overcoming of the duality passive-active: sociality is not inscribed in the passive/active alternative, but rather disturbs it. In this sense, sociality as facing is closely linked to what Levinas called "orientation," when he summarizes his thesis as being concerned with the "primacy of orientation" in *Totality and Infinity*, as well as its corresponding term in the later works: "approach."[28] We have seen that orientation, like the approach of proximity, expresses a movement without synchrony that gives sense and marks a relation without relation and without establishment. Indeed, in a later essay, Levinas connects proximity with 'facing,' and this connection shows once again the correlation between facing and sociality:

> In humanity, from one individual to another, there is established a proximity that does not takes its meaning from the spatial metaphor of the extension of the concept. Immediately, one and the other is one facing the other (*en face de l'autre*). It is myself for the other.[29]

Shortly, we will include Nancy in our discussion, when problematizing sociality in terms of community without a shared common (see Part III).

[27] The French that corresponds to 'facing' in its gerundive form could be '*en visageament*,' however Levinas does not use this expression.

[28] TI 215.

[29] "The Rights of Man and the Rights of the Other" (1985), in OS 124, HS 186. A similar comment regarding the "rectitude of facing" can be found in the essay "Diachrony and Representation" (1985): "The face of the Other—*under* all the particular forms of expression where the Other, already in a character's skin, plays a role—is just as much *pure expression*, an extradition without defense or cover, precisely the extreme rectitude of a *facing*, which in this nudity is an exposure unto death: nudity, destitution, passivity, and pure vulnerability. Such is the face as the very *mortality* of the other person. But through this mortality, which is also an assignation and obligation that concerns the ego—which 'concerns me,'—there is a 'facing up' of authority, as if the invisible death to which the face of the other person is exposed were, for the Ego that approaches it, *his*

Our critical points regarding sociality as a dual relation and sociality as face-to-face relation are more than just a matter of pedantry. They highlight the risk of thinking sociality in terms of symmetry, reciprocity and singular/plural or other/others dichotomies. Thought in these terms, sociality fails to express the inside-out dimension of the relation to the other(s), going against what Levinas has argued on so many occasions. Then, sociality as face-to-face becomes in certain ways similar with a relation 'side-by-side,' precisely that to which the face-to-face relation was supposed to offer an alternative. By proposing a notion of sociality as facing, we would like to avoid the risks involved in the face-to-face relation, and at the same time, develop a notion of sociality that, in a way, departs from Levinas's thought yet remains deeply connected to it. In the following part of the thesis we will continue to develop this notion of sociality by investigating the meanings revealed when sociality is thought in connection to community without a common ground.

business, implicating him before his guilt or innocence, or at least without his intentional guilt.," "Diachrony and Representation" (1985), in TO 107.

PART III
Un-common Sociality

In our quest to bring forth a Levinasian meaning of sociality, the first part of our thesis examined the unthematized and thematized relations to the other. We have seen that these correspond to two dimensions of the relation to the other, the inside-out, opened up by Levinas's notion of de-posed subjectivity, and the outside dimension, which reflects the way Levinas tackles the question of justice. Even though the word does not belong to Levinas's terminology, we have described these as *dimensions* in order to underline our argument that they do not designate different kinds of relations to the other, but only different ways of approach. Subsequently, the second part of the thesis was dedicated to discussing how the notion of sociality appears in Levinas's work. We found that in Levinas's writings sociality signifies an unthematized relation, one approached from the hither side. Nevertheless, the inconsistencies in Levinas's text have forced us to leave aside his conception of sociality in dyadic terms, and even sociality as the face-to-face relation. Instead, we have proposed sociality as *facing*, an expression that manages to maintain the importance of the face without, however, falling back into the singular/plural dichotomy, or running the risks of becoming a symmetrical or reciprocal relation.

Sociality as *facing*, we have shown to be very different from *facing each-other*, that is to say, from a side-by-side type of relation. A side-by-side type of relation already implies the sharing of that *something* towards which the self and the other are situated side-by-side. Sociality as facing, on the other hand, has nothing to share, not even itself since it is an unthematized relation. In this sense, we can say that sociality is without a shared common. It is this refusal of a sharing *something*, a refusal characteristic of sociality as facing, which captures our interest in this third part of the thesis. It will lead our discussion towards the debate on community thought otherwise than as grounded on a common *something*—a debate in which Levinas himself never fully took part. Connecting sociality as facing with the discussions on community without a shared common helps us to give shape to our notion of sociality inspired by Levinas, and, at the same time, it shows the importance of such a notion for a more contemporary debate on community.

We begin, in Chapter 9, by exploring Levinas's own understanding of community. There we argue that Levinas re-thinks community in the form of fraternal community, which expresses community interrupted by sociality. It becomes clear that, by engaging the interruptive character of sociality, Levinas criticizes a thinking of community in the determining terms of a shared common. This calls for an engagement with similar critiques; and thus, in Chapter 10 we address the more specific discussion on community outside communion, examining the approaches of Jean-Luc Nancy and Maurice Blanchot, who were among the first to raise this question. Then, Chapter 11 relates their debate to the notion of sociality inspired by Levinas, and hence enables us to further explore this notion of sociality by means of the ideas brought forth by both Nancy's and Blanchot's thinking on community.

We are about to show that the face-to-face relation is not radical enough to express the interruption of a side-by-side type of community, as Levinas intended, and that, instead, his notion of sociality needs to be thought further, as an un-common sociality of facing. In its turn, thinking sociality as facing reveals that ireciprocity and the inside-out dimension play a crucial role in thinking community without a common. In this way, the notion of un-common sociality, inspired by Levinas's philosophy but not always faithful to Levinas's wording, becomes a crucial aspect in thinking community without establishing it on a common foundation.

CHAPTER 9
Levinas's Community

In questioning the meaning of community, perhaps one of the first things that come to our mind is the model of community formed on the basis of a shared belonging: belonging to a certain society, collective, group or organization, but even also to humanity as a whole. This way of thinking community is determined (i.e. the community as such is defined by a shared *something*: nationality, state, territory, belief, etc.) and determining (i.e. the members of community are determined by the community they belong to). Nevertheless, as Roberto Esposito shows, the etymological origin of the word 'communitas,' *munus* already indicates something else, something other than determination. In the sense of its original meaning, the common of community is not characterized by a property, by *something*, but rather by a voiding and a lack of identification in itself, an expropriation of one's own subjectivity.[1] Although Levinas does not seem to explore directly the etymological meaning of community, the recognition of an insufficiency in understanding community based on a determined and determining common *something*, is, in our view, well reflected in his work. This insufficiency leads him to the importance of the face-to-face relation that replaces a 'side-by-side' community, and at the same time it involves the Levinasian notion of sociality deeply in the question of community.

---

[1] "The *munus* that the *communitas* shares isn't a property or a possession (*appartenenza*). It isn't having, but on the contrary, is a debt, a pledge, a gift that is to be given, and that therefore will establish a lack. The subjects of community are united by an 'obligation,' in the sense that we say 'I owe *you* something,' but not 'you owe *me* something.' This is what makes them not less than the masters of themselves, and that more precisely expropriates them of their initial property (in part or completely), of the most proper property, namely, their very subjectivity." Roberto Esposito, *Communitas. The origin and destiny of community* (1998), trans. Timothy Campbell (Stanford University Press, 2009), 6–7.

We begin this chapter by showing Levinas's dissatisfaction with community understood as a being side-by-side one another. As we are about to see, this way of thinking community hides within it a risk of totalization that is imbedded in the notion of community as communion (based on a shared *something*). Levinas proposes the face-to-face relation (which, we have seen is one of his ways of describing sociality) as that which interrupts community from forming a totality. Sociality interrupts community based on *something*, and this interrupted community takes the form, for Levinas, of fraternal community. However tempting it might be to identify the meaning of fraternity through its place in the slogan of the republic, Levinas reaches deeper than that, and explores the term in relation to sociality.[2] Thus, in the second part of the chapter, which is dedicated to the question of fraternal community, we argue that although the notion of fraternity generally remains problematic, when approached from the perspective of Levinas's later work, it reveals the important role of sociality in thinking community: sociality interrupts communion (totalization), and in this sense, makes community itself ungrounded, de-posed. It is in this way that Levinas's understanding of subjectivity becomes an important element in thinking community, and hence we will need to think the de-position, exile or groundlessness of the self characteristic of subjectivity, in connection with the meaning of sociality. This approach will also help us re-think Levinas's notion of sociality as an *un-common* sociality, that is to say, sociality which neither constitutes nor represents a common base or foundation, yet is necessary for re-thinking community in the way presented above. Nonetheless, the exploration of sociality as un-common remains incomplete in this chapter, as it calls for a deeper discussion on community without communion, a discussion to be undertaken in the last two chapters of this thesis.

---

[2] "Should not the fraternity that is in the motto of the republic be discerned in the prior non-indifference of the one for the other, in that original goodness in which freedom is embedded, and in which the justice and the rights of man takes on an immutable significance and stability, better than those guaranteed by the state?," "The Rights of Man and the Rights of the Other" (1985), in OS 125.

9.1. Side-by-side with a shared common

Given that Levinas is a Jewish thinker who was actively engaged in Talmudic readings and lectures, as well as in interpretational discussions of the Bible,[3] one would expect his thoughts on community to be linked to the Judaeo-Christian meaning of a confessional community tied by faith. In the following we attempt to show that the way Levinas describes community does not correspond to these expectations. Even in his confessional works, Levinas argues that, rather than being tied through a common foundation, community is brought by the face-to-face relation and by *my* infinite responsibility for the other—thoughts fully developed in his philosophical writings.[4] This way of approaching the question of community is well illustrated by the Talmudic reading "The Pact" (1982), which is focused on the covenant between God and the people of Israel.[5] We start our discussion with this essay.

---

[3] Here we refer to Levinas's Talmudic readings, but also his connection with Alliance Israélite Universelle, and his position as a director of École Normale Israélite Orientale; in addition, he had several discussions with Talmudic scholars at the *Colloque des intellectuels juifs de langue française*, where he gave his first Talmudic reading (1957), a colloquium attended by Vladimir Jankélévitch, André Neher, and Jean Halpérin, among others.

[4] Although it is a matter of debate whether or not it is adequate to make a separation between Levinas's philosophical and confessional writings, we have made the above distinction by considering Levinas's own remarks: "Among my publications there is a whole series of works drawn from this [his reading of Talmud], but I never run together my general philosophy with what I call the more confessional writings. I don't have the same publisher: the confessional writings are published by Minuit. But there's certainly some infiltration from one side to the other.," Interview with Emmanuel Levinas conducted by Raoul Mortley, in *French Philosophers in Conversation*, 13. Following Levinas, we will base our main argument on his philosophical texts, but without excluding his confessional writings either, when relevant.

[5] Regarding the question of the community of Israel, Levinas carefully specifies that the term "Israel" does not mean the state, territory, people of a certain ethnicity or of certain religious belief, but it designates precisely the priority of particular over the general, singularity over genus. Levinas says while commenting on Tractate *Baba Metsia*, 83a-83b: "What else could descendent from Abraham mean? Let us recall the biblical and Talmudic tradition relating to Abraham. Father of believers? Certainly. But above all the one who knew how to receive and feed men: the one whose tent was wide open all sides. Through all these openings he looked out for passerby in order to receive them. [...] So defined, the heirs of Abraham are of all nations: any man truly man is no doubt of the line of Abraham," "Judaism and Revolution" (1968), in NTR 99. This conception of the community of Israel, rather than advocating a totalizing inclusion of all religions into

In "The Pact" Levinas presents two ways of thinking community: on the one hand, the community of what he calls the "real" or "concrete" society, and on the other hand, the community of the face-to-face. The structure of society and our different roles in it, Levinas argues, makes us "come together side-by-side" rather than face-to-face, suggesting by this that the social community corresponding to a side-by-side type of relation (the "real" or "concrete" society) is different from sociality (here designated by the face-to-face).[6] Although we have not yet addressed directly the question of community, we have already shown that Levinas uses the expression "real society" in his early works in order to differentiate sociality from society as a structure.[7] We have seen, too, that in both *Existence and Existents* (1947)[8] and *Time and the Other* (1947)[9] Levinas points out the insufficiency of thinking the relation to the other exclusively in terms of a side-by-side.[10] Now, viewed within the context of community, a new aspect of Levinas's critique is being revealed, one which focuses this time on the insufficiencies that come from thinking community with an emphasis on a shared com-

---

one, is connected with Levinas's re-thinking of the meaning of religion. Religion is presented as the bond without totality to the other in *Totality and Infinity*: "We propose to call 'religion' the bond that is established between the same and the other without constituting a totality," TI 40. In *Otherwise than Being*, the word "religion" is reserved to the an-archic responsibility at the core of *me*: "exceeding the psychology of faith and of the loss of faith, 'religion' orders me in an anarchic way, without ever becoming or being made into a presence or a disclosure of a principle.," OB 168. Or in "The State of Israel and the Religion of Israel" (1951): "Religion and religious parties do not necessarily coincide. Justice as the *raison d'être* of the State: that is religion," in DF 219. (Here, we need to consider that the meaning of justice in Levinas's early writings corresponds to the unthematized relation of ethics from Levinas's later work. See Chapter 4.) Similarly to his notion of religion, which does not mean faith, but designates the ethical relation itself prior to justice (the relation without relation of the ethical responsibility that makes the self as *me* emerge in an-archy), Levinas understands the community of Israel not as the specific community of the State of Israel, but the very interruption of the totality that any specific community would form through the specificity that its people share (through their common bond). It might be helpful in this sense, to consider the essay "Levinas and Judaism" by Hilary Putnam, in which he explains the double movement of Levinas's universalization of Judaism, while keeping a resistance of universalization. (See Hilary Putnam, "Levinas and Judaism," in *The Cambridge Companion to Levinas*, 33–62).

[6] "The Pact" (1982), in BV 68.
[7] See Chapter 7.
[8] EE 95.
[9] TO 94.
[10] See Chapter 6.

mon. In "The Pact," the above mentioned expression, "[to] come together side-by-side," indicates the common sharing of a universal law which places us side by side, symmetrical and reciprocal toward one another, that is to say, one which makes us the same in front of the law. The law is applied to the whole community and, as such, it turns community into a whole, in the totality of the same; this is what Levinas means when a few lines later he says: "a concrete community capable of being taken in a gaze."[11] Perhaps the significance of this critique becomes more evident when we reformulate it in the following way: when the emphasis on thinking community is on the universal law that we all share, facing the law replaces facing the other.

Hence, the importance of the face-to-face *relation,* in the context of community, takes the form of the importance of the face-to-face *community*: "a community whose members are practically face-to-face should keep its interpersonal relationship when its members look outwards towards humanity."[12] The way Levinas frames his idea ("look outwards towards humanity"—humanity here implying universality[13]) points clearly at the dynamic between the inside-out and the outside dimension of the relation to the other—this is precisely what is at issue here. From the beginning of the essay, Levinas is searching for a notion of sociality different from a mere gathering around *something* in common. He proposes instead sociality in the form of the face-to-face community (in Levinas's formulation), or facing (the expression that we prefer to the face-to-face relation), corresponding to the inside-out dimension of the relation to the other. The universality of law, on the other hand, requires an outside perspective, and it is presented by Levinas in the form of the side-by-side type of community, or facing the law, which, if thought as the exclusive dimension of community, runs the risk of totalization. Our concern is not necessarily that Levinas finds the 'law' to be a possible way to reduce community to a totality. Rather we emphasize that the 'law' is a reference to a shared common, which is the true target of Levinas's critique. The side-by-side community from "The Pact" is very similar to the previously

---

[11] "The Pact," in BV 74.
[12] Ibid.
[13] However, this is not always the case in Levinas's works. The meaning Levinas gives to the human, and the question of the humanism in Levinas's work are complex, and cannot be undertaken here. In this sense, see Carl Cederberg, *Resaying the Human. Levinas Beyond Humanism and Antihumanism* (Stockholm: Södertörn Doctoral Dissertations, 2010).

mentioned "collectivity which says 'we,'" that designates the community where *I* is alongside the other, facing the shared common instead of facing the other.[14] In both cases, sociality (or, in Levinas's terminology the "face-to-face") is needed as a disruption of the totality that "we" or a shared common might form.

We have already emphasized the paradoxical intertwinement of ethics and justice, sociality and society, in other words, the inside-out and the outside dimensions of the relation to the other. Neither does Levinas forget to highlight, in this context, how the two ways to think community (the side-by-side, and the face-to-face), far from excluding each other, are in fact closely connected:

> [T]he distinction between community and society testifies only to a social thought that is not yet mature. The adoption of the Law on which this society is based would entail, for those men who adopt it correctly, the possibility of remaining face-to-face with one another.[15]

Inside-out and outside dimensions, the community of the face-to-face and the side-by-side, facing the other and facing the law: these are indeed different, but do not exclude each other, nor are they contradictory.[16] Their interconnection, according to Levinas, is reflected in the very ritual of the pact of the Covenant: those receiving the universal Laws of God stay on two mountains (Mount Gerizim and Mount Ebal) face-to-face with each other, and in this sense they are not just a society receiving the Law, but are also in sociality, facing, in the community of the face-to-face:

> In the Covenant, when it is fully understood, in a society that deploys all dimensions of the Law, society is also community.[17]

Thus, in "The Pact," just as in his philosophical writings, Levinas does not search for an exclusive alternative (either/or), nor does he propose an improved version of the side-by-side community, but rather points out the insufficiency of thinking community *exclusively* in terms of a side-by-side.

---

[14] See Chapter 6.
[15] "The Pact," in BV 75.
[16] This idea will become even clearer when Levinas considers community in terms of fraternal community (to be discussed in the next section).
[17] "The Pact,", in BV 84. Here, "community" refers to the community of the face-to-face.

The insufficiency of thinking community exclusively in terms of a side-by-side is reflected in a sense of being lost in our belonging to humanity as a whole. According to Levinas, the side-by-side type of community strengthens the sense of being lost in the universality of the social order.[18] By pushing Levinas's thoughts further, one can say that there is a sense of being lost in the very belonging to *something*. In this new context, sociality signifies precisely that which disrupts this belonging in such a way that we find ourselves in our not belonging. Thought in this way, the sense of being lost receives a positive connotation: there is a disruption of belonging, and with it comes a need for thinking community together with sociality that brings an inside-out dimension of the relation to the other, where the self is indeed lost, de-posed, but precisely as itself, as *me*. Thus, by arguing against the presupposition that Levinas would understand community on the basis of confessional belief, we have arrived at a deeper significance, namely, the insufficiency of thinking community based on a shared common, and its necessary disruption through sociality. This shared common can be a belief system, as in the case of religious community, but also a universal law, a common land, shared interests or any kind of common *something* that leads to communion, or in Levinas's terminology, totality.

The same critique of thinking community exclusively in terms of a shared common reveals itself through Levinas's objection to considering sociality as "community of a genus," a critique that is quite prevalent in his work.[19] By "community of a genus" Levinas means the union under a shared

---

[18] "[E]veryone has the impression of being simultaneously related to humanity as a whole, but also solitary and lost [...] Even within the family, human relationships are less alive and less direct because of the multiplicity of systems in which each person is caught, [...] hence the search for a more restricted society whose members would know one another. Some think that in order to achieve this, it is necessary to spend time together, to see one another regularly. Is this really the solution? [...] Will our sociality find fulfilment in a society of Sundays and leisure activities, in the provisional society of clubs?," "The Pact," in BV 68.

[19] We find an example of this approach in *Totality and Infinity* (1961): "The Other is not other with a relative alterity as are, in a comparison, even ultimate species, which mutually exclude one another but still have their place within the community of a genus—excluding one another by their definition, but calling for one another by this exclusion, across the community of their genus. The alterity of the Other does not depend on any quality that would distinguish him from me, for a distinction of this nature would precisely imply between us that community of genus which already nullifies alterity," TI 194. Or, even in Levinas's later work: "But we do not need this knowledge in the relationship in which the other is a neighbor, and in which before

common, which now, instead of the common law, as in "The Pact," is represented by common characteristics; in other words, me and the other are of the same kind, individuals of the same genus.[20] This new angle given by the critique as regards the community of a genus shows us yet more clearly the importance of making the differentiation between sociality on the one hand, and community based on a shared common, on the other hand. The community of genus places the emphasis on certain characteristics that are revealed and shared between me and the other. In this way, me and the other form a 'we,' while the reciprocity of sharing makes the other my counterpart, an alter ego. This is a form of determination of the other through relativeness, and one in which the meaning of alterity is lost. Moreover, thinking community based on a shared common not only goes against the alterity of the other, but also against the uniqueness of the self as *me*.[21] The uniqueness of the self is thought by Levinas outside the com-

---

being an individuation of the genus *man*, a *rational animal*, a *free will*, or any essence whatever, he is the persecuted one for whom I am responsible to the point of being a hostage for him," OB 59; or "Behind the reciprocal and formal alterity of individuals composing a genus, behind their reciprocal negativity (but in which, within the human genus, they are equals among themselves through the community of the genus, and endowed with reason, each one promised by Reason to peace 'for his part') a different alterity signifies.," "Uniqueness" (1986), in EN 192-3. In Chapter 3 we have shown that the refusal of thinking the self and the other as part of a genus has important repercussions regarding subjectivity. Hence Levinas's introduction of radical multiplicity, where the self and the other through their relation (through sociality) do not form a totality.

[20] However, this remains connected with the universality of the law, since those considered the same under the law, are in a sense considered as a part of the same genus.

[21] "The ego (*Moi*) is an incomparable unicity; it is outside of the community of genus and form, and does not find any rest in itself either, unquiet, not coinciding with itself," OB 8, AE 21. Here, we need to consider the different forms of self (I, ego, me) from Levinas's text (see Chapter 1). Previously, we have mentioned that '*Moi*' with a capital 'M' usually receives the English translation of 'ego' or 'I' because it often refers to the reflexive self, or the self as a concept. However, the unique self (the self which is always *my* self, the elected self in substitution), is usually noted by Levinas as '*moi*,' without capitalization. We can observe that in this fragment from *Otherwise than Being* the word '*Moi*' appears at the beginning of the sentence, which makes its sense puzzling: the capitalization is either intentional, belonging to the word '*Moi*,' or accidental, given by the fact that it is the beginning of the sentence. Considering the context it is more likely that Levinas refers to '*moi*' (what we have refered to as 'me' and not 'ego' as it appears in the translation), since what Levinas begins to describe in the cited phrase is precisely the uniqueness of the self, of me, and its resistance to generalization. The last sentence from the same paragraph gives even more strength to our interpretaion: "A unicity that has no

munity of genus. A community of genus represents a mere "plural of the I,"[22] with no regard of *me* emerging as a unique self. This implies a determinative way of thinking the self, where the subject is determined through its belonging to a genus. As we can see, the risks are high: for both the self and the other it becomes crucial to displace community constructed around a shared common where the emphasis falls on the common and not on difference; it is crucial to understand the disruption of the community formed as a totalizing genus where *we* stand side-by-side. Through its disruptive character, it is sociality that brings a different way to understand community, or rather it makes community different in the sense of non-indifferent, by disrupting it from coincidence and indifference. Let us evoke here Levinas's words from 1989, which give an excellent illustration of his efforts to differentiate between sociality, society, and community understood as communion:

> [E. L.] I feel that the neighbor is not a fall from coincidence, not a *modus deficiencies* of coincidence, regardless of what Plotinus thought. Throughout all of our literature, there has been the theme of two beings who may well coincide, yet do not get there—as if coincidence were the highest, the greatest value. Very important. Can one say, "sociability"? Can one say, "towards society"? I would like to find a more rigorous concept than "society." In French there is the word "socialité."
>
> Q: And how does it pertain to the difference—much discussed around the turn of the century—between "society" and "community"?
>
> E. L. "Community" is just as well the search for unity, for the coincidence of what is common among us. Seeking the place and position where one founds society on knowledge is Greek. Knowledge, common knowledge is "community."[23]

From the quotation above it becomes clear that Levinas is proposing sociality as that which disrupts the coincidence brought by a community of

---

site, without the ideal identity a being derives from the kerygma that identifies the innumerable aspects of its manifestation, without the identity of the ego (*moi*) that coincides with itself, a unicity withdrawing from essence—such is man," OB 8, AE 21.

[22] "The absolutely other is the Other. He and I do not form a number. The collectivity in which I say 'you' or 'we' is not a plural of the 'I.' I, you—these are not individuals of a common concept. Neither possession nor the unity of number nor the unity of concepts link me to the Stranger (l'Etranger), the Stranger who disturbs the being at home with oneself (*le chez soi*)," TI 39. (Note that here "we" gains a more positive meaning, and it does not designated unity).

[23] "Intention, Event and the Other" (1989), in IIRB 153.

genus, which is also referred to as 'knowledge'—knowledge that for Levinas designates determination and thematization. In a way, we find ourselves back at the paradox of the unthematized disrupting thematization, while neither belongs to thematization nor forms a separate realm. Thus, Levinas does more than just provide a critique. His thoughts on community are not exhausted by negative determinations (*not* communion, *not* genus), but he re-thinks community in the form of an interrupted community, through sociality.

The key issue, then, becomes the disruptive interplay between sociality and the community of genus. In what way does sociality make us re-think community? In the following we attempt to show that a more positive formulation of community is given in Levinas's work by the expressions 'fraternity' and 'fraternal community.'

9.2. Fraternal Community

The two expressions, 'fraternity' (*fraternité*) and 'fraternal community' (*communauté fraternelle*) are very close to each other in Levinas's work, and in some sense their meaning overlaps. Levinas strips fraternity from its meaning of biological kinship, and thinks it instead in the form of fraternal community. We find references already in *Totality and Infinity* that reveal the close connection between the two expressions,[24] and Levinas seems to remain faithful to this idea in his later works. The following lines from *Otherwise than Being* show clearly that fraternity, thought as fraternal community, outside its biological meaning, is differentiated from a community of genus, or the unity of the human race:

> Here there is a relation of kinship outside of all biology, "against all logic." It is not because the neighbor [le prochain] would be recognized as belonging to the

---

[24] "Human fraternity has then two aspects: it involves individualities whose logical status is not reducible to the status of ultimate differences in a genus, for their singularity consists in each referring to itself. (An individual having a common genus with another individual would not be removed enough from it.) On the other hand, it involves the commonness of a father, as though the commonness of race would not bring together enough. Society must be a fraternal community to be commensurate with the straightforwardness, the primary proximity, in which the face presents itself to my welcome." TI 214.

> same genus as me that he concerns me. He is precisely other. The community with him begins in my obligation to him. The neighbor is a brother.[25]

> Between the one I am and the other for whom I am responsible there gapes open a difference, without a basis in community. The unity of the human race is in fact posterior to fraternity.[26]

As we can see there are two uses of the term 'community' here. Firstly, the community with the other that begins "in my obligation to him," a formulation which designates community as it is re-thought by Levinas. Secondly, community is referred to as unity, as communion in *something* common (here, this *something* is the human race), which is the target of Levinas's critique and brings with it the need to re-think the meaning of community. In this sense, these lines resonate with Levinas's previously mentioned critique against thinking community as a community of genus, but they also raise the question about the relation between fraternal community and sociality. In looking for an answer to this question we will start by examining more closely Levinas's understanding of fraternity.

9.2.1. Thinking community through fraternity

Although we find references to fraternity relatively early in Levinas's work,[27] it was developed as a notion only later, in *Totality and Infinity*. There, as we saw in Chapter 7, leaving aside his strong emphasis on the erotic as a privileged relation, Levinas shifts his focus towards fecundity as the truly important aspect of the erotic love. Fecundity appears powerfully in *Totality and Infinity*, and the notion of fraternity finds its roots in it. Although still somewhat connected with Eros, fecundity now opens up another dimension: transcendence through the child, where the subject becomes other while remaining itself:

> [The subject] will be other than himself while remaining himself, but not across a residue common to the former and the new avatar. This alteration and

---

[25] OB 87.
[26] OB 166.
[27] It is mentioned already in *Existence and Existents*, in the context of social relation and the irreciprocal relation to the other. There, Levinas still sees Eros as a relation to the other and emphasizes that the reciprocal relation reflected by fraternity is "an outcome and not a point of departure, and refers back to everything implicated in eros," EE 96.

identification in fecundity—beyond the possible and the face—constitutes paternity.[28]

The parent's relation to the child, or paternity, in Levinas's terminology is a relation with a stranger, but also a stranger who I am,[29] and in this sense it undoubtedly has similarities with substitution, a notion developed later on in Levinas's work. In this early stage, however, Levinas's goal with his notion of fecundity is to emphasize the importance of the relation with the future. According to Levinas, fecundity is a relation with a future that is mine, but at the same time, an escape from self; it is my (the self's) future through the child. By means of fecundity I exceed my own possibilities, since my possibilities are both mine and not mine (they are also the possibilities of the beloved and the future of my child). This idea transpires in Levinas's quasi-definition of fecundity from *Totality and Infinity*:

> Both my own and non-mine, a possibility of myself but also a possibility of the other, of the Beloved, my future does not enter into the logical essence of the possible. The relation with such a future, irreducible to the power over possibles, we shall call fecundity.[30]

In this way, fecundity is transcendence, transcending oneself while remaining oneself; it is not reducible to a condition of possibility (in Levinas's own words quoted above: "does not enter into the logical essence of the possible") because it does not serve as a ground, origin or arche. We can say that the transcendence characteristic of fecundity is transcendence in immanence, similar to the hither side as an-archy from Levinas's later work. Thus, it is not a coincidence that fecundity also has a disruptive character in relation to time, just as an-archy has. Through the future of the child, fecundity, Levinas says, "opens up an infinite and discontinuous time."[31]

---

[28] TI 272. In Levinas's vocabulary, whenever he refers to the parent-child relation he speaks in terms of "father," "son," "filiality" or "paternity." We acknowledge that this constitutes a problem in Levinas's discourse and we will return to it briefly in the next section.

[29] "Paternity is a relation with a stranger who while being other [...] *is* me, a relation of the I with a self which yet is not me. In this 'I am' being is no longer Eleatic unity. In existing itself there is a multiplicity and a transcendence," TI 277.

[30] TI 267.

[31] TI 301.

The discontinuous time characteristic of fecundity makes the parent-child relation very different from a relation of causality. Instead of a causal relation between the parent and the child, Levinas speaks about "creation."[32] His decision to use this word shows us again the link between an-archy and fecundity: contrary to suggesting the existence of an entity from a higher order with the power to create, creation goes against order and established origin; it indicates non-originarity in itself. The child is created, but this does not invest the parent with some kind of power or dominating position regarding the child. Instead, it indicates going beyond causality and beyond originarity: if it were not created, it would be the *result* of something, it would have a *source* (an origin), and it would be integrated in a totality formed by a line of causality.[33] The son is unique, chosen, elected by the father, without however the father's fulfilling the role of a Creator. Election does not invest the parent with any specific power, but simply expresses the uniqueness of every child.[34] Filiality, the other side of fecundity, strengthens this non-causal relation with the parent. The child is separated through the temporal discontinuity, the rupture involved in filiality, but there is also a "recourse at the same time," Levinas explains[35]—and here one can see similarities with the recurrence of the self in an-archy from *Otherwise than being*.[36] While in the case of paternity the emphasis was on the transcendence through fecundity, we can observe that in the case of filiality, Levinas sees the parent-child

---

[32] "Creation contradicts the freedom of the creature only when creation is confused with causality. Whereas creation as a relation of transcendence, of union and fecundity, conditions the positing of a unique being, and his ipseity qua elected," TI 279.

[33] In *Otherwise than Being*, Levinas returns to the question of creation in the context of substitution and anarchy and shows again the strong link between the two: "It is not here a question of justifying the theological context of ontological thought, for the word creation designates a signification older than the context woven about this name. In this context, this said, is already effaced the absolute diachrony of creation, refractory to assembling into a present and a representation. But in creation, what is called to being answers to a call that could not have reached it since, brought out of nothingness, it obeyed before hearing the order. Thus in the concept of creation *ex nihilo*, if it is not a pure nonsense, there is the concept of a passivity that does not revert into an assumption. The self as a creature is conceived in a passivity more passive still than the passivity of matter, that is, prior to the virtual coinciding of a term with itself," OB 113-4.

[34] "The son is a unique son. Not by number; each son of the father is the unique son, the chosen son," TI 279.

[35] TI 278.

[36] See especially OB, Ch.IV.2.

relation with an emphasis on the uniqueness of every child. Now, it is the elected child that reflects Levinas's later thoughts on subjectivity. This side of the parent-child relation is also the one that sets out Levinas's developing of the notion of fraternity. If the father-son relation means that the son is unique, elected, fraternity means that the son is also equal with his brothers. Accordingly, in *Totality and Infinity*, fraternity is presented as a two-folded notion: one the one hand, through its connection to filiality it points towards the uniqueness of the elected self, characteristic of ethics, and on the other hand, the equality it entails connects fraternity to the order of justice. Levinas brings forth this idea through the paradox of the uniqueness and non-uniqueness of the child:

> The unique child, as elected one, is accordingly at the same time unique and non-unique. Paternity is produced as an innumerable future; the I engendered exists at the same time as unique in the world and as brother among brothers.[37]

Levinas's notion of fraternity makes us return to our earlier discussion of the relation between ethics and justice. We already pointed out the importance, for Levinas, of breaking down an exclusive type of thinking, and embracing instead the paradoxical intertwinement between the inside-out and outside dimension. In this context, the notion of fraternity problematizes precisely this intertwinement. Fraternity conveys equality and thus certain symmetry and reciprocity characteristic of the outside dimension of the relation to the other, while at the same time, through filiality, it brings forth the asymmetry and irreciprocity characteristic of an inside-out dimension. That is to say, fraternity reinforces our previous argument regarding the non-exclusiveness of ethics and justice. The following lines from *Totality and Infinity* come to support this argument:

> The I as I hence remains turned ethically to the face of the other: fraternity is the very relation with the face in which at the same time my election and equality, that is, the mastery exercised over me by the other, are accomplished.[38]

By now it has become clear that fraternity does not simply constitute the unity of a genus, yet one cannot deny that there is a certain fraternal bond through the figure of the father. Does not the father signify precisely a

---

[37] TI 279.
[38] TI 279.

common mediator for the "brothers"? How can fraternity refer to any kind of common while remaining outside a community of genus and thus without contradicting Levinas's effort of going against a totalizing communion? It is time now to address some of the difficulties encountered when dealing with the notion of fraternity.

9.2.2. Some problems with fraternity

One of the most noticeable problems arising from Levinas's notion of fraternity and its surrounding concepts consists in the use of a patriarchal language. Indeed, Levinas's account of fraternity is quite strikingly dominated by a masculine language: it is about "the son" and not "the daughter," "the father" and not "the mother," "paternity" and not "motherhood," "fraternity" and not "sorority." This critique addresses similar issues to the previously discussed problems raised by Levinas's thinking of the feminine and his early thoughts on love.[39] We acknowledge the importance of criticizing Levinas's patriarchal language, and certainly agree with its problematical nature. However, since this aspect of Levinas's work does not constitute the topic of our thesis, we will not develop this issue, as it would require a study of its own. Still, besides signaling our agreement with the inadmissibility of Levinas's patriarchal language, in order to do him justice, we also need to mention that, just as in the case of the feminine, Levinas seems to become more aware of these errors as his work develops. As a consequence, he puts more effort into making it clear that fraternity does not represent a biological brotherhood,[40] and that the emphasis is on "the fact that the son, and the daughter too, is other and is still, but only still, me."[41] Levinas underlines that biological fraternity alone does not offer sufficient ground for responsibility.[42]

---

[39] See Chapter 6, "Sociality and love."
[40] Levinas reassures us several times throughout his work that the notion of fraternity, as he understands it, is not based on biological relatedness. See for instance see "Interview with François Poirié" (1986), in IIRB 61, or even in *Totality and Infinity*: "The biological origin of this concept [fecundity] nowise neutralizes the paradox of its meaning, and delineates a structure that goes beyond the biologically empirical," TI 277.
[41] "Interview with François Poirié" (1986), in IIRB 59.
[42] "The biological human brotherhood—conceived with the sober coldness of Cain—is not a sufficient reason for me to be responsible for a separated being. The sober coldness of Cain consists in conceiving responsibility as proceeding from freedom or in terms of a

Derrida, who also noted the patriarchal resonance of the concept of fraternity,[43] extends this critique by problematizing the familial model implied by fraternity and the homogeneity that comes from that model. Although not necessarily implying a biological relatedness, the term "fraternity" has its roots in familial kinship; that is to say, it continues to imply a bond that unites on the basis of homogeneity. Derrida calls "fraternization" the building up of politics on the idea of fraternal bond.[44]

contract. But responsibility for the other comes from what is prior to my freedom," Levinas, "God and Philosophy" (1975), in OGCM 142.

[43] "Brothers have named themselves brothers in so far as they issue from one and the same mother: uterine brothers. But what will one say of brothers ('distantly related' or 'consanguine') who are thus called because they issue from the same father? And what about the sister? Where has she gone?" Jacques Derrida, *The Politics of Friendship* (1994), trans. George Collins (London and New York: Verso, 2005), 96. "Is it that 'son' is another word for 'child,' a child who could be of one or the other sex? If so, whence comes that equivalence, and what does it mean? And why couldn't the 'daughter' play an analogous role? Why should the son be more or better than the daughter, than me, the Work beyond 'my work'? If there were no differences from this point of view, why should 'son' better represent, in advance, this indifference? This unmarked indifference?" Derrida, "At This Very Moment In This Work Here I Am" (1980), in *Re-reading Levinas*, 39–40.

[44] "Democracy has seldom represented itself without the possibility of at least that which always resembles—if one is willing to nudge the accent of this word—the possibility of a *fraternization*," Derrida, *The Politics of Friendship*, viii; "Everything in political discourse that appeals to birth, to nature or to the nation—indeed, to nations or to the universal nation of human brotherhood—this entire familialism consists in a renaturalization of this 'fiction.' What are we calling 'fraternization,' is what produces symbolically, conventionally, though authorized engagement, a *determined politics*, which, be it left- or right-wing, alleges a real fraternity or regulates spiritual fraternity, fraternity in the figurative sense, on the symbolic projection of the real or natural fraternity," Ibid., 93). Needless to say that Derrida's considerations do not stop here; he goes forward towards discussing politics and "democracy to come." For more on Derrida and his discussion on fraternity see for example John D. Caputo, "Who is Derrida's Zarathustra? Of Fraternity, Friendship, and a Democracy to Come," in *Research in Phenomenology* 29, no. 1 (1999): 184–198. On Derrida's critique of fraternity see also A. J. P. Thomson, "Against Community: Derrida contra Nancy," in *The Politics of Community*, ed. Michael Strysick (Aurora: Davies Group Publishers, 2002), 67–84. Although the stake of the article is Derrida's critique of Nancy, the author points out the critique of fraternity presented by Derrida, according to which fraternity would always set a limit, there are brothers, but there are those outside this fraternity; this would turn fraternity or friendship based on brotherhood limited in number. Nevertheless, we are not addressing this critique here since we have already shown at the beginning of this chapter Levinas's strong emphasis on the particularism over universalism that his understanding of community implies.

Along with this there always comes a certain threat of homogenization that the notion of fraternity in general carries. If any notion of fraternity leads to homogeneity, as Derrida suggests, that would create serious difficulties for Levinas's re-thinking of community. Levinas must have been aware that the notion carries the connotation of relatedness, of a certain bond, even if it is not a biological one. If the fraternal bond is created by certain similarities or by a shared common element, then fraternal community can easily become a homogeneous unity—that is, the notion would emphasize sameness and communion based on this sameness. This would go against Levinas's own efforts to overcome a notion of community thought in terms of belonging to a genus, of communion and totalizing unity.[45]

A similar problem arises due to the important role of filiality and paternity in Levinas's way to address fraternity, and the monotheistic type of thinking that it implies. Fraternity thought in terms of monotheism might be problematic as it suggests the necessity of a father representing the common ground for fraternity:

> On the other hand, it [human fraternity] involves the commonness of father, as though the commonness of race would not bring together enough. Society must be fraternal community to be commensurate with the straightforwardness, the primary proximity, in which the face presents itself to my welcome. Monotheism signifies this human kinship.[46]

The contextualizing of fraternity in a father-son relational structure, as Levinas seems to do, has been criticized both for its theological and for its ethical monotheism. Critchley reproaches Levinas for involving monotheism in thinking fraternity because "the universality of fraternity is assured

---

That is to say, it is not about belonging to a group (with certain number of individuals), but precisely the breaking down of belonging itself.

[45] This is exactly the danger of totalization that Levinas describes in *Totality and Infinity*: no matter if it is the result of a relation to the other based on similarities, or a negative description where the other and the self form a dialectical couple, or even a definition forced upon the other that would make it knowable (thus, assimilated through comprehension), in all these cases the self would in fact remain in a relation with itself, in the Same: "[…] the radical separation between the same and the other means precisely that it is impossible to place oneself outside of the correlation between the same and the other so as to record the correspondence or the non-correspondence of this going with this return. Otherwise the same and the other would be reunited under one gaze, and the absolute distance that separates them filled in," TI 36.
[46] TI 214.

through the passage to God."[47] This means, according to Critchley's interpretation, that fraternity implies the mediation of God. We can see why thinking fraternity based on mediation would be a problem: it would transform the whole concept of fraternity into a mediated relation (representing solely the outside dimension of the relation to the other, and thus losing its emphasis on the importance of the inside-out). In Llewelyn's reading, although fraternity is not sharing a common genetic relation to the father (the author acknowledges that fraternity disrupts the idea of a common genus), there is still an "ethical monotheism" where a self-identical father holds an important role for the identity of the self.[48]

In agreement but also complementary to Critchley's and Llewelyn's reading, let us point out that the risk of thinking fraternity and fraternal community in the light of the Father (which remains a very important figure in *Totality and Infinity*) is two-fold. Firstly, if the father is considered a common reference, a mediator, then the face-to-face relation would be transformed from facing the other to each facing the same *common* father. The relation of fraternity would become a relation alongside one another, and fraternal community would turn into an uninterrupted side-by-side type of community. Secondly, the emphasis on the father leads to thinking society based on the model of the family, which means that society would be reduced to an extended version of the small core represented by the family. We have already seen that Derrida criticizes the notion of fraternity for maintaining the familial model. Nancy gives a similar critique to fraternity as a model of community shaped according to the prototype of the family.[49] The family, in this sense, would constitute an ideal model for community and thus the community that is based on it would carry the "consciousness of lost community" (in this case, the "lost community" would be the ideal model of the family).[50] In our next chapter we will examine in detail how Nancy questions a community based on a consciousness of lost community;

---

[47] Simon Critchley "Five Problems in Levinas's View of Politics and the Sketch of a Solution to Them," *Political Theory* 32, no. 2 (2004): 174.

[48] "The identity of each is in part defined by a relation to a self-identical father," John Llewelyn, *Emmanuel Levinas: The Genealogy of Ethics* (Florence, KY: Routledge, 1995), 137.

[49] For a comparative reading of Nancy's and Derrida's critique of fraternity as a model of community see Marie-Eve Morin, "Putting Community Under Erasure: Derrida and Nancy on the Plurality of Singularities," *Culture Machine*, 8 (2006), http://www.culture-machine.net/index.php/cm/article/viewarticle/37/45.

[50] IC 9–10.

for now, it is suffice to say that a community defined by its striving to achieve an ideal original community remains, according to Nancy, an enclosed community united by the very idea that it is striving for. When community is enclosed in this way, its very plurality is dissolved, or rather melted together, since it lacks the openness to an outside. When we transfer this concern to Levinas's philosophy, we can see that an enclosed community, lacking openness towards exteriority, leads, again, to totalization—that is to say, it would go against the very point that Levinas tries to make through his notion of fraternity. In a more recent work, Nancy presents another side of fraternity which would not fall in the trap of his previously emphasized enclosure: "to be together without a consistent cause of being together."[51] At first glance, this interpretation is very close to the way that Levinas describes fraternity.[52] For Nancy, nevertheless, and contrary to Levinas, in order to escape the 'lost' ideal community and its risk of enclosure, the father should not carry any importance for fraternity. Moreover, he says, "my only argument is that fraternity is precisely without the father. Fraternity starts when the father is dead."[53] A similar thought is also reflected in his short essay dedicated to fraternity, where he relates the notion of fraternity to nourishment rather than to brotherhood and family relatedness.[54] "'[F]raternity'—Nancy claims—does not in itself carry the

---

[51] Nancy and Sá Cavalcante Schuback, *Being With the Without*, 31.

[52] Howard Caygill, in his article "Bearing Witness to the Infinite: Nancy and Levinas" (*Journal for Cultural Research* 9, no. 4 (2005): 351–357) shows an interest in this connection through a comparison of Levinas's and Nancy's understanding of community/fraternity. Although Caygill's article focuses mainly on Nancy's work, towards the end of the text he draws a parallel between Nancy's approach regarding the Christian moment of the resurrected Christ's visitation of Magdalene, and Levinas's notions of illeity and the trace. Caygill argues that in both cases there is an absence (the untouchable body of Christ, and, respectively, the untouchable face), which ultimately stays at the core of community and fraternity. "Placing absence at the heart of community produces for both Levinas and Nancy a more complicated understanding of fraternity, not as the incarnation of a community, but as a site of witness for the absent God and the joyful promise of an other than fraternal community," Ibid., 356.

[53] Nancy and Sá Cavalcante Schuback, *Being With the Without*, 31. Then he continues by reinforcing his previous point: "But the truth of fraternity is precisely to be *without* any common thing," Ibid.

[54] "'[B]rothers' are not originally those united by the same blood. For "blood" is nothing but the symbol of filiation through the transmission of semen (of a natural identity or conformity), and filiation itself is represented according to an ancient scheme in which the mother lacked any generative power of her own (and was instead seen simply as an incubator). 'Blood' is by no means a sufficient explanation of what comprises generation

values of the masculine and the parental as we ordinarily understand them."⁵⁵ This idea, however, remains rather far from Levinas's early conception of fraternity (the one predominant in *Totality and Infinity*), where the father still occupies an important role.

As we can see, fraternity, and with it, fraternal community, approached from the perspective of a familial model and a paternal structure, remain problematic concepts. In an effort to develop our thoughts on Levinas's notions of fraternity and fraternal community in a fruitful way, it seems reasonable to distance ourselves from this approach. Thus, instead of settling on the context of the father-son structure characteristic for *Totality and Infinity*, in the following we propose to take a different angle and consider the notion of fraternity in relation to Levinas's account of subjectivity and the question of thematization developed in his later works. In doing so, our goal is to reveal a deeper meaning of Levinas's fraternal community, one that is somewhat detached from the father-son monotheistic and patriarchal schema. This will help us elaborate on the earlier mentioned meaning of fraternity as the intertwinement between ethics and justice. At the same time, it enables us to investigate more clearly the relation between the meaning of fraternal community and the notion of sociality.

---

and filiation. Sons and daughters are not so much those united by blood —pater incertus, said the Roman law — but rather those united by the community of maternal nursing —mater certissima: whether it be real or symbolic, nursing does not consist in the internal, continuous and immediate transmission of a vital principle, but in the external, discontinuous and mediated gift of a nourishing substance.," Jean-Luc Nancy, "Fraternity," *Baltic Worlds* (Special Theme: Voices on solidarity), Vol. VIII, 1-2, Centre for Baltic and East-European Studies (CBEES), Södertörn University (April 2015): 99.

⁵⁵ Ibid. Nancy goes on to explain that fraternity, linked to nourishment rather than suggesting a "blood" connection through the father, refers to an outside: outside oneself and outside the law (outside the authority figure of the father). We find it interesting that these ideas presented by Nancy bear some similarity to Levinas's notion of fraternity as it appears in his later work. As we will see in the next section, Levinas's later works reveal a more complex notion of fraternity, where the outside (exteriority) is signaled, and fraternity becomes the very Unsaying of the Said, carrying the trace and sense of the unthematizable. Nancy's closing thoughts on fraternity are strikingly similar: "'Fraternity' is certainly an insufficient term, even if not necessarily a dangerous one. Nevertheless it is a signal: it alerts us to the fact that the social, juridical and political order cannot assume the register of sense. It can only provide the framework of sense. But it is essential that it should do so, and that in order to do so, it is able by itself to indicate that it is beyond the law, in a place where sense emerges," Ibid., 100.

9.2.3. Fraternal community and sociality

From the 1970's onwards, the patriarchal language of Levinas's writings surrounding fraternity seems to weaken, and the notions of fecundity, paternity and filiality slowly start to fade away. In an interview from 1981 Levinas himself acknowledged this change:

> What I wrote in *Totality and Infinity* about the meaning of 'the son' (*Totality and Infinity*, 287ff./ *Totalité et infini* 255ff.) has also become less important. The father-son structure is released from the biological relationship and forms an interpersonal relationship, namely that of 'fraternity.' The fraternal bond between people is not explained, as I feel now, by the fact that we are children of the same father. The fraternity of 'All people are brothers' is prior to a pure biological brotherhood. I am taking more and more distance from the terminology related to the erotic that I used before. What was formerly central, has become marginal.[56]

Although fecundity and paternity tend to disappear from Levinas's later work, the notion of fraternity is maintained. While not so powerfully present as in *Totality and Infinity*, we still find it in *Otherwise than Being* and later essays,[57] however there is a definite change of context. With the development of substitution Levinas seems to replace what in *Totality and Infinity* signified the birth of the child, with the 'birth' of the self; hence, in *Otherwise than Being*, fraternity is closely connected to substitution. The structure of the-one-for-the-other—Levinas claims—is inscribed in human fraternity, it is the very signification of fraternity.[58] The connection between substitution and fraternity means that, in Levinas's later works, community is re-thought through the question of subjectivity.

Even when detached from the model of the family, fraternity retains its two-fold character. On the one hand, it does not entail the unity of a genus,[59] and on the other hand, fraternity means equality among the "brothers":

---

[56] "What one asks of oneself, one asks of a saint," 20.
[57] For example in God and Philosophy (1975); The Meaning of Meaning (1980); Notes on Meaning (1981); Peace and Proximity (1984); The Rights of Man and the Rights of the Other (1985).
[58] OB 166-7. One can find a similar reference in "The Meaning of Meaning," in OS 92-3.
[59] "The unity of the human race is in fact posterior to fraternity," OB 166.

> The other is from the first the brother of all the other men. (Cf. *Totality and Infinity*, pp. 212ff.) The neighbor that obsesses me is already a face, both comparable and incomparable, a unique face and in relationship with faces, which are visible in the concern for justice.[60]

Fraternity, "the brother of all the other men," implies equality, yet it does not coincide with the order of justice. Instead it expresses the carrying of uniqueness, the ethical, into justice. That is to say, it reflects precisely the non-exclusiveness of the two dimensions inside-out and outside of approaching the relation to the other. Similarly, fraternal community does not coincide with the way that Levinas describes society as the collectivity of the 'we,' the common life of us.[61] Instead, fraternal community goes beyond thinking community as sharing *something* in common. The great change that Levinas brings in *Otherwise than Being* regarding fraternal community consists in the fact that he no longer needs the model of the family from *Totality and Infinity* since, through his development of subjectivity and the de-posed subject, a de-rootedness of fraternity also takes place. This interpretation is indeed supported by Levinas's remark that the unthematized one-for-the-other is "inscribed" in fraternity,[62] and fraternity does not arise from thematization.[63] In the de-position and de-rootedness of both subjectivity and community (fraternity), the ambiguous interplay between the thematized and the unthematized, between the Saying and the Said is revealed. This thought suggests a connection between sociality as an unthematized relation and fraternity, and so we proceed with its closer examination.

It is no mere coincidence that Levinas, in his later work, takes up the question of fraternal community with reference to the problem of thematization. We have previously seen that the unthematized relation, in which the relation to the other is approached from the inside-out, has sense through giving sense to the thematized.[64] In other words, the unthematized

---

[60] OB 158.
[61] Regarding Levinas's critique of the collectivity of the 'we,' see Chapter 7.
[62] Ibid., 166.
[63] "Representation does not integrate the responsibility for the other inscribed in human fraternity; human fraternity does not arise out of any commitment, any principle, that is, any recallable present. The order that orders me to the other does not show itself to me, if not through the trace of its reclusion, as a face of a neighbor.," OB 140, translation altered according to the original, AE 220.
[64] See Chapter 4.

makes sense when it actually makes (gives) sense, through its trace. We cannot reach the unthematized, but we find its trace in the thematized, without this trace actually leading us to the unthematized; that is to say, the trace cannot be tracked in the usual sense. The mode of signification that Levinas proposes can only be thought from the thematized towards the unthematized, and not the other way around. In other words, it needs an Unsaying of the Said so that the signification of the Saying can come forth. When Levinas introduces the question of fraternity in this setting, it becomes clearer that fraternal community has the role of unsaying community as communion. This idea is revealed in the following fragment from the beginning of *Otherwise than Being*:

> But how is the saying, in its primordial enigma, said? How is time temporalized such that the dia-chrony of transcendence, of the other than being, is signalled? How can transcendence withdraw from esse while being signalled in it? In what concrete case is the singular relationship with a past produced, which does not reduce this past to the immanence in which it is signalled and leaves it be past, not returning to a present nor a representation, leaves it be past without reference to some present it would have "modified," leaves it be a past, then, which can not have been an origin, a pre-original past, anarchical past?[65]

Just a few lines below, Levinas responds to his question through the notion of fraternity:

> But the relationship with a past that is on the hither side of every present and every re-presentable, for not belonging to the order of presence, is included in the extraordinary and everyday event of my responsibility for the faults or the misfortune of others, in my responsibility that answers for the freedom of another, in the astonishing human fraternity in which fraternity, conceived with Cain's sober coldness, would not by itself explain the responsibility between separated beings it calls for.[66]

Fraternity signifies "the extraordinary and everyday event," through which the Saying is signaled in the Said. The Saying is Said with fraternity, due to its double-folded character (expressing equality and also non-coincidence), and the uniqueness that it maintains. Fraternity carries the signification of the Saying into the Said without losing the inside-out dimension of

---

[65] OB 10.
[66] Ibid.

responsibility. Levinas's notion of fraternity carries in itself "the responsibility between separated being," but fraternity by itself does not "explain" it—that is to say, the sense (meaning) of responsibility is not given by fraternity. Here again, we are dealing with an essential ambiguity: it is the ambiguity of reciprocity, a posited self "with" the other, and also elected, unique self, the ambiguity of *between* but also *separated* beings. The word "between" expresses the possibility of reciprocity—reciprocity which ensures the equality—needed by politics. "Cain's sober coldness," we have seen,[67] points towards the posited self as *I*.[68] *Separateness* expresses the refusal of totalization: those in fraternal relation are neither defined by similarities, nor by dialectical opposition, nor do they form an alliance through sharing *something*. Separateness indicates that in fraternal community the resistance to determination is maintained (the other is my 'brother' but at the same time a stranger).

Thus, fraternal community neither annuls the inside-out dimension of the relation to the other (as a community of genus would), nor is it the source of *my* responsibility. In other words, it neither goes against, nor coincides with sociality. In the essay "God and Philosophy" from 1975, by appealing yet again to the Cain-Abel relationship, Levinas explains that the inside-out dimension of the relation to the other, "to be one's brother's keeper," "does not come from fraternity, but fraternity denotes responsibility for another."[69] We see here that the interplay between the Saying and the Said, between the unthematized and thematization, corresponds to the interplay between the un-common and common. In terms of community, the role of the Unsaying is given to fraternal community; it is a

---

[67] See Chapter 4.
[68] It is not a coincidence that Levinas exemplifies the double-folded character by referring to the Cain-Abel story. From early on, he uses fratricide as an illustration of this ambiguity. In one of his early notes (published posthumous), written sometime before *Totality and Infinity* (most probably around 1956), Levinas speaks about the possibility of fratricide by explaining that the self as son is posited against the others who are my brothers. Nevertheless, this positedness also means that I am *with* the others, and that I am elected: "Comme fils je suis posé contre les autres (mes frères) et par conséquent avec les autres. Je me pose contre les autres, car comme fils je suis élu et par conséquent élu parmi d'autres fils, mes frères, mais pour cela, précisément, toujours incertain de mon élection et, par conséquent, contre mes frères.," *Œuvres complètes Tome 1. Carnets de captivité et autres inédits*, eds. Rodolphe Calin et Catherine Chalier (Paris : Grasset, 2009), 309, emphasis by Levinas.
[69] "God and Philosophy" (1975), in OGCM 72.

way to signal, without ever determining sociality. The an-archical interruption of community from becoming a totalizing unity is expressed on the societal level *through* fraternal community, where community is interrupted from melting together in a communion, and being determined by the unity of a genus, or in "the tribal" as Levinas puts it in a later text ("The Vocation of the Other" [1988]):

> Alterity is strangeness, as I said earlier. The other has a tribal link with no one. That is precisely his departure from the community of genus, the total alterity. The moment in which fraternity attains its full sense is when, in the brother himself, the stranger is recognized: the beyond-the-tribal. It is not that the tribal is proscribed; it comprises many virtues. But in principle, the human is the consciousness that there is still one more step to take: to appease the tribal, scandalous exigency![70]

"[T]he tribal" is yet another way in which Levinas expresses the community of having something in common, and the term helps him point out that this common cannot be the source of community itself.[71] However, Levinas does not hesitate to specify: "It is not that the tribal is proscribed; it comprises many virtues"—meaning that there is a need for the common in community, but this common does not constitute the basis for community. Fraternal community holds together the need for a common and the interruption by the un-common sociality, from which it receives its sense ("The moment in which fraternity attains its full sense is when, in the brother himself, the stranger is recognized"). Just as fraternity marks the intertwinement between ethics and justice, fraternal community marks the intertwinement between the shared common, and the un-common. It expresses a positive understanding of community, where the difference is maintained despite the bond. Nevertheless, it is not fraternity that interrupts, nor that which keeps community from becoming totality—sociality has this role.

Thus, Levinas's understanding of fraternal community brings forth the important role that sociality plays in his re-thinking of community. From Levinas's refusal to think community exclusively in terms of communion

---

[70] "The Vocation of the Other" (1988), in IIRB 109.
[71] The expression "beyond the tribal link" also shows how Levinas addresses the question of community beyond its meaning of Jewish community—earlier, we have already argued for this reading.

emerges the need for an un-grounding sociality, an un-common sociality that has nothing to share, but, on the contrary, interrupts the grounding in a shared common. In the end, for Levinas, "the unique to unique relation is higher than fraternity,"[72] which gives sociality a non-ordinal priority over fraternity. The notions of fraternity and fraternal community, although interrupted, include in themselves the symmetry and reciprocity of the brothers.[73] Even though the notion of fraternal community is important as a form of re-thinking community, its importance is only due to sociality. Levinas highlights, in his notion of fraternity, precisely the uniqueness of the brother, despite the common, despite sharing, and this means even despite the sharing of the same father. In this *despite* lies the true signifycance of sociality for the question of community: despite that we might share a common in a community or several communities of genus, this is always interrupted by the ungrounding un-common.

Fraternal community is not an ideal to achieve, it is not an alternative to the community of common genus, but it describes community as such, any community. It becomes, however, exceptional for Levinas, for in his view the notion of fraternal community shows that the community of common genus is indeed *interrupted*, that even if it seems to express nothing more than communion under equality, fraternal community is an *interrupted* community by a sociality that resists communion. This already introduces the importance of the un-commonness of a sociality that interrupts the shared common of community, while the sense of any community is given precisely through this interruption. In the remaining chapters, our goal is to bring forth more clearly this meaning of sociality as the un-common.

---

[72] "The Vocation of the Other," in IIRB 108. We have seen in the previous part of our thesis that, at occasions, Levinas refers to sociality as a face-to-face, unique-to-unique or one-to-one relation. Although we have found serious objections against these expressions, this does not change the fact that Levinas still associates them with sociality. As such, when he claims, "the unique to unique relation is higher than fraternity" he means that sociality is higher than fraternity.

[73] See also TI 280, where fraternity is strongly connected with equality and "solidarity with all the others" (as in the relation between the equal "sons").

Without a Common

In the previous chapter we argued that, in objecting to thinking community as totalizing unity, Levinas is laying down a firm critique against founding community on *something* in common. This critique has revealed that sociality plays the crucial role of interrupting community based on communion. In order to continue our examination of sociality and its interruptive role, we need to address more deeply the question of community without a foundation on *something* in common. Undertaking this task is the purpose of the present chapter.

In pursuing our task we will consider, owing to their exceptional contribution to the topic, Jean-Luc Nancy's and Maurice Blanchot's conceptions of community as respectively, "inoperative" and "unavowable": their debate from 1983-4 is one of the first to be preoccupied extensively with the problem of community not founded on *something* in common. As a consequence, we draw back for a moment from Levinas's own text, and centre our attention on the dialogue between Nancy and Blanchot, which takes place in *The Inoperative Community* (*La communauté désœuvrée*) (1983) and *The Unavowable Community* (*La communauté inavouable*) (1983). The goal of this chapter is neither an exhaustive exposition of the otherwise complex philosophies of Nancy and Blanchot, nor to follow their discussions in terms of political philosophy or literary theory. Instead, we will focus on the more specific question of community without an underlying common ground, as part of our efforts to bring forth the dimension of sociality as the interruptive un-common.

10.1. Inoperative community

Nancy's essay from 1983 *The Inoperative Community* (*La Communauté désœuvrée*)[1] was inspired both by Bataille's critique of community as work, and by Blanchot's account of writing as absence of work (or inoperativeness);[2] indeed he borrows the expression "inoperative" (*désœuvré(e)*) from Blanchot in order to describe his own conception of community.[3] The expression proves to be especially resourceful, as it envelopes an array of meanings: on the one hand, the French word *oeuvre*, similarly to the English word *work*, can express an artistic or literary work, but also a task or undertaking; on the other hand, the composite word "désœuvré(e)" (or "désœuvrement") allows room for a play on the multiple meaning of the word "*oeuvre*," and can mean both the interruption of the literary or artistic work, but also 'out of work,' idle, unemployed or inoperative.[4] In Nancy's case, *work* gains its specific meaning in the context of community.

The starting point of Nancy's essay is a reflection on the contemporary problem regarding the way we are forced to re-think community with reference to today's context of global society. As Esposito put it some years later, the problem lies in that "political philosophy tends to think community as a 'wider subjectivity'; as, and this in spite of the presupposed opposition to the individualist paradigm, such a large part of neo-communitarian philosophy ends up doing, when it swells the self in the

---

[1] The essay was first published in 1983 in *Aléa*, 4. Then it was republished in 1986 as a part of a book with the same title.

[2] Blanchot has employed the expression "inoperative" already in his earlier texts such as *The Space of Literature* (1955) or *Infinite Conversations* (1969).

[3] "'Unoccupancy' (*désœuvrement*) was taken from Blanchot, thus very nearly from Bataille, from the community or communication called 'friendship' and 'endless conversation' between the two," Jean-Luc Nancy, "The Confronted Community" *Postcolonial Studies* 6, no. 1 (2001/2003): 30. Evidently, Nancy is referring to Blanchot's works, *Friendship* (1971) and *The Infinite Conversation* (1969). However, for us, it is important to mention that Blanchot's work in general, and *The Infinite Conversation* in particular is highly influenced by Levinas's philosophy. We will return later to the closeness between Levinas and Blanchot.

[4] The difficulty of finding an English equivalent with similar potential gave rise to different translations, depending on the context; among them, perhaps the most popular ones are "unworking," "idle," "inertia," "unoccupancy" and "inoperative." We will opt here for the word "inoperative" for consistency reasons, as it was the one adopted by Peter Connor when translating into English Nancy's *La communauté désœuvrée*, the text which remains here our main source of reference.

hypertrophic figure of 'the unity of unities.'[5] This problematic tendency of neo-communitarian political philosophies is expressed right at the beginning of Nancy's essay through a short discussion around the word 'communism.'[6] He argues that the meaning of this word has been betrayed by creating a unifying identity of community through *work*.[7] The *work of community* is seen by Nancy as the production of *something* that defines community.[8] A typical example is given in the form of the nostalgia for a lost community. This nostalgia presupposes the construction (or production) of an ideal community which was supposedly lost sometime, somehow, and which is considered to represent the original meaning of community. Inspired by Bataille, who "understood the ridiculous nature of nostalgia for communion,"[9] Nancy argues that *the consciousness of a lost community* carries the nostalgia for a lost social bond prior to the present society, similar to the idea that a *Gesellschaft* had dissolved a prior *Gemeinschaft*.[10] This is a form of nostalgia that expresses the striving for a past state, and at the same time points towards a utopian future. Nancy reminds us that our history gives many examples of such "lost" communities in the form of utopian, ideal community as a goal to aspire to, or ideas of the immortal community of the dead in the form of an afterlife.[11] What these communities have "lost," Nancy says, "is lost only in the sense that such a 'loss' is constitutive of 'community' itself."[12] The nostalgic picture of the lost community (in the form of the idyllic but lost social bond which needs to be achieved) has a role of satisfying our need to establish an

---

[5] Roberto Esposito, *Communitas. The origin and destiny of community*, 2.
[6] For more from Nancy on the topic of communism see his essay "Communism, the word," in *The Idea of Communism*, eds. Costas Douzinas and Slavoj Žižek (London and New York: Verso 2010), 145–154.
[7] "But the schema of betrayal is seen to be untenable in that it was the very basis of the communist ideal that ended up appearing most problematic: namely, human beings defined as producers (one might even add: human beings *defined* at all), and fundamentally as the producers of their own essence in the form of their labor or their work," IC 2.
[8] "[T]his something, which would be the fulfilled infinite identity of community, is what I call its 'work.' All our political programs imply this work: either as the product of the working community, or else the community itself as work," IC XXXIX.
[9] IC 17.
[10] See IC 9–12.
[11] See IC 12–13. Nevertheless, for Nancy, death takes a different meaning to which we will return shortly.
[12] IC 12.

identity for community, that is to say, to bring a foundational essence to it in the form of communion, of a unifying bond represented by *something*.

Thus, in the context of the nostalgia for an ideal community, *work* is understood as the operation of producing that *something* that represents the essential bond and which gives meaning and identity to community. However—and here lies the core of Nancy's argument—the very operation itself of producing this *something* eventually comes to fulfill the role of fundamental identity. Again, we are led to an essentialist definition of community, this time however not in the form of a particular ideal (of something), but as the *work* itself undertaken by the community in producing its own identity.[13] Through this move, the meaning of *work* is taken to a different level: the very process of constructing an essence, or the work of community, becomes the essence of community. This movement of identification through the very production of identity, according to Nancy, is "totalitarianism" and "immanentism," a movement in interiority that keeps the meaning of community in interiority.[14] Hence, there is a risk that lies in the way neo-communitarian political philosophies think community: the risk of inscribing the notion of community in an enclosed, totalitarian mode of thinking.

The same risk of thinking community as a movement in interiority is revealed from the individualist point of view as well. Individualism, in Nancy's view, reflects a new kind of atomism that addresses individuality, or more precisely the sovereignty of the individual, in terms of an absolute detached atom originating from itself.[15] Nevertheless, this new kind of atomism, Nancy argues, although seeming to rely on Epicureanism, fails to import the key element of 'clinamen' that in Epicureanism indicates an inclination of the atom outside its trajectory, a deviation from itself (from its own trajectory).[16] In other words, the new kind of atomism (which we can easily recognize in the form of liberalist individualism), according to

---

[13] "In the work, the properly 'common' character of community disappears, giving way to a unicity and a substantiality. (The work itself, in fact, should not be understood primarily as the exteriority of a product, but as the interiority of the subject's operation)," Ibid., XXXIX.

[14] Ibid., 3.

[15] "By its nature—as its name indicates, it is the atom, the indivisible—the individual reveals that it is the abstract result of a decomposition. It is another, and symmetrical, figure of immanence: the absolutely detached for-itself, taken as origin and as certainty," Ibid., 3.

[16] Ibid., 3–4.

Nancy, fails to think the individual outside itself. This inevitably leads to an enclosed individuality, and thus it repeats the totalitarian move of thinking community as work. The absurdity of an enclosed individuality is expressed by the contradiction that being alone implies: "to be absolutely alone, it is not enough that I be so; I must also be alone being alone—and this of course is contradictory," says Nancy.[17] All this confirms the need for an intrinsic opening of the self outside itself, an inclination towards outside. When it lacks this inclination, its clinamen, individualism remains enclosed in itself, just as the neo-communitarian community encloses itself as work.

The two sides of Nancy's critique (one from the perspective of neo-communitarian political philosophies, and the other from the perspective of the new atomist individualism) show the close connection between the critique of community and the critique of subjectivity. In Nancy's examples, both community and the subject are enclosed in a movement inside interiority, a movement that in fact represents the work of essence-construction. The essence-construction, in its turn, is the essentializing, first, of community, and then of subjectivity. It essentializes, not in the sense of universality, but in being its own source of origin and determination—essence as the very production or *work* of essence.[18] Thought in this way, both the subject as individual and the community as work are infinite, yet an enclosed infinity. Due to the production of essence (work), and because this creation of essence is absolute and infinite, we have an *operative* (*working*) *immortality*: a community of immortals enclosed upon itself.[19] As the title of his essay already suggests, Nancy's task becomes one of challenging this *operative* (*working*) community and of showing instead the

---

[17] Ibid., 4. Nancy's argument is questioned by Todd May who, whilst agreeing with the idea behind it, finds the argumentation itself inadequate. "If Nancy is right here, - May observes - then not only is exposure a necessary aspect of individuality, but the denial that it is, is logically impossible. […] I am not convinced that the denial of that exposure is self-contradictory. Wrong, but not self-contradictory." Todd May, *Reconsidering Difference: Nancy, Derrida, Levinas and Deleuze* (University Park, PA: Pennsylvania State University, 1997), 26. He brings as an example of a not self-contradictory scenario the Hobbesian inspired form of social contract theory.

[18] Although Nancy does not use the exact expression "the work of essence," the formulation seems to be appropriate, given that Nancy often refers to Bataille and even borrows the expression "work of death": "Bataille went through the experience of realizing that the nostalgia for a communal being was at the same time the desire for a work of death," IC 17.

[19] Ibid., 3.

"un-working" of community, which breaks the enclosedness of the absolute. This 'absolute' is very different from Levinas's 'absolute,' meaning the refusal of the relative determination of self and the other.[20] We can observe already that with Nancy we are dealing with a rather different terminology. For him, ab-solute means a movement closed-up in interiority, enclosure that ultimately closes upon enclosure itself.[21]

The *operative immortality*, which brings together the critique of community and subjectivity, places the problem of death at the centre of Nancy's thoughts on community. Thinking the community *of* the dead, as a community of afterlife which would give an original all-encompassing meaning to community, makes community absolute, infinite, and it makes the dead, paradoxically, immortal. When re-thinking community, Nancy refuses to consider death in terms of *work*, that is to say, as an essence-constructing essence. Instead of an *operative immortality* Nancy proposes community as *inoperative mortality*—it is through death, through finitude that community is inoperative:

> The death upon which community is calibrated does not *operate* the dead being's passage into some communal intimacy, nor does community, for its part, *operate* the transfiguration of its dead into some substance or subject—be these homeland, native soil or blood, nation, a delivered or fulfilled humanity, absolute phalanstery, family, or mystical body. Community is calibrated on death as on that of which it is precisely impossible to *make a work* (other than a work of death, as soon as one tries to make a work of it). Community occurs in order to acknowledge this impossibility, or more exactly—for there is neither function nor finality here—the impossibility of making a work out of death is inscribed and acknowledged as "community."[22]

---

[20] For more on Levinas's understanding of the 'absolute,' see Chapter 3.
[21] "This ab-solute can appear in the form of the Idea, History, the Individual, the State, Science, the Work of Art, and so on. Its logic will always be the same inasmuch as it is without relation. A simple and redoubtable logic will always imply that within its very separation the absolutely separate encloses, if we can say this, more than what is simply separated. Which is to say that the separation itself must be enclosed, that the closure must not only close around a territory (while still remaining exposed, at its outer edge, to another territory, with which it thereby communicates), but also, in order to complete the absoluteness of its separation, around the enclosure itself," IC 4.
[22] Ibid., 14–5.

For Nancy, death is "always the singular death"[23] and with this he not only renders community inoperative, but also replaces the subject with the singular finite being—instead of subjectivity we have now *singularity*. The singular being is neither a subject nor an individual or single resulting from a process of singularization—i.e. it is not derived "*from out of* or as *an effect of*" something.[24] Singularity does not emerge from a separate ground or underlying foundation, nor does it emerge from itself, for that would bring it back to the nonsensical notion of the isolated individual. Instead of a stable ground, there is a sharing of singularities of *the like* (*le semblable*) while not being an alter-ego or the copy of an original *I*.[25] In this sense, singularity is neither originary, nor deduced, but *co-originary*, sharing the plurality of origins, without however this co-originarity constituting a common origin. By being co-originary the self is not anymore an origin for itself and, in this sense, we can say that it is an-archical—this move coincides with the de-essentialization of the subject, replaced already in Nancy's terminology by the notion of singularity. "There is no original, or origin of identity."[26] What is thought to be the problem of the origin of the subject or individual, according to Nancy, is a false problem; we are already in-common, that is to say, Being is always being-with. From the start we *are* already *with*, we are *in-common*. The question of *the* origin is thus replaced

---

[23] "What forms a future, and consequently what truly comes about, is always the singular death—which does not mean that death does not come about in the community: on the contrary [...]. But communion is not what comes of death, no more than death is the simple perpetual past of community," IC 13.

[24] "There is no process of 'singularization,' and singularity is neither extracted, nor produced, nor derived. Its birth does not take place *from out of* or as an *effect of*: on the contrary, it provides the measure according to which *birth,* as such, is neither a production nor a self-positioning, the measure according to which the infinite birth of finitude is not a process that emerges from a ground *(fond)* or from a fund *(fonds)* of some kind. The 'ground' is itself, through itself and as such, *already* the finitude of singularities.," IC 27. For more on the way Nancy introduces his notion of singularity, see Ibid., 6.

[25] "A like-being (*le semblable*) resembles me in that I myself 'resemble' him: we 'resemble' together, if you will. That is to say, there is no original or origin of identity. What holds the place of an 'origin' is the sharing of singularities." IC 33, CD 82. Without introducing Levinas in our discussion at this point, we need to note that, as we have seen, Levinas, too, prefers singularity in the sense of uniqueness (and not as the one among the many), and in this sense is close to Nancy. On the other hand, we can easily see that the "like me" would be something very problematic for Levinas due to the symmetry that it implies—again, we are dealing with a very different conceptual reservoir.

[26] IC 33.

by the (non-countable) plurality of origins—this is what the meaning of co-originarity reflects.

> [W]e are brought into the world, each and every one of us, according to a dimension of "in-common" that is in no way "added onto" the dimension of "being-self," but that is rather co-originary and coextensive with it. But this does not mean that the "common" is a substance uniformly laid out "under" supposed "individuals," nor is it uniformly shared out among everyone like a particular ingredient.[27]

That we are in-common is not a pure empirical fact, but it has an ontological weight: Being is in-common.[28] For Nancy, *in-common* does not refer to a common property. There is a significant difference between *being-in-common* and *having something in common*; or, in Nancy's words, "being-in-common is not a common being."[29] In this way, co-originarity does not mean a single shared origin, but a plurality of origins, just as being-in-common is not a shared common property, not in communion, but in common.[30] Similarly, the 'with' from 'being-with' should not be conceived as *something* in its own right (e.g. a term or a mediator); there is nothing substantial in the 'with.' It is not a "connecting tissue," says Nancy, nor a "bridge."[31] The *with* breaks down the presentable/unpresentable alternative, as it is not presentable in itself, but it is not un-presentable, withdrawn presence either. It escapes any form of definition, since it is not a subject.[32] *With* functions as a pre-position without having a position of its own; Even

---

[27] IC xxxvii.

[28] Jean-Luc Nancy, "Of Being-in-Common," translated by James Creech, in *Community at Loose Ends*, eds. Miami Theory Collective (Minneapolis: University of Minnesota Press, 1991), 1.

[29] IC 29.

[30] The introductory passage from Nancy's essays "Of Being-in-Common" explains with precision this issue: "What could be more common than to be, than being? We are. Being, or existence, is what we share. When it comes to sharing nonexistence, we are not here. Nonexistence is not for sharing. But being is not a thing that we could possess in common. Being is in no way different from existence, which is singular each time. We shall say then that being is not common in the sense of a common property, but that it is in common. Being is in common." Jean-Luc Nancy, "Of Being-in-Common," 1.

[31] BSP 5.

[32] "Undoubtedly, the *with* as such is not presentable. I have already said so, but I have to insist upon it. The *with* is not 'unpresentable' like some remote of withdrawn presence, or like an Other. If there is a subject only with other subjects, the 'with' itself is not a subject," BSP 62.

using the definite article '*the* with' can already be misleading.³³ In other words, Nancy refuses to substantialize *with* in both grammatical and ontological meanings of substantialization: on the one hand, he wants to maintain "with" as a preposition and not as a substantive (*the* with),³⁴ and on the other hand, he refuses to insert any determining substance in conceiving the 'with.'³⁵ Read in this way, 'with' from 'being-with' does not form a ground, neither for singularity nor for community. According to Nancy, instead of an essential ground or foundation of community, there is a 'groundless ground.'³⁶

In-common, but without communion, without forming a common ground (a 'common being'), community instead of homogenization, it "make[s] possible a being-separated"³⁷, an exposition that exposes the self "outside-of-self."³⁸ This 'outside-of-self,' which Nancy calls *ex-posure*, is what was missing from both the neo-communitarian and the individualist views on community.

> "To be exposed" means to be "posed" in exteriority, according to an exteriority, having to do with an outside *in the very intimacy* of an inside. Or again: having access to what is *proper* to existence, and therefore, of course, to the proper of *one's own* existence, only through an "expropriation"³⁹

This exposure comes before identification, before determination.⁴⁰ For Nancy, it is the finitude given by death what provides an interruption and a shattering that opens up both the self and community, without this finitude

---

³³ "In fact, one should not say the 'with'; one should only say 'with,' which would be a preposition that has no position of its own and is available for every position," Ibid.
³⁴ Nevertheless, probably due to grammatical constrictions necessary in order to give coherence to a text, Nancy continues using the articulated form, 'the with' (*l'avec*).
³⁵ We consider to be fruitful for our purpose to continue discussing the complex problematic of Nancy's notion of 'with' by relating it to Levinas's critique of the 'between' and 'with.' With this in mind, we leave for now the question of the 'with,' only to take it up again in the next chapter.
³⁶ IC 27, "un 'fond' sans fond," CD 70.
³⁷ IC xxxvii.
³⁸ Ibid., 19.
³⁹ Ibid., xxxvii.
⁴⁰ "Exposure comes before any identification, and singularity is not an identity. It is exposure itself, its punctual actuality. (But identity, whether individual or collective, is not a sum total of singularities; it is itself a singularity.)," Nancy, "Of Being-in-Common," 7.

coagulating into the form of an essence.[41] Community exposes finitude, and it becomes nothing more than exposition.[42] Instead of an enclosed community of immortals, Nancy proposes an exposed community of mortals. In the context of the *inoperative community* death interrupts the enclosedness of community and shatters it, disabling it from the construction of its essence, from grounding itself in itself. There is no particular ground or positedness of community, but it is dis-location, the unstable and undetermined "places of communication":

> "These 'places of communication' are no longer places of fusion, even though in them one *passes* from one to the other; they are defined and exposed by their

---

[41] The importance that Nancy attributes to death, his rejection of subjectivity, the very way in which Nancy's thoughts on community unravel, show the closeness between his thinking and Heidegger's philosophy. In fact, in several works, Nancy's ideas have their starting point in a critique of Heidegger. In *Being Singular Plural*, for example, the question of origin is introduced through a critique directed towards the originarity of Dasein in Heidegger's philosophy. The problem of the "co-originarity of Mitsein," Nancy argues, becomes only a concern of a second degree for Heidegger. For Nancy, by contrast, "it is not the case that the 'with' is an addition to some prior Being; instead, the 'with' is at the heart of Being. In this respect, it is absolutely necessary to reverse the order of philosophical exposition, for which it has been a matter of course that the 'with'—and the other that goes with it—always comes second, even though this succession is contradicted by the underlying (*profonde*) logic in question here. Even Heidegger preserves this order of succession in a remarkable way, in that he does not introduce the co-originarity of *Mitsein* until after having established the originary character of Dasein.," BSP 30-1. This argument is recurrent in Nancy's work. For example, in "The being-with of being-there," a short essay from 2008, Nancy gives his critique in a succinct yet clear formulation: "*Dasein* is essentially *Mitsein*. This means that *Mitsein* is essential to *Dasein*: it is Being-with unlike the putting together of things, but an essential with.," Jean-Luc Nancy, "The being-with of being-there," *Continental Philosophy Review* 41, no. 1 (2008):3. The core of Nancy's critique is formulated as follows: "Despite the presence of the term *Mitsein* and *Mitdasein* in the text [Being and Time], no lengthy or rigorous analyses of the concept are provided as in the case of the main concept—far from it. Yet, *Mitsein* and *Mitdasein* are posited as co-essential to *Dasein*'s essence, that is, to its property as an existent for which Being is not its ontological foundation but rather the bringing into play of its own sense of Being as well as of the sense of Being itself." Ibid., 2. In this way, *co-originarity* and *Being-with* (*Mitsein*) in Nancy's view are essential to *Dasein*, moreover, they carry the very sense of Being. *Mitsein* is re-thought as being-in-common yet without communion—meaning that being is being-in-common without this very common being substantialized.

[42] "Community does not sublet the finitude it exposes. Community itself, in sum, is nothing but this exposition," IC 26.

dislocation. Thus, the communication of sharing would be this very dis-location.[43]

We can see that both "communication," and "place" receive here a specific meaning: the place is dis-location, groundless ground, while communication is without *something* communicated, a non-determinatory communication, or as Nancy says: "'communicating' by not 'communing,'"[44] and a few lines later he continues: "What 'there is' in place of communication is neither the subject, nor communal being, but community and sharing."[45] This understanding of dis-location, of communication, of sharing without sharing *something*, is intensified by the two-fold meaning of the French word for 'sharing,' *partage*, which expresses both sharing and division, separation. The two-fold meaning of sharing points yet again towards a breakdown of the logic of alternatives, something that we have already witnessed in the case of the 'with.' However, this time, the breakdown that is emphasized is the disruption of the separateness/union alternative. Here it becomes even clearer that the critique of community necessarily goes together with a critique of subjectivity, not only the atom-like closed-up individual but also the essentialized notion of the sovereign subject. Both the subject and community are ex-posed to the outside, without finding their 'place' in the outside or the inside, but in communication without communion, which is dis-location itself.[46]

Hence, Nancy understands community and, with it, singularity, beyond the movement in interiority around essence, that is to say, beyond imamnentism. In this sense, he seems to re-think community as transcendence.[47] At the same time, the inoperative community is characterized by finitude, not because community itself is limited, but because it is the community of

---

[43] IC 25.
[44] Ibid.
[45] Ibid.
[46] "Only in this communication are singular beings given—without a bond *and* without communion, equally distant from any notion of connection or joining from the outside and from any notion of a common and fusional interiority. Communication is the constitutive fact of an exposition to the outside that defines singularity. In its being, as its very being, singularity is exposed to the outside. By virtue of this position or this primordial structure, it is at once detached, distinguished, and communitarian. Community is the presentation of the detachment (or retrenchment) of this distinction that is not individuation, but finitude compearing," Ibid., 29.
[47] Ibid., 35.

mortals.⁴⁸ The singularity of each death is what interrupts the infinite or absoluteness of immanentism. In this sense, it is the infinite finitude of singularity that makes community break from unity; it is what makes it plural. Consequently, infinity is placed at the level of immanence, while finitude marks transcendence. Nancy changes the customary settings of transcendence and immanence in such a way that we end up with a closed infinite in immanence and an open finite in transcendence; meanwhile, the key element in this change is the interrupted community revealed as "the uninterrupted passage through singular ruptures."⁴⁹ The "singular ruptures" signify the re-thinking of subjectivity in terms of singularity, without however giving priority to the singular being. Nancy rejects the priority of the individual, of the subject, or of the Other. None of these are more original, since there is no hierarchy of originarity or determination; there is only co-originarity and co-determination. Placing the emphasis on the Other, Nancy argues, would only create a relative relation between the same and the other, "the same and the other, refer to one another" and deviate the focus from the 'with' and the plurality that it implies.⁵⁰ Thus, for Nancy the entire problem raised by the Same and the Other is a false problem. Community cannot be a question of the Same and the Other, of me and you. Instead of me and you there is one-another—in other words, primordial plurality.⁵¹

Before we examine Nancy's critique, which evidently targets Levinas's philosophy (we will do this in the next chapter), Blanchot needs to be introduced into our discussion as he, contrary to Nancy, through the problematic of death, reinstalls the importance of the other. As we are about to see, this makes him re-think community without communion in terms of dissymmetry.

---

⁴⁸ "It is the community of finite beings, and as such it is a *finite* community. In other words, not a limited community as opposed to an infinite absolute community, but a community *of* finitude, because finitude 'is' communitarian, and because finitude alone is communitarian," IC 6–7.
⁴⁹ Ibid., 35.
⁵⁰ BSP 81.
⁵¹ Ibid., 67.

10.2. Unavowable community

Shortly after the first publication of *The Inoperative Community*, Blanchot published the book *The Unavowable Community* with two essays, the first of which ("The Negative Community") directly addresses Nancy's *The Inoperative Community*. Blanchot's many approving references to Nancy's text create the impression of consensus. Nevertheless, as Robert Bernasconi rightly points out,[52] there are some crucial differences in their approach. Blanchot's work has a critical side, which in its turn asked for a response from Nancy. Nevertheless, Nancy's answer to Blanchot's critique came only much later. Regarding their polemic, Gregory Bird argues that Nancy's critique of the priority given to the Other (in such works as *Being Singular Plural* [1996], or *La Comparution/The Compearance* [1991] is in fact a response to Blanchot's emphasis on the importance of introducing the question of the other in conceiving community without communion (in *The Unavowable Community*).[53] Nancy himself explicitly announces his response to Blanchot in two later works, "The Confronted Community" (2001) and *La communauté désavouée* (The Disavowed Community) (2014).

In *The Unavowable Community*, Blanchot quickly puts the reader in deep water by raising the question of the other, of the irreciprocal relation and of dissymmetry just a couple of pages into the beginning of his first essay:

> However, if the relation of man with man ceases to be that of the Same with the Same, but rather introduces the Other as irreducible and — given the equality between them — always in a situation of dissymmetry in relation to the one looking at that Other, then a completely different relationship imposes itself and imposes another form of society which one would hardly dare call a "community." Or else one accepts the idea of naming it thus, while asking oneself what is at stake in the concept of a community and whether the community, no matter if it has existed or not, does not in the end always posit the *absence* of community.[54]

This paragraph is commented upon by both Bernasconi and Bird, though in differing ways. Bernasconi questions whether there are two "hard"

---

[52] Robert Bernasconi, "On Deconstructing Nostalgia for Community within the West: The Debate between Nancy and Blanchot," *Research in Phenomenology* 23, no. 1 (1993): 3–21.
[53] Gregory Bird, "Community Beyond Hypostasis: Nancy responds to Blanchot," *Angelaki* 13, no.1 (2008): 3–26.
[54] UC 3.

alternatives presented here, and suggests that Blanchot "prefers not to have to choose," and yet gets closer to Levinas by introducing the Other into Nancy's argument and by his Levinasian reading of Duras (which we will also discuss shortly).[55] Bird sees the above quotation as "a rhetorical alternative: turn to the Other or get caught up in the hypostasis of language." He considers the two sides as "productive alternatives," in the sense that "his [Blanchot's] attempt to privilege the first option at the expense of the second option leads him to posit the Other, not-community, and another type of society as his move beyond the hypostasis of community vis-à-vis society."[56] Whilst we agree with both Bernasconi's and Bird's readings of Blanchot in that they indicate that, at least to some extent, Blanchot is taking into consideration both alternatives,[57] we propose to view Blanchot's words as an attempt to reach further. In the way in which he questions the meaning given to the word 'community' and tries to re-think community with regards to the other, irreciprocity and dissymmetry, it seems that he aims precisely to dissolve the alternatives he apparently displays. Read in this way, the "or else" does not mark a disjunction, but rather indicates Blanchot's invitation to re-think community as the absence of community—that is, as the absence of something in common—while paying attention to the problematic of the other. Blanchot's move can be read as more of a disruption of alternatives than as a taking of sides. This interpretation gains more significance when we take into consideration that both Nancy and Levinas seek to break down thinking in alternatives.

As the above quotation shows, Nancy's community without communion is seen by Blanchot as the absence of community, in the sense that it does not share anything specific; the meaning of absence, here, does not negate community itself, but suggests instead the absence of communion, of

---

[55] Bernasconi, "On Deconstructing Nostalgia for Community within the West: The Debate between Nancy and Blanchot," 7–8.

[56] Bird, "Community Beyond Hypostasis: Nancy responds to Blanchot," 7.

[57] We need to note here that as Bernasconi's article develops, he draws more and more distance between the two thinkers, Blanchot and Nancy, placing Blanchot closer to Levinas and thus widening the gap between the two alternatives set out by Blanchot: "The trajectory that Nancy has followed and the extent to which he believes that the task to think community can be met only by an ontology, and specifically an ontology of largely Heideggerian inspiration, has served to strengthen the extent to which one is obliged to choose between the alternatives set out by Blanchot at the beginning of *The Unavowable Community* quoted earlier.," Bernasconi, "On Deconstructing Nostalgia for Community within the West: The Debate between Nancy and Blanchot," 11.

something in common. Blanchot borrows the expression "the absence of community" from Bataille, yet criticizes Bataille for making it *mine* ("my absence of community") and by this reinstalling appropriation.[58] Although this particular term ("the absence of community") is indeed borrowed, Blanchot's use of the expression "absence" is rather typical of his general terminological choices, and in this sense, his thoughts on community become consistent with his oeuvre.[59] In the tribute that he gave on the occasion of the 100th anniversary of Blanchot's birth, Nancy explained the "absence" in Blanchot's oeuvre as the refusal of any establishment of a meaning, this implying a nihilism in Blanchot. Absence, for Blanchot, is neither a negation nor a state, says Nancy, but a movement, "an absenting."[60] The movement involved here hinders absence from being stabilized—a stability which would be given by any specific meaning, even if that meaning is a negation of meaning. Blanchot insists, just as Nancy does, on the de-essentialization of community. He considers that giving community an established meaning by avowing it turns community into communion under that very established (avowed) form.[61] Thus, for Blanchot community without communion must be *unavowable community* (hence the title of his book).[62]

---

[58] It remains appropriation even if it is only in the form of an appropriation of death (as *my* death), see UC 4.

[59] The thematic of *absence* is to be found throughout Blanchot's writing. A good example in this sense is "The Absence of the Book" from *The Infinite Conversation* (1969) where Blanchot discusses the absence of the book, not as an established meaning or negation of meaning but as a reference to an outside of the book. Thinking the book as absence goes together with the "unworking" of writing, that is to say, writing without it becoming a "work" (without having a purpose and self-contained meaning)—hence writing becomes the "absence of work" (see Blanchot, *The Infinite Conversation*, 422–434.) Nancy points out that the importance of absence is already felt in the early novel *Thomas the Obscure* (1941): "The prodigious absent, absent from me and from everything, absent also for me" (see Jean-Luc Nancy's tribute to Maurice Blanchot on the 100th anniversary of his birth, http://this-space.blogspot.se/2007/09/maurice-blanchot-1907–2003-by-jean-luc.html).

[60] Jean-Luc Nancy, "Tribute to Maurice Blanchot on the 100th anniversary of his birth," trans. Charlotte Mandell, *This Space* (blog), http://this-space.blogspot.se/2007/09/maurice-blanchot-1907–2003-by-jean-luc.html.

[61] UC 19–20.

[62] Towards the end of the essay "The Negative Community" Blanchot expresses the limits of thematization, and the unavowability of community: "'The infiniteness of abandonment,' 'the community of those who have no community.' Here perhaps we touch upon the ultimate form of the communitarian experience, after which there will be

So far, Blanchot's unavowable community seems to correspond to Nancy's inoperative community. The unavowability means the refusal of determination, of the giving of essence to community (even if that essence is its own construction of essence, its very avowal). Nevertheless, it remains somewhat different from the "inoperative," and Nancy, in a preface written to the Italian edition of Blanchot's *The Unavowable Community* and published some good years later as *The Confronted Community* (2001), recognized in it a subtle critique.[63] In this response, Nancy addresses Blanchot's critique that the inoperative community still carries in itself a "work," even if only in the background, and even if only as a reference or the simple "assumption" of the word *désoeuvré* itself.[64] Although he appears to be addressing the question directly only rather late, Nancy had, in a sense, already reacted to it much earlier, when he turned his focus towards the "with" and the "co-" of community.[65] This is Nancy's way of not being

---

nothing left to say, because it has to know itself by ignoring itself," UC 25. We need to add here Blanchot's closing words of the second essay "The Community of Lovers" (and of the book itself *The Unavowable Community*), which again express nicely the problematic of the unavowable: "*The unavowable community*: does that mean that it does not acknowledge itself or that it is such that no avowal may reveal it, given that each time we have talked about its way of being, one has had the feeling that one grasped only what makes it exist by default? So, would it have been better to have remained silent? Would it be better, without extolling its paradoxical traits, to live it in what makes it contemporary to a past which it has never been possible to live? Wittgenstein's all too famous and all too often repeated precept, 'Whereof one cannot speak, there one must be silent'—given that by enunciating it he has not been able to impose silence on himself—does indicate that in the final analysis one has to talk in order to remain silent," Ibid., 56.

[63] "I have never completely clarified this reserve or this reproach, either in a text or for myself, and not in correspondence with Blanchot either. I am speaking of it here for the first time in this preface." Nancy, "The Confronted Community," 30.

[64] "That work around the 'with' will perhaps lead me anew toward Blanchot's book. This new Italian edition is a first opportunity. As if Blanchot, across the years that have passed and other signs exchanged between us, once more admonished me: 'Be on your guard against the unavowable!' I believe I understand it thus: beware any assumption of community, be it by the name of 'unoccupied' [désoeuvré]. Or else, you must follow even further in the direction that this word points. Unoccupancy [désoeuvrement] comes after work but also comes from it." Nancy, "The Confronted Community," 32.

[65] "In effect, I have preferred to substitute, little by little, the graceless expressions, 'being-together,' 'being-in-common,' and finally 'being-with.'[...] It was clear that the emphasis placed upon a necessary but as yet under-elaborated concept went at least hand in hand, during this period, with a reviving of communitarian and sometimes fascist urges. [...] I therefore preferred, in the end, to focus the work around the 'with':

satisfied with a mere negation of work as un-working, and finding it necessary to develop his thinking around "a secret of the common that is not a common secret."[66] It is the secret that, according to Nancy, Blanchot himself suggests with the *unavowable* community. Unavowable, in this sense, is a secret that is shared but not divulged.

Besides the subtle but important difference between "unavowable" and "inoperative," there is another significant distinction between Blanchot and Nancy's thought, which is revealed through their different approaches to the question of death. Just as for Nancy, death is central for Blanchot—it is not in this aspect that they differ—nevertheless, contrary to Nancy, he placed the emphasis on the other's death.[67] Nancy acknowledges Blanchot's different standpoint and remarks that dying, for Blanchot, has rather the meaning of surviving than of the end of life.[68] Indeed, we find a very illuminating example in this sense in Blanchot's discussion of the march in the memory of those killed by the police at Charonne subway station (nine people were killed while demonstrating in support of an independent

---

almost indistinguishable from the 'co-' of community, it brings with it however a clearer indicator of the removal at the heart of proximity and intimacy," Ibid., 31–2.

[66] Ibid., 31.

[67] This importance of this difference is considered "crucial" by Bernasconi: "The crucial point of difference between Nancy and Blanchot is located at this point where, at first sight, they seem closest: in the course of their discussion of the death of the Other.," Bernasconi, "On Deconstructing Nostalgia for Community within the West: The Debate between Nancy and Blanchot," 8.

[68] "The 'dying' of which Blanchot speaks - and which is not at all to be confused with the cessation of living, but which on the contrary is the living or 'sur-viving' named by Derrida so close to Blanchot - shapes the movement of the incessant approach to absenting as true meaning, annulling in it any trace of nihilism.," Nancy, *Tribute to Maurice Blanchot on the 100th anniversary of his birth*. These thoughts depicting "surviving" as a more important concept than death, are close to both Levinas's and Derrida's approach: Levinas, who shows the importance of survival through his attitude towards suicide: "Before defining the man as the animal that can commit suicide it is necessary to define him as capable of living for the Other and being on the basis of the Other who is exterior to him." (TI 149), and Derrida, who was mentioned in Nancy's comment and who in his last interview emphasized "survival" as an original concept, which is not defined through death: "[S]urvival is an original concept, which defines the structure itself of what we call existence, the Da-sein, if you will. We are, structurally speaking, survivors, marked by this structure of the trace, of the testament. That said, I would not endorse the view according to which survival is defined more by death, the past, than by life and the future. No: deconstruction is always on the side of the affirmative, the affirmation of life," Jacques Derrida, *The Last Interview*, SV. Derrida, *Le Monde* (August 2004).

Algeria). The crowd gathered in the memory of the dead, in Blanchot's view was not a totality, nor a number of people, but the form of community without communion, "as an extension of those who no longer could be there (those assassinated at Charonne)."[69]

The importance given to the death of the other is explained by Blanchot through Bataille's principle of insufficiency, according to which "the sufficiency of each being is endlessly contested by every other."[70] Rather than something that would compensate for this insufficiency by making it sufficient, at the heart of the insufficiency there remains an "excess of a lack."[71] Blanchot formulates this insufficiency that needs to be maintained in its insufficiency as a putting of itself "radically and constantly into question"[72]—and this is where the importance of the death of the other comes into play. The question that puts me in question, Blanchot argues, cannot originate from myself, nor from a unity in which I partake (i.e. a collective through communion); it needs to come from an outside. Again, we find this very similar to the opening up to the outside of community and of subjectivity proposed by Nancy. However, contrary to Nancy, for whom this outside was not the other, but exposure, for Blanchot, while also relying on the notion of exposure, this becomes "exposure to some other (or to the other)."[73] For him, a *radical* outside is needed, which he finds in the absence of the other through its death:

---

[69] UC 32.

[70] This is the larger context of how Bataille explains his principle of insufficiency in the essay "The Labyrinth" (1930): "At the basis of human life there exists a *principle of insufficiency*. In isolation, each man sees the majority of others as incapable or unworthy of 'being.' There is found, in all free and slanderous conversation, as an animating theme, the awareness of the vanity and the emptiness of our fellowmen; an apparently stagnant conversation betrays the blind and impotent flight of all life toward an indefinable summit. The sufficiency of each being is endlessly contested by every other. Even the look that expresses love and admiration comes to me as a doubt concerning my reality." George Bataille, "The Labyrinth" (1930), in *Visions of Excess: Selected Writings, 1927–1939* (Minneapolis: University of Minnesota Press, 1985), 172.

[71] UC 8.

[72] Ibid.

[73] UC 8. "L'exposition à un autre (ou à l'autre)," CI 20.

> What, then, calls me into question most radically? Not my relation to myself as finite or as the consciousness of being before death or for death, but my presence for another who absents himself by dying.[74]

The above lines show clearly that for Blanchot the death of the other is not like any other death. While keeping in focus the importance of thinking community in a de-essentialized way, Blanchot carefully re-interprets Nancy's ideas in a way that places much more emphasis on the death of the other. This move is announced already a few pages earlier, when Blanchot evokes Nancy's words regarding the inoperative community revealed in the death of the other.[75] Although, as we have shown, Nancy places the emphasis on finitude and not on the other, Blanchot sees here the overall importance for community of the death of the other:

> Two essential traits emerge at this stage of the reflection: 1) the community is not the restricted form of a society, no more than it tends toward a communitarian fusion; 2) it differs from a social cell in that it does not allow itself to create a work and has no production value as aim. What purpose does it serve? None, unless it would be to make present the service to others unto/in death, so that the other does not get lost all alone, but is filled in for (supplé) just as he brings to someone else that supplementing (*suppléance*) accorded to himself. Mortal substitution is what replaces communion.[76]

It is worth noting here Blanchot's reference to substitution, which can be interpreted as a direct link to Levinas's philosophy.[77] Blanchot's allusion to this Levinasian notion becomes even more interesting when we take into consideration a line that in Nancy's essay precedes the ones commented upon by Blanchot: "Community is what takes place always through others and for others."[78] It is interesting to see the striking similarities with the way Levinas describes the notion of substitution as "for the other," "through the other."[79]

Hence, for Nancy it is not the otherness of the other, but the singularity of its finitude that prevents community from being reduced to communion,

---

[74] UC 8–9.
[75] IC 15, UC 11.
[76] UC 11.
[77] Blanchot's closeness to Levinas regarding the notion of substitutions is also pointed out by Bernasconi (see Bernasconi, "On Deconstructing Nostalgia for Community within the West: The Debate between Nancy and Blanchot," 10.)
[78] IC 15.
[79] See Chapter 1.

and the other, as well as the self, from becoming essentialized subjects;[80] it is in this sense that the death of the other becomes significant for Nancy: "It [community] is not the space of the egos—subjects and substances that are at bottom immortal—but of the *I*'s, who are always *others* (or else are nothing)."[81] For Blanchot however, death takes its profound meaning only when it is the other's death, since only the absence of the other can take the form of a radical outside and thus maintain the questioning and bring an interruption of essentialization.[82] My death is not radical enough to open an outside. Only the death of the other, the absence of the other, can make a separation that opens me to the openness of community.[83] The opening to the outside and the opening to the other is described by Blanchot as a movement similar to fission, and perhaps more importantly, this interruption disturbing the sovereignty of the *I* is characterized by Blanchot through *dissymmetry*:

> an opening to the outside and an opening to others, a movement which provokes a violent dissymmetry between myself and the other: the fissure and the communication[84]

Just as it does for Nancy, the critique of community, for Blanchot, goes hand in hand with a critique of subjectivity.[85] For Blanchot as well, the breaking with an established *I* is tightly linked with a re-thinking of community.

---

[80] "The genuine community of mortal beings, or death as community, establishes their impossible communion. Community therefore occupies a singular place: it assumes the impossibility of its own immanence, the impossibility of a communitarian being in the form of a subject," IC 15.

[81] Ibid.

[82] "the exposure to death, no longer my own exposure, but someone else's, whose living and closest presence is already the eternal and unbearable absence, an absence that the travail of deepest mourning does not diminish. And it is in life itself that that absence of someone else has to be met," UC 25.

[83] "To remain present in the proximity of another who by dying removes himself definitively, to take upon myself another's death as the only death that concerns me, this is what puts me beside myself, this is the only separation that can open me, in its very impossibility, to the Openness of a community," UC 9, and a few pages later he continues: "That is what founds community. There could not be a community without the sharing of that first and last event which in everyone ceases to be able to be just that (birth, death)," Ibid., 9.

[84] UC 22.

[85] "the isolated being is the individual, and the individual is only an abstraction, existence as it is represented by the weak minded conception of everyday liberalism," Ibid., 18.

Conceiving the self in terms of individuality is rejected, while the 'contestation' given by the other's death comes to question the essentialization of the self.[86] However, as the above quotation suggests, there is something very different from Nancy's approach: according to Blanchot, the interruption given by the absence of the other in the form of a contestation (a putting under question) makes the relation between the *I* and the other dissymmetrical. In this way, dissymmetry becomes a very important element in Blanchot's re-thinking of both the self and community.

It is quite apparent by now that, in thinking community, Blanchot involves aspects that are familiar to us from Levinas's philosophy. Besides raising the importance of the other and of dissymmetry, a whole range of clues signal Levinas's presence in the background of Blanchot's work. We have earlier seen Blanchot evoking 'substitution' for the other's death as an expression for his way of thinking community—this being a fairly direct allusion to Levinas's notion of substitution. Another example in this sense is the call (*l'appel*) of the other's death, calling me in question, which again finds its equivalent in Levinas's thoughts on subjectivity where the other calls the *I* into question electing the unique *me*. Indeed, Levinas and Blanchot were very close, both in terms of personal relationship and in their work. In addition to being good friends, their philosophies intersect at many points, and we can hear Levinas's echo in Blanchot's several works, sometimes even accompanied by direct references to Levinas.[87] In his turn, Levinas dedicated a number of essays to Blanchot, their year of publication ranging from 1956 to 1975 (later collected in the volume *Sur Maurice Blanchot* [1975]).[88] Unsurprisingly, the closeness between the two philoso-

---

[86] "A being does not want to be recognized, it wants to be contested: in order to exist it goes towards the other, which contests and at times negates it, so as to start being only in that privation that makes it conscious (here lies the origin of its consciousness) of the impossibility of being itself, of subsisting as its *ipse* or, if you will, as itself as a separate individual: this way it will perhaps ex-ist, experiencing itself as an always prior exteriority, or as an existence shattered through and through, composing itself only as it decomposes itself constantly, violently and in silence. The existence of every being thus summons the other or a plurality of others.," Ibid., 6.

[87] We can take for example *The Infinite Conversation*, especially the part entitled "Plural speech," where Blanchot not only explicitly comments on Levinas's work, but he experiments with Levinas's thoughts on plurality by transposing them so they are reflected not only by the content (the theme), but also by his style of writing; by this Blanchot explores further the question of the unthematizible Saying.

[88] *Sur Maurice Blanchot* (Montpellier: Fata Morgana, 1975). The English translation was included in the volume *Proper Names*, from 1996 (PN 127–170), volume which in its

phers has not remained unnoticed in the secondary literature.[89] Our purpose here is neither a general comparison between Blanchot and Levinas, nor to explore their undoubted closeness on different topics. We need to keep the focus on their connection in the context of community, and in that context, our interest lies in the two aspects that seem to distance Blanchot from Nancy, namely the importance of the other and dissymmetry.

What Blanchot means by "the other" remains unclear in the first essay of the volume *The Unavowable Community*, which addresses Nancy's essay. In the second essay however, "The Community of Love," he pursues an examination of community from the perspective of the couple with the help of Marguerite Duras's novel "The Malady of Death." The topic of absence and death remains of primal importance, yet here we also encounter a more direct discussion about the meaning of other. When referring to Duras's novel, the way Blanchot describes the character of the woman borrows many aspects from Levinas's terminology. More recently, in *La communauté désavouée* (2014), Nancy provides an overview and interpretation (at times, with a harsh critical tone) of Blanchot's *The Unovowable Community*, further highlighting the closeness between Blanchot's thoughts on community and Levinas's ethics, especially in relation to his commentary on Duras's text. Nancy sees in Blanchot's dissymmetry and irreciprocity something very similar to Levinas's ethical relation.[90]

It seems that in his understanding of the other, Blanchot follows Levinas's early work, as he associates otherness with the feminine. Indeed, it is quite clear that the woman in this fictional couple corresponds to the way Levinas presented his understanding of the other. We find her (the woman

---

original French edition published in 1976 did not include the essays dedicated to Blanchot. (See *Noms Propre*, [Montpellier: Fata Morgana, 1976]).

[89] See for example Jeffrey L. Kosky, "Maurice Blanchot and Levinas Studies," in *Levinas studies: An Annual Review*, Vol. 1, eds. Jeffrey Bloechl and Jeffrey L. Kosky (Pittsburgh: Duquesne University Press, 2006), 157–172, who discusses the similarities and differences between Blanchot and Levinas, as well as secondary literature overview; Kevin Hart, "Ethics of the Image," in *Levinas studies: An Annual Review Vol.* 1, 119–138, writing on the question of the "Image" in the relation between Blanchot and Levinas; William Large, *Emmanuel Levinas and Maurice Blanchot: Ethics and the Ambiguity of Writing* (Manchester: Clinamen Press 2005), on Levinas and Blanchot in the light of literature; or more generally on Blanchot's inspiration from Levinas in Ulrich Haase and William Large, *Maurice Blanchot* (New York: Routledge, 2001), or Leslie Hill, *Maurice Blanchot: Extreme Contemporary* (London: Routledge, 1997), and the list could continue.

[90] Jean-Luc Nancy, *La communauté désavouée* (Paris: Galilée, 2014), 67–8.

from the novel) described by Blanchot as vulnerable, fragile, weak, offering herself, one who can be killed, moreover "beckoning murder," and at the same time, precisely her weakness makes her resist murder, becoming strong in her ordering not to kill.[91] All of these characterizations lead our thoughts towards Levinas's work, where the face of the other is described as "weak," "exposed," "naked," and "destitute," holding in itself "an incitement to murder, the temptation to go to the extreme, to completely neglect the other—at the same time (and this is the paradoxical thing) the Face is also 'Thou Shall not Kill.'"[92] We recognize a matching pattern between Levinas and Blanchot even regarding the double role of the face [visage]. As we have seen, in Levinas's case, the face is described as "epiphany," where under the visible face, subject of the senses, lies the trace of the Infinite, which cannot find its correspondence through the senses or consciousness, the naked face stripped bare from categories. Similarly, Blanchot's account of the woman character's face from Duras's novel is described as invisibility in the visible, close and distant, naked and still inaccessible: "her face (*visage*) is a face which in its absolute visibility is its own invisible evidence" says Blanchot, adding: "her constant nakedness, the closest and most distant nakedness, the inaccessible intimacy of the outside."[93] The affiliation between Levinas's philosophy and Blanchot's words is clear, yet still in an implicit way. Soon enough, just a few pages later in the same essay ("The Community of Love"), the connection between Levinas and Blanchot becomes explicit when Levinas's contribution to ethics is acknowledged:

> That is what I read in this récit devoid of anecdote where impossible love (no matter its origin) can be translated by an analogy with the first words of an ethics

---

[91] "Two further traits give her a reality—that nothing real would suffice to limit: the fact that she is without defenses, the weakest, the most fragile, exposing herself through her body offered ceaselessly, as her face is, a face which in its absolute visibility is its own invisible evidence—thus beckoning murder (*"strangulation, rape, ill usage, insults, shouts of hatred, the unleashing of deadly and unmitigated passions"*), but, due to her very weakness, due to her very frailty, she cannot be killed, preserved as she is by the interdiction which makes her untouchable in her constant nakedness, the closest and most distant nakedness, the inaccessible intimacy of the outside (*'you look at this shape, and as you do so you realize its infernal power* [Lilith], *its abominable frailty, its weakness, the unconquerable strength of its incomparable weakness'*).," UC 37, CI 63. Emphasis by Blanchot.
[92] "Philosophy, Justice and Love" (1982), in EN 104.
[93] UC 37.

(words Levinas has uncovered for us): an infinite attention to the Other, as for the one whose destitution puts him above all and any being[94]

By connecting his reading of Duras's story to Levinas's ethical relation, Blanchot makes a clear path leading to a Levinasian understanding of responsibility, at which he arrives shortly after describing the other. For Blanchot, just as for Levinas, responsibility is not an obligation dictated by law, but one which comes as an obligation to respond to the other, who puts *me* in question "to the point of being able to respond to it only through a responsibility that cannot limit itself and that exceeds itself without exhausting itself. A responsibility or obligation towards the other that does not come from the Law but from which the latter would derive."[95] Blanchot comes so close to Levinas that he finds the dissymmetry of the erotic love to be easily capable of being confused with the irreciprocal ethical relation, yet remaining an "imitation" of it.[96] By again making a direct reference to Levinas, Blanchot compares the irreciprocal relation, characteristic of the ethical, with the dissymmetry between the lovers in Duras's novel. Just as Levinas gives priority to love without concupiscence in his later work, Blanchot finds erotic love insufficient. Love as lost, Blanchot argues, is the only kind of love where the primordial relation to the other is revealed. This loss makes us return, along with Blanchot, to the question of death:

> And thus, eternally separated, as if death was in them, between them? Not separated, not divided: inaccessible and, in the inaccessible, in an infinite relationship.[97]

Thus, the two major points in which Blanchot's thoughts on community differ from that of Nancy's, namely the importance of the other and dis-

---

[94] Ibid., 43.
[95] Ibid.
[96] "Is it the same dissymmetry that, according to Levinas, marks the irreciprocity of the ethical relationship between the other and me, I who am never on equal terms with the Other, an inequality measured by this impressive thought: The other is always closer to God than I am (whatever meaning one gives that name that names the unnamable)? This is not certain, and neither is it clear. Love may be a stumbling block for ethics, unless love simply puts ethics into question by imitating it. Likewise the distribution of the human between male and female creates problems in the various versions of the Bible," Ibid., 40.
[97] Ibid., 43.

symmetry, share a Levinasian inspiration; nevertheless, in Blanchot we find them reframed in terms of absence of the other (or the death of the other), and of loss.

Despite his connection with Levinas, whose work is seemingly quite far from Nancy's approach (we will return to this question in the next chapter), the very effort of re-thinking community otherwise than in terms of a common *something*, and with it the de-essentialization of the subject, itself keeps Blanchot close to Nancy. Both Blanchot and Nancy are questioning community as communion, while the questioning as such is posed in different terms. Some have argued that the different position of the two philosophers reflects their different affiliations: ethics in Blanchot's case, and ontology in Nancy's case. For instance Robert Mitchell[98] gives such a reading when he compares the two philosophers and their re-thinking of Mitsein, finding in Nancy's and Blanchot's different considerations on Acéphale an important moment of departure in two different directions: the ethical and the ontological.[99] On the other hand, the question is whether it is fair to make such a radical division. Ian James[100] argues that although there seems to be a significant difference between Nancy and Blanchot—the ontological language that Nancy employs indeed differs from Blanchot's terminology in that the latter thinks community as unavowable, and thus differently from a language of presence—it is more a difference in gesture than a radical disparity in their understanding of community.[101] This latter approach challenges not only the categorization of Nancy and Blanchot as representatives of ontology and ethics respectively, but also raises questions regarding Levinas's under-

---

[98] See Robert Mitchell, "Fraternal Anonymity: Blanchot and Nancy on Community and Mitsein," in *The Politics of Community*, ed. Michael Strysick (Aurora: Davies Group Publishers, 2002), 85–105.

[99] "Yet the example of Acéphale is also important insofar as it allows him to differentiate his 'ethical' understanding of the role of the other's death from that Nancy's 'ontological' reading," Mitchell, "Fraternal Anonymity: Blanchot and Nancy on Community and Mitsein," in *The Politics of Community*, 99.

[100] Ian James, "Naming the Nothing: Nancy and Blanchot on Community," *Culture, Theory and Critique* 51, no. 2 (2010): 171–187.

[101] "Perhaps the distance which separates Nancy and Blanchot on the question of community is, in fact, a matter of words, a matter of choosing the right order to mark an absence, empty space, or opening into nothing. This distance amounts very little. It is a difference in philosophical or rhetorical strategy, a difference in gesture. [...] They are, after all, trying to say the same thing in different terms. Or rather, they are both trying to think an instance, that is, an originary absence or withdrawal of essence which escapes any logic of the same," Ibid., 177.

standing of ontology and whether his general critique of ontology would also apply to Nancy's inoperative community. In the next chapter, we propose to continue this conversation by involving the notion of sociality. Our intention is to explore further the meaning of sociality as the un-common that displaces community from its ground in itself.

CHAPTER 11
Sociality and the Un-common

In this third part of this thesis, we have thus far discussed Levinas's efforts at giving a positive meaning to community through fraternity, revealing the importance of interrupting community from founding itself on a common *something*, or in a more Levinasian terminology, from becoming an exclusive side-by-side community. We have suggested the "un-common" aspect of sociality, which gives the interruptive character of community, although this thought have remained underdeveloped. In order to gain the necessary tools for developing it further, we have attempted a deeper exploration of the problem of community without a shared common foundation through the writings of Nancy and Blanchot. In the light of community thought as inoperative, and as unavowable, our goal in this chapter is to think further the un-commonness of sociality in term of interruptive facing. We shall approach the question of un-common sociality as a way of expressing the disturbance of determination, without sociality itself becoming a determining ground. We will pursue this approach in the second part of this chapter. In the first part, however, we need to address some seemingly problematic aspects in the dialogue we attempt to create when engaging Nancy's and Blanchot's thoughts on community in a Levinasian context.

11.1. Thinking the un-common with Levinas
11.1.1. Beyond the ontology/ethics alternative

Due to Nancy's closeness to Heidegger (through his re-thinking of being-with) and to Levinas's and Blanchot's emphasis on the other and on asymmetry (or dissymmetry in Blanchot's case), the temptation is high to distinguish two separate camps: Nancy, as an ontological thinker, on the one hand, and Levinas and Blanchot, as ethical thinkers, on the other.

Indeed, in the context of community Blanchot writes that "An ethics is possible only when—with ontology (which always reduces the Other to the Same) taking the backseat—an anterior relation can affirm itself."[1] This suggests that Blanchot shares Levinas's critique of ontology and his efforts to think otherwise than being. At the same time, for Nancy, the groundless ground for community is being-in-common, and hence, for him, a refusal of thinking in terms of being would also mean a refusal of thinking community without a common foundation. However, before rushing to the conclusion that Nancy and Levinas come from opposite directions, and thus that their critique of thinking community founded on *something* in common must be incompatible, we might want to see from what kind of ontology Levinas tries to escape through ethics, what kind of ontology is put forward by Nancy, and perhaps even more importantly, what kind of relation they suggest between ethics and ontology.

Precisely this relation is problematized by Stella Gaon, who instead of the ethics/ontology division, recognizes a more significant distinction between Nancy and Blanchot given their approach to the very relation between ethics and ontology. Gaon suggests that while Blanchot keeps ethics and ontology separated, Nancy thinks Being itself in an ethical register—an approach that leaves its imprint on their problematization of community.[2] The author does not hide her preference for Nancy's approach, and argues that an emphasis on the ethics/ontology distinction would precisely undermine the very interruption of community from communion because it would congeal thinking community either as ontology or as ethics.[3] According to Gaon, both Blanchot and Nancy try to

---

[1] UC 43.

[2] The article does not seem to specify exactly what kind of ethics Nancy puts forth, but we can assume that it is ethics that regards the heteronomous relation with others. We draw this assumption from claims such as "More specifically, being-with exceeds ontology in the direction of ethics insofar as it avows without saying our asymmetrical, heteronomous relation with others, just as it exceeds ethics in the direction of ontology insofar as that relation (is) the spacing (arche-writing) through which is what *is* (will have) come(s) to be," Stella Gaon, "Communities in Question: Sociality and Solidarity in Nancy and Blanchot," *Journal of Cultural Research* 9, no. 4 (2005), 400.

[3] "It is precisely when the ethical and the ontological are distinguished in a radical way - such that, for example, ethics is understood *either* metaphysically as the 'practical effectuation of the political' (Fraser 1984, p. 135), *or* 'ethically' (in a Levinasian sense) as ontology's absolute, radical outside (as 'essence' divorced from appearance, for example) —that the political purchase of deconstruction is missed.," Gaon, "Communities in Question: Sociality and Solidarity in Nancy and Blanchot," 398.

articulate "the community-in-question," a fundamental interrogation of the classical understanding of community of sovereign individuals, as well as "a questioning that is itself 'communal' or 'social' in a certain sense of those terms."[4] Yet in Nancy's case this interrogative move becomes more successful, Gaon argues, because of his interconnection between ethics and ontology. Moreover, she implies that Nancy's *being singular plural* represents a "beyond Being" in the Levinasian sense, since it is not a win of ontology over ethics, but "undoes radically, at its roots, the ethics-ontology contest."[5] Ian James also argues that Nancy goes beyond a language of ontology,[6] and that, in a way, his re-thinking of the question of community leads to a re-thinking of ontology, otherwise than the Heideggerian ontology.[7] We agree with Gaon and James in their efforts to articulate Nancy's ontology differently than as the totalizing ontology that in Levinas's case calls for an "otherwise." In no way, however, are we seeking to equate Levinas and Nancy, as they clearly differ on several points. Instead, in the following we attempt to argue that the tendency that is found in Nancy's philosophy to break up the ethics/ontology division is not so far from Levinas as one might think. This disintegration of the ethics/ontology division proves to be an important component of thinking community without foundation in *something* in common, as it highlights Levinas's resistance to think in alternatives.

Levinas's famous declaration of ethics as first philosophy might indeed suggest a radical division between ethics and ontology. Nevertheless, the essay that bears this title expresses the *insufficiency* of thinking in terms of thematization, rather than aiming for a radical turn away from this way of

---

[4] Ibid., 397.

[5] Ibid., 400.

[6] According to James, although it is clear that Nancy persists in a language of ontology in many of his works, he still "does so within the demand that ontology be fundamentally refigured," James, "Naming the Nothing: Nancy and Blanchot on Community," 181.

[7] "Nancy is not simply repeating and 'reforming' Heidegger's thinking of being as a more fundamental being-with, and, crucially he is not seeking to retrieve or enclose absence or nothing within the logos of an ontological discourse. The Heideggerian idiom enters into a resonance with a range of other non-Heideggerian terms and can only be read in relation to its resonance with those terms. This, then, is a community of writing which turns around the very nothing of community itself, and in that play something else emerges: a thinking of the 'exposure' or sharing of singular being which *is* otherwise than Heideggerian being," James, "Naming the Nothing: Nancy and Blanchot on Community," 180.

thinking. Published in 1984, "Ethics as First Philosophy" is in fact a slightly modified version of the earlier essay "The Bad Conscience and the Inexorable" (1981), where Levinas proposes a non-intentional consciousness or "bad" consciousness, in order to question the presupposed exclusiveness of the thematizing intentional consciousness.[8] Both the ambiguity of the interplay between the Saying and the Said (between the unthematized and thematization that we have previously shown) and also Levinas's general avoidance of dialectical thinking, suggest that he tries to overcome oppositions rather than building them.[9] The strict separation of ethics leads to formalism, which, we have seen, was one of Levinas's reproaches to Buber's I-Thou relation.[10] It is thus rather unlikely that Levinas's intention is to create a separation between ethics and ontology. Instead of promoting these as two separate alternatives, it is more likely that what Levinas is attempting is a critique of ontology and Being as totality, or interiority as enclosed upon itself—which seems to stay close to Nancy's critique of immanentism. However, before firmly declaring such a connection, we need to investigate further.

The question of Levinas's understanding of Being and his critique of ontology deserves to be studied on its own, due to the complexity of the problem. Here we confine ourselves to examining Levinas's critique of ontology in its relation to our more specific quest for sociality; that is to say, the threat of totalization without the interruption brought by sociality. It is important to keep in mind that interruption, for Levinas, does not mean 'to

---

[8] We have discussed this topic in more details in Chapter 2.

[9] As seen in the first part of this thesis, Levinas insists on the importance of the third and the necessity of the outside dimension of the relation to the other. His insistence is due precisely to the strong interconnection between ethics and justice, which takes the form of an ambiguity. We have shown that their paradoxical intertwinement does not permit making ethics and justice (or ethics and politics) two separate realms. See especially Chapter 4.

[10] One can, however, argue that the ethical language itself that Levinas is engaging in serves the purpose of precisely establishing his philosophy as ethics (and not ontology). Indeed, as we have also pointed out several times, the so called "ethical language" became predominant in Levinas's later work. This however, is a way of showing the refusal to be shown, thematizing the un-thematizible. The "ethical language," Levinas says in *Otherwise than Being*, "does not arise out of a special moral experience," instead it is a way of expressing a paradox that Levinas embraces. The an-archical, characteristic to the ethical relation, "is possible only when contested by language - Levinas says -, which betrays, but conveys, its anarchy, without abolishing it, by an abuse of language," OB 194, note 2.

bring to an end,' 'to stop' but a continual discontinuity, a diachrony opened up by sociality itself.[11] Viewed in terms of uninterrupted Being, ontology *unites* the incomparables in community, and as such, it makes community a communion—that is to say, community is thought *exclusively* on the basis of a shared common, or, in a more Levinasian terminology, it means an *exclusive* side-by-side type of community.

> Essence, the being of entities, weaves between the incomparables, between me and the others (*entre moi et les autres*), a unity, a community (if only the unity of analogy), and drags us off and assembles us on the same side, chaining us to one another like galley slaves, emptying proximity of its meaning.[12]

In this way of thinking ontology, the self would be a sovereign self, not because it is alone, but because it auto-proclaims itself (a movement in interiority).[13] Thus, Levinas's search for the otherwise than being can be translated as a critique of totalizing, uninterrupted Being enclosed in itself that refers to itself by turning back upon itself. In a way, this bears similarities with Nancy's thoughts on the dis-location of community, through its groundless ground. Similarly to the groundless ground that suggests a shattering not only at the level of community, but also at the level of the self, Levinas describes the subject in substitution as null-site (non-lieu), out of its place, expelled, inside-out, without locus or dwelling, deposed. When we turn to Nancy's essay *L'intrus/The Intruder* published in 2000, we find him describe the stranger intruding in me, in every inch of me, up to the point at which the self is nothing else but the thread between strangeness.[14] In an interview from 2007, Nancy again emphasizes that the outside is at the very heart of the inside: "The real outside is not another

---

[11] See Chapter 2 on diachrony, and Chapter 6 where sociality is discussed in relation to temporality.
[12] OB 182, AE 279.
[13] Levinas often expresses it as "folding back upon itself" (*le repliement de l' être sur soi*). This return to itself must not be confused with Levinas's notion of "recurrence." For more on this topic, see Part I.
[14] "An intruder is in me, and I am becoming a stranger to myself.[…] I end/s up being nothing more than a fine wire stretched from pain to pain and strangeness to strangeness.," "L'intrus/The Intruder" [2000], in *Corpus*, trans. Richard A. Rand (New York: Fordham University Press, 2008), 167, 169. It needs to be noted that here Nancy uses strangeness as "étrangeté" and not as bizarreness, oddity (*bizarrerie*) as he uses it in *Being Singular Plural*.

inside than this *inside*: it is at the heart (you can say that again!) of the *inside* [...] We are beside ourselves [hors de nous], essentially."¹⁵ Yet again, in his work from 2002 entitled "Listening," Nancy's distinction between listening (*écouter*) and hearing (*entendre*) brings forth the interplay between inside and outside in relation to a non-substantial self. While Nancy links hearing to understanding and apprehending, he finds listening to be a much deeper relation to the self, or rather to "the relationship in self," where "the 'self' is precisely nothing available (substantial or subsistent) to which one can be 'present' but precisely the resonance of a return (*renvoi*)."¹⁶ Through listening, and the "omni-dimensional" sonorous space, Nancy argues, the self is opened from itself and towards itself, from the inside and from the outside, "from without and from within," "from one to the other and from one in the other."¹⁷ What is suggested in these works is not a simple (even if necessary) relation of the self with exteriority, but a dis-location, a shattering of the self as interiority, and with it the breaking down of inside/outside opposition.

Despite the similarities regarding the necessary interruption of enclosed interiority, for Nancy, ontology has a rather different meaning than for Levinas. Being, Nancy argues, cannot be simply singular as its name ("Being") might suggest, since it cannot be something previous to existence;

---

[15] Jean-Luc Nancy, "The real outside is 'at the heart' of the inside: Interview," in *ATOPIA* (2007), www.atopia.tk. This brings to our mind Levinas's expression according to which the other is "under my skin": "This being torn up from oneself in the core of one's unity, this absolute non-coinciding, this diachrony of the instant, signifies in the form of one-penetrated-by-the-other. The pain, this underside of skin, is a nudity more naked than all destitution"(OB 49). The "skin," besides expressing corporeity (and Levinas do not deny the importance of the body and embodiment), has a direct connection to vulnerability and the self as vulnerability. If sociality discussed as the "correction" of Buber's I-Thou was presented in terms of solicitude where the other is in need, the other is vulnerable, here, vulnerability is the vulnerability of the self; it is the self that is de-cored, de-nuded of his own skin by having the other already under the skin, in the sense of already in its very core, as that which gives the very selfness of the self (the *me*).
[16] Jean-Luc Nancy, *Listening* (2002), trans. Charlotte Mandell (New York: Fordham University Press, 2007), 12.
[17] Nancy, *Listening*, 14. "Car elle [écouter] s'ouvre en moi tout autant qu'autour de moi, et de moi tout autant que vers moi: elle m'ouvre en moi autant qu'au dehors et c'est par une telle double, quadruple ou sextuple ouverture qu'un 'soi' peut avoir lieu. Être à l'écoute, c'est être *en même temps* au dehors et au-dedans, être ouvert *du* dehors et *du* dedans, de l'un à l'autre et de l'un en l'autre.," Nancy, *A l'écoute*, (Galilée: Paris, 2002), 33, emphasis by Nancy.

and existence is plural. Being is singular plural (hence the title of his book *Being Singular Plural*), and in this formulation he recognizes "the most formal and fundamental requirement" of ontology.[18] Essence is not totalizing, but it is co-essence, and this "co-" confers its very interruption, or destabilization, shattering at the core of Being.[19] Nancy argues that in an ontology dominated by Being (and not by being-in-common), being-with would be considered only secondary to the question of Being and would remain formulated as a "question of social Being." Reacting against this view, Nancy places the question of being-with at the centre of his thought, and for him, it becomes *the* ontological question.[20] In this way, his philosophy gives a different understanding of ontology from that which Levinas criticizes; it becomes an ontology for which the question of ethics (here understood simply as the relation to the other) is not a separate question. This is the sense in which we dare to say that Nancy goes "beyond" or "otherwise than" the ontology of Being.

Interestingly, Nancy himself comments on Levinas's otherwise than being, a comment that, although unlikely to have been intended to signal a closeness to Levinas, might nonetheless be viewed that way:

> But what he [Levinas] understands as "otherwise than Being" is a matter of understanding "the ownmost of Being," exactly because it is a matter of thinking being-with rather than the opposition between the other and Being[21].

In our view, the above quote can be read differently than as a mere critique of Levinas. Nancy seems to place Levinas's philosophy in an ontology-ethics conjunction, not by diminishing the importance of Levinas's efforts for an

---

[18] "The most formal and fundamental requirement [of ontology] is that 'Being' cannot even be assumed to be the simple singular that the name seems to indicate. Its being singular is plural in its very Being," BSP 56.
[19] "Being singular plural means the essence of Being is only co-essence. [...] [I]f Being is being-with, then it is, in its being-with, the 'with' that constitutes Being: the with is not simply an addition. [...] Therefore it is not the case that the 'with' is an addition to some prior Being; instead the 'with' is at the heart of Being." Ibid., 30.
[20] "It follows then, that not only must being-with-one-another not be understood starting from the presupposition of being-one, but on the contrary, being-one (Being as such, complete Being or ens realissimum) can only be understood by starting from being-with-one-another. That question which we still call a 'question of social Being' must, in fact, constitute the ontological question." BSP 56–57, emphasis by Nancy.
[21] BSP 199, n. 37.

otherwise than Being, but on the contrary, by acknowledging on the one hand the significance of interrupting a totalizing Being and re-thinking ontology, and on the other, the importance of breaking up thinking in terms of ethics/ontology alternatives. According to this line of thought, instead of a divergence we can find more of a meeting point between Nancy and Levinas through their critique of totalization and their efforts to overcome dialectical thinking. What might be confusing is the two philosopher's very different use of some of their key concepts. Levinas understands the *beyond*, which remains the core of his project, as transcendence given by the idea of the infinite in the finite. For Levinas, infinity is not the *realm* of *the* Infinite, but is what precisely provides an escape from enclosedness in any realm; in other words, preventing fusion. For Nancy, on the contrary, the Infinite means immanence and enclosedness, while it is finitude that brings the transcendence of Nancy's "outside." Perhaps it is too much to say that the two concepts (infinite and finite) are used in exactly the opposite way by the two thinkers, cancelling the difference between them; just as it would be too much to say that Nancy's ontology corresponds with Levinas's ethics. Nevertheless, the similarity in their line of thought, in particular in their respective attempts at overcoming thinking in dialectical terms, and the importance they confer to interrupting the fusion or communion, bring them closer to one-another on the specific topic of community without a common foundation.

11.1.2. On the same and the other

The closeness between Nancy and Levinas that we have pointed out so far is seriously challenged by Nancy's critique of prioritizing the other over the self (or the self over the other), which quite explicitly targets Levinas's philosophy. *Being Singular Plural* displays clearly the two aspects of his critique of prioritizing the other over being-in-common. In the first place, he lays out a critique against the dialectical type of thinking for which "the identification of the self as such […] can only take place once the subject finds itself or poses itself originarily as other than itself."[22] In this case, although alterity or rather alteration of the self is needed, this alterity is

---

[22] BSP 77.

ultimately enveloped by the self through a dialectical move: the dialectic of the Same and the Other. This movement is described by Nancy as "dis-alienating and reappropriative" and invests the self with primordiality both over the other and over the "with." Thus, it places the self as the ultimate originarity.[23] Secondly,—and this is the critique that interests us, since this is where we see Levinas's philosophy becoming a target—Nancy criticizes the Other (with capitalized "O") as an infinitely withdrawn other. Thinking community by placing at its centre the Other, according to Nancy, leads to communion.[24] As in the first case, in which the self occupies a privileged position, when, on the other hand, the privileged position is accorded to the Other, we arrive yet again at the Same/Other dichotomy. The Same and the Other become counterparts, the Same being thought relative to the Other and vice versa. As one would expect, Nancy refuses both these lines of thought; neither the Same nor the Other is more originary, he argues, since there is no such thing as a hierarchy of originarity and there is no order of determination; there is only co-originarity and co-determination, yet without relativeness. This makes the problem of the Same and the Other,

---

[23] "It [the dialectic of the same and the other] reveals that the power of the negative which holds the self to the other, the dis-alienating and reappropriative power of alienation itself as the alienation of the same, will always be presupposed as the power of the self, or the Self as this very power," BSP 78.

[24] "The Other is the place of *community as communion*," Nancy claims, and then he adds, "In this world the mystery of communion announces itself in the form of the *nearby* [prochaine] (the neighbor)," BSP 79. We can immediately recognize a Levinasian terminology emerging, and soon after this, Nancy discusses proximity with a critical tone. Proximity, as the nearer and nearer towards something that cannot be reached is a keeping alive of the "loss" and an aspiration to recuperation (even if it is impossible), but at the same time, because it is a loss in the midst of the self, ultimately it leads us back to the same/other dialectic; it is "the infinite relation of the same to the same as originarily other than itself," Nancy writes. (Ibid., 80.) Although, here, Nancy criticizes the idea of proximity as being a part of constructing a lost community (and in this way proximity leads to community as communion), he does not seem to renounce the idea of a de-posed self (not by the other, but through its being-with) and formulates a positive understanding of proximity. In proximity "where distancing and strangeness are revealed—Nancy says—[we] are each time an other, each time with others.," Ibid., 35. In a more recent book *Being With the Without* Nancy discusses the "co-" as a non-visible social link, and he goes as far as saying that in fact there is no link per se, but proximity as *touching*: "In the touching, there is no link, there is proximity but no link," *Being With the Without*,15–16. Indeed, Nancy refuses proximity as the one *in* the other, (BSP 5–6.), because that would form another essence by emphasizing the "in," the very place of meeting; as such, it would melt together, and destroy both the one and the other.

according to Nancy, a false problem that connects the self to the other through negation and invests either the self or the other with primordiality over the "with."[25] For Nancy the other is not Other (with a capital "O") which is thought in opposition to Being and outside being-with. Nancy links alterity to the singularity of origin. "The alterity of the other is its being-origin" he says.[26] The origin of the other is inassimilable, and the other is alterity, not because it is other, but because it is origin.[27] However, we need to keep in mind that origin, for Nancy, means co-origin, which functions as the very disturbance of originarity (it is an-archy).[28] Nancy's lower case "other" is one among many, yet this one is more than one.[29] In this way, for Nancy, co-originarity becomes a much more important concept than alterity. In the course of his argument, Nancy presents

---

[25] In *Being Singular Plural*, Nancy states clearly his distance from a philosophy governed by the question of the Other: "[T]here are two different measures of the incommensurable to be found within the very depths of our tradition, two measures that are superimposed, intertwined, and contrasted. One is calibrated according to the Other; the other is calibrated according to the 'with.' Because the intimate and the proximate, the same and the other, refer to one another, they designate a 'not being with,' and in this way, a 'not being society.' They designate an Other of the social where the social itself— *the* common as *Being* or as a common *subject*—would be in itself, by itself, and for itself: it would be the very sameness of the other and sameness as Other. In contrast, being-with designates the other that never comes back to the same, the plurality of origins," BSP 81.

[26] Ibid., 11.

[27] Ibid., 6.

[28] For Nancy, the singular plural, co-originarity is what interrupts unity, it repeats itself at each moment of what it originates. It is "continual creation" (Ibid., 82-3).

[29] *More than one* is the title of Nancy's essay from 2012 in which he discusses one of Derrida's favourite phrases ("more than one") and finds in it the very birth of the multiple. *More than one* does not signify simply the addition of another *one*, of another unit of the same kind, but here the addition "is also the distance between one and two, the gap that divides one at the same time as it supplements it.," "More than One" (2012), in *Politics of the One. Concepts of the One and the Many in Contemporary Thought*, edited by Artemy Magun (New York: Bloomsbury, 2013), 3-4. At the same time, this very *more than one*, introduces multiplicity and difference from the start, and the one itself is born through the *more than one*. This aspect of Nancy's "more than one" is strikingly familiar to us from Levinas's radical multiplicity. There *my* (the self's) primordial relation to the other is radical multiplicity—not because it already implies the third party and with it, the plurality of human beings, but precisely because it implies a multiplicity which exceeds both the many and the dyad. For Levinas as well, we have seen, multiplicity is not measured by addition, yet it is not a dyad either - it is in this sense, more than one.

Levinas's philosophy as an example of prioritizing the Other, and he is in fact quite explicit on this point.

> Despite what Hegel maintained, 'soi' is not just the 'soi' of self-consciousness needing to be recognized in order to recognize *itself*. Nor is it merely, as Levinas claims, hostage to others.[30]

Christopher Watkins views Nancy's philosophy as successfully disengaging from a Levinasian Same/Other dichotomy, but without eliminating the ethical aspect of being-with. Watkins argues that for Nancy the self is not "the Same" to begin with, and his philosophy is not inscribed in the Same/Other framework, which according to him, is represented by Levinas's and Derrida's philosophy.[31] Reading Levinas with exaggerated emphasis on the Same/Other distinction is not so uncommon.[32] The same reading has generated the critique according to which "the Other" is an empty concept resulting from an ethics of alterity where the Other prevails over the phenomenality of being-together.[33] It is very likely that these readings are fuelled by Levinas's early- and middle-period work, (especially *Totality and Infinity*) where the separation of the Other from the Same is indeed quite accentuated.[34]

---

[30] Nancy, "Of Being-in-common," 4.

[31] Christopher Watkins, "A Different Alterity: Jean-Luc Nancy's 'Singular Plural,'" *Paragraph* 30, no. 2 (2007): 61.

[32] Another example would be the interpretation given by Harold Durfee, who sees the same and the other as "extreme polarities." See Harold A. Durfee, "War, Politics and Radical Pluralism," in *Philosophy for Phenomenological Research*, 35, no. 4 (1975): 549–558.

[33] In this sense, see for example the rather destructive critique of Alain Badiou, (Alain Badiou, *Ethics: An Essay on the Understanding of Evil* (1998), trans. Peter Hallward [London and New York: Verso, 2001]), or Luce Irigaray's article from 1991, ("Questions to Emmanuel Levinas. On the Divinity of Love," in *Re-reading Levinas*, 109–119) in which Irigaray questions Levinas's notion of the other and considers it abstract, by asking what we think to be an illegitimate question: "Who is this other?." As a response to Irigaray's critique see Kate Ince, "Questions to Luce Irigaray (on Irigaray and Levinas)," *Hypatia: a journal of feminist philosophy* 11, no.1 (1996): 122–140.

[34] Nevertheless, Levinas tries to avoid a relative reading of the Same/Other distinction in *Totality and Infinity*: "The metaphysician and the other do not constitute a simple correlation, which would be reversible. The reversibility of a relation where the terms are indifferently read from left to right and from right to left would couple them the *one* to the *other*; they would complete one another in a system visible from the outside. The intended transcendence would be thus reabsorbed into the unity of the system, destroying the radical alterity of the other. Irreversibility does not only mean that the same

Despite the discourse of *Totality and Infinity* remaining framed by the Same/Other distinction, we feel encouraged to interpret Levinas's thought as a refusal of the negative determination of the other, for reasons similar to Nancy's own argument: describing the other as a simple negation of 'me' (the other as non-me) or relative to the self (the other as alter-ego) would maintain a dialectical thinking which Levinas firmly opposes—this we have pointed out on several occasions. Nancy and Levinas's different terminology makes less apparent their similar argument. With this in mind, we need to point out that, although Levinas did engage the Same/Other separation, in *Totality and Infinity* a radical multiplicity already appears, radical multiplicity that disrupts the self/other dyad. By the time of *Otherwise than Being*, the earlier distinction between the Same and the Other has become substitution, the-other-in-the-same: the dichotomy is broken (the self and the other are bind together forming one word) yet without ending up in fusion (hence the hyphen). The *in* from this formula is not *something*, not a mediator or a common, nor a meeting place (as Nancy would see it), but it marks diachrony and interruption itself.[35] The other is presented neither at the top of a hierarchical order of originarity, nor at the height of sovereignty, simply because it is not a matter of origin— it is anarchical. We propose here a reading of Levinas's philosophy that emphasizes neither the self nor the other, but sociality as anarchical interruption; sociality, which is not a relation as such, and is not the *Relation* between the self and the other. Sociality as interruption disrupts the Same/Other dichotomy. In this sense, the withdrawal of the other does not represent something/someone lost or hidden in another world inaccessible to me, which would then be caught by a consciousness in the form of a lack, as Nancy's critique suggests. On the contrary: it marks a disruption of a common measure between me and the other, it precisely disrupts com-

---

goes unto the other differently than the other unto the same. That eventuality does not enter into account: the radical separation between the same and the other means precisely that it is impossible to place oneself outside of the correlation between the same and the other so as to record the correspondence or the non-correspondence of this going with this return. Otherwise the same and the other would be reunited under one gaze, and the absolute distance that separates them filled in," TI 35–6.

[35] "[D]iachrony is like the *in* of the other-*in*-the-same—without the other ever entering into the Same.," GDT 19. This *in* is similar to the *in* from I*n*finite: i*n*finite is interrupting the finite, without being something beyond, above or on the other side of the finite. See also GDT 110.

munion.³⁶ Clarifying these aspects helps us move forward, in the direction of engaging the debate on community between Nancy and Blanchot in discussing the meaning of an un-common sociality.

11.2. Un-common and irreciprocal facing

Previously we have examined Levinas's dissatisfaction with thinking community merely as a common genus, or side-by-side type of community, and showed that he introduces the face-to-face relation as its interruption. At the same time, we have expressed our preference for thinking sociality as *facing* instead of the face-to-face relation. In the following we continue our discussion on the notion of sociality as facing, and with the help of the Nancy-Blanchot debate on community, emphasize its role of interrupting a common foundation. Nancy's and Blanchot's thoughts on community enable us to re-think Levinas's sociality in terms of un-grounding, which signifies the shattering of the determination of community. This shattering does not form a ground of its own, but it is a groundless ground.

Even if Nancy, as we have seen, is deeply preoccupied with the question of community as groundless ground, he does not find it appropriate to call it "sociality."³⁷ Nancy does not work with terms such as 'sociality' or 'intersubjectivity,' because he identifies them with the 'social ties' that propagate communion, and, in this sense, it is related to a metaphysics of the subject, its essentialization.

> The motif of the revelation, through death, of being-together or being-with, and of the crystallization of the community around the death of its members, *that is to say around the "loss" (the impossibility) of their immanence* and not around their fusional assumption in some collective hypostasis, leads to a space of thinking incommensurable with the problematics of sociality or intersubjectivity

---

[36] "The withdrawal is not a negation of presence, nor its pure latency, recuperable in memory or actualization. It is alterity, without common measure with a presence or a past assembling into a synthesis in the synchrony of the correlative," OB 90.

[37] "Community means, consequently, that there is no singular being without another singular being, and that there is, therefore, what might be called, in a rather inappropriate idiom, an originary or ontological 'sociality' that in its principle extends far beyond the simple theme of man as a social being (the *zoon politikon* is secondary to this community)," IC 28.

(including the Husserlian problematic of the alter ego) within which philosophy, despite its resistance, has remained captive.[38]

As we have seen, Nancy always carefully specifies that the 'with' does not designate an established common which would mark communion, but is rather the shattering, or in a more Levinasian terminology, the interruption, that is signified by the 'with.' This gives the 'in-common,' paradoxically, the meaning of resistance to communion. For Nancy, community *confronts* within itself, it is a 'confronted community' breaking within itself, and in this way, carrying within itself the fissure of being without communion, the absence of an essence of community (or even essence as this very absence).[39] It is a noteworthy detail that *facing* as 'in the face of' ('en face de' in Levinas's terminology), can also be understood as *in front of*. Thus, sociality as *facing* could also take on the stronger meaning of confronting. In one of his later essays, Levinas even uses the expression "powerless af-fronting (*affrontement*)" which means (con)*fronting* the other.[40] This expression, indeed, coincides with Nancy's expression of *confronted community* from his essay "The Confronted Community" ("*La communauté affrontée*") which was the preface for the Italian edition of Blanchot's *The Unavowable Community*.[41]

---

[38] IC 14. Emphasis by Nancy

[39] "Once 'the' community sets itself to stammering a strange uniqueness (as if there should only be the one, and as if it should possess a unique essence of the common), then 'the' community takes in the fact that it is the community itself that gapes—yawningly open to its unity and to its absent essences—and that it confronts within itself this break. [....] That this confrontation with self may be a law of being-in-common and its very meaning, this is what is on the task sheet for the work of thought," Nancy, "The Confronted Community" (2001), 24–5.

[40] "The Bad Conscience and the Inexorable," in OGCM 175–6. See also Chapter 8.

[41] Moreover, in Nancy's discussion on community we find co-presence taking the form of compearance (co-appearing) [com-parution]. In *The Inoperative Community* Nancy describes compearance as "presenting itself before the judgement of community as law" (IC 28) while communication is this compearance (Ibid., 29). The meaning of the word "compearance," again, places the emphasis on co-appearing *in the front of*. Despite the fact that compearing—understood as the appearance in front of a judge—would seem to assign the judge as exteriority, being-with does not appear (compear) to something other than itself, but it compares or co-appears in the face of itself. (See Jean-Luc Nancy and Tracy B. Strong, "La Comparution /The Compearance: From the Existence of 'Communism' to the Community of 'Existence'" [1991], *Political Theory* 20, no. 3 [1992]: 371–398.) On the topic of Nancy's notion of com-pearing see also BSP 53–65.

Nevertheless, read through the Levinasian terminology, both 'being-with' and 'confronting' implies the thematization given by 'with' and 'co-,' and makes community susceptible to fusion. Already in *Existence and Existents,* Levinas sees the "collectivity of the with" to be "set up around a third term which serves as intermediary."[42] Thus, from early on, he distances the notion of sociality not only from the side-by-side community, but also from any kind of collectivity that might imply a sharing and thus the introduction of a reciprocal relation. It is this refusal of mediation that ultimately leads Levinas to reject a discussion that focuses on togetherness itself, or 'betweeness.' "'Between' is a mode of being: co-presence, co-esse,"[43] Levinas says, and by this inscribes the "between" in the movement of union or fusion—something, we previously seen, Levinas assigns to a totalizing ontology. Levinas remains faithful throughout the years to his critique of the 'with,' as we find him repeating essentially the same critique in both the early works[44] and in later writings.[45] His consistency makes us conclude that Levinas's closeness to Nancy, in his effort to disrupt the ethics/ontology and Same/Other dichotomies, does not bring them too close. When approached through a Levinasian framework, reciprocity is inscribed in the "with" and remains characteristic of a side-by-side community. In bringing Levinas into dialogue with Nancy, Critchley pinpoints precisely this problem. He criticizes Nancy's conception of the being-with as risking to reduce intersubjectivity to reciprocity and symmetry:

> Nancy's conception of being-with risks reducing intersubjectivity to a relation of reciprocity, equality, and symmetry, where I rub shoulders or stand shoulder to shoulder with the other, but where I do not *face* him.[46]

---

[42] EE 94.

[43] "Martin Buber, Gabriel Marcel and Philosophy"(1978), in OS 23. We need to add here that despite his critique regarding "betweeness," Levinas is using the expression *between* when he discusses love, or the ethical relation. He is even using it in the title of one of his collection of essays "Entre Nous" (between us).

[44] An example of this is EE 94–5, which we have discussed in Chapter 6.

[45] See for example a text from 1982: "'Mit' is always being next to … it is not in the first instance the Face, it is zusammensein [being-together], perhaps zusammenmarschieren [marching-together]," "Philosophy, Justice and Love" [1982]), in EN 116.

[46] Critchley, "With Being-With? Notes on Jean-Luc Nancy's Rewriting of *Being and Time,*" 66.

Critchley recognizes that the 'being-with' that stands at the core of Nancy's thought, instead of bringing forth community without fusion, transforms it into community where I "stand shoulder to shoulder with the other"—in other words, the side-by-side community, which for Levinas signifies community as fusion. The singular self, *I*, is not only 'with,' continues Critchley, but is also 'without,' and he emphasizes the dimension of the other that cannot be thematized:

> The face-to-face risks effacing itself in the reciprocity of the "with" and it is therefore a matter - ontologically, ethically, politically—not of thinking without the "with," but of thinking the "without" within this "with."[47]

Thus, in Critchley's critique, an important problem is resurfacing, one which we have seen to be a key point in the Nancy-Blanchot debate: the question of irreciprocity and asymmetry (or dissymmetry) brought forth by Blanchot. Nevertheless, in order to give a fair reading to Nancy, we need to point out that he does not consider the 'with' in terms of reciprocity, but of *mutuality*.[48] According to him, mutuality has nothing to do with a transaction where *something* is exchanged. In this sense, it is very different from the Levinasian reciprocity, and does not lead to fusion under *something* in common. So, although Critchley's comments are valuable, his critique goes too far when simply equating Nancy's mutuality with reciprocity. Watkins, who does not agree with Critchley's comments regarding the reciprocity of the 'with,' highlights the difference between mutuality and reciprocity: "Being-in-common is not a space of reciprocal transaction, but a mutual sharing," he argues, and continues by saying that Nancy's ethics is an "ethics of mutuality" where "I am not *in* relation; I *am* singular plural relation."[49] Mutuality, in contrast to reciprocity, has nothing in particular to share. This also means that, in Nancy's sense, mutuality does not imply plain resemblance (as symmetry would). It is a "like-being" (*le semblable*), but "the like is not the same," says Nancy:

> The like is not the same *(le semblable n'est pas le pareil)*. I do not rediscover *myself*, nor do I recognize *myself* in the other: I experience the Other's alterity, or

---

[47] Ibid.
[48] "The 'with' is the measure of an origin-of-the world *as such*, or even of an origin-of-meaning as such. To-be-with is to make sense mutually, and only mutually," BSP 83.
[49] Watkins, "A Different Alterity: Jean-Luc Nancy's 'Singular Plural,'" 61.

> I experience alterity in the other together with the alteration that "in me" sets my singularity outside me and infinitely delimits it.[50]

In being-in-common the very 'in-common,' which expresses the resistance to communion, implies mutuality as mutual *exposure*.[51] Ex-posure reflects the dis-location, de-position, and in this sense, *exile*. Even though Nancy's dis-location, the outside "at the heart of the inside" is, in a sense, similar to Levinas's de-position, for Nancy, being-with means co-originarity, a co-appearing which cannot inscribe itself in the irreciprocal inside-out dimension. Exile, as thought by Levinas in connection to subjectivity, through the de-position that it implies, opens up the inside-out dimension of sociality. For Levinas, irreciprocity presupposes the approach of the relation from the hither side (the inside-out dimension).

In order to remain within the Levinasian framework, we need to distance ourselves from the mutuality of the 'with' and to problematize sociality in irreciprocal terms, or more precisely, in terms of the inside-out dimension that irreciprocity presupposes. That is to say, it is not enough to highlight the refusal of fusion under a shared common ground; considering sociality in terms of inside-out is crucial when thinking the notion with Levinas. The connection between ungrounding and the inside-out dimension is expressed through Levinas's view on exile as 'no-ground' and 'turning inside out':

> It [the I approached in responsibility] does not posit itself, possessing itself and recognizing itself; it is consumed and delivered over, dis-locates itself, loses its place, is exiled, [...], emptying itself in a no-grounds, to the point of substituting itself for the other, holding on to itself only as it were in the trace of its exile.[52]

Or:

> The subject in saying approaches a neighbor in expressing itself, in being expelled, in the literal sense of the term, out of any locus, no longer *dwelling*, not stomping any ground [...] The subject is not *in itself*, at home with itself, such that it would dissimulate itself in itself or dissimulate itself in its wounds and its

---

[50] IC 33.
[51] This mutual exposure is reflected in the meaning of compearing.
[52] OB 138.

exile, understood as *acts* of wounding or exiling itself. Its bending back upon itself is a turning inside out.[53]

As the inside-out dimension is opened-up through the de-posed subject and carried by sociality, Levinas thinks both subjectivity and sociality in an asymmetrical and irreciprocal way. The inside-out denotes both the de-position of the self and the de-position of sociality from any foundation. Yet again we find the interconnection between rethinking the self and rethinking sociality. Here, the role of sociality as radical multiplicity, which surpasses the distinction between singular and plural, becomes clearer. *My relation to the other, from inside-out, cannot be described in terms of singularity ("I"), duality (me and one other), or in terms of the many (society).* Similarly, sociality neither forms an enclosed unity, nor does it express a community of addition: sociality is different from a "total and additive sociality."[54]

We have preferred to denote sociality as "facing" instead of "face-to-face," precisely due to the importance of keeping the inside-out dimension and the irreciprocity that comes with it. By replacing sociality as face-to-face with sociality as facing we depart from a relation of facing each other, towards *me* facing the other, where *me* is nothing else but *facing*. Through its gerundive form, facing becomes an irreciprocal movement that does not permit substantialization. Although we leave aside the face-to-face relation, in this way we still remain faithful to Levinas's description of sociality as not being side-by-side "around a common content," but facing the other without any common content.[55] Sociality as facing reveals both the self and the community in their de-position, and in this way, it is ungrounding and groundless. We have chosen the expression "un-common" to signal this specific aspect of sociality.

---

[53] Ibid., 48–9.
[54] See EI 79–80.
[55] "Contre cette notion du social, nous avons cherché à décrire un rapport social qui se fait entre sujets qui ne sont pas côte à côte autour d'un contenu commun, mais l'un pour l'autre—l'un en face de l'autre sans l'intermédiaire d'un contenu commun.," *Œuvres complètes Tome 2. Parole et silence et autres conférences inédites*, eds. Rodolphe Calin et Catherine Chalier (Paris: Grasset, 2011), 94, emphasis by Levinas. The excerpt is the rewriting from of conference paper entitled "Parole et Silence" originally held at the Collège philosophique in 1948, and it is estimated to be dated sometime the second half of the 1950's.

The expression "un-common," though inspired by Nancy's "in-common," to the extent that it expresses the refusal of communion, the replacement of the "in-," from Nancy's "in-common," with an "un" has important significance. The "in" of the "in-common" makes sense if we follow a Nancian 'logic.' The breakdown of the inside/outside boundaries, here, is represented by finding the outside, that which breaks communion, already *in* the inside. Both prefixes, 'in-' and 'un-,' go beyond a mere negation, and suggest the re-thinking of the common (here understood in the sense of communion). Yet the 'un' seems to escape the reciprocity and symmetry that the possible interpretation of the "in-common" can lead to, and thus, the expression "un-common" manages to carry the inside-out dimension within its meaning. Despite the grammatical negative, the un-common sociality does not express a negation in the usual sense, as part of the dialectic between affirmation and negation. The prefix 'un,' with its origin in the Greek 'an,' carries the meaning of 'without' in the same way that the an-archical (without origin). Just as the an-archical, in Levinas's understanding, is not in opposition to arche, it is not disorder, so too, the un-common does not enter into the common/uncommon dialectic either. In this sense, the un-common is not a dismissal; its function is not that of exclusion, but as we have argued, that of a necessary interruption. At the same time, the un-common (as in the everyday use of the word "uncommon") suggests the meaning of the exceptional, of what is un-ordinary. This again, should not be taken in the sense of exception among the usual (the unexceptional). Its un-ordinariness is not thought against the ordinary. Instead, through its an-archical character, the un-commonness of sociality breaks down the very thinking in terms of order and ordinary. Un-common as exception, does not suggest other *than* the ordinary, but it is closer to its etymological roots, as ex-ception from *ex-cipere*, meaning that Levinas himself suggestively uses to express the de-position of the self.[56] This reflects the de-position of community through the disturbance that sociality entails, and that only through de-position can be possible the positioning of community, its common.[57] In order to have reciprocity at all, we need irreciprocity, just as we need community without a common, the un-common,

---

[56] "In its identity invoked the one is irreplaceable, and does not return to itself; in its bearing of itself, it is an expiation for the other, in its "essence" an ex-ception to essence, or a substitution.," OB 141.
[57] In this sense, we can say that sociality is a pre-supposition, where sup-position indicates positioning a foundation, grounding.

for any communion to be possible. Nevertheless, this is a different kind of possibility than one which implies groundedness. We could see its meaning transpire in the already discussed relation between the unthematized and thematization in the context of the intertwinement between ethics and justice, and the radicalized and non-radicalized multiplicity corresponding to them. There we have argued that there cannot be a "politics of radical multiplicity" or a "society of radical multiplicity" for in that way the unthematized would be thematized, since the Saying would form a separate *realm* (hence falling into thematization). Saying does not designate something more original, or more authentic than the Said, but it assures the interruption of the Said, in a way that can never be detected in itself, but only the sense, the direction that it gives, through the interruption by its untraceable trace or unheard echo. It is communication as ex-posure, without having *something* to communicate.[58] "It is not the common content that made communication possible, but communication is what has to make possible the common content," Levinas says.[59]

What Levinas proposes is a new way of approaching the question of possibility. The measure of possibility is not anymore the reflection on the self, the for-itself. By substitution, the one-for-the-other breaks its identity (made by self-identification), "to the hither side or beyond being and the possible."[60] Levinas suggests a different way of thinking possibility than as part of the possible/impossible couple, or possibility as an origin, grounding. Instead, in a move typical to his thought, he tries to escape thinking in dualities or in terms of arche, proposing instead the use of expressions such as "probably" or "perhaps."[61] Derrida remarks that Levinas's use of "probably" or "perhaps" are far from a sign of approximation. Instead, through them, essence is freed from certainty and opened up towards probability, risk, and uncertainty.[62] In using these words ('probably' and

---

[58] This aspect gets close to Nancy's understanding of community as communication.

[59] "Ce n'est pas le contenu commun qui rendait la communication possible mais la communication doit rendre possible le contenu commun," *Œuvres complètes Tome 2. Parole et silence et autres conférences inédites*, 94.

[60] OB 113.

[61] See for example " The revelation of the beyond being is perhaps indeed but a word, but this 'perhaps' [peut-être] belongs to an ambiguity in which the anarchy of the Infinite resists the univocity of an originary or a principle.," OB 156, AE 224., or "'perhaps' is the modality of an enigma, irreducible to the modalities of being and certainty," "Enigma and Phenomenon" (1965), BPW 75.

[62] Derrida, "At This Very Moment In This Work Here I Am" (1980), 23.

'perhaps'), Levinas breaks from the concerns regarding conditions *of* possibility, which characterizes the language of being-present. When we translate this thought to our question of community, we need to conclude that the un-common is neither the condition nor the bases of the common. The un-common sociality does not form any kind of *base* or foundation, and does not coagulate into essentialization. Thinking the relation between the common and un-common is not about priorities. Instead, it indicates the necessity of interruption; it suggests that the interruptive movement of facing and the sense that it entails is inseparable from concreteness that always brings the shared common into play. As we have argued, the inside-out dimension of *my* relation to the other and an outside perspective upon the relation are in an ambiguous intertwinement. We should keep this in mind when considering un-common sociality. Thought in these terms, the un-common sociality cannot generate a different *kind* of politics, a different *kind* of society or a different *kind* of community. There is no un-common society or un-common community, but only un-common *sociality* that cannot congeal itself in a community, but is signaled in any community. It gives sense, orientation to community through an interruptive movement. Sociality is not something *towards which* society or community orients themselves, but, as we have previously seen, it is the very orientation. That is to say, there is nothing that we could or should do to attain an un-common sociality. As its etymological meaning suggests, socia*lity* is an always already socius.

The different approach to possibility and to condition without conditioning entails a different approach towards temporality. The un-common sociality is not constrained to contemporaneity. When thought through Levinas's notion of diachrony, we get perhaps a clearer glimpse of the way in which sociality as interruption escapes priorities. Diachrony, for Levinas, means a loss of time, a lapse, "despite oneself,"[63] not a "work of the subject."[64] Blanchot, who as we have seen is close to Levinas in thinking the unavowable community in terms of dissymmetry,[65] describes the "loss" of community as an out of phase, a resistance to synchrony:

---

[63] See OB, Chapter II 4 c.
[64] OB 51.
[65] For Blanchot, however, dissymmetry becomes double dissymmetry, and ultimately takes the form of the neutral. "it [the redoubling of irreciprocity] signifies a double dissymmetry, a double discontinuity, as though the empty space between the one and the other were not homogeneous but polarized: as through this space constituted a non-

> [T]hat is to say realizing itself by losing not what has belonged to you but what one has never had, for the "I" and the "other" do not live in the same time, are never together (synchronously), can therefore not be contemporary, but separated (even when united) by a "not yet" which goes hand in hand with an "already no longer."[66]

The "not yet" and the "already no longer," which keeps the separation between the "I" and the "other," correspond to Levinas's thoughts on the anarchical past—a past that is not a recollectable present that had a past. In this sense, the anarchical past is "not yet" (because it is never present) and at the same time "already no longer" (because it cannot be re-presented through memory). Blanchot's "loss," which does not designate a former belonging to something but interrupts any binding or possibility of original belonging, expresses something similar to the out of time, yet opening-up time itself, characteristic of the Levinasian sociality.[67] In the context of death, we find Blanchot even using the expression so familiar to us from Levinas's work, "most passive passivity."[68] In his conference essay from 1987 entitled "Dying for...," Levinas, as elsewhere, takes up the problem of death through the death of the other. Yet this time around, through a reference to the biblical verse (a eulogy for Saul and Jonathan dying together), he points out the importance of not only "dying for the other," but also of "dying together," suggesting that sociality is not "undone" through death:

> "Dying for," "dying for the other." I also considered calling my remarks "dying together." [...] A biblical verse came to mind—II Samuel 1:23, a verse of the funeral chant of the prophet weeping for the death of King Saul and his son Jonathan in combat: "Saul and Jonathan were lovely and pleasant in their lives, and in their death they were not divided; they were swifter than eagles, they were stronger than lions." As if, contrary to the Heideggerian analysis, in death, all relationship to the other person were not undone. I do not think this verse alludes to "another life" that, after death, can unite those who are no longer there. But neither do I think that these words on "non-separation in death" in

isomorphic field bearing a double distortion, at once infinitely negative and infinitely positive, and such that one should call it neutral if it is well understood that the neutral does not annul, does not neutralize this double-signed infinity, but bears in it the way of an enigma.," Blanchot, *The Infinite Conversations*, 70–1.

[66] UC 42.
[67] See Chapter 6 and 7.
[68] "The impossibility of death is its most naked possibility [...] suspended until the end of time the illicit action in which the exaltation of the most passive passivity would have been affirmed," UC 14.

the verse amount to nothing more than a metaphorical way of speaking to exalt the love between father and son, which would thus be "stronger than death," and a symbol or sign or image in the impressive simultaneity of their final hours in combat.[69]

Levinas's comments above can be seen as opening up the dimension of un-common sociality towards a community with the dead. This would not correspond to an afterlife, but to an un-common that surpasses the living synchronous time.

Inspired by Derrida's discussion of friendship, in which he places the time of friendship in a future anterior,[70] it seems to be fruitful to interpret Levinas's an-archy in this context, similarly to the "curling of time" suggested by Derrida: past without present (absolute passivity) but also a future; signifying, in other words, a future anterior. In *Totality and Infinity*, the "not yet" is presented as the absence without anticipation. It is not the possible, not because it would be impossible, but because it is beyond anticipation.[71] This opens up a way of thinking temporality differently than the "banal thought that extrapolates one's own duration; it is the time of the other."[72] Sociality is not only a relation (without relation) to the contemporary other(s), but also, to the other(s) *before me*, in front of me in a future (yet without determinatory anticipation), and in a past never present—one could say: already in front of me, already facing. In this sense, the past that was never present is also a future that has already past. Perhaps the notion of fecundity, from Levinas's early- and middle-period work, gives a good illustration of this idea; but even its successor from Levinas's later writings, the syntagma "the other in me," can be interpreted in terms of my relation with the future, unborn other. Seen in this light, Levinas's discussion on maternity in the context of substitution receives the additional meaning of breaking up the restraints of contemporaneity.[73] Thus, we find in Levinas's

---

[69] "Dying for…"(1987), in EN 215.
[70] Jacques Derrida, "The Politics of Friendship," *The Journal of Philosophy*, Vol. 85, No. 11 (1988): 638, and Derrida, *The Politics of Friendship* (1994), 249–50.
[71] This is mentioned in relation to the caress, which seeks for the not-yet. See TI 257–260.
[72] "The Trace of the Other" (1963), 349. As mentioned earlier, this essay was later integrated in the volume *The Humanism of the Other* (1972), which to us suggests that Levinas did not give up this idea in his later thinking.
[73] See OB, especially Chapter III.5 and IV.2.

philosophy the possibility of thinking sociality beyond contemporaneity, a diachronous sociality that cannot exclude the unborn and the dead.[74]

In 1982, just a year before the first publication of Nancy's *The Inoperative Community* and Blanchot's *The Unavowable Community*, Levinas claims: "My idea consists in conceiving sociality as independent of the 'lost' unity."[75] Here, he expresses quite explicitly the need to think sociality differently than as the striving for a lost unity, or, in Nancy's terminology, the "nostalgia" for communion. The question of community without a common ground in *something*, addressed by Nancy and Blanchot, has helped us to develop a Levinasian notion of sociality in terms of ungrounding, while remaining faithful to the main strands of Levinas's philosophy.

[74] Marcia Sá Cavalcante Schuback's essay, "Hermeneutics of tradition" (in *Rethinking Time: Essays on History, Memory and Representation*, eds. Hans Ruin and Andrus Ers [Stockholm: Södertörn Philosophical Studies, 2011]) on "tradition as common life after death and before," although not refer directly to Levinas, inspired our interpretation.
[75] "Philosophy, Justice and Love" (1982), in EN 112. The same idea is repeated in an essay from 1983: "A sociality not to be confused with some weakness or deprivation in the unity of the One," "From the One to the Other" (1983), in EN 149.

Instead of a Conclusion: Un-common Turned Inside-out

In our quest to develop a notion of sociality inspired by Levinas, we have discovered that Levinas's efforts to think community without fusion transpose his well-known thoughts regarding the de-posed subjectivity onto the question of sociality. Sociality, as anarchical interruption, also means a de-position, a disturbance and trembling of its very foundation. It reflects the shattering in the grounding of both the self and its relation to the other. This disturbance, at the level of both subjectivity and community, is a turning inside-out, opening up a dimension from within: neither inside, nor outside, without a place, in permanent exile. It is what we have called the *inside-out dimension*.

The turn inside-out, although disruptive, is not a destructive movement. On the contrary, the disturbance of the inside-out dimension brings forth, without determination, sociality as *facing*. Despite Levinas's emphasis from his early- and middle-period works on the face-to-face relation, we have argued that the expression as such, 'face to face,' never really escapes the suspicion of a dual relation; it endangers the inside-out dimension opened up by the exiled self, because it assigns both to the other and to me a 'face'; in this sense, it brings synchrony and symmetry, even if it is just the synchrony of the faces, and the symmetry of having faces. Sociality as facing has the role of disrupting synchrony, and a Levinasian notion of sociality cannot be considered either a dyad (me in relation with one other), or a third (indicating the society of the many)—both of these would presuppose the dialectical synchrony of the other/others, singular/plural distinction.

Synchrony is unifying, it brings fusion, while its disturbance gives resistance to fusion. In our context of facing, this means having nothing (no-*thing*) in common, not even the movement of facing. Facing is an interruptive, diachronic movement; it interrupts the establishment and determination that the subject or community would subsume; and, through its interruptive movement, facing itself also escapes determination. Hence, the significance of the inside-out dimension becomes even more evident when sociality is problematized in terms of un-groundedness and community without a common ground in *something*.

The question of community without a common ground in *something* helps us think a notion of sociality with Levinas, yet in terms that are not problematized by Levinas himself: sociality as un-common. The un-common sociality marks the interruption of community and subjectivity, and, paradoxically, through this interruption, it opens up community and subjectivity, and makes them 'possible.' In this way, we remain faithful to Levinas's paradoxical mode of thinking. At the same time, the development of a notion of sociality with an emphasis on turning inside-out brings another dimension (an inside-out dimension) to thinking community. Exploring a notion of sociality inspired by Levinas helps us to give voice to Levinas on the question of community without a common ground, a topic and a debate where he has been until now unjustly disregarded. Even if for this task we would have to leave behind some of Levinas's own words, his philosophy nonetheless enables the notion of sociality to open up towards the un-common.

References

Works by Levinas

The Theory of Intuition in Husserl's Phenomenology [1930]. Translated by André Orianne. Evanston IL: Northwestern University Press, 1995.

De l'existence à l existant [1947]. Paris: Vrin, 1990/2004. (Seconde édition augmentée)

Existence and Existents [1947]. Translated by Alphonso Lingis. Dordrecht: Kluwer Academic Publishing, 1978/1995 (Third printing).

Time and the Other [1947]. Translated by Richard A. Cohen. Pittsburgh, PA: Duquesne University Press, 1987.

En découvrant l'existence avec Husserl et Heidegger [1949]. Partially translated by Richard A. Cohen and Michael B. Smith. *Discovering Existence with Husserl.* Evanston, IL: NorthWestern University Publishing, 1998.

"Place and Utopia" [1950]. In *Difficult Freedom* [1976]. Translated by Seán Hand. Baltimore: The John Hopkins University Press, 1990, pp. 99–102.

"Is ontology fundamental?" [1951]. In *Entre Nous. Thinking of the Other* [1991]. Translated by Michael B. Smith and Barbara Harshav. New York: Columbia University Press, 1998, pp. 1–12.

"The State of Israel and the Religion of Israel" [1951]. In *Difficult Freedom* [1976]. Translated by Seán Hand. Baltimore: The John Hopkins University Press, 1990, pp. 216–220.

"The I and the Totality" [1954]. In *Entre Nous. Thinking of the Other* [1991]. Translated by Michael B. Smith and Barbara Harshav. New York: Columbia University Press, 1998, pp. 13–38.

"Philosophy and the Idea of Infinity" [1957]. Translated by Alphoso Lingis. In *Emmanuel Levinas. Collected Philosophical Papers.* Dordrecht: Martinus Nijhoff Publishers, 1987, pp. 47–59.

"Martin Buber and the Theory of Knowledge" [1958/1963]. In *Proper Names* [1975]. Translated by Michael B Smith. Stanford CA: Stanford University Press, 1996, pp. 17–35.

Totalité et infini [1961]. Paris: Le Livre de Poche, 1990.

Totality and Infinity. An essay on exteriority [1961]. Translated by Lingis, Alphonso. Pittsburgh, PA: Duquesne University Press, 1969.

"The Trace of the Other" [1963]. Translated by Alphonso Lingis. In *Deconstruction in Context*, edited by Marc C. Taylor. Chicago: University of Chicago Press: 1986, pp. 345-359.

"The Temptation of temptation" [1964]. In *Nine Talmudic Readings*. Translated by Annette Aronowicz. Bloomington IN: Indiana University Press, 1990/1994, pp. 30-50.

"Enigma and Phenomenon" [1965]. In *Basic Philosophical Writings*, edited by Adriaan Peperzak, Simon Critchley and Robert Bernasconi. Bloomington, IN: Indiana University Press, 1996, pp. 65-78.

"Dialogue with Martin Buber" [1965]. In *Proper Names* [1975]. Translated by Michael B Smith. Stanford CA: Stanford University Press, 1996, pp. 36-39.

"'As Old as the World?'" [1966]. In *Nine Talmudic Readings*. Translated by Annette Aronowicz. Bloomington IN: Indiana University Press, 1990/1994, pp. 70-88.

"A Man-God" [1968]. In *Entre Nous. Thinking of the Other* [1991]. Translated by Michael B. Smith and Barbara Harshav. New York: Columbia University Press, 1998, pp. 53-60.

"Martin Buber's Thought and Contemporary Judaism" [1968]. In *Outside the Subject* [1987]. Translated by Michael B. Smith. Stanford, CA: Stanford University Press, 1993, pp. 4-19.

"Judaism and Revolution" [1968]. In *Nine Talmudic Readings*. Translated by Annette Aronowicz. Bloomington, IN: Indiana University Press, 1990/1994, pp. 94-119.

"Substitution" [1968]. In *Basic Philosophical Writings*, edited by Adriaan Peperzak, Simon Critchley and Robert Bernasconi. Bloomington, IN: Indiana University Press, 1996, pp. 79-98.

"No Identity" [1970]. Translated by Alphoso Lingis. In *Emmanuel Levinas. Collected Philosophical Papers*. Dordrecht: Martinus Nijhoff Publishers, 1987, pp. 141-152.

Humanisme de l'autre homme. Montpellier: Fata Morgana, 1972 ; L.G.F., Le Livre de poche. Biblio essais, 1987.

Humanism of the Other [1972]. Translated by Nidra Poller. Urbana and Chicago: University of Illinois Press, 2003.

Autrement qu'être ou au-delà de l'essence [1974]. Paris: Le Livre de Poche, 1978.

Otherwise than Being or Beyond Essence [1974]. Translated by Alphonso Lingis. Pittsburgh, PA: Duquesne University Press, 1999.

Sur Maurice Blanchot. Montpellier: Fata Morgana, 1975.

"God and Philosophy" [1975]. In *Of God who Comes to Mind* [1986]. Translated by Bettina Bergo. Stanford, CA: Stanford University Press, 1998, pp. 55-78.

Dieu, la mort et le temps [1975-6]. Paris: Grasset, 1993.

God, Death and Time [1975-6]. Translated by Bettina Bergo. Stanford, CA: Stanford University Press, 2000.

Noms Propre. Montpellier: Fata Morgana, 1976.

"Desacralization and Disenchantment" [1977]. In *Nine Talmudic Readings*. Translated by Annette Aronowicz. Bloomington, IN: Indiana University Press, 1990/1994, pp. 136-160.

"Hermeneutics and the beyond" [1977]. In *Entre Nous. Thinking of the Other* [1991]. Translated by Michael B. Smith and Barbara Harshav. New York: Columbia University Press, 1998, pp. 65-76.

"Questions and answers" [1977]. In *Of God who Comes to Mind* [1986]. Translated by Bettina Bergo. Stanford, CA: Stanford University Press, 1998, pp. 79-99.

"Utopia and Socialism" [1977]. In *Alterity and Transcendence*. [1995]. Translated by Michael B. Smith. New York: Columbia University Press, 1999, pp. 111-118.

"Martin Buber, Gabriel Marcel and Philosophy" [1978]. In *Outside the Subject* [1987]. Translated by Michael B. Smith. Stanford, CA: Stanford University Press, 1993, pp. 20-39.

"The Word I, the Word You, the Word God" [1978]. In *Alterity and Transcendence*. [1995]. Translated by Michael B. Smith. New York: Columbia University Press, 1999, pp. 91-96.

"Manner of Speaking" [1980]. In *Of God who Comes to Mind* [1986]. Translated by Bettina Bergo. Stanford, CA: Stanford University Press, 1998, pp. 178-182.

"The Meaning of Meaning" [1980]. In *Outside the Subject* [1987]. Translated by Smith, Michael B. Stanford, CA: Stanford University Press, 1993, pp. 90-95.

"The Old and the New" [1980]. In *Time and the Other and additional essays*. Translated by Richard A. Cohen, Pittsburgh, PA: Duquesne University Press, 1987, pp. 121-138.

"What one asks of oneself, one asks of a saint" [1980-81]. Interview conducted and translated by Johan F. Goud. In *Levinas Studies: An Annual Review. Volume 3*, edited by Jeffrey Bloechl. Pittsburgh, PA: Duquesne University Press, 2008, pp. 1-33.

"La mauvaise conscience et l'inexorable." *Exercises de la Patience 2*, Paris: Editions Obsidiane, 1981.

"Bad Conscience and the Inexorable" [1981]. In *Of God who Comes to Mind* [1986]. Translated by Bettina Bergo. Stanford, CA: Stanford University Press, 1998, pp. 172-177.

"Everyday Language and Rhetoric without Eloquence" [1981]. In *Outside the Subject* [1987]. Translated by Michael B. Smith. Stanford, CA: Stanford University Press, 1993, pp. 135-143.

"Notes on Meaning" [1981]. In *Of God who Comes to Mind* [1986]. Translated by Bettina Bergo. Stanford, CA: Stanford University Press, 1998, pp. 152-171.

"Préface a la deuxième édition" [1981]. In *De l'existence à l'existant*. Paris: Vrin, 2004, p. 10–14.

"Philosophy, Justice, and Love" [1982]. Remarks recorded by R. Fornetand A. Gómez. In *Entre Nous. Thinking of the Other* [1991]. Translated by Michael B. Smith and Barbara Harshav. New York: Columbia University Press, 1998, pp. 103–122.

"Ethics and Politics" [1982], radio interview with Shlomo Malaka on Radio Communauté, 28 September 1982. Translated by Romney, Jonathan. In *The Levinas Reader*, edited by Seán Hand. Basil Blackwell: Blackwell Publishing, 1989, pp. 289–297.

Ethics and Infinity. Conversations with Philippe Nemo [1982]. Translated by Cohen, Richard A. Pittsburgh, PA: Duquesne University Press, 1985.

"The Pact" [1982]. In *Beyond the Verse. Talmudic Readings and Lectures*. Translated by Gary D. Mole. Bloomington IN: Indiana University Press, 1994, pp. 68–85.

"Apropos of Buber: Some Notes" [1982]. In *Outside the Subject* [1987]. Translated by Michael B. Smith. Stanford, CA: Stanford University Press, 1993, pp. 40–48.

"Useless Suffering" [1982]. In *Entre Nous. Thinking of the Other* [1991]. Translated by Michael B. Smith and Barbara Harshav. New York: Columbia University Press, 1998, pp. 91–102.

"De l'Un à l'Autre. Transcendance et temps." *Archivio di filosofia*, vol. 51, No. 1–3, 1983.

"From the One to the Other: Transcendence and Time" [1983]. In *Entre Nous. Thinking of the Other* [1991]. Translated by Michael B. Smith and Barbara Harshav. New York: Columbia University Press, 1998, pp. 133–154.

"La conscience non-intentionnelle." *Philosophes critiques d'eux-mêmes*, vol. 10, (1983), pp. 143–171.

"Nonintentional consciousness" [1983]. In *Entre Nous. Thinking of the Other* [1991]. Translated by Michael B. Smith and Barbara Harshav. New York: Columbia University Press, 1998, pp. 123–132.

"Éthique comme philosophie première." *Justifications de l'éthique*, Bruxelles: Editions de l'Université de Bruxelles, 1984.

"Ethics as First Philosophy" [1984]. In *The Levinas Reader*, edited by Seán Hand. Basil Blackwell: Blackwell Publishing, 1989, pp. 75–87.

"Transcendence and Intelligibility" [1984]. In *Basic Philosophical Writings*, edited by Adriaan Peperzak, Simon Critchley and Robert Bernasconi. Bloomington, IN: Indiana University Press, 1996, pp. 11–32.

"Peace and Proximity" [1984]. In *Basic Philosophical Writings*, edited by Adriaan Peperzak, Simon Critchley and Robert Bernasconi. Bloomington, IN: Indiana University Press, 1996, pp. 161–170.

"Dialogue with Emmanuel Levinas" [1984]. Interview conducted by Richard Kearney. In *Face to Face with Levinas*, edited by Richard A. Cohen. Albany, NY: State University of New York Press, 1985, pp. 13–34.

"Diachrony and Representation" [1985]. In *Time and the Other and additional essays*. Translated by Richard A. Cohen, Pittsburgh, PA: Duquesne University Press, 1987, pp. 97–120.

"Who Shall Not Prophesy" [1985]. Translated by Bettina Bergo. In *Is it Righteous to Be?*, edited by Jill Robbins. Stanford, CA: Stanford University Press, 2001, pp. 219–227.

"The Rights of Man and the Rights of the Other" [1985]. In *Outside the Subject* [1987]. Translated by Michael B. Smith. Stanford, CA: Stanford University Press, 1993, pp. 116–125.

De Dieu qui vient à l'idée [1986]. Paris: Vrin, 2004. Seconde édition augmentée. Quatrième tirage.

"The Paradox of Morality: An Interview with Emmanuel Levinas" [1986]. Interview conducted by Tamra Wright, Peter Hughes and Alison Ainley. Translated by Andrew Benjamin and Tamra Wright. In *The Provocation of Levinas. Rethinking the Other*, edited by Robert Bernasconi and David Wood. London and New York: Routledge, 1988/2003, pp. 168–180.

"Interview with François Poirié" [1986]. Translated by Jill Robbins, Marcus Coelen and Thomas Loebel. In *Is it righteous to be?*, edited by Jill Robbins. Stanford, CA: Stanford University Press, 2001, pp. 23–83.

"The Proximity of the Other" [1986]. Translated by Bergo, Bettina. In *Is it righteous to be?*, edited by Jill Robbins. Stanford, CA: Stanford University Press, 2001, pp. 211–218.

"Uniqueness" [1986]. In *Entre Nous. Thinking of the Other* [1991]. Translated by Michael B. Smith and Barbara Harshav. New York: Columbia University Press, 1998, pp. 189–196.

Hors Sujet. Montpellier: Fata Morgana, 1987.

"Dying for…" [1987]. In *Entre Nous. Thinking of the Other* [1991]. Translated by Michael B. Smith and Barbara Harshav. New York: Columbia University Press, 1998, pp. 207–218.

"Being-Towards-Death and 'Thou Shall Not Kill'" [1987]. Interview conducted by Florian Rötzer. Translated by Andrew Schmitz. In *Is it righteous to be?*, edited by Jill Robbins. Stanford, CA: Stanford University Press, 2001, pp.130–139.

"Dialogue on Thinking-of-the-Other" [1987]. In *Entre Nous. Thinking of the Other* [1991]. Translated by Michael B. Smith and Barbara Harshav. New York: Columbia University Press, 1998, pp. 201–206.

"Sociality and money" [1987]. Translated by François Bouchetoux and Campbell Jones. In *Buisness Ethics: A European Review*, Vol. 16, No. 3 (July 2007): 203–207.

"*Totality and Infinity*. Preface to the German Edition" [1987]. In *Entre Nous. Thinking of the Other* [1991]. Translated by Michael B. Smith and Barbara Harshav. New York: Columbia University Press, 1998, pp. 197–200.

"The Other, Utopia, and Justice" [1988]. In *Is it righteous to be?*, edited by Jill Robbins. Stanford, CA: Stanford University Press, 2001, pp. 200-210.

"The Vocation of the Other" [1988]. Translated by Jill Robbins. In *Is it righteous to be?*, edited by Jill Robbins. Stanford, CA: Stanford University Press, 2001, pp. 105-113.

"Philosophie et transcendance." In *Encyclopédie philosophique universelle*. Presses Universitaires de France. 1989.

"Philosophy and Transcendence" [1989]. *Alterity and Transcendence*. [1995]. Translated by Michael B. Smith. New York, NY: Columbia University Press, 1999, pp. 3-38.

"Intention, Event and the Other" [1989]. In *Is it righteous to be?*, edited by Jill Robbins. Stanford, CA: Stanford University Press, 2001, pp. 140-157.

"In the Name of the Other" [1990]. In *Is it righteous to be?*, edited by Jill Robbins. Stanford, CA: Stanford University Press, 2001, pp. 188-199.

Entre Nous. Essais sur le penser-à-l'autre. Paris: Grasset, 1991.

Interview with Emmanuel Levinas conducted by Raoul Mortley. In *French Philosophers in Conversation*, edited by Raoul Mortley. London and New York: Routledge, 1991. http://epublications.bond.edu.au/french_philosophers/2

Altérité et transcendance. Montpellier: Fata Morgana, 1995.

Alterity and Transcendence. [1995]. Translated by Michael B. Smith. New York, NY: Columbia University Press, 1999.

"Responsibility and Substitution" [1996]. Interview conducted by Augusto Ponzio. Translated by Gedney, Maureen. In *Is it righteous to be?*, edited by Jill Robbins. Stanford, CA: Stanford University Press, 2001, pp. 227-233.

Œuvres complètes Tome 1. Carnets de captivité et autres inédits, edited by Rodolphe Calin et Catherine Chalier. Paris : Grasset, 2009.

Œuvres complètes Tome 2. Parole et silence et autres conférences inédites, edited by Rodolphe Calin et Catherine Chalier. Paris: Grasset, 2011.

Other references

A Dictionary of Prefixes, Suffixes, and Combining Forms from Webster's Third New International Dictionary, Unabridged. Merriam-Webster, 2002.

Atterton, Peter and Matthew Calarco. "Editors' Introduction: The Third Wave of Levinas Scholarship." In *Radicalizing Levinas*, edited by Peter Atterton and Matthew Calarco. Albany: SUNY Press, 2010, pp. ix-xviii.

— "Levinas and Our Moral Responsibility Toward Other Animals." *Inquiry: An Interdisciplinary Journal of Philosophy*, (2011): 633-649.

Badiou, Alain. *Ethics: An Essay on the Understanding of Evil* [1998]. Translated by Peter Hallward. London and New York: Verso, 2001.

Bataille, George. "The Labyrinth" [1930]. *Visions of Excess: Selected Writings, 1927-1939*. Minneapolis: University of Minnesota Press, 1985, pp. 171-177.

Bergo, Bettina. *Levinas Between Ethics and Politics. For the Beauty that Adorns the Earth*. The Hague: Martinus Nijhoff Publishers, 1999.

— "Ontology, Transcendence, and Immanence in Emmanuel Levinas' Philosophy." *Research in Phenomenology* 35, 1 (2005): 141-180.

— "'When I Opened He had Gone'": Levinas' substitution as a reading Husserl and Heidegger," *Discipline Filosofiche 1* (2014): 97-118.

Bergson, Henri. *Time and Free Will* [1889]. Translated by F. L. Pogson. London: George Allen and Unwin, 1910.

— *Matter and Memory* [1896]. Translated by Nancy Margaret Paul and W. Scott Palmer. London: George Allen and Unwin, 1911.

— "Introduction to Metaphysics" [1903]. In *The Creative Mind*. Translated by Mabelle L. Andison. New York: Philosophical Library, 1946, pp. 187-237.

— *The Creative Mind*. Translated by Mabelle L. Andison. New York: Philosophical Library, 1946.

Bernasconi, Robert. "'Failure of communication' as a Surplus: Dialogue and Lack of Dialogue between Buber and Levinas." In *The Provocation of Levinas. Rethinking the Other*, edited by Robert Bernasconi and David Wood. London and New York: Routledge, 1988/2003, pp. 100-135.

— "Skepticism in the face of philosophy." In *Re-reading Levinas*, edited by Robert Bernasconi, Simon Critchley. Bloomington and Indianapolis, IN: Indiana University Press, 1991, pp. 149-161

— "On Deconstructing Nostalgia for Community within the West: The Debate between Nancy and Blanchot." *Research in Phenomenology* 23, 1 (1993): 3-21.

— "The Third Party. Levinas on the Intersection of the Ethical and the Political." In *Journal of the British Society for Phenomenology*, 30, 1 (January 1999): 67-87.

— "What is the question to which 'substitution' is the answer?." In *The Cambridge Companion to Levinas*, edited by Simon Critchley and Robert Bernasconi. Cambridge: Cambridge University Press, 2002, pp. 234-251.

— "No Exit: Levinas' Aporetic Account of Transcendence." In *Research in Phenomenology* 35, 1 (2005): 101-117.

— "Levinas's Ethical Critique of Levinasian Ethics." In *Totality and Infinity at 50*, edited by Scott Davidson & Diane Perpich. Pittsburgh, PA: Duquesne University Press, 2012, pp. 253-270.

— and Stacy Keltner. "Emmanuel Levinas: The Phenomenology of Sociality and the Ethics of Alterity." In *Phenomenological Approaches to Moral Philosophy: A Handbook*, edited by John Drummond. Dordrecht: Kluwer, 2002, pp. 249-268.

Bernet, Rudolf. "Levinas' Critique of Husserl." In *The Cambridge Companion to Levinas*, edited by Simon Critchley and Robert Bernasconi. Cambridge: Cambridge University Press, 2002, pp. 82-99.

Bevis, Kathryn. "'Better than metaphors'? Dwelling and the Maternal Body in Emmanuel Levinas." In *Literature and Theology* 21, 3 (2007): 317–329.

Bird, Gregory. "Community Beyond Hypostasis: Nancy responds to Blanchot." *Angelaki* 13, 1 (2008): 3–26.

Blanchot, Maurice. *Thomas the Obscure* [1941]. Translated by Robert Lamberton. Station Hill Press, 1973/88.

— *The Infinite Conversation* [1969]. Translated by Susan Hanson. Minneapolis and London: University of Minnesota Press, 1992.

— *La communauté inavouable*. Paris: Les éditions minuit, 1983.

— *The Unavowable Community* [1983]. Translated by Pierre Joris. Barrytown, NY: Station Hill Press, 1988.

— *The Space of Literature* [1955]. Translated and Introduction by Ann Smock. Lincoln, London: University of Nebraska Press, 1982.

Brady, Bernard V. *Christian Love*. Washington DC: Georgetown University Press, 2003.

Buber, Martin. *I and Thou* [1937]. Translated by Ronald Gregor Smith. Edinburgh: T. and T. Clark: Scribners, 1958/86.

— "Replies to My Critics." In *The Library of Living Philosophers*. Volume XII. *The Philosophy of Martin Buber*, edited by Paul A. Schlipp and Maurice Friedman. La Salle, IL: Open Court Publishing Company, 1967.

Butler, Judith. *Parting Ways: Jewishness and the Critique of Zionism*. New York: Columbia University Press, 2012.

Caygill, Howard. *Levinas and the Political*. New York, NY: Routledge, 2002.

— "Bearing Witness to the Infinite: Nancy and Levinas." *Journal for Cultural Research* 9, 4 (October 2005): 351–357.

Caputo, John D. "Who is Derrida's Zarathustra? Of Fraternity, Friendship, and a Democracy to Come." *Research in Phenomenology* 29, 1 (1999): 184–198.

Casey, Damien. "Levinas and Buber: Transcendence and Society." *Sophia* 38, 2 (1999): 69–92.

Cederberg, Carl. *Resaying the Human. Levinas Beyond Humanism and Antihumanism*. Stockholm: Södertörn Doctoral Dissertations 52, 2010.

Chalier, Catherine. "Ethics and the Feminine." In *Re-reading Levinas*, edited by Robert Bernasconi, Simon Critchley. Bloomington and Indianapolis, IN: Indiana University Press, 1991, pp. 119–129.

Chanter, Tina. "Levinas and Impossible Possibility: Thinking Ethics with Rosenzweig and Heidegger in the Wake of the Shoah." *Research in Phenomenology* 28 (1998): 91–110.

— ed. *Feminist Interpretations of Emmanuel Levinas*. University Park, Pennsylvania: The Pennsylvania State University Press, 2001.

Ciocan, Cristian and Hansel, Georges. *Levinas Concordance*. Dordrecht: Springer, 2005.

Cohen, Richard A. "Translator's introduction." In *Time and the Other and additional essays*. Translated by Richard A. Cohen, Pittsburgh, PA: Duquesne University Press, 1987, pp. 1-28.

— (ed.) *Face to Face with Levinas*. Albany, NY: State University of New York Press, 1985.

— "Foreword" [1998]. In *Otherwise than Being or Beyond Essence*. Translated by Alphonso Lingis. Pittsburgh, PA: Duquesne University Press, 1999, pp. xi–xvi.

— *Levinasian Meditations: Ethics, Philosophy, and Religion*. Pittsburgh, PA: Duquesne University Press, 2010.

Copenhaver, Brian P. ed. *Hermetica: The Greek Corpus Hermeticum and the Latin Asclepius*. Cambridge: Cambridge University Press, 2002.

Critchley, Simon. *The Ethics of Deconstruction: Derrida and Levinas*. West Lafayette, IN: Purdue University Press, 1992/1999.

— *Ethics, Politics, Subjectivity: Essays on Derrida, Levinas and Contemporary French Thought*. London: Verso, 1999.

— "Five Problems in Levinas's View of Politics and the Sketch of a Solution to Them." *Political Theory*, 32, 2 (April 2004): 172-185.

— "With Being-With? Notes on Jean-Luc Nancy's Rewriting of *Being and Time*." *Studies in Practical Philosophy*, 1, 1 (1999): 53-67.

Derrida, Jacques."Violence and Metaphysics" [1964]. Translated by Alan Bass. In *Writing and Difference* [1967]. London and New York: Routledge, 2001, pp. 97-192.

— *Anne Dufourmantelle invite Jacques Derrida à répondre : De l'hospitalité*. Calmann-Lévy, 1997.

— *Adieu to Emmanuel Levinas*, [1997]. Translated by Pascale-Anne Brault, and Michael Naas. Stanford: Stanford University Press, 1999.

— "At This Very Moment In This Work Here I Am" [1980]. Translated by Ruben Berezdivin. In *Re-reading Levinas*, edited by Robert Bernasconi and Simon Critchley. Bloomington and Indianapolis, IN: Indiana University Press, 1991, pp. 11-48.

— "The Politics of Friendship." *The Journal of Philosophy*, 85, 11 (1988): 632-644.

— *Of Hospitality. Anne Dufourmantelle Invites Jacques Derrida to Respond*. Translated by Rachel Bowlby. Stanford, CA: Stanford University Press, 2000.

— *The Politics of Friendship* [1994]. Translated by George Collins. London, New York: Verso, 2005.

— *The Last Interview*, SV. Derrida, *Le Monde*, August 2004.

Drabinski, John E. *Sensibility and Singularity: The Problem of Phenomenology in Levinas*. Albany, NY: State University of New York Press, 2001.

— "The Possibility of an Ethical Politics" [2000]. In *Emmanuel Levinas. Critical Assessments of Leading Philosophers*, Vol 4: *Beyond Levinas*, edited by Claire Katz and Lara Trout. New York: Routledge, 2005, pp. 188-212.

— "Wealth and Justice in a U-topian Context." In *Addressing Levinas*, edited by Eric S. Nelson, A. Kapust and K. Still. Evanston, IL: Northwestern University Press, 2005, pp. 185-198.

— *Levinas and the Postcolonial: Race, Nation, Other.* Edinburgh, Scotland: Edinburgh University Press, 2011.

Duncan, Roger. "Emmanuel Levinas: Non-intentional consciousness and the status of representational thinking." In *Analecta Husserliana XC*, edited by A.T. Tymieniecka. Springer: Netherlands, 2006, pp. 271-281.

Durfee, Harold A. "War, Politics and Radical Pluralism." *Philosophy for Phenomenological Research* 35, 4 (June 1975): 549-558.

Eisenstadt, Oona and Claire Elise Katz. "The Faceless Palestinian: A History of an Error." *Telos* 174 (Spring 2016): 9-32.

Ernour, A. and A. Meillet. *Dictionnaire Etymologique de la Langue Latine*. Paris: Librairie C. Klincksieck, 1951.

Esposito, Roberto. *Communitas. The origin and destiny of community* [1998]. Translated by Timothy Campbell. Stanford, CA: Stanford University Press, 2009.

Formosa, Paul. "Levinas and the Definition of Philosophy: An Ethical Approach," in *Crossroads. An Interdisciplinary Journal for the study of history, philosophy, religion and classics*, 1, (2006): 37-46.

Frank, Didier. *L'un -pour-l'autre. Levinas et la signification.* Paris: Puf, 2008.

— "The Sincerity of the Saying." In *Between Levinas and Heidegger*, edited by John E. Drabisnki and Eric S. Nelson. Albany, NY: State University of New York Press, 2014, pp.75-84.

Gaon, Stella. "Communities in Question: Sociality and Solidarity in Nancy and Blanchot." *Journal of Cultural Research* 9, 4 (October 2005): 387-403.

Gibbs, Robert B. "Substitution." *Philosophy & Theology* 4 (Winter 1989): 171-85.

— *Correlations in Rosenzweig and Levinas*. Princeton, New Jersey: Princeton University Press, 1994.

Haase, Ulrich and Large, William. *Maurice Blanchot*. New York: Routledge, 2001.

Hand, Seán. *Emmanuel Levinas. Routledge Critical Thinkers*. London: Routledge, 2009.

Hart, Kevin. "Ethics of the Image." *Levinas studies: An Annual Review*. Vol. 1, edited by Jeffrey Bloechl and Jeffrey L. Kosky. Pittsburgh, PA: Duquesne University Press, 2006, pp. 119-138.

Hayat, Pierre. *Emmanuel Levinas, éthique et société*. Paris: Édition Kimé, 1995.

Heidegger, Martin. *Being and Time* [1927]. Translated by John Macquarrie and Edward Robinson. New York: Harper Collins Publishers, 1962.

Hill, Leslie. *Maurice Blanchot: Extreme Contemporary*. London: Routledge, 1997.

Ince, Kate. "Questions to Luce Irigaray." *Hypatia: a journal of feminist philosophy* 11, 1 (Spring 1996): 122-140.

Irigaray, Luce. "Questions to Emmanuel Levinas. On the Divinity of Love." Translated by Margaret Whitford. In *Re-reading Levinas*, edited by Robert Bernasconi and Simon Critchley. Bloomington and Indianapolis, IN: Indiana University Press, 1991, pp. 109-118.

James, Ian, "Naming the Nothing: Nancy and Blanchot on Community," *Culture, Theory and Critique*, 51, 2 (July 2010): 171-187.

Jay, Martin. "Hostage Philosophy: Levinas's Ethical Thought." *Tikkun* 5, 6 (1990): 85-87.

Kant, Immanuel. "Idea for a universal history with a Cosmopolitan aim" [1786]. Translated by Allen W. Wood. In *Kant's Idea for a Universal History with a Cosmopolitan Aim. A Critical Guide*, edited by Amélie Oksenberg Rorty and James Schmidt. Cambridge: Cambridge University Press, 2009, pp. 9-23.

Katz, Claire Elise. *Levinas, Judaism, and the Feminine: The Silent Footsteps of Rebecca*. Bloomington IN: Indiana University Press, 2003.

Keenan, Denis King. *The Question of Sacrifice*. Bloomington: Indiana University Press, 2005.

Kelley, Andrew. "Reciprocity and the Height of God: A Defense of Buber against Levinas" [1995]. *Levinas and Buber—Dialogue and Difference* edited by Peter Atterton, Matthew Calarco and Maurice S. Friedman. Pittsburgh, PA: Duquesne University Press, 2004, pp. 226-232.

Kosky, Jeffrey L. "Maurice Blanchot and Levinas Studies." *Levinas studies: An Annual Review*. Vol. 1, edited by Jeffrey Bloechl and Jeffrey L. Kosky. Pittsburgh, PA: Duquesne University Press, 2006, pp. 157-172.

Large, William. *Emmanuel Levinas and Maurice Blanchot: Ethics and the Ambiguity of Writing*. Manchester: Clinamen Press, 2005.

Levin, David Michael. *The Philosopher's Gaze: Modernity in the Shadows of Enlightenment*. Berkeley: University of California Press, 1999.

Lawlor, Leonard. *Challenge of Bergsonism*. London: Continuum International Publishing, 2003.

Lingis, Aphonso. "Objectivity and of justice: A critique of Emmanuel Levinas's Explanations." *Continental Philosophy Review*, 32, 4 (1999): 395-407.

— *The Community of Those Who Have Nothing in Common*. Bloomington IN: Indiana University Press, 1994.

Lipari, Lisbeth. "Listening for the Other: Ethical Implications of the Buber-Levinas Encounter." *Communication Theory* 14, 2 (May 2004): 122 - 141.

Llewelyn, John. *Emmanuel Levinas: The Genealogy of Ethics*. Florence, KY: Routledge, 1995.

Lumsden, Simon. "Absolute Difference and Social Ontology: Levinas Face to Face with Buber and Fichte." *Human studies* 23, Kluwer Academic Publisher, (2000): 227-241.

Maloney, Philip J. "Levinas, substitution, and transcendental subjectivity." *Man and World* 30 (1997): 49–64.

May, Todd. *Reconsidering Difference: Nancy, Derrida, Levinas and Deleuze.* Univesity Park, PA: Pennsylvania State University, 1997.

Marsh, Jack, "Lévinas en Amérique du Nord aujourd'hui. Trois vagues et deux écoles," *Cahiers d'Etudes Lévinassienes.* Vol 11 (2012): 193–211.

Mitchell, Robert. "Fraternal Anonymity: Blanchot and Nancy on Community and Mitsein." In *The Politics of Community*, edited by Michael Strysick. Aurora, CO: The Davies Group Publishers, 2002, pp. 85–105.

Moran, Dermot. *Introduction to Phenomenology.* London and New York: Routledge, 2000.

Morin, Marie-Eve, "Putting Community Under Erasure: Derrida and Nancy on the Plurality of Singularities," *Culture Machine*, Vol 8 (2006), http://www.culture machine.net/index.php/cm/article/viewarticle/37/45

Nancy, Jean-Luc. *La communauté désœuvrée*, éditeur Christian Bourgois. Paris: Galilée, 1986 (1990).

— "The Inoperative Community" [1983/1986]. Translated by Peter Connor. In *The Inoperative Community*, edited by Peter Connor. Foreword by Christopher Fynsk. Minneapolis, London: Minneapolis University Press, 1991, pp. 1–42.

— "Shattered Love" [1986]. Translated by Lisa Garbus and Simona Sawhney. In *The Inoperative Community*, edited by Peter Connor. Foreword by Christopher Fynsk. Minneapolis, London: Minneapolis University Press, 1991, pp. 82–109.

— "Of Being-in-Common." Translated by James Creech. In *Community at Loose Ends*, edited by Miami Theory Collective. Minneapolis: University of Minnesota Press, 1991, pp. 1–12.

— and Tracy B. Strong. "La Comparution /The Compearance: From the Existence of "Communism" to the Community of "Existence"'" [1991]. *Political Theory*, 20, 3 (Aug., 1992): 371–398.

— *Being Singular Plural* [1996]. Translated by Robert D. Richardson and Anne E. O'Byrne. Stanford, CA: Stanford University Press, 2000.

— "L'intrus/The Intruder" [2000]. In *Corpus*. Translated by Richard A. Rand. New York: Fordham University Press, 2008, pp. 161–170.

— "The Confronted Community" [2001]. Translated by Amanda Macdonald. *Postcolonial Studies*, 6, 1 (2003): 23–36.

— *A l'écoute.* Paris: Galilée, 2002.

— *Listening* [2002]. Translated by Charlotte Mandell. New York: Fordham University Press, 2007.

— "Tribute to Maurice Blanchot on the 100th anniversary of his birth." Translated by Charlotte Mandell, *This Space*, http://this-space.blogspot.se/2007/09/maurice-blanchot-1907-2003-by-jean-luc.html

— "The real outside is "at the heart" of the inside." *ATOPIA* (2007). www.atopia.tk

— "The being-with of being-there." *Continental Philosophy Review*, 41, 1 (2008): 1–15.

—. "Communism, the word." In *The Idea of Communism*, edited by Costas Douzinas and Savoj Žižek. London and New York: Verso, 2010, pp. 145–154.

— "More than One." In *Politics of the One. Concepts of the One and the Many in Contemporary Thought*, edited by Artemy Magun. New York and London: Bloomsbury Academic, 2013, pp. 3–12.

— and Marcia Sá Cavalcante Schuback. *Being With the Without*. Stockholm: Axl Books, 2013.

— "Fraternity." *Baltic Worlds* (Special Theme: Voices on solidarity), Vol. VIII, 1–2, Centre for Baltic and East-European Studies (CBEES), Södertörn University, (April 2015): 98–100.

— *La communauté désavouée*. Paris: Galilée, 2014.

Overgaard, Søren. "On Levinas's Critique of Husserl." In *Metaphysics, Facticity, Interpretation: Phenomenology in the Nordic Countries*, edited by Dan Zahavi, Sara Heinamaa, and Hans Ruin. Netherlands: Springer, 2003, pp 115–138.

Powell, Jeffrey. "Levinas Representing Husserl on Representation." *Philosophy Today* 39, 2 (1995: Summer): 185–97.

Peperzak, Adriaan. *To the Other: An Introduction to the Philosophy of Emmanuel Levinas*. West Lafayette, IN: Purdue University Press, 1993.

Putnam, Hilary. "Levinas and Judaism." In *The Cambridge Companion to Levinas*, edited by Simon Critchley and Robert Bernasconi. Cambridge: Cambridge University Press, 2002, pp. 33–62.

Raffoul, François. "The Subject of the Welcome." *Symposium* 2, 2 (1998): 211–222.

Ricoeur, Paul, "Otherwise: A Reading of Emmanuel Levinas's 'Otherwise than Being or beyond Essence.'" [1997]. Translated by Matthew Escobar. *Yale French Studies*, No. 104, Encounters with Levinas (2004): 82–99.

Robbins, Jeffrey W. "Thinking Transcendence with Levinas: From the Ethico-Religious to the Political and Beyond." *Analecta Hermeneutica*, Vol 2 (2010).

Rolland, Jacques. "Postscript." In *God, Death and Time* [1975–6]. Translated by Bettina Bergo. Stanford, CA: Stanford University Press, 2000, pp. 234–5.

Rosato, Jennifer. "Woman as Vulnerable Self: The Trope of Maternity in Levinas's Otherwise Than Being." *Hypatia*, 27, 2 (Spring 2012): 348–365.

Sá Cavalcante Schuback, Marcia. "Hermeneutics of tradition." In *Rethinking Time: Essays on History, Memory and Representation*, edited by Hans Ruin and Andrus Ers. Stockholm: Södertörn Philosophical Studies, 2011, pp. 63–74.

Sallis, John. "Levinas and the Elemental" [1998]. In *Radicalizing Levinas*, edited by Peter Atterton and Matthew Calarco. Albany: SUNY Press, 2010, pp. 87–94.

Sandford, Stella. "Levinas, feminism and the feminine." In *The Cambridge Companion to Levinas*, edited by Simon Critchley and Robert Bernasconi. Cambridge: Cambridge University Press, 2002, pp. 139–160.

— *The Metaphysics of Love: Gender and Transcendence in Levinas*. London and New Brunswick, New Jersey: The Athlone Press, 2000.

Schütz, Alfred. *The Phenomenology of the Social World* [1932]. Translated by G.Walsh and F. Lehnert. Evanston: Northwestern University Press, 1967.

Shaw, Joshua James. *Emmanuel Levinas on the Priority of Ethics: Putting Ethics First*. Amherst, New York: Cambria Press, 2008.

Simmel, Georg. "The Sociology of Sociability." Translated by Everett C. Hughes. *American Journal of Sociology*, 55, 3 (Nov., 1949): 254–261.

Simmons, William Paul. "The Third. Levinas's theoretical move from an-archical ethics to the realm of justice and politics." *Philosophy and Social Criticism*, 25, 6 (1999): 83–104.

Strasser, Stephan. "Buber and Levinas: Philosophical Reflections on an Opposition." In *Levinas and Buber—Dialogue and Difference*, edited by Peter Atterton, Matthew Calarco and Maurice S. Friedman. Pittsburgh, PA: Duquesne University Press, 2004, pp. 37–48.

Thomson, A. J. P. "Against Community: Derrida contra Nancy." In *The Politics of Community*, edited by Michael Strysick. Aurora, CO: The Davies Group Publishers, 2002, pp. 67–84.

Villarmea, Stella. "The Provocation of Levinas for Feminism." *The European Journal for of Women's Studies*. Vol. 6, No. 3. (1996): 291–304.

Watkins, Christopher. "A Different Alterity: Jean-Luc Nancy's 'Singular Plural.'" *Paragraph* 30, 2 (2007): 50–64.

Wehmeier, Sally, ed. *Oxford Dictionary*. Oxford University Press, 2005. (Seventh edition).

Zahavi, Dan. *Husserl's Phenomenology*. Stanford, CA: Stanford University Press, 2003.

— "Inner Time-Consciousness and Pre-reflected Self-awareness." In *New Husserl: A Critical Reader*, edited by Donn Welton. Bloomington, IN: Indiana University Press, 2003, pp. 157–180.

Žižek, Slavoj, "Neighbors and Other Monsters: A Plea for Ethical Violence." In *The Neighbor: Three Inquiries in Political Theology*, edited by Slavoj Žižek, Eric L.Santner and Kenneth Reinhard. Chicago, IL: University of Chicago Press, 2006/2013, pp. 134–190.

Södertörn Doctoral Dissertations

1. Jolanta Aidukaite, *The Emergence of the Post-Socialist Welfare State: The case of the Baltic States: Estonia, Latvia and Lithuania*, 2004
2. Xavier Fraudet, *Politique étrangère française en mer Baltique (1871–1914): de l'exclusion à l'affirmation*, 2005
3. Piotr Wawrzeniuk, *Confessional Civilising in Ukraine: The Bishop Iosyf Shumliansky and the Introduction of Reforms in the Diocese of Lviv 1668–1708*, 2005
4. Andrej Kotljarchuk, *In the Shadows of Poland and Russia: The Grand Duchy of Lithuania and Sweden in the European Crisis of the mid-17th Century*, 2006
5. Håkan Blomqvist, *Nation, ras och civilisation i svensk arbetarrörelse före nazismen*, 2006
6. Karin S Lindelöf, *Om vi nu ska bli som Europa: Könsskapande och normalitet bland unga kvinnor i transitionens Polen*, 2006
7. Andrew Stickley. *On Interpersonal Violence in Russia in the Present and the Past: A Sociological Study*, 2006
8. Arne Ek, *Att konstruera en uppslutning kring den enda vägen: Om folkrörelsers modernisering i skuggan av det Östeuropeiska systemskiftet*, 2006
9. Agnes Ers, *I mänsklighetens namn: En etnologisk studie av ett svenskt biståndsprojekt i Rumänien*, 2006
10. Johnny Rodin, *Rethinking Russian Federalism: The Politics of Intergovernmental Relations and Federal Reforms at the Turn of the Millennium*, 2006
11. Kristian Petrov, *Tillbaka till framtiden: Modernitet, postmodernitet och generationsidentitet i Gorbačevs glasnost' och perestrojka*, 2006
12. Sophie Söderholm Werkö, *Patient patients?: Achieving Patient Empowerment through Active Participation, Increased Knowledge and Organisation*, 2008
13. Peter Bötker, *Leviatan i arkipelagen: Staten, förvaltningen och samhället. Fallet Estland*, 2007
14. Matilda Dahl, *States under scrutiny: International organizations, transformation and the construction of progress*, 2007
15. Margrethe B. Søvik, *Support, resistance and pragmatism: An examination of motivation in language policy in Kharkiv, Ukraine*, 2007
16. Yulia Gradskova, *Soviet People with female Bodies: Performing beauty and maternity in Soviet Russia in the mid 1930–1960s*, 2007
17. Renata Ingbrant, *From Her Point of View: Woman's Anti-World in the Poetry of Anna Świrszczyńska*, 2007
18. Johan Eellend, *Cultivating the Rural Citizen: Modernity, Agrarianism and Citizenship in Late Tsarist Estonia*, 2007
19. Petra Garberding, *Musik och politik i skuggan av nazismen: Kurt Atterberg och de svensk—tyska musikrelationerna*, 2007

20. Aleksei Semenenko, *Hamlet the Sign: Russian Translations of Hamlet and Literary Canon Formation*, 2007
21. Vytautas Petronis, *Constructing Lithuania: Ethnic Mapping in the Tsarist Russia, ca. 1800–1914*, 2007
22. Akvile Motiejunaite, *Female employment, gender roles, and attitudes: the Baltic countries in a broader context*, 2008
23. Tove Lindén, *Explaining Civil Society Core Activism in Post-Soviet Latvia*, 2008
24. Pelle Åberg, *Translating Popular Education: Civil Society Cooperation between Sweden and Estonia*, 2008
25. Anders Nordström, *The Interactive Dynamics of Regulation: Exploring the Council of Europe's monitoring of Ukraine*, 2008
26. Fredrik Doeser, *In Search of Security After the Collapse of the Soviet Union: Foreign Policy Change in Denmark, Finland and Sweden, 1988–1993*, 2008
27. Zhanna Kravchenko. *Family (versus) Policy: Combining Work and Care in Russia and Sweden*, 2008
28. Rein Jüriado, *Learning within and between public-private partnerships*, 2008
29. Elin Boalt, *Ecology and evolution of tolerance in two cruciferous species*, 2008
30. Lars Forsberg, *Genetic Aspects of Sexual Selection and Mate Choice in Salmonids*, 2008
31. Eglė Rindzevičiūtė, *Constructing Soviet Cultural Policy: Cybernetics and Governance in Lithuania after World War II*, 2008
32. Joakim Philipson, *The Purpose of Evolution: 'struggle for existence' in the Russian-Jewish press 1860–1900*, 2008
33. Sofie Bedford, *Islamic activism in Azerbaijan: Repression and mobilization in a post-Soviet context*, 2009
34. Tommy Larsson Segerlind, *Team Entrepreneurship: A process analysis of the venture team and the venture team roles in relation to the innovation process*, 2009
35. Jenny Svensson, *The Regulation of Rule-Following: Imitation and Soft Regulation in the European Union*, 2009
36. Stefan Hallgren, *Brain Aromatase in the guppy, Poecilia reticulate: Distribution, control and role in behavior*, 2009
37. Karin Ellencrona, *Functional characterization of interactions between the flavivirus NS5 protein and PDZ proteins of the mammalian host*, 2009
38. Makiko Kanematsu, *Saga och verklighet: Barnboksproduktion i det postsovjetiska Lettland*, 2009
39. Daniel Lindvall, *The Limits of the European Vision in Bosnia and Herzegovina: An Analysis of the Police Reform Negotiations*, 2009
40. Charlotta Hillerdal, *People in Between – Ethnicity and Material Identity: A New Approach to Deconstructed Concepts*, 2009
41. Jonna Bornemark, *Kunskapens gräns – gränsens vetande*, 2009
42. Adolphine G. Kateka, *Co-Management Challenges in the Lake Victoria Fisheries: A Context Approach*, 2010
43. René León Rosales, *Vid framtidens hitersta gräns: Om pojkar och elevpositioner i en multietnisk skola*, 2010
44. Simon Larsson, *Intelligensaristokrater och arkivmartyrer: Normerna för vetenskaplig skicklighet i svensk historieforskning 1900–1945*, 2010
45. Håkan Lättman, *Studies on spatial and temporal distributions of epiphytic lichens*, 2010 [report]

46. Alia Jaensson, *Pheromonal mediated behaviour and endocrine response in salmonids: The impact of cypermethrin, copper, and glyphosate*, 2010
47. Michael Wigerius, *Roles of mammalian Scribble in polarity signaling, virus offense and cell-fate determination*, 2010
48. Anna Hedtjärn Wester, *Män i kostym: Prinsar, konstnärer och tegelbärare vid sekelskiftet 1900*, 2010
49. Magnus Linnarsson, *Postgång på växlande villkor: Det svenska postväsendets organisation under stormaktstiden*, 2010
50. Barbara Kunz, *Kind words, cruise missiles and everything in between: A neoclassical realist study of the use of power resources in U.S. policies towards Poland, Ukraine and Belarus 1989–2008*, 2010
51. Anders Bartonek, *Philosophie im Konjunktiv: Nichtidentität als Ort der Möglichkeit des Utopischen in der negativen Dialektik Theodor W. Adornos*, 2010
52. Carl Cederberg, *Resaying the Human: Levinas Beyond Humanism and Antihumanism*, 2010
53. Johanna Ringarp, *Professionens problematik: Lärarkårens kommunalisering och välfärdsstatens förvandling*, 2011
54. Sofi Gerber, *Öst är Väst men Väst är bäst: Östtysk identitetsformering i det förenade Tyskland*, 2011
55. Susanna Sjödin Lindenskoug, *Manlighetens bortre gräns: Tidelagsrättegångar i Livland åren 1685–1709*, 2011
56. Dominika Polanska, *The emergence of enclaves of wealth and poverty: A sociological study of residential differentiation in post-communist Poland*, 2011
57. Christina Douglas, *Kärlek per korrespondens: Två förlovade par under andra hälften av 1800-talet*, 2011
58. Fred Saunders, *The Politics of People – Not just Mangroves and Monkeys: A study of the theory and practice of community-based management of natural resources in Zanzibar*, 2011
59. Anna Rosengren, *Åldrandet och språket: En språkhistorisk analys av hög ålder och åldrande i Sverige cirka 1875–1975*, 2011
60. Emelie Lilliefeldt, *European Party Politics and Gender: Configuring Gender-Balanced Parliamentary Presence*, 2011
61. Ola Svenonius, *Sensitising Urban Transport Security: Surveillance and Policing in Berlin, Stockholm, and Warsaw*, 2011
62. Andreas Johansson, *Dissenting Democrats: Nation and Democracy in the Republic of Moldova*, 2011
63. Wessam Melik, *Molecular characterization of the Tick-borne encephalitis virus: Environments and replication*, 2012
64. Steffen Werther, *SS-Vision und Grenzland-Realität: Vom Umgang dänischer und „volksdeutscher" Nationalsozialisten in Sønderjylland mit der „großgermanischen" Ideologie der SS*, 2012
65. Peter Jakobsson, *Öppenhetsindustrin*, 2012
66. Kristin Ilves, *Seaward Landward: Investigations on the archaeological source value of the landing site category in the Baltic Sea region*, 2012
67. Anne Kaun, *Civic Experiences and Public Connection: Media and Young People in Estonia*, 2012
68. Anna Tessmann, *On the Good Faith: A Fourfold Discursive Construction of Zoroastripanism in Contemporary Russia*, 2012

69. Jonas Lindström, *Drömmen om den nya staden: stadsförnyelse i det postsovjetisk Riga*, 2012
70. Maria Wolrath Söderberg, *Topos som meningsskapare: retorikens topiska perspektiv på tänkande och lärande genom argumentation*, 2012
71. Linus Andersson, *Alternativ television: former av kritik i konstnärlig TV-produktion*, 2012
72. Håkan Lättman, *Studies on spatial and temporal distributions of epiphytic lichens*, 2012
73. Fredrik Stiernstedt, *Mediearbete i mediehuset: produktion i förändring på MTG-radio*, 2013
74. Jessica Moberg, *Piety, Intimacy and Mobility: A Case Study of Charismatic Christianity in Present-day Stockholm*, 2013
75. Elisabeth Hemby, *Historiemåleri och bilder av vardag: Tatjana Nazarenkos konstnärskap i 1970-talets Sovjet*, 2013
76. Tanya Jukkala, *Suicide in Russia: A macro-sociological study*, 2013
77. Maria Nyman, *Resandets gränser: svenska resenärers skildringar av Ryssland under 1700-talet*, 2013
78. Beate Feldmann Eellend, *Visionära planer och vardagliga praktiker: postmilitära landskap i Östersjöområdet*, 2013
79. Emma Lind, *Genetic response to pollution in sticklebacks: natural selection in the wild*, 2013
80. Anne Ross Solberg, *The Mahdi wears Armani: An analysis of the Harun Yahya enterprise*, 2013
81. Nikolay Zakharov, *Attaining Whiteness: A Sociological Study of Race and Racialization in Russia*, 2013
82. Anna Kharkina, *From Kinship to Global Brand: the Discourse on Culture in Nordic Cooperation after World War II*, 2013
83. Florence Fröhlig, *A painful legacy of World War II: Nazi forced enlistment: Alsatian/Mosellan Prisoners of war and the Soviet Prison Camp of Tambov*, 2013
84. Oskar Henriksson, *Genetic connectivity of fish in the Western Indian Ocean*, 2013
85. Hans Geir Aasmundsen, *Pentecostalism, Globalisation and Society in Contemporary Argentina*, 2013
86. Anna McWilliams, *An Archaeology of the Iron Curtain: Material and Metaphor*, 2013
87. Anna Danielsson, *On the power of informal economies and the informal economies of power: rethinking informality, resilience and violence in Kosovo*, 2014
88. Carina Guyard, *Kommunikationsarbete på distans*, 2014
89. Sofia Norling, *Mot "väst": om vetenskap, politik och transformation i Polen 1989–2011*, 2014
90. Markus Huss, *Motståndets akustik: språk och (o)ljud hos Peter Weiss 1946–1960*, 2014
91. Ann-Christin Randahl, *Strategiska skribenter: skrivprocesser i fysik och svenska*, 2014
92. Péter Balogh, *Perpetual borders: German-Polish cross-border contacts in the Szczecin area*, 2014
93. Erika Lundell, *Förkroppsligad fiktion och fiktionaliserade kroppar: levande rollspel i Östersjöregionen*, 2014
94. Henriette Cederlöf, *Alien Places in Late Soviet Science Fiction: The "Unexpected Encounters" of Arkady and Boris Strugatsky as Novels and Films*, 2014
95. Niklas Eriksson, *Urbanism Under Sail: An archaeology of fluit ships in early modern everyday life*, 2014

96. Signe Opermann, *Generational Use of News Media in Estonia: Media Access, Spatial Orientations and Discursive Characteristics of the News Media*, 2014
97. Liudmila Voronova, *Gendering in political journalism: A comparative study of Russia and Sweden*, 2014
98. Ekaterina Kalinina, *Mediated Post-Soviet Nostalgia*, 2014
99. Anders E. B. Blomqvist, *Economic Natonalizing in the Ethnic Borderlands of Hungary and Romania: Inclusion, Exclusion and Annihilation in Szatmár/Satu-Mare, 1867–1944*, 2014
100. Ann-Judith Rabenschlag, *Völkerfreundschaft nach Bedarf: Ausländische Arbeitskräfte in der Wahrnehmung von Staat und Bevölkerung der DDR*, 2014
101. Yuliya Yurchuck, *Ukrainian Nationalists and the Ukrainian Insurgent Army in Post-Soviet Ukraine*, 2014
102. Hanna Sofia Rehnberg, *Organisationer berättar: narrativitet som resurs i strategisk kommunikation*, 2014
103. Jaakko Turunen, *Semiotics of Politics: Dialogicality of Parliamentary Talk*, 2015
104. Iveta Jurkane-Hobein, *I Imagine You Here Now: Relationship Maintenance Strategies in Long-Distance Intimate Relationships*, 2015
105. Katharina Wesolowski, *Maybe baby? Reproductive behaviour, fertility intentions, and family policies in post-communist countries, with a special focus on Ukraine*, 2015
106. Ann af Burén, *Living Simultaneity: On religion among semi-secular Swedes*, 2015
107. Larissa Mickwitz, *En reformerad lärare: konstruktionen av en professionell och betygssättande lärare i skolpolitik och skolpraktik*, 2015
108. Daniel Wojahn, *Språkaktivism: diskussioner om feministiska språkförändringar i Sverige från 1960-talet till 2015*, 2015
109. Hélène Edberg, *Kreativt skrivande för kritiskt tänkande: en fallstudie av studenters arbete med kritisk metareflektion*, 2015
110. Kristina Volkova, *Fishy Behavior: Persistent effects of early-life exposure to 17α-ethinylestradiol*, 2015
111. Björn Sjöstrand, *Att tänka det tekniska: en studie i Derridas teknikfilosofi*, 2015
112. Håkan Forsberg, *Kampen om eleverna: gymnasiefältet och skolmarknadens framväxt i Stockholm, 1987–2011*, 2015
113. Johan Stake, *Essays on quality evaluation and bidding behavior in public procurement auctions*, 2015
114. Martin Gunnarson, *Please Be Patient: A Cultural Phenomenological Study of Haemodialysis and Kidney Transplantation Care*, 2016
115. Nasim Reyhanian Caspillo, *Studies of alterations in behavior and fertility in ethinyl estradiol-exposed zebrafish and search for related biomarkers*, 2016
116. Pernilla Andersson, *The Responsible Business Person: Studies of Business Education for Sustainability*, 2016
117. Kim Silow Kallenberg, *Gränsland: svensk ungdomsvård mellan vård och straff*, 2016
118. Sari Vuorenpää, *Literacitet genom interaction*, 2016
119. Francesco Zavatti, *Writing History in a Propaganda Institute: Political Power and Network Dynamics in Communist Romania*, 2016
120. Cecilia Annell, *Begärets politiska potential: Feministiska motståndsstrategier i Elin Wägners 'Pennskaftet', Gabriele Reuters 'Aus guter Familie', Hilma Angered-Strandbergs 'Lydia Vik' och Grete Meisel-Hess 'Die Intellektuellen'*, 2016
121. Marco Nase, *Academics and Politics: Northern European Area Studies at Greifswald University, 1917–1992*, 2016

122. Jenni Rinne, *Searching for Authentic Living Through Native Faith – The Maausk movement in Estonia*, 2016
123. Petra Werner, *Ett medialt museum: lärandets estetik i svensk television 1956–1969*, 2016
124. Ramona Rat, *Un-common Sociality – Thinking sociality with Levinas*, 2016
125. Petter Thureborn, *Microbial ecosystem functions along the steep oxygen gradient of the Landsort Deep, Baltic Sea*, 2016

Södertörn Philosophical Studies

1. Hans Ruin & Nicholas Smith (eds.), *Hermeneutik och tradition: Gadamer och den grekiska filosofin* (2003)
2. Hans Ruin, *Kommentar till Heideggers Varat och tiden* (2005)
3. Marcia Sá Cavalcante Schuback & Hans Ruin (eds.), *The Past's Presence: Essays on the Historicity of Philosophical Thought* (2006)
4. Jonna Bornemark (ed.), *Det främmande i det egna: Filosofiska essäer om bildning och person* (2007)
5. Marcia Sá Cavalcante Schuback (ed.), *Att tänka smärtan* (2009)
6. Jonna Bornemark, *Kunskapens gräns, gränsens vetande: En fenomenologisk undersökning av transcendens och kroppslighet* (2009)
7. Carl Cederberg & Hans Ruin (eds.), *En annan humaniora, en annan tid/Another humanities, another time* (2009)
8. Jonna Bornemark & Hans Ruin (eds.), *Phenomenology and Religion: New Frontiers* (2010)
9. Hans Ruin & Andrus Ers (eds.), *Rethinking Time: Essays on History, Memory, and Representation* (2011)
10. Jonna Bornemark & Marcia Sá Cavalcante Schuback (eds.), *Phenomenology of Eros* (2012)
11. Leif Dahlberg & Hans Ruin (eds.), *Teknik, fenomenologi och medialitet* (2011)
12. Jonna Bornemark & Hans Ruin (eds.), *Ambiguity of the Sacred* (2012)
13. Brian Manning Delaney & Sven-Olov Wallentein (eds.), *Translating Hegel* (2012)
14. Sven-Olov Wallenstein & Jakob Nilsson (eds.), *Foucault, Biopolitics, and Governmentality* (2013)
15. Jan Patočka, *Inledning till fenomenologisk filosofi* (2013)
16. Jonna Bornemark & Sven-Olov Wallenstein (eds.), *Madness, Religion, and the Limits of Reason* (2015)
17. Björn Sjöstrand, *Att tänka det tekniska: En studie i Derridas teknikfilosofi* (2015)
18. Jonna Bornemark & Nicholas Smith (eds.), *Phenomenology of Pregnancy* (2016)

Södertörn Philosophical Studies is a book series published under the direction of the Department of Philosophy at Södertörn University. The series consists of monographs and anthologies in philosophy, with a special focus on the Continental-European tradition. It seeks to provide a platform for innovative contemporary philosophical research. The volumes are published mainly in English and Swedish. The series is edited by Marcia Sá Cavalcante Schuback and Hans Ruin.

www.ingramcontent.com/pod-product-compliance
Lightning Source LLC
Chambersburg PA
CBHW031314160426
43196CB00007B/522